M000232998

HOW NOT TO
BE A POLITICIAN

Also by Rory Stewart

The Places in Between

Occupational Hazards: My Time Governing in Iraq

The Marches: Border Walks with My Father

HOW NOT TO
BE A POLITICIAN

A Memoir

RORY STEWART

Penguin Press | New York | 2023

PENGUIN PRESS
An imprint of Penguin Random House LLC
penguinrandomhouse.com

Copyright © 2023 by Rory Stewart
Penguin Random House supports copyright. Copyright fuels creativity,
encourages diverse voices, promotes free speech, and creates a vibrant culture.
Thank you for buying an authorized edition of this book and for complying with copyright
laws by not reproducing, scanning, or distributing any part of it in any form without
permission. You are supporting writers and allowing Penguin Random
House to continue to publish books for every reader.

ISBN 9780593300329 (hardcover)
ISBN 9780593300336 (ebook)

Printed in the United States of America
1st Printing

To Shoshana

Me debeo quid ego nunc interiora nostra et recondita consilia sermonesque arcanos eruam, ut repentinis nuntiis ad praesentia et inminentia pericula evocatus tuis consiliis conservatus sim, ut neque audacius experiri casus temere passa sis, et modestiora cogitanti fida receptacula pararis.

(from 'Laudatio Turiae', first century BC)

Why must I now expose all our most intimate chats, our personal plans, and private conversations: how it was only your good judgement which saved me when a sudden message pulled me into immediate and present danger; how you did not allow me recklessly to tempt fate by an even more risky step, but instead created for me a safe and more modest place for reflection.

Contents

Author's Note

Facts, narration, prejudices

Many colleagues will be angry with what I have chosen to include. And with reason. All professions expect colleagues to be discreet about their experiences within the workplace. MPs are often proud of their records in government and their roles in Parliament, and many will be hurt that I have criticised things which they valued deeply. Some will feel I am unfair, bitter and ungrateful.

To which I can only answer that our government and Parliament, which once had a reasonable claim to be the best in the world, is now in a shameful state. And this is in part because other insiders – whether concerned for their friendships, their reputations and their future careers, or simply more tactful than myself – continue to conceal its horrifying decline. Government of, by, and for the people should be exposed properly to the public eye.

I have protected the identities of intelligence officers, and special forces personnel and the details of their operations. I have not included the names of junior civil servants, when the story is not to their credit – they should be able to give confidential advice to ministers without worrying about their reputations. I have kept the names of many backbenchers anonymous, because I think their stories can illustrate problems of parliamentary life, without having to indict an individual. I have also concealed the names of some MPs whom I admired and who were immensely helpful to me, because it might not benefit their future careers to be praised by me. But I have named those people in public life who I thought were senior enough to bear responsibility. And generally, given a choice between discretion and honesty, I have chosen the latter.

There will be mistakes in this account. This book is based in part on my diary entries, checked against documents, emails, WhatsApp messages, press reports, Hansard and video recordings of House of Commons proceedings, and memoirs by, and interviews with, others. With this assistance, I have tried to confirm my memories of events. But many descriptions still rely on my ability to recall accurately words and scenes. I have tried to be honest about my own vanity, ambitions and failures, but I will have often failed to judge myself in the way that I judge others. I can see no way, however, of entirely avoiding the risks of personal memory in reconstructing a decade of life. The alternative would be blandness, evasion or silence. If I may not always have recorded what is true, I have not written what I know to be false.

This is a highly condensed version of my experience. The first draft of this book was 220,000 words long and still covered only a fraction of the events between 2010 and 2019. I have since cut half of that material entirely. Anyone interested in my involvement as a backbencher in Libya or the campaign for community hospitals, my speeches inside and outside the House of Commons, my arguments as a minister over Yemen policy and rewilding, my fight with the government over Covid policy, or my run as an Independent to be mayor of London, would have to get their hands on the unpublished draft. For those stories are no longer included. Nor are my detailed attempts to analyse Boris Johnson, populism, the hope for the centre ground, or the place of ethics in politics.

I left politics with a deep love for my constituency, respect and admiration for the intelligence, competence, imagination and courage of many of my colleagues, and enduring friendships. But my final sense is one of shame. And my regret is often not about my openness but about not being able to be more forceful in my condemnation.

In case it is of help to readers who are unfamiliar with the complications of British politics, I have added a Dramatis Personae and Glossary at the end of the book.

Prologue

We are seated on unstable, cream-leather bar stools, arranged in a shallow curve. 'Our Next Prime Minister' is printed on the floor. There is no live audience – nor any room for one on this narrow studio stage. A wall, however, is occupied by a giant screen on which citizens will appear. 'Five men. One job,' says the presenter Emily Maitlis to one of the cameras. She is dressed in imperial purple. 'How they answer tonight will help decide who will become your next prime minister.' It is 18 June 2019. One of us will be prime minister on 24 July.

'I hope,' murmurs Boris Johnson, settling into his seat, 'that this is not all going to be about Brexit.'

'No,' says the presenter reassuringly, 'we will keep the Brexit section short.'

'Wait a second,' I interrupt from across the room, 'I hope that we are going to have a lot on Brexit.'

'Don't worry, Rory, we will have quite enough, I think.'

Behind us flicker fragmentary images of 10 Downing Street, with cubist glimpses of Parliament and Big Ben, through oddly shaped windows. We are live. One camera is zoomed in tight. Another shows us all: making us seem, with our legs coyly looped over the footrest of the bar stools, like diminutive nightclub crooners. The cameras do not reveal how easy it would be to fall.

Since the shot will hover on each of us in turn for a few long seconds, we have had to choose an expression to hold. Jeremy Hunt, the Foreign Secretary – four inches taller than the rest of us and the only one good-looking enough to pass as an American politician – has apparently opted for noble determination. It is perhaps the look his father the admiral adopted on the quarter-deck. Michael Gove, the Environment Secretary, two seats to my

right – who may be the cleverest of us and certainly the most
excessively polite, and right-wing – has one side of his mouth
pulled up in a smirk, making him resemble a grammar-school
master, presented with a comical error in Latin composition. Sajid
Javid, the Home Secretary, the most likeable of us, has his hands
perfectly folded on his lap and is conveying meditative serenity. I
keep closing my eyes. And Boris Johnson – ever the punchline –
looks as though he is a celebrity contestant bracing for a custard
pie in the face.

More images tumble over the giant screen: protesters in face paint,
young women in burqas, the Downing Street cat, and finally twelve
faces – apparently the people waiting to ask questions. One of the
women seems angry; the imam, in his prayer cap, merely disapprov-
ing. As Emily works her way through her lengthy introduction, our
expressions remain frozen – the cameras panning back and forth to
check that we still resemble waxworks.

Finally, a vast amiable face with a hearing aid and a grey plaid
shirt appears on the screen and is introduced as 'Lee from Norwich'.
As we stare at him, trying to compute the precise texture of his political loyalties, he stares back at five middle-aged men in dark suits
and white shirts, four of whom are Oxford graduates, and all of
whom have been Conservative Cabinet ministers. Difficult perhaps
to tell the difference between us.

But we are more distinct than we appear. Two of us were born
outside the United Kingdom. One of us chose to live and work in
Japan, another in Singapore, a third in Afghanistan, a fourth in Brussels. We speak more than a dozen languages between us. One of us
was adopted as a child; another watched his mother beaten by his
father; a third's brother recently killed himself.

'My question to you all is,' says Lee, 'can you guarantee to get
your Brexit plan through Parliament by 31 October?'

I wince. Boris Johnson leans forward soberly on his chair to
reassure him.

The task that faces the winner of this contest is significant. We
will be taking responsibility in five weeks' time for the fifth largest
economy in the world, and for a population larger than that of the

Roman Empire at its peak. We will govern more lives than did Julius Caesar, reaching into far more dimensions of those lives. For this is not Rome at the birth of Christ; this is Britain in the early twenty-first century, where the state touches almost everything. More than half of the population receives some form of state benefit from the government. For 10 million families, benefits make up more than half of their income. The rest rely on the state for saving their lives, helping them in sickness, and keeping the sewers open. Our values and instincts as prime ministers will determine how free, how equal or how prosperous our society becomes. We will control a budget of close to £1 trillion a year, directing the military and the police in the full coercive role of the state. It's still by a large margin one of the most powerful jobs in the world. Power failures matter.

But equally, this is not America. Britain grows only half the food we eat, produces less than half the energy we consume. Russia and Ukraine help to keep us fed and warm. We are dependent on Taiwan for 90 per cent of our advanced semiconductor chips and 50 per cent of our normal semiconductor chips, and on China for our clothes, our laptops and most of the rare earth metals on which our devices depend. We are in debt and borrowing more. A single misstep could destroy our currency, wipe out the gilt markets, spark inflation, and drive much of our country to the edge of bankruptcy almost overnight. That is before we think about the threat posed by a small dirty bomb in London, or a new pandemic.

Nor is it 2005 any more. It is 2019. We have been through the humiliations of Iraq and Afghanistan, the financial crisis and the Arab Spring. Populism is sweeping across Europe, Asia, the United States and Latin America. Three years have passed since Britain voted for Brexit. Parliament had rejected every deal with Europe, and there is no consensus on what to do for our economy or security in Northern Ireland. We are trapped by the rigidity and shallowness of our political parties, the many weaknesses in our Civil Service, and the lack of seriousness in our political culture. We are trapeze artists, stretching for holds, on rusty equipment over fatal depths. A slip is easy.

I do not trust any of the other four middle-aged men, teetering on bar stools over that mirrored floor to be prime minister. I don't trust myself either. I am standing because I feel the country is in crisis, and I believe I can forge a more workable Brexit, and fight for reality and compassion in the centre ground of a country that is painfully divided. But I don't consider my brain, or that of any of the others, adequate for our historical moment. Our life as politicians has rewired our synapses, just as profoundly as the study of London streets has enlarged the hippocampuses of London cabbies. In our case, the profession has developed not an expanded memory centre, but a capacity for shortcuts and sinuous evasions. Our brains have become like the phones in our pockets: flashing, titillating, obsequious, insinuating machines, allergic to depth and seriousness, that tempt us every moment of the day from duty, friends, family and sleep.

Each of us has a group of admirers, who find it almost inconceivable that anyone could think that Sajid, or Jeremy, or Michael, or Rory isn't exactly what the country needs, and they believe that each of us can win. The latest opinion poll, for example, suggests I am the most popular candidate with the general population – and so the argument goes, the most likely to win a general election. But Sajid's own polls suggest he leads among younger people and minorities. Michael's focus groups suggest that it must be him, because he was the most fervent proponent of Brexit three years earlier. Jeremy has the second-largest number of supporters amongst MPs. In the latest betting odds, I am the second favourite to win, with Jeremy, Michael and Sajid behind me, but a week earlier, our positions had been reversed. And Boris – well Boris – is by far the most popular both with the MPs and with the more than 100,000 members of the Conservative Party, who will choose between the final two.

These members of the Conservative Party have not worked with us. They have only vague notions of the dozens of ministerial roles through which we have each been reshuffled, and what they know has been filtered by TV producers, wrapped and packaged by newspapers, and promoted through the hidden algorithms of Twitter and Facebook. Machiavelli cannot have been the first to observe that the public cannot see the real conduct of the politician behind the palace doors. The public see the appearance that someone else chooses to share. But the party members may not care how much they know about our real achievements. Some, at least, are fed up with politicians who pretend to know better, and would like to throw one of us like a hand grenade at the entire system.

PART ONE

I.

Suddenly Coming Alive

(2003–2009)

My journey into domestic politics began in Iraq. Later I realised how many of the people I had worked with in different parts of the world wanted to make a similar journey. A man who had been a political adviser to a governor in Afghanistan, an officer who wrote on the Helmand tribes, a UN staffer specialising in the Sahel, and a conflict-resolution specialist from Myanmar all approached me for advice on how to become members of the British Parliament. But that was much later. At the time my journey felt more unusual.

I had first entered government service in 1991 as an eighteen-year-old Scottish infantry officer on a short-service limited commission. I had been in Indonesia as a British diplomat for the fall of President Suharto in 1998; had played a part in the international interventions in Bosnia and Kosovo and Afghanistan; and had spent a year and a half walking, twenty to twenty-five miles a day, across Iran, Afghanistan, Pakistan, India and Nepal. My early career was spent in a world which seemed to be becoming rapidly less violent, and less poor, and where it even seemed possible to 'make poverty history'.

When the US and the UK invaded Iraq in 2003, I was appointed to an Iraqi province, where I operated at first as the acting governor. Our money was apparently limitless – in my case delivered in vacuum-packed bricks of a million dollars in bills, which I could spend without audit. When things got sticky, 100,000 troops and AC-130 Spectre gunships stood by to back us up.

I had entered Iraq supporting the war on the grounds that we could at least produce a better society than Saddam Hussein's. It was one of the greatest mistakes in my life. We attempted to impose programmes made up by Washington think tanks, and reheated in air-conditioned palaces in Baghdad – a new taxation system modelled on Hong Kong; a system of ministers borrowed from Singapore; and free ports, modelled on Dubai. But we did it ultimately at the point of a gun, and our resources, our abstract jargon and optimistic platitudes could not conceal how much Iraqis resented us, how much we were failing, and how humiliating and degrading our work had become. Our mission was a grotesque satire of every liberal aspiration for peace, growth and democracy.

Most striking was not the failure, but the failure to acknowledge our failure. Politicians, 'experts' on Iraq and counter-insurgency and many liberal advocates for state-building, continued to insist it was working – or if it wasn't, this was simply because it wasn't being 'done right': that some new team with a new strategy could make it alright. The hysterical optimism at the highest levels was shadowed by the most profound cynicism on the ground. Too often, I and my colleagues, whether civilian or military, were encouraged to shy away from precise and honest descriptions of our failure, and instead to perpetuate worthless and extravagant projects designed to placate the imagined tastes of our political masters.

I lived these paradoxes as a relatively senior official in the occupation government. On the one hand, I felt that someone like me should never have been governing an Iraqi province. On the other, I was completely immersed in the work. During the days, I chaired meetings with senior Iraqi officials, visited schools we had funded, and tried to reason with crowds who sometimes waved banners calling for my death. In the evening I retired to my shipping container, which was wrapped, since a mortar had come through the roof without detonating, in a tea-cosy of sandbags. The trays in the dining hall and the shower blocks seemed a natural extension of the life I had known since my father – who had himself been a colonial administrator and British diplomat – sent me aged eight from our home in Malaysia to a boarding school in Oxford. But the many moments of individual courage and achievement, which I witnessed in a place of bombs and death and power far from home, were components of an illegitimate occupation.

It took two years before my bewilderment at these failures and hypocrisies, and my part in them, drove me finally to resign from government service. I did not return to Britain. Instead, having been part of an attempt to make Iraq more like the United States, I decided to try to preserve what was unique about Afghanistan. I swapped the shipping containers and airbases in Iraq for a mud fort in Kabul, and set up a small charity on behalf of the Prince of Wales, who had developed a deep love of Afghan calligraphy and woodwork. We worked to rebuild some of the houses of the old city of Kabul and support traditional craftsmen and women.

The environment in central Kabul was worse than anything I had seen in Iraq. The old city had not been rebuilt after the bombardments a decade earlier. Collapsed buildings lay eight feet deep in the street and the lanes ran with oil-thick sewage. Recently returned refugees, possessing little except a few tin pots, huddled behind curtains of rough blankets, strung across the gaps in the mud walls. There was no clinic or primary school, adult life expectancy was thirty-seven, one in five children were dying before the age of five, and almost everyone was unemployed.

Yet, stooping beneath the cracking lintels, and following the worn staircases, I found rooms decorated in ancient spirals of limestone plaster, set with glimmering glass. The inner facades of the buildings were panelled with blackened screens of cedar wood, carved into roses and lilies. Abdul Hadi who was selling bananas in the street was a master of all the forms of Kabuli carving, and a former cabinetmaker to the king. Tamim, a miniaturist – who had been tortured by the Taliban, when they found his drawings – was trying to offer private art lessons.

I started with a loan of £40,000 and one employee – my driver, whom I called my 'logistics manager'. My second employee – now called 'chief engineer' – found a hundred spades and wheelbarrows and within a day we had employed all the unemployed men in the community, clearing garbage. Within a month, they had dropped the street level by six feet. Within six weeks, we were running craft lessons for women and men. The team went on to restore over a hundred buildings, constructing along the way an art institute, a clinic and a primary school.

Working in big government jobs – governing an Iraqi province of a million people, for example – had not begun to prepare me for a start-up and running an NGO. The Prince of Wales was engaged and immensely helpful. But I got a lot wrong. The clinic that I had resisted creating ('it is not in our strategic plan') became the most successful part of the entire project, seeing 27,000 patients a year. I almost ran out of money twice.

But it was the most fulfilling work I had ever done. I liked working with Afghans. The work was the antithesis of the Iraqi occupation and its utopian dreams. We worked quickly. The young foreign volunteers who came to help on the project made me fall in love with Britain and the US again. I admired how hard they worked on their Dari, and in some cases on Pushtu and Arabic as well; how they put up with hand grenades and bombs; how they walked, and sometimes skied, in remote rural areas; collected books and plants. They were practical, effective and funny, with an ironic sense of their own limitations, honest about their lack of expertise, and sensitive and respectful to Afghans.

First among them was Shoshana, formerly a middle-school science teacher in the poorest areas of New York and Boston, who became my deputy and, much later, my wife. Without this partnership between Afghans and foreigners the community would have left; Abdul Hadi would have died without passing on his woodworking skills to a new generation, and all those buildings would have been demolished and cleared for the mayor's East German-style plan. So, the project made me optimistic about Afghans, and through the lens of the volunteers, about the West, and even about myself.

Afghanistan itself, four years after 9/11 and my walk across the country, seemed transformed. In the highlands, where on my 2001–2 walk I had seen village after village burnt to the ground by the Taliban, I now found clinics and schools. More than a million girls were going to school for the first time. Mobile phones seemed suddenly everywhere. Health and life expectancy were far better. Millions of Afghan refugees were choosing to return home. All this seemed to be a much better trajectory than Iraq, and I credited it to foreigners staying out, and keeping only a very light military footprint in Afghanistan.

Except, my former government colleagues were reaching the opposite conclusion. They told me that Afghanistan was a corrupt, violent, drug-riddled catastrophe, which only they could save. A new generation of American heroes was posted to Kabul to fulfil this dream – generals who got up at 4 a.m. to sprint eight miles around their airbase. They were not simply trying to pick up garbage in the old city. They were parachuting in, like turnaround CEOs, to fix the whole country.

The immense confidence in US and UK power to transform Afghanistan was apparently unaffected by how difficult it had been to do anything in Iraq. Perhaps if they had been seeking to turn around lives in an ex-coal town in Durham or to work with Native American tribes in South Dakota, they would have paid more attention to the history of local communities, and been more modest about their position as outsiders. They might have understood that messiness was inevitable, and patience and humility essential. But somehow in Afghanistan – a place far more traumatised, impoverished and damaged than the very poorest community at home – US and increasingly British officials were insisting that there could be a formula for success, a 'clearly defined mission', and an 'exit strategy'.

I still believed deeply in the work of the charity, and felt very lucky to be able to be part of it, but I could sense that the nation-builders were about to turn Afghanistan into as much of a mess as Iraq, and I didn't feel I could stay much longer. I had now spent fifteen years in other people's countries, touching the extremity of their politics: political revolutions and coups, invasions and civil wars. However deeply I had tried to immerse myself in rural culture, however many friends I made, I had always ultimately remained a foreigner. The laws passed by politicians, the generals and officials they appointed, their personal obsessions or unpardonable ignorance, their aggression or their absent-mindedness, could efface everything I was trying to achieve in an instant. This charity, and indeed every job I had ever done, circled around the black hole of politics.

So when Harvard University offered me a chance to be a professor and the director of a centre focused on human rights policy and

global governance, I accepted. I concentrated on building a platform to influence politicians and change US Afghan policy. The
many American politicians, whom I met through Harvard, seemed
much more serious figures than their British equivalents. John
Kerry, for example, invited me to debate him on Afghanistan in
front of 2,000 people at the National Cathedral in Washington, and
a few weeks later I joined him for dinner. Al Gore had been invited
too, and these two tall presidential candidates with magnificent
hair, the sonorous tone of Old Testament prophets and white-
toothed smiles designed to be seen by crowds of thousands, seemed
a little big for a small sitting room and a gathering of ten.

Over the main course, Kerry spoke for twenty minutes about
Afghanistan, beginning with North Waziristan and the early
nineteenth-century Popalzai federation, and finished with 'but of
course Rory you know much more about this than I do, and I should
be listening to you'. Before I could get a word in, still less suggest he
might have confused Pushtu and Panshir, he set off for another ten
minutes of 'we need to understand that what works in Mazar-e-
Sharif, a predominantly Uzbek city that fought the Taliban tooth
and nail in the 1990s, is very different from what works in Kandahar,
a Pashtun city . . .' He was not a charming dinner guest. But there
was no denying his determination to master a topic, and when
Kerry and Gore started lecturing each other on carbon parts per
million I felt I was glimpsing what it might have been like to dine
with Roman senators on their way to becoming marble statues.

I served in the diplomat Richard Holbrooke's group focusing on
Afghanistan and Pakistan, preparing a strategy for President Obama.
Secretary of State Hillary Clinton cleared time in her diary for long
discussions in her office and at dinner, in which she probed me both
on the charity and on what I had seen of the military operations.
Holbrooke lectured me exuberantly at New York lunches and in
Washington hotels, thinking nothing of waking me with calls at
one in the morning to say 'it's down to you Rory – this is Vietnam
1968 – you are the only one who can stop it. I'm sitting you next to
Hillary again tomorrow night. It is you who has to speak truth to
power.' He praised, cajoled and threatened me till my head spun.

But we failed. Hillary Clinton listened courteously but ultimately agreed with John Kerry that we needed a surge. Richard Holbrooke, who had once compared his experiences in Vietnam with mine in Iraq, suddenly turned on me at the dinner table and caricatured me as a tired British imperial throwback – Lawrence of Arabia without the tribes. I watched from Harvard, as the US force grew from 10,000 to 100,000 soldiers. $100 billion a year formed an Afghan military reliant on American technology and advisers, and supercharged corruption. Military operations killed tens of thousands. The presence of international troops in rural villages allowed the Taliban – which had been a weak and fragile group when I first returned to Afghanistan – to present itself as fighting for Afghanistan and Islam against a foreign occupation. The more troops that were killed, the more strident the speeches from Western politicians.

It was already clear what would happen when the rhetorical Ponzi scheme collapsed. As they failed to fulfil their fantasies as saviours of Afghanistan, the United States, the United Kingdom and their allies were beginning to ignore all that had actually been achieved in the cities and the highlands for women, and for public services. They had promised so much that they were no longer able to acknowledge their more humble achievements. They were lurching from insane optimism, through denial, into despair. And I could sense they were already tempted to simply slam the door and leave – blaming the chaos not on their own deadly fantasies, but on the corruption, ingratitude and cowardice of the Afghans themselves.

Cycling every day from my house to my office in Harvard, I knew that I would not be able to stop any of this if I remained an academic. Having dreamt all my life of quite different things – of being a soldier, a writer, an edgier sort of diplomat, an explorer (even, in my most pretentious moments, a philosopher or a monk) – I began to wonder whether the only way of effecting fundamental change in our states and societies was to become a politician.

The chair to which I had been appointed at Harvard had been held immediately before me by Michael Ignatieff, a journalist, political philosopher and novelist. He had written a beautiful, intimate portrait of his friend Isaiah Berlin that showed capacity for reverence, and for discipleship. He had felt more at ease at Harvard than I did. But he was also an unusual professor: clean-cut, six foot, handsome: part irreverent, self-deprecating Canadian, part worldly Russian nobleman. He knew Obama and Mario Vargas Llosa. He had applied political philosophy to difficult modern realities, sat with Serbian warlords, been in Kabul just after the fall of the Taliban, and spent time with the Kurdish survivors of Saddam's massacres. He was brave, prepared to say very difficult things and get things badly wrong – his initial support for the Iraq War, for example – and then acknowledge his mistakes.

I had inherited his centre and his position at Harvard, because two years earlier, he had chosen to leave the university and stand in Canadian politics. He had done it in his late fifties, having lived outside Canada for thirty years, with almost no connection with Canadian politics since he was eighteen. And on the basis of reputation, charisma and ability, he had become within two years the leader of the Canadian Liberal Party, the traditional ruling party of Canada, and, since the Conservatives were on the ropes, the likely next prime minister. It was a fairy tale, a public intellectual transported into politics, in the footsteps of men he knew and deeply admired: other writers turned politicians like Carlos Fuentes in Mexico, Mario Vargas Llosa in Peru and Vaclav Havel in what had been Czechoslovakia.

The person I met, when I went to stay with him in Toronto, two years after he had left Harvard, seemed to have changed. The gentle stooping figure who had entertained undergraduates with his wife Zsuzsanna, serving good French cheese in their flat in a Harvard hall of residence and taking me for walks around the blazing sugar maples in Mount Auburn cemetery, had gone. The irony, charm and flashes of honesty were still there, but there was also a new rawer energy. His hair was coiffed, and he was wearing an immaculate handmade suit. I was not quite sure whether a part of him was being suffocated, or whether he was suddenly coming alive.

'Nothing requires so much of you,' he smiled. 'Politics demands more of your mind, of your soul, of your emotions than anything on earth.' As he said this he gestured from his feet to his head, indicating the call on every muscle in his frame. 'This is by a very long shot harder than being a professor at Harvard, harder than being a freelance writer, harder than anything I've ever done, the hardest job any country has to offer. It's combat.'

'Is it really more intellectually demanding than being a professor?' I asked.

'In ways no professor can imagine. But no one in politics is interested in your thinking. You and I were trained to speculate, to ruminate, to muse about things, we are engaged in the business of showing how clever we are. The public isn't interested in how clever you are. They are not interested in your thinking; they want to know where you stand.'

I was surprised that he had somehow wrapped me into this conversation. So was politics, I asked, what I too should be doing with my life?

He was silent for a moment. 'There is a lot of gripping hands and putting on shit-eating smiles. But it also tests your capacity for self-knowledge in a way, teaches you things about yourself, that nothing else can. It is a chance to stop being a spectator, to leave the stands and get in the game.'

'Does it suit you?'

'Yes, I think it does, says an otherwise sensible person who has turned his life upside down.' He pursed his lips. 'There are moments of exaltation. And there are thrills. But I'm very pleased I came to it later in life, when there is some wine laid down in the cellar, and I have done enough to sometimes think, you know . . .' His voice became a little gruffer, 'I've done a lot of things. I'm not a kid any more. I know some things about human beings.'

'So is this what we should all be doing?'

He looked at me. 'I know your father, and I had a father like that.' He had been particularly struck meeting my eighty-six-year-old father: a mischievous, tough, supremely competent, D-Day veteran, who had served as a colonial officer in Malaya and ended his government career as a very senior figure in the British Secret

Intelligence Service. Michael saw in him a powerful image of an older Scotland, an older Britain. He sensed how much I loved my father, and seemed to suspect that, despite my attempts at contemporary irony, I was still shaped by his reading me Kipling's *Kim*. Michael's father had been a very senior Canadian diplomat.

'We both come,' Michael continued, 'from people with a calling for public life. But our lives are not a tradition inherited, a way of living up to family imperatives, which are anyway half-invented. It doesn't matter what your father expects of you. And I'm pretty sure, he doesn't expect this. And, in any case, it is the wrong answer to why you go into politics. You don't do it to live up to them. You do it for you.'

I was puzzled by his answer. I hadn't been thinking of my father or my family when I asked the question.

'So why,' I asked, 'did you go into politics?'

'Apart from self-dramatisation, self-importance, and hubris?' he grinned. 'Forget your childhood, your father's heroes, your books, your distinguished career in public service and the rest. No one cares.' But despite his words, I sensed that his admiration for his father's generation of public servants was deep, and there was still nostalgia and tradition, behind this progressive liberal, perfectly brushed for his appearance on hi-definition TV. 'And if you do do it,' he said, 'be honest about who you are and where you come from. Okay you are an upper-middle-class Scot and you believe in public service. So what? Fuck 'em.'

I grinned.

'In politics,' he continued, 'you earn your support one handshake at a time. And there can be only one answer to that question and they want to hear you say it . . .'

'Say what?'

'What you say, what you always say, is that you want to make a difference. People want to hear you say that you are in it for them.'

A scandal broke in the UK over parliamentary expenses in the spring of 2009. It seemed that the whips had encouraged Members of Parliament to put as much as they could on their expenses, as an alternative to voting for a salary rise. Few MPs seemed troubled. Until, at least, someone downloaded the millions of pieces of correspondence between the fees office and each Member of Parliament, including the handwritten comments scrawled in margins, and Post-it notes, and sold them to the *Daily Telegraph*. The *Telegraph* turned the cache into a daily reality show: 'the Welsh Secretary splashed out more than £3,000 on a new hot water system for his second home, explaining in a letter to the parliamentary fees office that his water was too hot'.

On they went, emailing a few MPs at noon every day, giving them five hours to reply, recording their conversations – and slowly drip-feeding the stories onto their front page. Half a million extra readers bought the *Daily Telegraph*. The office of the Home Secretary, Jacqui Smith, had submitted a £67 claim for Internet, into which was bundled a television subscription, and two £5 purchases for 'additional features': a euphemism for pornography, apparently paid for by her husband when she was travelling. The *Sunday Express* front page ran: 'World Exclusive: Jacqui Smith put adult films on expenses'.

The papers were full of new jargon, taken from the expenses rule book. But it was the substance of the claims, rather than their technical category, that caught the public's attention. How David Cameron had claimed for the 'pruning of his wisteria', Douglas Hogg for cleaning his moat, and Peter Viggers for a floating duck-house. In the polling, 66 per cent of the public said MPs cared most about serving their own personal interest, and 70 per cent that they were out of touch with the day-to-day lives of their constituents.

In the midst of this, I was invited to see the former MP and leader of the Liberal Democrats, Paddy Ashdown, in the House of Lords. An aide led me into a narrow corridor. Ashdown emerged and seized my hand, and drew me into a small office with claustrophobic wallpaper, thorny with vines of fruit and heraldry. He said he had liked my books on Iraq and Afghanistan. 'I haven't walked across Afghanistan like you. In fact, I have never visited. But my great-grandfather,' he growled, smile lines breaking across his tanned face, 'was in the Second Anglo-Afghan War. At Maiwand.' He fancied we had reached similar conclusions about intervention,

and he wanted my support to become the senior civilian administrator in Afghanistan.

Put on the spot, half-enthralled, and feeling, to my surprise, awkwardly keen to impress, I said that I understood the importance of
his experience from Bosnia, where he had been the UN High
Representative.

'Do you think it is relevant?' he said, his blue eyes squinting from
beneath flamboyantly bushy eyebrows.

'Yes – after all so much of it is about knowing people,' I pattered
on, somehow repressing my firm conviction that someone like him
or indeed me should never be trying to rule Afghanistan.

There was a lull. He gazed like an emperor out of the window,
down onto Parliament Square. I explained that I had been a Labour
Party member at eighteen but had voted Lib Dem in 1997. 'Do you
think,' I asked coyly, 'I should be an MP?' Now it was his turn to
encourage my ambitions and flatter me as I had him. With perhaps
as little conviction. 'Absolutely,' he said, 'it is the best, the only, the
great game. But for God's sake don't become a Lib Dem, the point
is to be a minister,' said the former leader of the Lib Dems. 'Lib
Dems get nothing done.'

Returning to New York, I sat with my friend Indrani in a diner.
While I sipped a refill of weak coffee and she went off to the bagel
selection, I looked at the paper. An article said that David Cameron
was calling for people who had not been involved in politics before
to become Members of Parliament.

'What do you think about my becoming an MP?' I asked
Indrani.

'I think that is a very bad idea,' she said.

She meant becoming an MP. But she probably also meant the
Conservative Party. I was closer, I knew, to Labour positions on
immigration, and criminal justice, the Civil Service and probably
poverty. The only visiting British politician I had warmed to in
Afghanistan was the Labour Foreign Secretary David Miliband.
But I blamed the Labour government for what I had seen in Iraq.
I felt that the technocratic fantasies, and indifference to tradition

and local communities which I had seen there and in Afghanistan, reflected something in New Labour's attitude to Britain. I was suspicious of big government and the obsession of progressive think tanks with inappropriate and inapplicable models from Scandinavia.

I had grown up revering the military, the monarchy, and many aspects of traditional Britain, with which my Labour friends had little sympathy. My community work in the Murad Khane district of Kabul seemed much closer to what the Conservative leader David Cameron called the 'Big Society'. If forced to spell out a political philosophy, I would have said that I believed in limited government and individual rights; prudence at home and strength abroad; respect for tradition, and love of my country. In short, as a fellow academic who was applying to be a Labour MP observed, I was perhaps if not a Conservative, then at least a Tory.

2.

Gajumaru Trees

I was in Kabul in 2009 when an email arrived telling me I had been given fifteen minutes in the diary of the Conservative leader, David Cameron, in London. In the Kabul departure lounge, a friend said, 'You know more about Afghan politics than you do about British. But I'm not even sure how much you really know about Afghanistan. What you think you have learned about politics in Indonesia or Iraq has nothing to do with politics in Britain.'

I had met Cameron only once before, and that had been in Afghanistan in 2006. The call from the British Embassy in Kabul had come when I was in a bear hug with the local seller of mystical amulets, Kaka Azim, who was pressing the sharp edges of his turquoise necklaces into my chest. I was delayed by long, intricate greetings from the blacksmith, and the man who fried goat's brains. In a triple-length shipping container in the guarded embassy compound, I found the heads of the larger NGOs. But David Cameron didn't arrive for another half an hour. When he entered, he was finishing a sentence apparently about how well the British military were doing. I noticed how fine his hair was.

'Good afternoon,' he said in a light baritone, sitting down and looking at the Americans, Australians and Afghans around the table. 'Normally right at this moment I would be drinking a cup of tea with eight sugars in it.' He paused with an easy smile. The NGO directors looked at each other. 'A tip I got from William Hague. Although,' he added in a stage whisper, 'don't tell him, I don't actually do it.' At this point he was perhaps becoming conscious of the fact that none of us had any idea what he was talking about. 'You see, it is Prime Minister's Questions at this moment.' Then he leaned back in his chair. This was not the kind of opening that any of us were accustomed to in the many briefings which we had all been asked to attend at other embassies: neither the fierce, rapid fire of facts from General Petraeus, nor General McChrystal's sincere, infectious enthusiasm, nor Ambassador Holbrooke's gruff criticism, and cunning questions.

An Australian woman spoke first about the snowfall in Bamiyan and explained that unless the UK provided emergency assistance, 100,000 could starve. Others made brief speeches about the antipathy towards the Afghan police in rural areas, and the ways in which the foreign military operations were creating more Taliban insurgents. I said we might be able to contain the Taliban, but we could not defeat them.

When we had finished, we waited. We were accustomed from other meetings to the principal guest taking notes, and then testing their theories on counter-insurgency, development and corruption. (John Kerry, of course, did this at considerable length.) But Cameron, who was rumoured to be sceptical about nation-building projects, only nodded, and then looking confidently up and down the table said, 'Well, at least we all agree on one extremely straightforward and simple point, which is that our troops are doing very difficult and important work and we should all support them.'

It was an odd statement to make to civilians running humanitarian operations on the ground. I felt I should speak. 'No, with respect, we do not agree with that. Insofar as we have focused on the troops, we have just been explaining that what the troops are doing is often futile, and in many cases making things worse.' Two small red dots appeared on his cheeks. Then his face formed back into a smile. He thanked us, told us he was out of time, shook all our hands, and left the room.

Later, I saw him repeat the same line in interviews: 'the purpose of this visit is straightforward . . . it is to show support for what our troops are doing in Afghanistan'. The line had been written, in London, I assumed, and tested on focus groups. But he wanted to convince himself it was also a position of principle.

'David has decided,' one of his aides explained, when I met him later, 'that one cannot criticise a war when there are troops on the ground.'

'Why?'

'Well . . . we have had that debate. But he feels it is a principle of British government.'

'But Churchill criticised the conduct of the Boer War; Pitt the war with America. Why can't he criticise wars?'

'British soldiers are losing their lives in this war, and we can't suggest they have died in vain.'

'But more will die, if no one speaks up . . .'

'It is a principle thing. And he has made his decision. For him and the party.'

'Does this apply to Iraq too?'

'Yes. Again he understands what you are saying, but he voted to support the Iraq War, and troops are on the ground.'

'But surely he can say he's changed his mind?'

The aide didn't answer, but instead concentrated on his food. 'It is so difficult,' he resumed, 'to get any coverage of our trip.' He paused again. 'If David writes a column about Afghanistan, we will struggle to get it published.'

'But what would he say in an article anyway?' I asked.

'We can talk about that later. But how do you get your articles on Afghanistan published?'

I remembered how US politicians and officials had shown their mastery of strategy and detail, I remembered the earnestness of Gordon Brown when I had briefed him on Iraq. Cameron seemed somehow less serious. I wrote as much in a column in the *New York Times*, saying that I was afraid the party of Churchill was becoming the party of Bertie Wooster.

Now, three years had passed since our meeting in Kabul and that article. In that time, Gordon Brown had replaced Tony Blair as prime minister, the global financial system had crashed, and David Cameron had moved the Conservative Party from its long flirtation with an anti-European, anti-immigration ideology back to the middle ground. He had embraced more socially liberal policies – particularly on the environment, international aid, and gay marriage – and Gordon Brown's struggle with the economy had helped to put Cameron well ahead in the opinion polls.

I had been told to report for our meeting in an extension to Parliament called Portcullis House. From the outside it was a glass and stone cube capped with a cluster of thick dark chimneys – as though a 1980s retail block was experimenting with the identity of an Edwardian power station. Its inner atrium consisted of a line of gajumaru trees – rented through some private-public partnership, which was said to have already cost the taxpayer £250,000. I knew these trees in Indonesia as the haunts of beautiful demons who ripped your eyes out with their nails.

I was led from the glass terminal into an older building, which had once been a police headquarters. Four men sat in Cameron's outer office, with floppy hair and open-necked white shirts: speech-writer, head of strategy, chief of staff, chancellor's chief of staff, all Old Etonians. I knew them because I had also gone to Eton, and I liked some of them. But I was astonished that Cameron could have filled his private office in this way. I employed 300 people in Kabul, including thirty foreigners, and not one had been to my school.

Outside this office, Cameron had launched a campaign to bring in women and people from working-class and minority-ethnic backgrounds to be MPs – people like the British Asian public affairs professional Priti Patel, or the state-educated think-tank director Liz Truss. He would promote them fast so that he could announce, proudly, to the media that his Cabinet was the most diverse in history. Nor did he ever miss a chance to insist that 'diversity makes government better'. And yet his real inner team, and his closest friends, with whom he developed policy, were drawn from an unimaginably narrow social group. There were exceptions: Kate Fall, his deputy chief of staff, and George Osborne, his shadow chancellor, only appeared to have gone to Eton.

This inner office, however, seemed to consist exclusively of that tiny slice of right-wing Old Etonians who had been engaged with Conservative politics since their twenties. I'd seen nothing like it in almost twenty years of working life. I was gestured through to an inner office, where Cameron sat in an open-necked, white shirt with its cuffs unbuttoned, leaning backwards on a green sofa. He indicated, without warmth, a small armchair, in which I sat primly, while he walked out to chat to his staff. When he returned, and I introduced myself, he nodded as though I were a total stranger.

Here, far from Kabul, we were on his ground, and I was the petitioner eager to please. I apologised for taking his time and tried to explain why my experience might be relevant for his government. I explained that I had set up and run a charity in a tough place. I had managed large budgets, run Iraqi provinces. I had worked in the government, in different roles, for many years. I suggested that my knowledge of Asia or America could be useful for a country that was a permanent member of the Security Council, that was entangled in Afghanistan, and whose economy depended on the US and China.

But I assured him I wasn't simply a technocrat. I loved Britain, its institutions, its history and its landscape. Scotland, not Afghanistan, was my home. My father had fought in the war. My grandfather had been a doctor at the creation of the NHS. And although it wasn't my place to say it, I could think reasonably clearly, speak in public, manage teams, handle a crisis. And I cared. I didn't want to be rich, or famous. The only thing that had ever really motivated me since I was a small child was the idea of public service.

When I finished, I hoped for some warm words. I got none. He stared at me with the air of a man who had been talked reluctantly into accepting a meeting, forgotten about it, and then been annoyed to find it in his diary. I could have placed Paddy Ashdown easily as a tanned Marines colonel or a piratical intelligence chief, but looking at Cameron's fine hair, pink full cheeks, narrow eyes and blurred features, I struggled to imagine him in any other profession.

I could already sense that my speech had irritated him, that he did not want me, and that he felt that he had met dozens of people like me before who wondered whether they should not, late in life, 'give back' and become a politician, who assumed that politics was simply a charitable endeavour that could be picked up as easily as clicking on a newsletter. Unlike him, we had never fought the street fights of democracy, had never been flattened by the insouciant brutality of the press, begged a wealthy donor, kowtowed to a drunken party whip, or endured the daily insolence of the voters. We were amateurs in a professional game – dangerous amateurs who probably imagined we were somehow above such things.

Politics had been Cameron's life from the very moment he had joined the Conservative Research Department as a twenty-one year-old, in 1988. He had been shortlisted for a seat in Kent in 1994, but was not chosen; was selected for Stafford in 1996, but failed to take the seat in the 1997 general election; failed to make the shortlist for Kensington in 1999, was shortlisted but not selected for Wealden, and only won a seat in 2001.

While I had been on boats in the Java sea or in Iranian mosques he had been serving his time as a special adviser, or sitting patiently on the back benches mastering parliamentary procedure. He had been in the party when Thatcher fell, had served Major's Cabinet, and had been a special adviser in the Treasury when the pound collapsed and George Soros and the short-sellers looted the Bank of England. He had absorbed the scale of Tony Blair's victory and learned to imitate his techniques. He had held his nose to vote for the right-wing leader Iain Duncan Smith in the dark days, served in the shadow Cabinet, and now was within reach of becoming the youngest prime minister in 200 years. He was a veteran of life on Mars, who knew exactly what that planet cost its inhabitants, and here was I proposing to fly in, expecting to be welcomed, as though I were volunteering in a soup kitchen.

But Michael Ignatieff had been clear that before I gave up my chair at Harvard, I needed to know where I stood. 'You have to look him in the eyes and see if he wants you. Don't take the job if he doesn't.' So I said as politely as I could to Cameron that I didn't understand the system but I would like some sense of whether he thought it was likely that if I became an MP, I might at some point anyway be promoted to be a minister. Because really, I felt my skills and interests lay more in management.

Finally he spoke, and his voice was a reprimand, 'If you are lucky enough to find a seat, and be elected, you will find that being a backbench Member of Parliament is the greatest honour you can have in life. I may be lucky enough to become prime minister but when I cease to be prime minister I will return with great pride to the back benches as Member of Parliament for Witney, for the rest of my life.'

There was a silence. We exchanged another couple of sentences, then he said goodbye, picked up some papers and walked back to chat to the team in the outer office. I had learnt whether Cameron was interested in making me a minister. Seven years later, when Cameron resigned as prime minister, and then almost immediately resigned from his seat on the back benches, I learnt something more about him.

But I was now too interested in the idea of politics to back out. Looking at the whole golden block of Parliament, from Big Ben to Victoria Tower, I felt that none of my public life to date would make sense unless I at least tried to enter what Michael had called 'the arena'. Being a civil servant was not enough; it was only via Parliament that I really had a hope of preserving what I still loved, and repairing what was shameful about British policy at home and abroad. And so I set off to try to learn about constituencies, and see if I might be chosen as an MP.

3

The Livestock Ring

(2009–2010)

Entering Parliament means winning a primary and then an election for a parliamentary seat. I had only the vaguest idea about what this might entail. I quickly discovered that my home constituency, which included my and my parents' house in Scotland, had long ago selected an active local campaigner as their candidate, as had all the neighbouring areas. The nearest seat to my home that seemed a possible option was Penrith and the Border, the most remote, sparsely populated, isolated and beautiful constituency in England, running along the Scottish border. It had a sitting conservative MP, David Maclean. But he had led the campaign in Parliament to prevent the publication of MPs' expenses, and, after being defeated by the courts, had found himself the target of the *Evening Standard* headline: 'One wife, two mistresses . . . and a quad bike on Commons expenses.' There seemed a good chance that he might not run again, but he had not yet announced anything.

Since I felt I learned best about places by walking, I decided I would walk the 150 miles down to Penrith from my home in Scotland, the week after my meeting with Cameron. It took six days, crossing the Ochils beyond Auchterarder, over the Forth Road Bridge, through the lowlands, and then up into the border hills above Traquair. I entered England and this constituency over the great stone bridge by Longtown, and spent much of that morning asleep beneath a hawthorn hedge. Strengthened by a bacon butty, bought from a van, I continued across the heavy clay fields of the Cumberland plain, trespassing on the gardens of a frontier castle, and then followed the Eden river along a bright-watered gorge, whose sandstone cliffs were smooth as clay on a wheel. I encountered little except a hazel coppice and a kingfisher. The only man I met lived in a caravan, and had moved to the area a few months earlier. Walking, it seemed, was not an efficient approach to political campaigning.

On the second night, a Cumbrian connection by marriage gave me a bed. Over pheasant stew that evening, he and his wife encouraged me to read the back issues of the *Cumberland and Westmorland Herald*, and over the next few days, walked me through the housing estates in Penrith, tested me on the prices in the agricultural fairs, introducing me to dairy farmers, and to teachers. I set up a meeting with the small Bangladeshi community in Penrith, but only two or three tired men came to see me. They explained that many of them were working nights and resting during the day. After the meeting, an elderly lady stopped me in the street and said, 'You hardly see a white face in Penrith any more.' The statistics suggested Penrith and the Border was 98 per cent white.

Many constituents in Penrith and the Border seemed to have accepted their MP's defence that he had needed to buy a quad bike on expenses because he had been diagnosed with multiple sclerosis. But fewer seemed to forgive him for leaving his wife, who had run the local association on his behalf for twenty years. The few Conservative activists I met seemed to have forgotten the decades they had spent alongside the MP, canvassing and door-knocking, in their fight not just to hold Penrith, but to win the neighbouring seat in Carlisle. The local press reporting was hostile. I was not surprised when, not long after my walk, he announced that he would be stepping down after twenty-seven years, citing ill health.

There was now, therefore, a vacancy. But to have a chance of filling it, I would have to pass through half a dozen tests, each controlled by different levels of the national or local Conservative Party. The party had just over 100,000 members nationally: 0.2 per cent of the British population – a catastrophic decline from the 2.5 million members when my mother was a young member. With 400 members Penrith and the Border was considered a reasonably large local party. I began to try to meet some of the members. They included a retired police dog handler, a group of dairy farmers with gleaming SUVs, a postman and a shy landowner who decorated his table with silver pheasants. Most of them seemed to be quiet, old-fashioned people, with a gentle interest in politics and a deep pride in their county. They combined their participation in the Conservative Party with fundraising for local charities. But the party had hardly attracted a new member in twenty years, and the shrinking association was dominated by local councillors, mostly retired men and women who had run small businesses, and who dedicated their lives to the daily doorstep fight against Labour and the Liberal Democrats.

The councillors were not, it seemed, looking for someone like me. They told me that they preferred MPs who joined the party young, who volunteered in elections, served as local councillors, and then contested unwinnable parliamentary seats, before they thought of applying for a winnable seat. They wanted younger people to help them with local campaigning and so it suited them to make this a prerequisite for becoming an MP. This was a common view across Britain and meant that convincing an association to accept you as a candidate was usually a long path even for the most favoured. Cameron – the quintessential insider – had applied for seven years to multiple constituencies before he was finally elected. Michael Howard, Cameron's predecessor as Conservative leader, first stood unsuccessfully for Parliament seventeen years before he actually won a seat. Another MP, who entered Parliament with me, had served as a councillor for thirty years, fighting nine local council elections, before entering the House of Commons at the age of sixty.

The curious personalities that emerged in Parliament at the end of this process were, I was beginning to realise, the product of a Darwinian process of party selection and rejection. The particular compound of canniness and ignorance, fluency, misdirected loyalty and awkward dishonesties which made the modern MP, had evolved to survive the demands of the dominant party members, just as much as the unsanitary habits of wrinkle-lipped free-tailed bats were formed by their long years in deep Bornean caves.

I asked the Conservative candidate who had been selected for my home seat in Scotland to introduce me to campaigning. He invited me to join him on a Saturday morning. I arrived, looking for a campaign headquarters packed with volunteers, posters and tele-phones, and found five people assembled outside Argos. It was 10 a.m. With my mother, whom I had persuaded to accompany me, we totalled seven. All bar the candidate and me were over sixty; one lady was in her eighties.

The candidate, however, seemed to fit the part: tall and confi-dent, with a well-tailored suit and sweeping black hair, fascinated by American as much as British politics and an expert on Obama's and George W. Bush's electoral campaigns. Importantly – in a political culture often suspicious of outsiders parachuting in – this was his home. One of the volunteers whispered that his family grew half the daffodils in Scotland.

We were arranged in two teams. Blue rosettes, the size of small plates, were pinned to our raincoats, and we were provided with rain-spattered photocopies of a local map, on which the campaign manager had highlighted certain streets in acid yellow. Our leaflets depicted David Cameron with flawless airbrushed skin, beneath a cartoon oak tree. A shopper passed, and one of our volunteers scur-ried after her, calling 'I'm from the Scottish Conservative Party. I wonder if I might ask you a couple of questions.' The shopper shook her head violently, hunched her shoulders into the drizzle, and accelerated towards Costa Coffee. The volunteer trotted back, with the air of a spaniel who has failed to retrieve a duck.

The candidate pointed to the empty shopfronts. He had spent the previous Saturday with 'his team', putting up some children's art-work in the windows. The artwork had fallen down. There was a discussion about whether to use Blu Tack, instead of glue. We moved to the residential streets and, being directed towards number 15, opened the low gate, walked up the short path, and knocked on the door. There was no answer, so we pushed a leaflet through the letter box, and proceeded to number 17. A man opened the door and said he was too busy to talk. A woman three doors down said she was looking after a baby; and at the next address, a couple claimed to be 'having dinner'. After half an hour we were yet to elicit a sin-gle piece of information. Seven of us were canvassing the 60,000 voters in this constituency. This, the candidate said, was not unusual.

In 650 constituencies across the country, Conservative, Labour and Lib Dem candidates were doing the same. Just before a general election the number of active volunteers might creep up to thirty.

After an hour, one of the older volunteers shouted across the street, 'I suggest you stop knocking on doors. No one likes being bothered on a weekend. And no one is going to give you their mobile number. How about just pushing a leaflet through every door?'

The candidate, eager both to please the central party by sticking to their template, and to placate this volunteer, who was reporting on his performance, suggested one more street. Perhaps the candidate was hoping that some voters might conclude from his progress down each cul-de-sac that he was a man of energy and diligence. But no voters were to be seen.

Finally, a door was opened by a large man in shorts, with veined biceps, and a tight white T-shirt. 'Ah,' he said, 'I've been waiting for you. I'd like to talk to the candidate, please . . .'

I smiled, and called the candidate over.

'Another corrupt MP eh?' he began, 'Up to your snout in the expenses scandal. What you claiming for at the moment? Your bath plug? Your Walkman? Probably claiming for visiting me, no?'

'No, no,' the candidate explained quickly, 'I'm not an MP yet, I'm—'

'Just waiting your chance then, eh? In training. What you gonna buy first?'

'I'm as disappointed as you are—'

'Are you now?'

'I am—'

'Are you now indeed?'

'That's right, if I'm elected—'

'Conservative? Mrs Thatcher, eh? You gonna ride police horses into the face of the working man?'

'No, I—'

'I don't know how you sleep at night,' the man said with joyful finality, and closed the door with a bang.

★

I had still not even been approved for the candidates' list, and the application form gave me little hope. In the section entitled 'Party Membership', I could put nothing. Under 'Political Experience' I had written about my daily work in Kabul and organising elections in Iraq. In section 9, 'Have you at any time been a member of a Political Party, Society or Organisation other than the Conservative Party?', I wrote 'The Labour Party' and added for exoneration, '(as a young student in 1991)'.

It was already becoming clear to me that in any normal year I would have been rejected almost immediately. But this was not a normal year. The fifty Conservative MPs who were stepping down had resigned in the expenses scandal *after* the party had already allocated its favoured candidates to the vacant parliamentary seats. Cameron – insisting that 'our political system needs radical change' – had reopened the candidates' list. With the Conservatives now leading the Labour government by ten points in the polls, he seemed to need many more Members of Parliament.

So, on 26 August 2009, I was invited to the assessment centre, in a grey-carpeted conference centre in the suburbs of Cambridge. I found myself among older men in heavy suits, younger men in pointed brown shoes, and a few women. They were mostly local councillors who had already given tens of thousands of hours of unpaid service to the party. Upstairs in what seemed to be called 'Milling Area 1', we were asked to make recommendations about a road bypass, draft letters to citizens and role-play chairing a committee. I recognised the type of test from the Civil Service selection board I had sat fifteen years earlier. The party was already planning to replace this test with an analysis of candidates' 'campaigning report from the last general election', which would have suited my competitors more. But I was benefitting from the older system, which seemed to have been designed more to predict people's potential as administrators. The process ended with an interview with a sitting MP. Instead of speaking, I asked him questions. Grateful for the opportunity to be listened to, the MP talked at length and then endorsed me. Perhaps because of the extraordinary number of vacant seats created by the expenses scandal, or perhaps because

I was practised in this kind of assessment, I was told that I was allowed to apply to any vacant seat in the country, rather than being restricted on my first attempt to Labour-held seats.

From the selection board, I was passed on to a set of party meetings in the south, where I was briefed on electoral regulations, and on the process for printing leaflets. Here I began to meet future colleagues, most of whom, it seemed, had already fought and lost at least once before. A would-be MP for a London seat explained that she had stood four times. Almost all had given up decently paid jobs, and taken on debt. Each, it seemed, had dedicated hundreds of mornings to pacing streets with their blue rosettes, their afternoons to defending party scandals on local radio, and their evenings to chatting over sizzling sausages with elderly activists. The central party had measured them on how many leaflets they had delivered, and on how many mentions they had achieved in the local paper. Sometimes the party had demanded they do things which cost them their seats. The tall candidate who had taken me round my home seat, for example, had been pushed by the party to make claims on VAT, which proved to be misleading, and which lost him the seat after two years of work.

None of this was unique to the Conservative Party. If they had been running for Labour they would have had to win over an equally small and unrepresentative local party association – compete with local councillors who had consumed a decade trying to stitch up their selection, neutralise the Trotskyite left, fight challenges on their income and ideological purity – and then settle into years of almost identical local campaigning purgatory, and party micro-management. Many feared they would never make it to Parliament.

A candidate who was a doctor told me that his medical qualifications were ignored, and that he was discriminated against as a white man; a Sikh businessman said he was conscious of how white the party remained. Some felt despised for having not been to Oxford or Cambridge, others for having been there; some for having been long-serving local councillors, and others for not having been councillors. Jacob Rees-Mogg had stood unsuccessfully for Parliament in 1997 and 2001 – it was now 2009 – and his sister had just been thrown off the candidates' list. But twenty other people in the room felt the party was biased in favour of people exactly like Rees-Mogg.

No one felt that the party valued them for their personality, their intelligence, or their experience. Nor for their ability to make a speech, to analyse policy, or to lead a country. Instead, they were prized for their ability to protect leaflets from the rain; enter a locked apartment block using the caretaker's code; partner with eighty-year-old male members, and understand their needs for lavatory breaks; and protect their fingertips from the sprung letter box and the teeth of a silent dog.

To be selected for a shortlist I now needed to win over the committees of local Conservative associations. It was suggested that I apply to many. One candidate encouraged me to focus on seats with larger minority-ethnic populations – with 'your years in Asia and the Middle East – your ability to speak some Asian languages'. I applied to two such seats, but neither invited me for an interview.

I was, however, shortlisted for Bracknell, whose sitting MP had resigned after a televised public meeting in which he was accused of being a 'thieving toad'. An ex-Cabinet minister told me that Bracknell was ideal, and I should forget Penrith: 'You are interested in international affairs. Penrith is too far from Heathrow.'

Bracknell is a new town of the 1950s, forty miles from London. I travelled up the day before the interview and found that at its centre lay a complex of concrete piazzas, towers and tunnels, planned for a future of space-suited residents in hoverjets, and fronted for the time being by faded department stores, and empty lots. No one I met who worked in Bracknell lived there; and no one who lived there worked there. People seemed to be passing through on their way either back to London or further out into the country.

I was on the shortlist with Iain Dale, a veteran Conservative Party member, radio host and commentator, and Phillip Lee, councillor, 2005 parliamentary candidate, and a doctor with a local practice. The final question in the Blue Mountain Golf Centre was what our greatest ambition would be as MPs. I produced a convoluted vision of transforming education and foreign policy. Phillip said, 'To be the first MP to score a century at Lord's.'

Phillip was selected.

Less than nine months remained until the next election. Cameron had been making it clear that he did not want me in Parliament. He had said this to Michael Ignatieff, not knowing he was my friend, adding 'Rory is a modern Julian Amery.' Amery was an exotic figure from another age, a partisan fighter in Albania, a friend of foreign potentates, a drinker, on the wrong side of history over Suez, with a reputation for being more keen on desert adventures than on visiting his constituency. Another friend had been in a party meeting in which Cameron snapped 'Rory Stewart is exactly the kind of person we don't want in Parliament.' Paradoxically, however, this seemed to help me. I was told that a senior party official was pushing my candidacy out of irritation at Cameron's opposition. But I was warned that this could not happen more than once and that, if I didn't get the next seat I applied for, I was finished.

Three hundred of us applied for Penrith and the Border, the seat to which I had walked from Scotland. The likeliest candidate was a tweed-jacketed councillor who ran a dairy business in the Eden Valley. He had been the youngest member of the Penrith and the Border association in 1990, and was still the youngest member in 2009. He had attended perhaps 400 local Party meetings, and seemed to effortlessly balance his farming with campaigns about rubbish collection and saving public toilets. He had supported the previous MP for twenty years, pounding the streets with a voter-registration sheet in his hand, a rosette on his chest, and leaflets in his bag. I was told he had a better chance than me because unlike me, he was married.

Then there was Tom Lowther. The Lowthers had been in the Lowther Valley so long that no one knew whether the valley was named for them, or they for the valley, whether they were descended from Viking chiefs, or earlier Iron Age chieftains. Fifty Lowthers had represented the seat since the early Middle Ages. Until the 1980s, all non-Lowther MPs had acknowledged this by marking election day with a champagne breakfast at Lowther Castle and riding to the Penrith count in a Lowther carriage wearing not a blue rosette but a yellow rosette in the Lowther colours. Tom was the grandson of the Lowther earl, and a farmer. He was a Conservative county councillor like his father before him.

But when the shortlist was published, both the dairy farmer and Tom Lowther were excluded and I made it through. I never worked out why. Had some of the local councillors on the committee, who had worked with them for decades, been jealous of one of their own going through? Or had the candidates been blocked, as they believed, by Central Office?

The other five on the Penrith shortlist were long-standing party activists from the Midlands and the north. Three were sitting Conservative councillors, who had run for Labour-controlled, northern parliamentary seats in the last 2005 election. They stressed their 'local' connections in Penrith, making the most of cousins, and half-forgotten holidays in the Lake District, in carefully composed leaflets, fronted with a photograph of them by the Penrith town clock, proclaiming their support for the local agricultural college and the dualling of the A66. Two of them, sensitive to a farming constituency, described themselves as farmers. Their opponents whispered that one rented out a couple of fields for sheep and the other sold hamsters with his husband at Hexham mart.

I spent a great deal of time talking to John Hatt, a retired publisher who lived in an old restored farmhouse on the edge of the Howgills. John could summon roe deer by blowing through a blade of grass, make wild tawny owls swoop to feed from his hand, and spot otter spraint at 200 yards. He knew the tribal areas of Orissa/Odisha, and river dolphins on the Irrawaddy and jaguars in Brazil, and had stood once as a Conservative local councillor in what he described as a 'rough part of Wandsworth'. He sent me clippings from the *Daily Mail*, and the *Cumberland and Westmorland Herald* – quizzed me, and trained me by making a dozen bets, on which political figures would be fired, and which would survive. He suggested a list of forty people to meet – from the head of the local auction mart, to neighbouring party chairmen, and the editor of the local newspaper. He began to reach out across Cumbria, and encourage his friends to attend to vote for me.

Meanwhile, my more experienced opponents spent evenings in the Conservative Club, went canvassing for the local elections, and worked their way through all the office holders in the local association, to pick up hints on what would count in the final vote. Normally, theirs would have been the only sensible approach to selection, but I was the beneficiary of a Cameron innovation, an open primary, in which not just local party members but every voter in the constituency, regardless of party membership, was entitled to vote. This made some democratic sense: the choice of a candidate for a safe Conservative seat, which almost guaranteed a place in the House of Commons, should have been made by more than a few elderly members of the local association. But it enraged local party members, who felt they had paid their £25 a year membership precisely for the privilege of selecting a candidate.

I wondered how Cameron had come by the idea. Perhaps it was something that he had encountered as an undergraduate, or perhaps someone had convinced him that it was more likely to result in a diverse and loyal group of MPs. In any case, it was one of those ideas on constitutional reform that occasionally occurred to him. He did it in only a few places and, troubled perhaps by the kind of candidates that it produced, dropped the idea at the next election.

The final selection meeting took place on a Sunday evening, 25 October 2009, in Penrith auction mart which, like most of the other livestock rings in the constituency, was shaped like a Roman theatre. The audience sat on the semicircle of concrete benches, looking down at the stage. On my last visit, there had been seven jittery Swaledale sheep in the ring – one held by a curling horn, that could have graced an ibex – overseen by a barrel-chested, white-aproned man with a crackling microphone. Now the droppings had been scrubbed from the concrete floor and we, the candidates, were to speak precisely where the Texels and mules had skittered and jumped. I could still smell the rich but not unpleasant odour – a blend of milk, manure, grass and strong soap – of people who had washed well after milking.

Barely 200 people were present. The elderly farmers in caps at the back, with the air of aficionados waiting for the matador, appeared not to have moved since viewing the sheep. Other groups, I guessed from the clothing – stiff new jackets in one case, soft and faded tweed in another – were a combination of Conservative councillors and landowners. The groups in hiking anoraks seemed to be Lib Dems, there for the fun. Someone whispered that one of my rivals, a key member of the conservative Christian network, and an anti-abortion campaigner, had packed the stands with evangelical church people. Perhaps half of 1 per cent of the adults in the constituency had turned up, where in a US primary the turnout would be generally at least 15 per cent. I was astonished that more people had not come, because whoever was selected in this safe Conservative seat would almost certainly become the next Member of Parliament.

As I walked towards the auction office, which served as a green room, a councillor caught my arm. 'Let me tell you who we are looking for,' he said. 'We want a local man. We want a married, family man. We want someone who understands this area. Preferably we want a farmer. And we want a good Conservative. I'm not sure you fit the bill, do you?'

In the side office, I shared a tea urn with the other candidates. It was the first time I had met them, but they seemed to know each other well. One woman told me she had been to a dozen previous selection meetings. 'You don't win the first few times,' she explained, 'your time will come . . .' I worked my way through packets of custard creams, and drank black tea. We were called into the arena one by one so that I could hear nothing that was happening in the hall.

When I was summoned, I stood with the curving steel rails in front of me and the auctioneer's box behind. The spotlights were in my eyes, and it was difficult to see the audience. I gave the speech I had practised on my father six times, in a Penrith hotel, that afternoon. A retired MP and minister, Tristan Garel-Jones, had suggested the structure.

'It was my speech forty years ago. Then, the party wanted MPs who were in favour of capital punishment and against Europe. And I didn't fit the bill. But I developed tricks. If I were asked "What would you do if someone killed your sister?" I would say "I am not in favour of capital punishment, but I would kill the man myself." And they would cheer. Or I would say "I am personally in favour of the single market, but if the European Union,"' here he winked, ' "ever tried to abolish the Queen I would lead the march on Brussels myself." You will still need my guaranteed structure which never failed. It goes: "I am going to answer three questions – why me, why this constituency, why the Conservative Party . . ."'

So I did a bit of that. But I also spoke about why I was disgusted by the British policies in Afghanistan and Iraq; and about why landscape mattered; and how I had learned from communities in Afghanistan. I talked about Richard III in Penrith Castle and sleeping under hedgerows. Under the bright lights, I could just make out a heavy-set man in an open-necked short-sleeved shirt, a bald head, and a silver necklace, tight around his neck. He was a district and a county councillor, and a prominent member of the local party, and from his expression he didn't seem to like my speech. Another councillor – now in his eighties, who had once sold milking machines – asked me how much it cost to produce a litre of milk. I replied that it depended a little on your production system, but I thought it unreasonable to expect to produce under 20p a litre.

A third councillor asked me if I would back the Sainsbury's supermarket in the town centre. This was the latest Lowther misfortune. The Lowther earl of the first half of the twentieth century had paid for a brass band to greet him at every train station between London and Penrith, hosted the kaiser with his own troop of uniformed cavalry and, despite stealing a fortune from a fund intended for distressed jockeys (John Hatt's alternative version was that he had plundered a hospital), had left a castle, whose roof was stripped and whose great gardens were converted to growing tomatoes, and commercial timber. His great-great-nephew had tried to build a new district on some of their land in Penrith. The scheme had misfired, and the Lowthers had declared that particular company bankrupt, and retreated back to their valley. The council, left with a hole in the ground and £1 million of debt, had concluded that the only way to recoup this money was to allow Sainsbury's to build a giant supermarket on the site.

Many of the councillors in the audience supported this proposal. It was rumoured that some were now employed by Sainsbury's as consultants. But the building would be, I felt, a disaster. Penrith had somehow maintained life and variety in its medieval streets when so many other British high streets were a half-abandoned parade of hairdressers and charity shops. Another giant supermarket on the fringes of town seemed certain to kill the smaller shops. So I spoke fiercely against it. 'Only incompetence or corruption,' I said, 'could justify such a scheme.' The scowling councillor crossed his arms and legs. Because of the spotlights in my eyes, I could not see the reactions of the rest.

My father was waiting outside when I finished. I said that it looked as though I would continue to teach at Harvard after all. He said that he wouldn't be so sure. Meanwhile, out of sight and hearing, the 200 or so who had bothered to turn up – Christian evangelists, conservative councillors, rambling Lib Dems, and friends of John Hatt – were ranking their preferences. At each round of voting, the candidate with the fewest votes was excluded, and the preferences reallocated, until a majority was reached. It took forty-five minutes. I won.

John Hatt, who had watched the whole event, said it had been close. He had particularly warmed to a woman who farmed in Northumberland. 'Your speech about Richard III was incomprehensible. But I think people may have liked the fact you weren't patronising them. You won, I think, because you were braver than the others about the supermarket development. And some felt they would have fun with you . . . And you were the only candidate who managed to finish his last answer with a bit of a "bang".' On my way to the car, a Conservative councillor approached me to tell me that in his view I should never have been chosen.

I didn't grasp then quite how lucky I had been. I was lucky that the party was still using the old Civil Service assessment board system: lucky that David Cameron had annoyed someone by trying to block my progress; lucky that he had allowed non-Conservative Party members to vote in the primary. And above all lucky that the expenses scandal had suddenly created, so late in the day, dozens of unexpected vacancies for safe seats, allowing someone like me to move so quickly through the system. Over the following years, almost every one of these loopholes was sealed up, guaranteeing that an increasing number of MPs were party professionals with long years of campaigning and service as local councillors.

Soon after my selection, I climbed Wild Boar Fell on a clear day and saw the whole constituency laid out before me, between its mountain ranges, tracing the full meander of the Eden river, the faint smoke above Penrith, the low grey hills of the border, and the flash of sun far off on the Solway Firth. I was able to pick out perhaps half the villages and towns which I proposed to represent.

I moved into a cottage of sharp-edged, white-washed limestone, on a crag, like a miniature Iron Age fort above the open fell. The thin, twisted roof beams still retained their bark. When the rain was strong, the stream ran on its old route across the kitchen floor. The animals had long since been moved out of the room which was now my study, and an indoor lavatory had been built to replace the outhouse. But the west wall of the bedroom, two storeys high, was dry-stone without mortar.

Six months before the likely date of the general election, I resigned from Harvard and designed a walk to take me through all the one hundred villages, and most of the hundred additional hamlets. My diary tells me that I began from Dufton, on a rainy morning, crossing a military firing range and reaching Kirkby Stephen, fifteen miles away, for a town council meeting at 2.30, with a heavy pack and boots sodden from the wet fell. I had to jog a little to make up lost time and, arriving at the library, put my boots outside, and focused on the new child protection centre. I was told in five separate conversations that the people of Kirkby were Roundheads, and still hated Appleby for being on the Royalist side in the civil war. I walked awkwardly on my new blister to the church hall to attend another six meetings, and scored zero in the music round at the pub quiz that evening.

My journey was designed to coincide with market days or livestock sales. I had tried to identify in advance someone in every village prepared to host a meeting in their house, where I could deliver a speech to a dozen people. With experience, the speeches got shorter, but people still seemed to expect a speech. I invited people to walk with me, so I could learn as I moved. I was accompanied by a vicar – who had just left the army after a tour in Afghanistan – a painter, a trout fisherman and a lurcher called Prospero. I slept on a sofa bed adjoining the church at Morland; in a seventeenth-century yeoman's hall in the centre of Orton; in a pub in Threlkeld; and in the doctor's house at Castle Carrock.

I was beginning to feel that this constituency, to which I hoped to be elected, was almost a separate, independent nation. This was the heart of what had once been the independent kingdom of Cumbria – that pre-dated England and Scotland. It had a separate dialect and fragments of a separate language (the sheep-counting numerals used by at least one of the shepherds I knew ran not 'one', 'two', 'three' but 'yann', 'tann', 'tethera'), and its market town had the highest incidence of Viking DNA in the country. As I explained in my front-room speeches, their – our – ancient frontiers enclosed the largest most sparsely populated constituency in England, the highest number of self-employed, and the highest number of small businesses in Britain. Their – our – distinct, ancient identity could be found in the lyrics of Wordsworth, in the ballads of Walter Scott, and the peculiar construction of our dry-stone walls. I proposed a Border development plan, precisely tailored for 'the only constituency with Border in its name'.

Except, I discovered that very few of my voters knew or cared exactly where Penrith and the Border began and ended. People in Brampton felt much more in common with Wetheral, six miles away, outside my constituency, than they did with Kirkby Stephen – forty miles away but inside. Where I emphasised unity within the constituency, others saw differences. My neighbour, a tenant farmer in the Lowther Valley, observed that 'Here we are in wealthier parts.

But some areas of your patch are pretty primitive. If you go up north to Bewcastle, you can find old boys holding their trousers up with twine.' I liked the image, and, when I had seen those same farmers, I repeated it.

Although I was entranced by the older farming families, most of my constituents had moved to their towns and villages recently. I learned from one of countless local history projects, manned by volunteers and funded by the Lottery, that only five of the hundred people in my local village had been born in the village. There were thousands of East Europeans working in the hotel industry and care homes; and thousands of civil servants, nurses, and teachers, mostly from Manchester, who had chosen to retire to the Lakes. These 'new villagers' were often passionately energetic: hammering up and down the narrow lanes on racing bikes; cleaning the village hall; organising village fetes and half-marathons. Some developed strong views on rewilding the fellside, and on the import-ance of marsh fritillaries; went to the agricultural shows to admire the lavender-dyed Herdwick sheep; and photographed the perfect Neolithic stone circle at Castlerigg. But this did not mean they were originally from Cumbria. Meanwhile, the older farming families around me – Atkinsons, Warburtons, Wears, Smiths, Richardsons and Raines – seemed often more taken with rewatching *The Lord of the Rings* than with the medieval history of their parish.

Three weeks into my walk, the snow was thick as I left Alston. It was 21 December, the winter solstice. I passed a covey of grouse in a field, their feathers puffed out against the sleet. Approaching 2,000 feet I saw Mr Crabtree, the Alston policeman, and a gritter lying on its side, lights blazing. The road to Penrith was blocked and walking had a more practical point. The gritter driver seemed impervious to the blizzard. 'How do? That truck is crap. The Unimog was the right bit of kit.'

'Why did they get rid of it?' I asked, guessing that the Unimog was some other sort of vehicle.

'Don't ask me. I'm only paid to think from the neck down. Forgot your skis?'

The powder was light and deep, as I dropped slowly down the next 1,400 feet over long heather. Crossing a packhorse bridge, I panicked a flock of Rough Fell sheep, burrowing beneath the snow. At a farm whose fine ashlar masonry suggested it was made from a looted castle, or a Roman fort, I found Mr Dixon in a Russian tank commander's cap.

'Walked from Alston on a day like this? Conservative candidate? Monster Raving Loony more like.'

By New Year's night, the snow was thicker. Eighteen miles into the day's walk and just three miles short of the Scottish border, the full moon on the frost-crust illuminated hills twenty miles away. Arriving in a hamlet at nine at night, my companion, Tommy, was offered a sofa by the fire, and I a space on the nursery floor, under many blankets. Our hosts had been snowed in for four days.

The next morning, we turned west. Fine particles of frost-dust cut through the air. Old farmers stumbled through drifts after their sheep. Some had ancestors who had farmed this land in the four-teenth century. A few of these cattle-rustling, border-raiding, steel-bonneted men lay in the Bewcastle churchyard. 'Those,' one joked, 'who were not hanged at Carlisle.'

Such conversations implied unchanging antiquity. But in fact their life and landscape was subject to hectic change. They were old enough to remember when the government had paid them to drain their fields. Now they were being paid to flood them again – by destroying the very field drains which they had laid. They had begun as young men with small wet hedge-lined fields of longhorn cattle, then seen them transformed into open dry fields of Holstein dairy cows, and now back into sodden fields, edged with commercial for-estry. One set of European Union subsidies had incentivised them to tear out hedges, another set was now paying them to replant them. They had been driven in a single lifetime from farming long-horn cattle to sheep, to dairy, to native breeds, to forestry, and now into abandoning their land as wilderness.

No group which I had encountered prided itself so much on its independence as the farming community, nor was as nostalgic for a stable past. None was as dependent on the whims of markets, regulators, negotiators, environmental fashions and their place in European Union subsidies. Their vulnerability was exposed across each snow-lined ridge and the field boundaries, as though someone had cut open the chest of the landscape and exposed its lungs to the ravens.

As I made more connections, my walks slowed, and I formed a stronger idea of what needed to be changed. The district hospital, for example, was a disgrace, with one of the poorest cancer survival rates in the country. One older woman observed 'I don't need to pay to go to Switzerland if I want some euthanasia, I just have to check into the Cumberland Infirmary.' The number of people with Alzheimer's in the constituency had doubled in fifteen years. Twice on my walk, I knocked on a door, and after a long wait, found a man in a dressing gown, barely competent, who invited me into a house with the smell of food uncleared, and nappies undisposed of. Old people were entitled to see a carer for only fifteen minutes a day – hardly time to wash them, certainly not time to chat. None of the parties seemed willing to tackle this problem. It felt as though the communities I had worked with in Kabul looked after their elderly better than we did in Britain.

I promised that, if elected, I would transform the scandalously slow broadband. I would protect our network of cottage hospitals, fire and police stations, and ensure that the government schemes helped small family farms. But, although I knew what I wanted to do, I had little idea about how to do it.

The election was called in the early spring, and I now had eight weeks to get out the vote. There was a spending limit of £20,000 in the long campaign, and just over £10,000 for the whole of the final month. There were no TV ads, simply leaflets through doors, banners in fields and hustings in village halls or above pubs. Opponents watched very carefully, counting every T-shirt and banner to make sure I didn't break that limit. This meant – in stark contrast to a US campaign – that it was possible to fund the campaign from my savings and small donations, rather than from large donors.

There had been a large Conservative majority in Penrith, but it had almost been lost in the handover to my predecessor, and the formerly safe Conservative seat of Kendal, to my south, had been taken by the Lib Dems at the previous election. So, I was determined to campaign hard and, since only nine active local party members were prepared to canvas, I brought up friends, in relays of dozens. Young Afghans, who had never been to Cumbria, knocked on doors to explain my vision for the constituency.

My election campaign was a mixture of awkward stunts, party propaganda and literary irrelevancies, I milked cows, and rode through towns on a wooden-sided trailer, pulled by a blue tractor, I quoted T. S. Eliot in speeches, and endured the toe-curling slogan 'Rory the Tory'. Journalists watched me in a milking parlour at five in the morning being gently splattered with cow manure, and took many images of me riding a horse – a picture of a tweed-jacketed MP on a horse would be useful later, to illustrate articles attacking me as a Tory toff. The *Times* photographer placed me on a remote hill farm with British Blue cows, surrounded me with elaborate spotlights and reflectors, and then included the spotlights and reflectors in the photograph so that I appeared as the most fake of country campaigners.

Ian Parker of the *New Yorker* did a 15,000-word profile of me that took him many weeks. I introduced him to my parents and friends and spent days walking with him and perhaps twenty hours talking to him, giving him the most detailed and honest answers that I could manage. He was not much impressed:

> Stewart had been walking from farm to farm, beating on doors with an oddly heavy fist, as if he were in *Macbeth*, summoning a porter ... When a woman remarked that she no longer knew her neighbors well, Stewart began calling out names, as if helped by a telephone directory: 'The Atkinsons. The Warburtons. The Addisons – they're still around? The *Richardsons*?' It would be hard to imagine someone bringing a greater level of furrowed concentration to the business of being an affable neighbor.

He turned my understatements into sneers so that when the UK papers picked it up, the headlines ran 'Rory is pretty sure he's a

Tory', 'Rory thinks William Hague is "quite" clever'. In general, he seemed to find me insufferable. It was difficult in fact to see why he thought I had merited a profile in the *New Yorker* in the first place.

But perhaps those months of walking and our erratic, naïve, unpolitical campaign were not entirely wasted, or at least had not done much harm, for we discovered in the gym of the local leisure centre, as the plastic ballot boxes were emptied until four in the morning, that I had won a record majority.

4.

The Empty Hall

May 2010. With hindsight we were entering a radically different era. Thirteen years of Labour government were giving way to a long period of Conservative government. Ahead lay austerity, Brexit, and a very new form of British politics. After a period of global stability and democratic growth we were about to enter an era of democratic decline, and increasing violence, displacement and poverty. The Arab Spring was a year away, Xi Jinping's election would happen in two years, in four ISIS would seize Mosul, and in six, Donald Trump would be elected president of the United States. But that is not how it felt at the time. To me it was the first day in a new job.

The new Member of Parliament, now with a bed in his aunt's basement in London, put on his smartest dark suit and his least-scuffed brogues and, with his shoulders back and his chin up, marched into the Palace of Westminster. The policeman at the gate greeted me – to my delight – by name. They had all, I discovered later, been studying the photographs of the new members. I was shown to a cloakroom whose oak door was marked 'Members Only'. Someone had hung a plastic sword on the pink sword-ribbon next to his coat peg.

With half an hour before I was due to meet the other MPs, I continued up a marble staircase, through panelled corridors. Beyond an oak door marked 'Tea Room: Members Only', I glimpsed old men with carefully parted thinning hair and great chests, who looked like MPs, passing thinner people in blazers pushing trolleys, who did not. In another corridor, I passed a woman in eighteenth-century britches with a rapier at her waist. But no one seemed any more conscious of their costumes, or of the rodent that scurried across a corridor (I glimpsed it very briefly and afterwards could not quite be sure if it was a mouse or a rat), than they were of the coats of arms and statues, the stained glass of a Gothic palace, braced with Victorian iron, and all the other symbols of medievalism that surrounded them.

A hall lined with wooden cubbyholes, one now marked for me, led through to the new green carpets of the debating chamber. A guide seemed to be telling the visitors in French that the chamber was a 1950s copy of a nineteenth-century reimagining of an eighteenth-century conversion of a late medieval chapel. This seemed to me a good symbol of the blend of the naff, the antique and the pastiche in the British government and constitution.

Finally, I traced my way to the Victorian stone barn, poking into Parliament Square, in which we, the new MPs, had been gathered to learn our new responsibilities. There was much jostling, and chatting. I sat down in a row of stiff-backed wooden seats, upholstered in green leather with a gold portcullis crest. There was a general hushing, others took their seats, and a sixty-year-old MP, with a broad red face, short white hair and a blue suit buttoned tight over a considerable frame, walked onto a low stage. His jaw was firm; his eyes, through rimless spectacles, strikingly amiable; his voice flat Staffordshire, punctuated with many pauses.

'Good morning . . . ladies . . . and gentlemen . . . I am the chief . . . whip . . .'

At the longest pause, he looked around the room, at the 149 of us. The Conservative Parliamentary Party of 2010 remained a byword for narrow establishment uniformity – male, stale and the rest. But that was not how we saw ourselves. We felt very different from the MPs who had joined with the chief whip in the 1980s. For the first time a quarter of us – the new MPs – were women. Nine of us were from minority-ethnic backgrounds (only nine, but there had been none twenty years earlier) and almost all – Priti Patel, Sajid Javid, Nadhim Zahawi, Alok Sharma, Sam Gyimah and Kwasi Kwarteng – were talked about as future Secretaries of State. This was in part because the expenses scandal had given David Cameron and the party modernisers the chance to fast-track more diverse candidates. And this was not simply a change for the Conservative

Party: Labour had never had a Secretary of State from a minority-ethnic background either.

This diversity extended to people's working lives as well. I was seated in a row with the newly elected MP for Sittingbourne and Sheppey, who had started work as a stockroom assistant in Woolworths in 1963, a boy in his first suit, and a billionaire with a penchant for Texas Hold 'Em. I recognised others from the press reporting as GPs, farmers, a colonel, a hairdresser, and a woman with a doctorate in biochemistry.

But in one fundamental way our intake was less diverse. When the chief whip, a coal miner, son and grandson of miners, had been elected in a 1986 by-election, he was one of a hundred MPs in all parties from manual-worker backgrounds. None of us now came from manual backgrounds. We were mostly, with a few exceptions, professional politicians: survivors of the long hazing process of local party functions, local council chambers, doorstep canvassing, and runs at unwinnable or marginal seats.

I thought I knew what to expect in this initiation talk. I was waiting for the chief whip to tell us how privileged we were to join this ancient House; give us a history lesson, focused on parliamentary heroes; and tell us that we were to set an example, and act with dignity. In my initiation into a Scottish infantry regiment, nineteen years earlier, this had meant being told to slice, not scoop the Stilton. Above all, given the expenses scandal, he would tell us that we were expected to embody the seven standards of public life, determined by a committee in 1994 to be Selflessness, Integrity, Objectivity, Accountability, Openness, Honesty and Leadership. I looked forward to nodding earnestly.

But, to my disquiet, he talked about none of these things. The volume and pitch of his voice neither rose nor fell. 'If anyone . . . is interested . . . in history,' he said gruffly, 'you should book a . . . guide for a . . . parliamentary tour.' As he continued, certain hints on how he wanted Parliament to work glinted beneath the surface of his words, like shopping trolleys in a city canal. We should not regard debates as opportunities for open discussion; we might be called legislators but we were not intended to overly scrutinise

legislation; we might become members of independent committees, but we were expected to be loyal to the party; and votes would
rarely entail a free exercise of judgement. To vote too often on your
conscience was to be a fool, and ensure you were never promoted
to become a minister. In short, politics was 'a team sport'. Teamwork, he said, was vital for the manifesto to be delivered. 'I always
try to get consensus as chief whip,' the chief whip concluded, 'and
the consensus is that the prime minister is right.'

Six days after the election, he summoned us again to hear from
David Cameron. This time, the whole Parliamentary Party – more
than 300 of us – were tight-packed on benches and pews in an oak-
lined committee room, beneath Victorian oils of seventeenth-century
parliamentarians. The paintings were vast. Here, we were no longer
among fellow members of our new intake. Instead on every side sat
the heavier, older, more red-faced pre-existing half of the party. The
chief whip's cry of 'The prime minister' was bellowed with comic-
opera grandeur and Cameron strode through a door, to the sound
of hundreds of older members banging the oak furniture with
heavy fists.

Cameron looked around the room, waiting for the cheering and
banging to subside. I felt beside me the most ambitious of the new
intake gazing fanatically at him, hoping perhaps that he would catch,
in their eyes, their loyalty. He began in his steady competent briefing
voice. He did not seem to be the type of orator to be elated by the
mood in a room. He might almost have been addressing a camera.

We would, he said, 'put aside party differences' by forming a government with the Lib Dems. At this, we all banged the desks again
and cheered. Our disappointing performance in the election – in
which we had come twenty seats short of a majority, almost allowing Gordon Brown to form another government – seemed entirely
forgotten.

Cameron didn't talk about the details of the compromises he had
offered as part of the coalition agreement. Instead, he said that he
would 'work hard for the national interest'. Sarah Wollaston, the
GP beside me, said, 'Are we going to be given a chance to ask

questions about this deal?' Before I could answer in the negative, the PM turned to leave, and she was cut off by the deep booming roar of MPs chanting 'heeyarr heeyarr' – again in comic-opera bass voices, like Edward VII calling across a packed banquette to a chorus girl. Others seemed to be taking their tone from the football stands – a roar of rough, exaggerated aggression. On every side, I heard the hammering of 300 fists, knuckle-bruising against oak desks, the echoes short, slightly metallic and hollow – a tone and rhythm that existed before it was first recorded in Parliament in the seventeenth century – learned through rote like plainchant in a Benedictine monastery.

I spent the next few weeks exploring Parliament and learning about my new colleagues. I met them most often either in the glass atrium of Portcullis House, which looked like a Norwegian airport terminal, or in the tea room, by the chamber, which like much of Parliament looked like the billiard room of a Victorian plutocrat. Initially, I noticed four different groups of MPs among our 2010 intake. The most unexpected group were the authors, who settled on the desks in the House of Commons library, beneath Victorian histories of our parishes or 1970s academic essays on the potential for Scottish devolution. They were mostly historians: Ben Gummer, Chris Skidmore, Damian Collins, Kwasi Kwarteng, Jesse Norman: the writers who specialised in grim medieval narratives were easier to talk to than those who grappled with empire and the eighteenth-century Parliament.

Second were the middle-aged men and women whose families were back in their constituencies, who didn't know London well, and seemed to have little interest in getting to know it. They stayed in hotels around Westminster, or rooms at the Farmers Club, and gravitated in the evenings towards the bar and the smoking terrace above the river. Most of them knew my own constituency well and took family holidays there. They had grown up in the seats they represented, had spent many years as local councillors, and seemed comfortable in Parliament. They were astute and funny but not vicious about the ambitions of younger colleagues.

The third group had lived for years in London, were on easy terms with the Cabinet, and were more likely to be spotted briefing journalists in restaurants than in the House of Commons bar. These were the former aides to ministers, who had often joined the inner circle of the party, like David Cameron and George Osborne before them, straight from university. Of course, they were theoretically our equals, but no one thought they would be backbenchers for long.

One cheerfully showed me an academic paper that demonstrated you were ten times more likely to make it to the Cabinet if you had been a researcher or a ministerial aide than if you had been a local councillor, and much more likely if you were young when first elected than if you were old. And speed mattered: 93.1 per cent of MPs reaching Cabinet positions were promoted in their first term.

Aidan Burley, for example, who could occasionally be seen striding purposefully through the corridors in a dark boxy suit, seemed to be one of these high-fliers – management consultant, Conservative councillor, dedicated doorstep campaigner, aide to a respected Cabinet minister, favoured member of David Cameron's A-list. He seemed confident that he would soon climb the first unpaid rung on the promotion ladder, as a parliamentary private secretary. Matt Hancock, a former aide to George Obsorne, was even more certain to be promoted.

Finally, there was a group of older people who had entered politics later, from other longer careers: Sarah Wollaston, a Totnes doctor, disarmingly idealistic and quietly good-humoured; Bob Stewart, a boisterous full colonel from the Cheshire Regiment, who had commanded in Bosnia; and Sajid Javid, a quieter, earnest senior banker, who had put a real effort into trying to understand parliamentary procedure and patiently answered my many questions. Did I need to wear my pass? ('No.') How could I be called in a debate? ('Write a letter to the Speaker.') How would I know which amendment had been selected for a vote? ('No idea.')

Many of these people would have impressed me in their former lives. But I was already sensing that Parliament reduced us. Too many of the jokes in the tea rooms seemed to have the tone of prisoners laughing. Too few of our conversations were about policy, too much of our time was already absorbed in gossip about the promotion of one colleague, or the scandal engulfing another. Even four weeks in, I sensed more impotence, suspicion, envy, resentment, claustrophobia and *Schadenfreude* than I had seen in any other profession.

I had known only one new MP reasonably well before my election. Kwasi Kwarteng had been at school with me. I remembered talking to him when he was fourteen about T. S. Eliot and medieval architecture. I had hoped to restart a friendship with him in Parliament. But he seemed always in a hurry. When I tried to engage him in conversations about policy, he seemed to prefer throwing out pugnacious aphorisms – or teasing me as a wet, Europhile, out of touch with 'real people'. I could never get him to slow down. It was as though he were embarrassed to know me, or as though years of Conservative campaigning had sucked the patience out of him.

In the parliamentary chamber, for Prime Minister's Questions, however, all individual characters seemed to dissolve into a single mass: 300 middle-aged men and women crammed into benches designed for 200, thighs against thick thighs, elbows on elbows, faces flushed. I had adopted a place, squatting on the steps between the benches, and I could feel knees in my back, and a shoulder against my shin from the other MPs on the steps. There was a scent of stiff wet wool from a chalk-striped suit; and the expensive aftershave worn by Sir Peter Tapsell, the eighty-year-old Father of the House. I could smell the breath of smokers and heavy coffee drinkers. Some of the younger members were passing around altoid mints, or chewing on gum. Across the aisle: there seemed to be more women on the Labour benches, more young people.

The first Prime Minister's Questions began with John Bercow, the Speaker – a very small, broad-shouldered man, with a pale face and a mop of white hair – shouting 'Order' in the parade voice of a First World War artillery sergeant major, and holding the second syllable for three seconds. A tall MP stood, drawled 'Question number one, Mr Speaker,' and sat back down among a group of new

Conservative MPs in their late thirties and early forties, who were sitting attentively, with neatly brushed hair and crisp white shirts, heads bowed to write carefully on their order papers. On the edge of this group were older MPs, who despite twenty years in the House of Commons, still seemed strikingly ill at ease.

The prime minister got to his feet. There was a prolonged rising cry of 'Yeahh!!!!' from the Conservative benches. The Lib Dems looked at their feet. Labour crossed their arms.

Cameron began: 'Mr Speaker I am sure the whole house will want to join with me' – at this phrase, all cheering stopped, and faces became blank and wary for the cameras – 'in paying tribute to the soldiers who lost their lives in Afghanistan this week. From 40 Commando, Corporal Stephen Curley and Marine Scott Taylor. From the 4th Regiment Royal Artillery, Gunner Zak Cusack. These were men of outstanding courage, of skill and of selflessness.'

Cameron's delivery was flat, and his delicate hands floated, palm down over his notes, as though he were waving them over a magic potion. I waited to hear some more about Stephen Curley – a mountain-warfare specialist, who had saved another soldier, and then been caught by a bomb in an alley in Sangin. But Cameron did not give any more details. Instead, raising his fingers and beating the air slowly with his flat palm, he turned to a shooting in Cumbria.

The first question was called again. The tall MP, Douglas Carswell, stood and barked 'I welcome proposals to eliminate quangos and shift power away from unelected functionaries to elected representatives.'

The more conservative members shouted 'Hear hear.'

'The biggest quango of the lot is . . . of course . . .' We all waited for him to say 'the European Commission'. Except he continued . . . 'The House of Lords. Will my Right Honourable friend confirm he will bring together proposals in the next twelve months to make all our lawmakers accountable through the ballot box?'

The cheering stopped – MPs glanced uncertainly at each other, unsure on what the party position ought to be. Cameron, however, agreed so smoothly that it was difficult not to feel that he had planted the question. 'I have always supported a predominantly elected House of Lords . . .'

We looked at the shiny back of his grey suit, processing this, as he moved on to the second question ('What I would say in addition is this: that friends of Israel – and I count myself a friend of Israel – should be saying to the Israelis . . .') and the third question ('I know the Right Honourable lady cares very deeply about this issue, as do I . . .'). But it was that very first short answer, at his first PMQs, about the House of Lords that already suggested his unpredictable power. Cameron seemed to be determining, question by question, policy issues which we – the backbenchers – had hardly begun to consider, but for which we would all be held collectively responsible. And I could already sense from the bodies around me that my colleagues had not liked the prime minister's line on abolishing the House of Lords, and that he was already – at the very beginning of his tenure – in trouble.

I attended many other debates and ministerial questions. I became accustomed to watching ministers reading speeches from the despatch box, and when they sat down, to MPs standing and sitting, standing and sitting: until being selected by the Speaker, in no sequence that I could determine, they began to read their own speeches, often centred on constituency campaigns. Then suddenly, the Speaker would roar 'Division,' doors flew open, tall men in tail-coats barked into trumpet telephones and a hundred bells rang in a hundred corridors summoning MPs to the chamber to vote.

In an attempt to understand exactly what we were voting on, I began by requesting copies of each bill from the Table Office. I read through dozens of pages of clauses and subclauses, traced references to previous legislation, skimmed the explanatory sheets and the library notes, gathered different amendments and new clauses, and compared them to the legislation ('(2) Leave out subsection (2) and insert—') and then worked out how the amendments had been grouped. I tried to understand the debates at committee stages, the objections of NGOs, the controversies over legal drafting, whether primary legislation was necessary, or whether extraneous issues were being smuggled into the bill. Even with briefings from some very patient civil servants, mastering the details and intricacies of an individual bill seemed to take me at least forty hours. And yet we were expected to vote on a three-line whip many times a week.

Seven weeks into my time in Parliament I came across Amendment 58, relating to Clause 3, page 2, line 17 of the Finance Bill. It ran:

... and at the end add:
   (6) The Treasury shall prepare a report into the impact of the rise provided for by subsection (1) on mountain rescue services in the United Kingdom and lay it before the House of Commons.

This amendment mattered to me. I had more mountain rescue teams in my constituency than any other in Britain. I had just stood successfully to be chair of the All Party Parliamentary Group on Mountain Rescue, and had made a public statement calling for mountain rescue to be exempted from VAT. I could not possibly, I thought, oppose a request for an impact statement relating to VAT on mountain rescue. Except it was a Labour amendment, and as Conservatives we were on a three-line whip to vote against all Labour amendments. We had been told that the legitimacy of the government, the survival of the party and all our chances of promotion to ministerial office depended on never voting against a three-line whip. I went to the chamber to find someone from the Whips' Office.

A Member of Parliament was speaking at length about not very much – presumably because the whips wanted to delay the vote to get some more members back from a party engagement. I found the chief whip himself standing by the brass-bound oak doors and explained my problem.

'Don't worry,' he said amiably, 'that amendment has not been selected.' He meant, it seemed, that for some reason, the amendment was going to be dropped without Parliament being given a chance to express an opinion. Some deal perhaps had been cut with Labour, or the Speaker. 'In any case,' he continued, 'we will not

vote on it. You can keep voting at each division bell with a clear conscience. And without affecting your future.'

Seeing my Lib Dem colleague on the mountain rescue group in
the lobby I mentioned this to him. He told me I was mistaken. I hurried back to the chamber. Every more experienced MP I saw seemed
to be busy in conversation. But I felt the energy of a debate moving
towards its close.

'Excuse me,' I said to a member who had been elected five years
before me, 'has Amendment 58 been selected?'

'How on earth should I know?'

'Well how can I find out?'

'Ask the whips.'

'They have told me it hasn't been.'

'Well then if I were you, I would listen to them,' and he walked
away.

I got no more sense out of three other colleagues. Finally, I found
a much older MP, who told me to look at the list pinned to a wooden
chair near the entrance to the chamber. I did so. It said 58.

I found the chief whip. 'I'm afraid it's been selected.'

'Rory, my advice to you is just to go into the lobby and vote with
the rest of us—'

'But Amendment 58?'

'It's not been selected. We're doing 56.'

The division bell went.

I ran back to the chair and looked again. I checked with a doorkeeper. We were definitely voting on Amendment 58. I found the
chief whip again. By now he seemed a little preoccupied because he
was trying to shepherd MPs into the voting lobby before the doors
closed. 'It is 58,' I said.

'Well bugger off, then,' he said.

I walked away, moving against the flow of my colleagues who
were heading to vote, believing every eye was staring at me, walking the wrong way out of the division lobbies. I went into the tiny
men's loo, opposite the library, and locked myself in the cubicle. As
I sat on the closed loo seat waiting for the minutes to tick away, I
wondered whether this was really the issue on which I wanted to

make my stand against the government. My face burned with some embarrassment I could not quite place, compounded by righteous defiance and a cower in the gentlemen's lavatory. I emerged when the vote was over. I waited to see what would happen to me. Nothing happened.

The day after my underwhelming rebellion in the mountain rescue vote, I stood to make my maiden speech. Churchill celebrated his maiden speech as though it were a first cavalry charge, which might make a hero of a hussar. He had chosen to speak on the great foreign policy issue of his day, the Boer War, had put immense effort into composing his argument, and arranged for it to be printed verbatim on the front page of *The Times*, and the speech – a triumph – had laid the foundations for his rapid promotion. He lived in the midst of a cult of Parliament speeches.

The greatest parliamentary speeches of the eighteenth and nineteenth centuries had been quoted like lines from musicals, and bound in multivolume works. My great-grandfather had left me one called *Crowned Masterpieces of Eloquence*, with a white calfskin cover and gold lettering – and I had read it carefully. Speeches were prized because debating – taking the time to explore both sides of an argument – was vital for the values of reason, tolerance, and equality which were supposed to underpin all democracies. Their importance in Parliament was enshrined in its French name: a *parlement* was a talking shop. Gladstone owed his first promotions almost entirely to the quality of his speeches. Disraeli as prime minister had spent most of his days in the chamber: running the country and its overseas possessions from the midst of the debates. The Victorians, like the Greek, Roman and Renaissance thinkers before them, believed that someone who spoke thoughtfully and well, would govern well. And I could see their point.

For all these reasons, my maiden speech felt like a big deal to me. I would have liked to have launched myself on the Afghan War – a subject that mattered, and on which I felt I could speak confidently, independently and well. But no foreign policy debates had been placed on the agenda. And I did not want to remain mute on the back benches. So I chose to speak on a bill on academy schools. My wife Shoshana had worked as a teacher in such schools in the States, and believed they could transform the lives of some of the poorest students. I was pleased the government was backing them, and I was mistrustful of the Labour amendments, which seemed to be driven by the most conservative instincts of the teachers' unions.

I sat in Parliament for two hours, waiting to be called by the Speaker. The Labour spokesman talked very slowly, with all the enthusiasm of a man conducting a lengthy classroom roll-call, repeating, all the time like the White Rabbit, that he was in a hurry, 'we don't have the time Mr Speaker, we simply don't have the time . . .'

Called at last, I rose a little unsteadily to my feet, and began my maiden speech with a traditional tribute to my predecessor in the constituency, David Maclean. 'I remember,' I intoned, sounding immediately pompous, 'climbing up a snowdrift in December, feeling like Scott of the Antarctic, reaching an isolated farmstead to find that David Maclean, like Amundsen, had already been there before me.' I described him 'during the foot and mouth crisis, with his cromach in his hand, moving across our landscape, denuded of livestock, with funeral pyres burning on the border, defending his constituency, that ancient medieval frontier, like a warden of the Western March.'

The MP behind me, whose head was bowed over either his phone or order paper, winced.

Still a little unsettled, and concluding that I had better drop the antique imagery and focus on the details of legislation, I lurched to the Labour spokesman's amendment. Staring at the Labour spokesman, I told him it was otiose because it duplicated a previous amendment; that it touched on administrative issues not proper points of law, and was self-defeating because its mechanism would not achieve its objective.

Pleased that I had managed, I thought, finally to get a bit of bite into my speech, I sat down and waited for the compliments, which were traditionally given to all maiden speeches. But instead of 'hear hears' for the new member, there was silence. Some MPs seemed to have found important things to look at on their phones. The next speaker's tribute ran, 'Although I didn't agree with it, I still thought it was a reasonable speech, if that makes sense.'

Then another speaker stood and gave me a glimpse of what the modern Parliament might actually be looking for. This MP had begun as a Labour councillor and then drifted to the Lib Dems. He had been a local councilllor for forty years, and an MP for twenty-seven. He wore a dove-grey double-breasted suit and a brilliant pink tie. His full white beard was matched by a mane of blow-dried mullet-fringed white hair, as though an AI program had been asked to blend an image of a hippy and a dressy banker. A bright red silk handkerchief ballooned out of his breast pocket.

He spoke in a voice which blended Hampshire vowels with a Royal Shakespeare Company manner, delivering slow extended compliments to the three speakers before him, and to two departed MPs, meeting nods of approval from every side. He glanced roguishly at an older Labour MP across the aisles: 'It's not often that you feel *humbled*,' he said, 'by someone's commitment both to the issue that we're discussing and the amount of *knowledge* that they bring to it and the *forthright and passionate* way in which she presented her case today and it was indeed a *pleasure* to be a witness to that . . .'

He spoke, in almost the very middle of the gangway, looking directly at the Speaker, his hands behind his back, swaying right onto the balls of his feet, and glancing frequently around the chamber. He was easy, unhurried, piling on the flattery and the synonyms, and above all never touching on the detail of the amendment. Instead, he reminded us in a lisping tenor that he had always been 'on the side of children and parents'.

Eventually, people began to intervene. An intervention was supposed to be a one-sentence question. But there was rarely a question mark in sight. Instead, the interventions were leisurely opportunities for MPs to match his anecdotes with their own. After each intervention, the MP merrily answered questions that had not been put, and increased his compliments: 'Once again,' he chirruped, in response to the ninth intervention, '*in all the years* that I have been here I have seldom been in the House on an occasion where so much common cause has been put by people who care so passionately about the issue. Of course the honourable gentleman is right . . . When I was doing that job,' he announced, extending an arm so that the light glittered from his gold ring and gold watch, 'people used to ask me what do I do [pause] and I said, "I bully for people who cannot bully for themselves . . ."' He allowed a faint chorus of 'hear hear' before continuing, in his characteristic mush of the casual and the grandiloquent: 'It's the silver-tongued politicians that I'm worried about [laughter] who make the suggestions to people that this is like manna from heaven and that the whole world is gonna be changed. And sometimes politicians have more than once talked with forked tongue . . .'

A number of colleagues had raised concerns about this MP's pro-Kremlin allegiances because of his 'pro-Putin and pro-Medvedev position'. He had also been accused of failing to declare all of his visits to Russia, which he denied, protesting that he did not know exactly how many trips he'd made because his passport had fallen into the sea. He was now having an affair with his twenty-five-year-old Russian aide, who was helping to facilitate his work on the Defence Committee. But the MPs, who generally heckled the austere Labour MP Jeremy Corbyn, listened to this man as though he were a genial bearded Santa. I began to understand how it was possible in the 1980s for one of the MPs, who was widely believed to have murdered his wife, to still be warmly greeted by colleagues.

On the speaker went, never simply using a word like 'education' if he could deliver a quadracolon ('whether it was in nursery education, whether it was in primary, er, education, secondary education, and after er, er, erm education'), saying nothing about the amendment in fifty-five minutes.

Finally, I rose to my feet and snapped: 'I thank the honourable gentleman for giving way. What is the relevance of this to Amendment 71? I do not understand how it is relevant.'

If I had expected support from the Conservative benches, I was wrong. People looked embarrassed. The MP sprang quickly to his feet and then pausing theatrically, with his hands in his pockets, raised his eyebrows. 'That's more a question for the Deputy Speaker than you,' he pronounced. The House was delighted. They laughed so much that the next person to intervene could not be heard. 'How do I follow that?' she expostulated, while everyone chuckled again.

Then he returned to his riff: 'The honourable member for Penrith and the Border could be a bit difficult if he pulls that one too often in the committee stage of a bill . . . he won't be seen to be very popular if he starts asking about the relevance or otherwise of amendments that are not being spoken about, or are . . .'

Everyone smiled happily again. In total, he spoke for an hour. No one seemed to be in a hurry to be anywhere else.

Finally, the Conservative minister rose to his feet, and insisted like every other speaker that time was short and that he would speak briefly. First he suggested that Gedling, the Labour spokesman's seat, sounded like Gelding, although the man, he said, was 'a *stallion*'. 'On the subject of my friends on the opposition benches,' he continued, 'I count the honourable member for Hartlepool as a friend, and I have not yet had the chance to congratulate his daughter, Hattie, on her eighth birthday yesterday. I shall do so now, because I want to get it into Hansard. In addition, I want to mention that he has a number of other children and I hope that they enjoy *Toy Story 3* when they go to see it on Sunday. Moving on! Time is short.'

By the summer of 2010, I had spent hundreds of hours in the chamber and the corridors and the tea rooms. ('Poor you,' said my father, 'I fear you have become a very junior member of a talking shop.') Meanwhile, beyond our antique walls, the economic crisis was deepening. The crash of 2008 had triggered the first recession for seventeen years. Both David Cameron and Gordon Brown, who had promised 'no more boom and bust', had failed to predict the crisis. The journalist Rafael Behr remembered the first signs of this crisis 'as if I had just come from a NASA briefing about a meteor on a collision course with Earth, and all these people were partying like they had no idea'. The markets, so long praised for their sensitive, knowledgeable allocation of resources, had not only been unable to prevent the crash – they had caused it. The economic system designed by Thatcher and maintained under Blair had been humiliated. Public money had been used to bail out the banks, and no action had been taken against the bankers.

The economy had contracted by 7 per cent. The deficit was high, debt was growing. The financial services sector – which had been allowed to dominate much of the economy under Conservatives and Labour – had collapsed and might never fully recover. After decades in which UK per capita GDP growth and productivity had been the best in the developed world, productivity had collapsed – semi-permanently. Incomes were frozen. The only two options seemed to be to borrow more and spend more, or cut. The first was likely to cause debt problems in the medium term, and the other to choke growth in the short term.

My voters often spoke to me as though I could control the future of the economy. But my hands were far from the levers of power. My only early hint of government policy came from a parliamentary meeting, addressed by David Cameron, held this time not beneath the Victorian oil paintings in the old committee rooms, but in the concrete shell of Portcullis House. By the time I arrived in the Booth-royd room, people were already perched on windowsills and radiator grilles, and the whips were standing with roving eyes and necks stretched out, like stags in flight.

Again, the chief whip introduced the prime minister in his grand-est, deepest tones, and again we all beat on tables and walls, as Cameron entered through a corridor in the crowd cleared by the whips. He walked briskly, with brow furrowed. Behind him, in his Tyrian purple tie, at a much slower pace, chin tipped high, chest thrust out, looking slowly from side to side as though in a Roman triumph, strode George Osborne, the chancellor.

David Cameron began, 'I know there are a few who say that we should have sat tight, waited for our opponents to fall out, and brought in a minority government.' His loyal MPs shook their heads at this idea. 'But I disagreed.' So apparently did we. 'We are all in it together. Stronger together. Of course the cynics will say . . .' He explained that he would make radical reductions in public spending. 'There is no other responsible way. Look at the nightmare we've seen in Greece. Labour bankrupted our country. We are the party of fiscal responsibility. We are the party of the NHS. I'm not saying its going to be easy. But we must work together in the national interest.'

As he sat down, we all applauded. But I had now been in Parliament long enough to sense that not everyone applauding agreed, or had remotely similar visions of party or policy. In front of me sat an MP who had told me that conservatism was about the constitution, and the beauty of the countryside. Beside him was a moderniser who believed that constitutional issues were irrelevant, and that Conservatives should build over the green belt. To my right a colonel's son in an Airborne Division tie, with the easy open face and broad shoulders of a man comfortable carrying a Bren gun, was sitting beside Liz Truss: the daughter of a pacifist left-wing maths professor and teacher, who had once made a speech for the abolition of the monarchy. All applauded equally.

When George Osborne stood, he looked pale and tired. Raising his hands in front of his chest, long fingers and thumbs stretched wide to their limit, he told us that his plan was to eliminate 'the structural deficit' within one parliament. He was proud of having reintroduced the word 'austerity'. He thought it had an air of appealing astringence. And he saw it as one of three things – along with a commitment to spending 0.7 per cent of GDP on foreign aid, and legislating for gay marriage – which he believed would be his legacy.

I had now met him a few times in Parliament – once for a cup of tea. He reminded me of an eighteenth-century French cardinal: wryly observant of colleagues, capable of breathtaking cynicism, but also erudite, irreverent, poised, witty, self-mocking and engaged. But there was no hint of any of this in his public speaking voice. His mouth, which could often rise in a sly conspiratorial smile, was now set in a thin scowl. 'We will cut the budgets of unprotected departments by 25 per cent.' This meant, I guessed, that perhaps a million civil servants, including police officers and prison officers, would lose their jobs. 'Such cuts,' he said, 'would be beneficial to the economy, and would reward the hard-working.' He said he would not shift the debt burden onto 'our grandchildren'. 'This is a

Conservative government.' When he intoned the word 'Conservative', he leant backwards and lifted his nose for emphasis, as though posing for a statue, or anticipating a punch.

The MP beside me whispered, 'He is distancing himself from Cameron and whistling to the Conservative right, he's trying to build them as his supporters for the leadership.' If this was the case, it didn't seem to be working. Very few MPs were nodding. Some, like me, presumably feared these cuts were going too far. John Redwood – a right-wing academic and former Cabinet minister, scribbling frantic notes, three seats away from me – appeared from his muttering to want Osborne to cut more. But none of us was going to be consulted on any of this. Osborne continued, 'We need to let people know that we understand how unfair it is to wake in a housing estate, to go to work, and see neighbours' blinds still down all morning . . . while those on benefits are sleeping in.'

I could imagine others in the room, who had grown up on such estates, being judgemental about idle neighbours. But George? The George I knew seemed more likely to be amused by his friends who liked to sleep in in the morning.

Approaching his peroration, his red lips finally began to twitch towards a smirk, and he stared more confidently into the eyes around him. 'Although the policy seems unpopular,' he said, 'it will in fact win us the next election.' Civil servants voted Labour; people in the private sector, Conservative. The more civil servants who were let go from government and joined the private sector, the more Conservative voters. As he sat down, I whispered to a new colleague that this seemed distasteful and unrealistic. 'No,' he replied, banging the table loudly, 'he is right.' The meeting ended with polling experts presenting 'internal' polling which was markedly more positive than the public polls ('we have a better algorithm').

I walked out with Ken Clarke. He was in his seventies, heavy and slightly lame. We moved slowly towards the lifts, with others squeezing past us. 'These parliamentary meetings are bizarre,' he drawled. 'No discussion and very few ideas. And it's as bad in David Cameron's Cabinet.'

Clarke had been a whip in Heath's administration in the early

1970s, and then a minister under Thatcher, Major and Cameron. He had been Health Secretary, Home Secretary and Chancellor of the Exchequer. David Cameron had now made him Lord Chancellor and Justice Secretary. He seemed hardly interested in the things which captivated other colleagues. I never heard him gossip about the personalities of other MPs or meetings with famous people; he did not talk about political campaigning tricks and the patterns of promotion and demotion. He was fond of his colleagues and the slow, surreal rhythm of parliamentary lives. Failing three times to become leader had left him with no resentment or bitterness. But he was upset that voices and views of MPs and Cabinet ministers had been drastically muted since he entered Parliament, and British prime ministers were increasingly behaving as solitary presidents.

'Cabinet under Thatcher and Major would take up a whole morning each week. At least three hours, enjoyable, lively, open-ended and effective conversation.' The warmth, ease and rhythm of his voice gave a force to his precise, jargon-free adjectives. 'Cameron's Cabinet is short and *cursory*,' he continued. 'Now he has set up another thing called the "Political Cabinet", where we are supposed to be franker about politics. But that is a waste of time. It is dominated by the polling people talking about the state of public opinion.'

I asked for an example. He stopped just inside Westminster Hall, a stone chamber a millennium old, and turned his broad red face to me. At the other end of the hall, 240 feet away, were six statues of kings, fragments of orbs and sceptres in their broken arms – carved so long ago that no one could remember exactly who they had once been. Ken explained that as Justice Secretary he wanted to reduce the prison population, abolish short sentences, and simplify legal aid. But David Cameron wanted him to increase mandatory sentences, and thus the prison population, and was encouraging him to sit with Rebekah Brooks, the editor of the *Sun*, and listen to her proposals to establish prison ships. Twenty-five-year-old aides from Number 10 had lied about his health to get him excluded from television interviews.

He said that Cameron, while claiming to restore Cabinet

government and abolish the culture of spin, was obsessed with the daily news cycle, monthly polls, and the idea of the permanent political campaign. He relied on unelected special advisers barely five years out of university. Having been a young special adviser himself, he liked special advisers, perhaps because they were loyal and helpful, and could be brought in and pushed out at need. Whereas he found elected MPs and ministers inconvenient.

'It is a *disastrous* way to run a government,' Ken said, putting as always the full emphasis on his adjectives. 'It's all a reaction to the *hysterical* 24/7 chatter. I first met David when he was a special adviser when I'm afraid I had to let him go from the Treasury, and I'm not sure he has *entirely* changed.' The phrase 'I'm afraid' was delivered ruefully, gruffly and with a touch of nostalgia.

We continued slowly through Westminster Hall. This building meant more to me than I could acknowledge without embarrassment. I had been summoned to serve in a Parliament that contained the great feasting hall of the Norman kings, where the first Council of Ministers met and the supreme judicial courts of the kingdom had been fixed by Magna Carta; where Simon de Montfort held the first parliament of commoners in 1265; and where Shakespeare had spoken his only certain recorded words. Not all my reading about medieval cynicism and barbarity had quite eroded my sense that I had entered a tradition of ancient dignity and gravity: that I was following in the footsteps of heroes.

We passed the brass plaque which recorded the place where in 1649 – in the most intense compression of the English constitution – King Charles Stuart had stood as the great-great-great-great-great-great-great-great-great-great-great-great-great-great-grandson of Henry I who had held his wedding banquet in this hall. Here Charles had, with calm and simplicity, faced the Members of Parliament and the judges, to hear his own sentence of death.

Ken, seeing where I was looking, raised an eyebrow, and muttered 'He nothing common did or mean / Upon that memorable scene . . .' and then lapsed back into the present. 'All these special advisers and PR advisers – I'm afraid they are mostly rather out of their depth. They talk about "the grid" and "lines to take" and they seem to regard their sole mission to be to second-guess and direct the work of Cabinet ministers.'

This hall led to committee rooms, to spaces for preparing legislation, for debating, for researching, for processing correspondence, for eating, meeting, and for voting. But it had not been designed to accommodate Parliament. It was not even a workplace. Westminster Hall preceded work and Parliament itself. It was the hard bark around 1,000 years of British government and, although the state had changed over time, with limbs growing and breaking, the carapace of the hall remained, like the shell of a hollow oak, enfolding shadowy ideas of government and power, that refused to be separated or clarified, a constitution that was not a constitution, a monarchy that did not rule, a democracy that was not perhaps quite a democracy.

Now, stumping through it beside a man who was on course to be the oldest member of our Parliament – the Father of the House – I found this embodiment of living tradition as empty as a school gymnasium after hours. The only piece of furniture was a chipped reception desk, piled with leaflets for visitors. At the far end near the royal dais, a plywood box, eight feet long and three feet high, lined with a plastic sheet, had been placed to catch the rainwater dripping through the roof.

Almost every weekend, I travelled 300 miles back to Penrith and the Border by train, and stepped out on the platform into colder air, a different season and, I felt, a better country. I looked shyly along the platform at my new constituents, some of whom nodded. I dragged my bag through the underpass, perhaps trying to help someone else too and promising to try to get a station lift installed. I now had the beginnings of a constituency office, and generally Catherine Anderson, my office manager, was waiting at the station entrance with her saluki on a lead.

Catherine had read my Afghan book in Dharamshala, travelled from India to Alston, and offered to volunteer for my election campaign. I had replied there were no slots. She ignored me, came to the office, and within three weeks was running the leafleting teams, then the correspondence and finances. After the election, she took over the constituency office, found a cottage outside Penrith, restored the barn as an office, got a dog and built me a team who had all lived in the constituency since childhood. None had been Conservative Party members. One was a forester's daughter, married to a farmer, who ran her own kids' clothing business. Another's father and brother were farmers. All had dogs. The office housed a saluki, a Patterdale terrier, a Cairn terrier, a sheepdog, a cocker spaniel and three Labradors.

I would get into Catherine's Skoda, she would hand me a copy of the *Cumberland and Westmorland Herald* – proudly pointing out the number of our press releases– and then set off with me towards a primary school, or bakery business. We were soon running along narrow roads between high dry-stone walls, glimpsing distant flocks and crags, weaving past oversized royal blue tractors, and talking through the local Conservative councillors: 'Duncan may complain, but basically he sees you as an adopted grandson'; 'Marilyn feels you are not at enough local branch events'; 'You will have to take three northern surgeries next Friday . . .'

Travelling back and forth across the 1,200 square miles of the constituency, we met a child with severe learning difficulties forced to commute to a school fifty miles from their parents' home, when there was a good school five miles away; a blind person losing their disability payment on the grounds that they could work in a tea shop; and a farmer whose agricultural subsidy payment was withheld for twelve months, because of the dispute over whether a hedge was nine inches wider than marked. We called on elderly couples who had lost their savings. I met a man whose partner had been killed when a trailer came loose on a motorway, immigrants severed from their families, and children whose parents had died from neglect. I was struck by how often the government refused to apologise, and put great energy into defending its failings.

Every evening I returned to my loose-walled, whitewashed cottage with its collapsing roof. It existed in a different season, not only from London, but from my Cumbrian neighbours. The leaves on the sessile oaks were bright new green, weeks after the oaks in the south had matured into summer russet. My friends at Hutton in the

Eden Valley had smooth lawns, plump rich-voiced pigeons, plums against the garden wall – and at night a hedgehog, trotting anxiously beneath the exuberant skirts of the cedar of Lebanon. But here at my cottage, high on the fellside, my only ash tree was late to leaf, and its trunk was stained with calcium from limestone boulders.

If the constituency was defined by cold clear air over limestone crags, Parliament for me was defined by claustrophobia. The traditional parliamentary day had been designed to start in the afternoon, leaving the days free for ministers to focus on their departments, committees to meet, and for backbenchers to work on second jobs. Voting had taken place late at night, and some of the most dramatic moments had occurred in the early hours of the morning, with a packed House, and an audience craning from the galleries. This had been the atmosphere in which the half-sozzled Charles James Fox had delivered his brilliant invective on the American War of Independence, and Churchill his maiden speech. By trapping MPs in the building till the early hours, this schedule had fostered deep friendships and conspiracies – which were then developed over long summer holidays, often spent, at least in the nineteenth century, with each other.

But most of the public disliked the idea of MPs with long summer holidays and second jobs, and the MPs wanted to see more of their families in the evenings. So, about a week after I had arrived in Parliament, we were asked to vote for a new calendar. There were many competing options. Genial middle-aged members assured me that late sittings were vital for MPs to dine and get to know each other, young parents told me late sittings were unjust. A seventy-year-old braying barrister in a heavy suit told me that any time limit to debates and speeches was an outrage to democracy.

I and most of my colleagues responded to these contradictory visions by voting for a broken-back British compromise. Henceforth, we would aim to sit from 3.30 in the afternoon to ten o'clock at night on Mondays, then till seven on Tuesdays, six on Wednesdays, five on Thursdays. Cameron also extended the parliamentary year, inserting a new two-week session in September. This new schedule neither allowed MPs to retain a serious second job, nor gave MPs much chance to see their children before bed-time. Nor could MPs make plans around it, because the 'ten o'clock' or 'seven o'clock' was only when votes started, and you could still find yourself sitting till one in the morning, unable to leave the chamber.

Most days were compulsory, 'three-line' running whips. This meant that from the moment the House met, to the moment it adjourned for the night, there could be a vote at any time, and the doors were locked precisely eight minutes after the division bell was rung. My parliamentary office was on the fifth floor of a building, almost half a mile away, which meant I had to stop what I was doing and run as soon as I heard the bell, and never risk waiting for a lift. Only younger MPs were given these offices.

On most days, we could rarely leave the narrow corridors of Parliament. I was addicted to long walks in the open air. But now my only glimpse of the sky came on the narrow gravel paths above the car park or shivering on the terrace with the smokers, staring across the Thames. Often votes came in groups, with only fifteen minutes between them, which made it difficult to start any serious work, so when there were multiple votes, I took to sitting in the tea room waiting for the next bell.

Not long after my maiden speech and my first weekend in the constituency, I found myself again waiting for a vote in the tea room, exchanging pleasantries with a Labour MP, as I ordered my fried eggs, fried bread and tinned tomato. Picking up my mini pot of marmalade and mug of tea I headed towards the first oval table, laden with newspapers. Beneath the portrait of Ramsay MacDonald with a tartan blanket wrapped around his legs sat two older MPs. Neither looked up as I entered.

Veterans such as these – thirty years into their careers – had defined the culture of every organisation I had ever worked in. The British general in Basra, for example, who swore like a sailor, and roller-bladed around the base, had taught me how to be courteous to impatient sheikhs and not delay a decision. The head of my personal security detail, a New Zealand police officer, had shown that taking over the heavy machine gun on the roof, when the Sadrists were flinging in mortars, was compatible with modesty and good humour. And the British intelligence officer, with his deep brown eyes, flashes of irreverence and his darts of questioning sympathy, had shown me how to take responsibility. My vision of British government had been formed by the graces of such men.

But I was not being invited to learn from veteran MPs in the same way. These two MPs had entered Parliament together at the same time, almost thirty years earlier. Each had been ministers on the front benches under Margaret Thatcher. They had stayed in the House when their former colleagues had retired, entered the House of Lords, and become lobbyists. Neither had supported David Cameron in his leadership campaign, and Cameron, who had entered Parliament seventeen years after them and never been a minister, had left them on the back benches.

One of them, with the bland blinking features of a tall man, like a shambling vicar with hellfire beliefs, was, I knew, on the right of the party. He was opposed to gay marriage; sceptical of climate change; tough on crime and immigration; in favour of the death penalty; and of banning the burqa. These attitudes – almost mainstream when he was first elected – were now perceived by many of our new intake as the risible attitudes of a political dinosaur.

I had no idea of the political views of the other MP. But I had noticed during Prime Minister's Questions that while the first man scowled at Cameron, the second gazed at him with exaggerated loyalty, nodding and frowning as though the cameras were focused on his tiniest gesture, and he could not afford to let his enthusiasm lapse for even an instant. I had seen him almost every day since in the TV studios, defending every decision and catastrophe of the Cameron government; and demonstrating that he could be more brutal to Labour than anyone else. He was smaller, crisper, with neater grey hair, than the other man, more managing director than vicar.

The first man had apparently concluded that he was never going to be a minister again. So having been a loyal minister under Thatcher and Major, he had decided to become a professional rebel. He would be probably knighted 'for his services to Parliament', and would still be sitting on green benches, peering at another new intake, forty years after he first entered the House. The man beside him was also due to be a forty-year man with a knighthood, but he hoped that his strident displays of television loyalty would encourage David Cameron to forgive him and to make him a junior minister again, and then perhaps even a Cabinet minister – provided he could ride the tides of the long-forgotten scandals that often seemed to re-erupt and sweep across the biographies of the older MPs.

Neither seemed comfortable engaging with younger MPs. I felt that the generals or spymasters I had known would have sat in this canteen with easy confidence. But these men, with their unruly hair combed into place, red hands held awkwardly on their laps, seemed like middle-aged men who had somehow been forced to sit in the back row of a classroom. And they looked at me as an overgrown school-leaver might peer at a cocky new boy.

Professions shaped characters. If senior judges remained preternaturally analytic, journalists often remained good listeners, and primary school teachers came to address adults as infants, thirty years in Parliament apparently unsettled these MPs, branding them with a not entirely dignified pattern of disappointment and corroded ambition. And I feared, as they looked at me, I was looking at my future self.

Our briefings had told us that MPs could sit wherever they wanted in the chamber, provided no one had left a 'prayer card' in the brass holder at the back of the seat so, about three months into my time in Parliament, I moved towards an empty seat.

'This seat is reserved,' said a large man, well-lunched, sixty years old, and wrapped in a chalk-striped suit. He had been a special adviser who had been elected to Parliament five years before David Cameron, but had been made neither a minister nor a committee chair. His voice was deep, with a hint of a Scottish accent, behind exaggerated English vowels.

'But there is no prayer card,' I observed.

'I'm keeping it for a female friend of mine,' the man growled.

'But I'm afraid she's not here and there is nowhere else to sit.'

'Show some fucking respect,' he said, folding his arms, and looking away.

'I'm sorry,' I persisted, 'I don't understand, I thought the rules of the House were that you needed to put a prayer card in—'

'You,' he muttered, 'should be ashamed of yourself.'

'Why?'

He glared at me.

'Could you please explain what I am doing wrong?' I asked.

'Why don't you just fuck off.'

I didn't. Instead I sat next to him and felt the pulsing rage, from his right bicep to my left bicep, his right quad to my left quad – his gaze fixed completely forward. After about ten minutes, I left the debate.

Later, I asked someone else whether I had done anything wrong.

'No, you haven't – just ignore him – he's a total shit.'

And when I asked someone else, the same.

'No – that guy is just a shit.'

This seemed to be something to do with how he had treated his wife.

Later, I was told that he was angry that I had had the impertinence to stand for election to the Foreign Affairs Select Committee. Traditionally, the committees were appointed by the whips, and the Foreign Affairs and Defence committees, with their opportunities for foreign travel, were traditionally rewards for senior members only. But in 2010, parliamentary committees had been suddenly opened for election by secret ballot of MPs. I had put my name forward. I had not realised how controversial this was, until I read Guido Fawkes, the blogger, the following morning.

Rory running before he can walk

Word reaches Guido that a certain new MP is ruffling a few old-guard feathers with his arrogance and brutal determination to climb the ladder. Despite barely having an office and working phone, Penrith's Rory Stewart, the Conservatives' self-proclaimed bright star and Afghan rambler, is lobbying his colleagues hard for a spot on the

Foreign Affairs Select Committee. Though he failed to mention the time he spent as a Labour Party member he has bullet-pointed his 'career highlights' in a letter that has been snorted at by some old-timers.

Enough of my colleagues were, however, prepared to vote for me to be elected as the only new MP on the committee.

Guido Fawkes was, it seemed, not impressed. 'It's highly unusual for a freshman MP to be seeking a spot on such a powerful committee. But then again, Rory Stewart is a highly unusual little man,' one told Guido after lunch. At the bottom was the hashtag #TwatWatch.

A few months later, however, this man who had been unwilling to sit next to me in the chamber, invited me to speak in his constituency. I travelled out to the West Country. It was a big audience and they seemed to like my speech. I assumed that by doing him the favour of travelling to his constituency, we had reconciled. Then I gave a critical speech in the chamber on the British intervention in Iraq. After the debate, he approached me in a corridor, stood very close to me, smirked and drawled, 'A nice speech – of course it's complete bullshit.'

'I'm sorry?'

'A nice speech – of course it's complete bullshit,' he repeated, as though he needed to repeat it verbatim, his smirk now distorted into a scowl. 'It's bullshit to say that the Foreign Office didn't know enough about Iraq. That people didn't predict what was happening. It's complete bullshit,' he said.

I looked up at him. I sensed uncertainty, aggression and self-regard. He reminded me of an unstable teacher. A muscle in his jaw was twitching, and I felt mine twitch too.

'When were you in Iraq?' I asked.

'I have written a book about Iraq – I have studied all the documents.'

'When were you in Iraq?'

'I am very close to the man who was the key Foreign Office lead on Iraq. And it's bullshit to say that senior people did not predict everything that happened. He did.'

'Who on earth is he? Because frankly I have never heard of him. But if you want to know who didn't . . .' and I began to list British and American generals and ambassadors.

At this he took another step forward and barked, 'If you dare to speak to me like that again, I am going to punch you.' He paused. 'On the nose.'

Now I just stared at him. He stared at me. I wondered what it was going to be like to roll around with a 200-pound, sixty-year-old man, behind the Speaker's Chair. We kept staring at each other. And I could feel the muscle in my jaw still working, long after he walked off.

5

One Nation

I enjoyed the One Nation dining club. The club saw itself as the guardian of One Nation conservatism – a conservatism which we would have called moderate, centre-ground and compassionate, and which the right of the party called 'wet'. The club table was anchored at one end by Ken Clarke, who proved as sharp and provocative about Iraq and Afghanistan as he was about Cameron's special advisers, but never sanctimonious about colleagues – he never, for example, reminded the room that he was the only person present who had voted against the Iraq War.

In the tea rooms and in the corridors, I found gossip and jokes. Even ex-academics brushed aside any of my attempts to debate government policy and shifted the conversation on to personalities, promotions and power. But in the One Nation I was surrounded by MPs who had been in the House for decades, and occupied almost every Cabinet position, and liked to quiz fellow members on the intricacies of the German federal elections.

The Secretary of State for International Development Andrew Mitchell was almost always there, as was the Europe minister, David Lidington, who seemed to share my taste for herbal tea, served in silver-plated pots with scalding handles, and dark chocolate truffles, of which we usually contrived to lift the only two laid on the table. Andrew Mitchell, like four of the other members, was the son of an MP, and he saw Parliament as a long lifetime's vocation. When he was not talking about the Rwandan economic development or his love of 'the serpentine world of whipping that brings out the darker side of my nature', he often lamented the changed hours, which limited events like the One Nation dinner to Monday nights. He charted out a career for me. Before ever becoming a minister, I should spend years as a backbencher, mastering procedure, then more years in the Whips' Office. If I became a junior minister, I should cherish my private office, and when I was done with my department, I should return to the back benches and a world of select committees, with 'an authority born of independent thought'. It sounded as though he were describing the maturing of a 1982 claret in his late father's cellar.

In July 2010 David Cameron invited me to a seminar on Afghanistan at Chequers, the prime minister's country house, and I had my first brush with national policy. I should have been more conscious of the honour he was doing me, since he had not invited anyone else from my intake. But, having spent ten years working on Afghanistan, I took the invitation too much for granted, forgetting that I was still very much, and for the foreseeable future, a backbench MP.

It was now almost two years since Obama had decided to 'surge' 130,000 soldiers into Afghanistan with the double aim of winning a counter-insurgency campaign against the Taliban, and fixing the Afghan state. He had also set a deadline for troop withdrawal; and proposed an 'Af-Pak strategy' to reach a settlement with Pakistan, who were the main supporters of the Taliban. Three questions, I felt, now faced Britain. Did Obama's surge make sense? Was it possible to reach a political settlement with Pakistan? Could we withdraw without handing the entire country to the Taliban?

These were questions which many others had been thinking about for almost a decade. They required knowledge of what was happening in rural Afghanistan, a sense of what exactly the US had been up to over the previous nine years, and an instinct for the wishful thinking of soldiers and diplomats. I didn't think it realistic for David Cameron to try to tackle such details, when his diary was already filled with Health Secretary Andrew Lansley's reforms, and the plans to sell the public forest estate, debates about Trident, the 'bonfire of the quangos' and meetings on polling data. I had, therefore, expected him to appoint a Defence Secretary or even a minister for Afghanistan who had some of the relevant experience – even if it meant bringing someone in from the outside (just as Gordon

Brown had made one of the most senior UN diplomats his Africa minister).

But this had not been his approach. Instead, he seemed to intend to make the decision himself. He was not proposing to consult the Defence Secretary, the National Security Council, or the Cabinet, and he planned to announce the decision to the press not Parliament. But he was going to test his views against this seminar at Chequers.

We were sat in what seemed to be the ancestral dining room. A friend of Cameron's had told me that Cameron was proud of his expertise on Afghanistan. He claimed to have visited Afghanistan more than any other country, to know its history, its landscape, its lingo, and to have visited some of the worst trouble spots, hearing once 'the quietest rush of air as a stray bullet passed overhead'. And I imagined it was true that he had probably devoted more time to Afghanistan than he had to almost any other topic in his portfolio. But this simply revealed how little even a very energetic prime minister could hope to learn about a particular subject given all the other demands on his time. I felt that three years in Afghanistan barely equipped me to opine on the country. Cameron had been to Afghanistan three or four times for a total of eight or nine days in his life, and his glimpses of the landscape had been from a heavily defended rooftop, surrounded by soldiers. He had convinced himself that he knew 'what ordinary life was like for Afghan people' from little more than a few visits to British-funded development projects. And yet perhaps the position of British prime minister required him not to worry too much about his lack of knowledge.

He sat calmly and confidently at the great oak table, as I, David Richards, the Chief of the Defence Staff, and others gave our presentations. I repeated the arguments which I had made in articles and a book: arguing both against the surge, and against a total withdrawal. I feared leaving Afghanistan completely would risk a government collapse and a Taliban takeover. I believed in what others called 'a light footprint', sustained for the long term. Cameron apparently disagreed.

When we had finished, he made it clear that he had concluded that all of us fell into one of two familiar categories. I had known General Richards well in Afghanistan and we agreed on almost as many things as we disagreed on – notably that we would be unlikely to fix the Afghan state and that a total withdrawal would be disastrous. But Cameron confidently decided I was in the 'war can't be won' camp, and General Richards was 'stick with the mission'.

As the seminar ended, Cameron said he had seen a third option, which the rest of us had missed. He expressed it, as he expressed everything, in half-sentences, and truncated imperatives, as though he were dictating in the bath. 'A middle way. Don't leave immediately: job undone. Don't stay indefinitely: a war without end. Set some sort of deadline.'

This middle way – doing more, and getting out, as opposed to my middle way of doing less, and staying in – was conveniently identical to the position of President Obama. And this suited the British system. The US was spending $50 billion to our £3 billion and deploying over 100,000 troops to our 10,000. But Britain was reluctant to see itself as simply a junior partner, with no independent influence in a vast American war, when British lives were being lost. Instead the system wanted to feel that the US might be shaped by the British prime minister's insights from his sixteenth-century manor house.

Cameron concluded that we should be concentrating 'more on training the Afghan army and police as the route for our exit'. A few million pounds were allocated to this training. He ignored my statement that US General Caldwell had already spent $12 billion on trying to train the Afghan police and army, and that our contribution was a rounding error. Or that, as I had discovered on my last trip to a British police training school in Afghanistan, our best efforts were resulting in only eight out of a hundred of the latest recruits writing their names or recognising numbers up to five, or that 30 per cent of them deserted every year.

Cameron felt he was being hard-headed and pragmatic. Afghanistan, he said, needed the rule of law, property rights, decent government, fair elections. 'I call these things the "golden thread" of truly sustainable development.' He said he would help focus

President Karzai on making his government work, ensuring the country was run properly: appointing governors, passing basic laws and dealing with rampant corruption. And he felt that an exit date in Afghanistan, 'would force everyone's hand to reach a satisfactory and stable position'.

The Pakistani president had assured him that he would be quite willing to address the problem of terrorist safe havens, and rein in the Inter-Services Intelligence Agency (ISI). Cameron planned to invite both the Pakistani and Afghan presidents to stay, and to convince the latter, who had spent thirty years fighting Pakistani-backed militia, to trust the Pakistanis. He was confident that we could 'deliver security and some semblance of uncorrupt administration, get the relationship between Afghanistan and Pakistan right; and achieve a political settlement which demonstrates that all Afghans are welcome. And then withdraw.' There was a crisp jauntiness to the conclusion – it would have made a good end to an 800-word op-ed or an undergraduate Oxford PPE essay.

'The Afghan government didn't collapse in the 1990s when the Russians left . . .' he observed. 'I know my history.'

It was now becoming clear to me that despite this grand invitation to Chequers, I had been no more able to influence Afghan policy as an elected politician than I had been as a Harvard professor advising the Obama administration. In fact, I suspected I had less influence as an MP. My first chance to debate Afghanistan in the House of Commons emerged that autumn, my first year in Parliament, nine years after the intervention. Here, finally, after my speech on an amendment to the academies bill and my muffled rebellion on mountain rescue, was a chance to address the deepest questions of strategy and British identity, and touch on my strongest interests. Hundreds of British lives and tens of thousands of Afghan lives were at stake. It seemed to me at last an opportunity to challenge the strategy of David Cameron and Barack Obama.

Seven years had passed since Parliament had debated the Iraq War, with Tony Blair delivering an impassioned speech from the despatch box, and all the leading politicians responding to a full chamber and packed public galleries. This was the first time that Parliament had ever debated Afghanistan on a substantive motion. But the chamber was three-quarters empty, and the front benches were almost deserted, with only three government ministers, and one opposition spokesman. None of the ambitious high-fliers in my intake were in attendance. It seemed an occasion largely for men with shiny shoes and regimental ties. The Defence Secretary began: 'It has been fashionable in some quarters to say that the House of Commons is increasingly irrelevant in our national life, and that the executive have become too powerful. Today marks a very welcome departure.' Everyone nodded, while I looked round the almost empty chamber. 'No subject could be more important than Afghanistan.'

When the MPs began to intervene it sounded like I was watching a debate recorded many years earlier. The member for Colchester wanted to know if the Secretary of State agreed that 'this is not just a military operation'. The Secretary of State did. The former chair of the Foreign Affairs Committee gave us a recap of Holbrooke's three-year-old 'Af-Pak strategy', informing us sonorously: 'What we are dealing with in Afghanistan is not just about Afghanistan. It is also about Pakistan.' A member of the Defence Committee emphasised that the Taliban were a bad thing. I was pleased to hear a colonel declare that 'We have not made some decisions very well thus far,' but less pleased when he assured us that 'there is now great optimism that we will be able to reach the endgame, and get to a situation where our troops can come home and feel that they have given their lives for something worthwhile'.

The Defence Secretary could not have agreed more. 'Notable successes have been achieved. Good things are happening, progress on security, governance, economic growth, the rule of law, human rights, countering corruption and reconciliation. The Taliban have lost significant ground in their southern heartland. They are incapable of stopping the expansion of the Afghan national security forces. Their senior leadership is isolated, their training is deficient and supplies are limited.' I wondered whether this was how the US Senate had talked about Vietnam in 1969. Or 1965.

Many MPs seemed most concerned to get sound bites into their newspapers. The MP for Birmingham wanted the Defence Secretary to pay tribute to her local hospital, the MP for Colchester wanted the same for his garrison, and a Eurosceptic found his chance for imperial nostalgia:

> I am bound to observe that our greatest naval hero managed to command the fleet decisively on 21 October 1805 without the benefit of an arm and a leg, I am doing the man a disservice, I mean an arm and an eye [pause for laughter]; I am supposed to be speaking at a Trafalgar night dinner next month, and I had better get that right [looks jovially around the chamber]. The man was chronically sick for most of his career. I point that out simply as a cautionary note and to say in all candour that it is perfectly possible to be disabled and yet to participate in active service.

Then it was the turn of the leading lights of the Foreign Affairs and Defence select committees to gesture towards indefinable goals, wallow in misty optimism, enthusiastically misremember facts, and fall back on misleading analogies. Their criticism was reserved for chippiness about the US, whom they seemed to blame for all the problems. I remembered the confidence and clarity with which John Kerry had ranged over the history of the Popalzai and the ethnic composition of Mazar-e-Sharif, and felt ashamed.

There were three exceptions. A Conservative MP tried to argue for a long-term strategic base as an alternative to withdrawal, and two Labour MPs attacked the whole fiasco. But the Conservative was dismissed by colleagues as an over-earnest crank, and the latter two as ineffectual, loopily left-wing, and intellectually deficient. MPs who had revelled in their extravagant endorsement of our brave British soldiers lost interest when the conversation moved on to policy. If they remained in the chamber, they bent over their phones – waiting for their opportunity to rehearse their own incoherent platitudes.

Only one MP seemed willing to suggest that we didn't really know what we were talking about: 'I hope I speak as a relatively average backbench member who has followed these matters closely for a number of years when I say that I do not know in detail whether what we are doing in Afghanistan is right, wrong or indifferent,' he said. But he used this argument not to shame the House or encourage it to improve its level of knowledge, but simply to suggest that we weren't qualified to have the debate, and that we should just leave the conduct of the war up to the 'experts' in the government.

Finally, I was called by the Speaker. He allocated me six minutes to make my case. I tried to pack into that time all my arguments against the surge, to expose its absurdities, and warn against the risks of lurching from troop increases to a total withdrawal.

The member that followed me said genially, 'I am still not entirely sure that I follow the logic of what the honourable member for Penrith and the Border has said. Perhaps I shall return to that a little later.' He did not.

That winter of 2010, I travelled with the Foreign Affairs Committee to Afghanistan. It was nine years since I had walked from Kabul to Herat. We were lectured for two hours in a stuffy office in Victoria on what to do if a mine exploded under our vehicle (sit still until told to move), or if your driver was killed (sit still until told to move), and then set off in a ragged band to Heathrow to apply ourselves to the conduct of the war. On one side of me was a Scottish Labour MP, who had been a steelworker in Motherwell for sixteen years, and on the other an Essex MP who had joined the Conservative Party at fourteen, campaigned with a Union Jack-waistcoat-wearing bulldog, and was Parliament's most profoundly committed monarchist, and expert on flags. His constituency association meetings were reported to begin with singing all three verses of the National Anthem – including 'Confound their politics / Frustrate their knavish tricks'.

At check-in there was a strident attempt by our senior member to hold on to his bag, refusing to believe any reassurance that it would be collected at the other end. Only three of us were stopped at security and, although we travelled economy, some official had persuaded British Airways to let us into the lounge, where we grazed contentedly on the sandwich trays. Then our chair – a sprightly, tanned, smiling ex-naval officer turned lawyer with a youthful face and twenty-six years in Parliament – herded us anxiously towards the boarding gates.

Once landed in Kabul, I was placed in the middle seat of an armoured vehicle, in eighteen-pound Kevlar armour, feeling a heavy MP's Kevlar plate pushing into my left shoulder. The bullet-proof glass was too thick to see much through. The British driver got lost on the way to see the Speaker of the Parliament. I knew the Speaker and had been to his house, so I gave directions. But after a year in Afghanistan, the driver had still not learned the street names of the largest streets – instead he had been instructed to call them by a new NATO naming system which turned 'Jad-e-Nadr-Pushtun' into something like 'Route Red'. I tried to interest my colleagues in what we could glimpse through the window – a man selling fighting partridge, a Chinese brothel, a policeman lighting a spliff – but they seemed to prefer not to concentrate too hard on what was going on in the street.

Back at the headquarters, our ambassador to the NATO coalition produced a polished, confident and optimistic defence of the American military strategy – as though he were trying to win over a group of journalists, not briefing fellow members of the British state. I tried to get him to concede that not everything was going well, but the chair, who was a great believer in the principle that each MP should have only two questions, told me that I had said enough. Then we saw the normal collection of Afghan dignitaries – many of whom I had known for ten years. After the twelfth such meeting, the chair took me aside and asked how I knew all these people and whether I had been to Afghanistan before. During all this time Shoshana was in Kabul but the embassy security team would not let me visit her. Instead, I peered down from the window of the Finance Ministry at our project in Murad Khane and we co-ordinated by phone for her to wave to me from a roof.

Finally, we had an hour with Karzai. The president embraced and kissed me and announced to the group that, 'As Rory knows, the entire Western counter-insurgency strategy is a mistake. If I lived in

southern Afghanistan,' he continued, 'I would join the Taliban. All
your military operations are just making things worse.'

On the way out the ambassador said, 'Well, that was an excellent
meeting.'

'But,' I protested, 'the president just said that our entire counter-
insurgency strategy is wrong, that we should be withdrawing troops
from Helmand and that his sympathies are with the Taliban.'

'Well, he is wrong about that of course.'

'But he's not a commentator,' I persisted. 'He is the president and
the commander-in-chief of the Afghan army . . .'

The chair interrupted tactfully to enquire about the guest list for
dinner.

Back in London I worked on drafts of the committee report with
the clerks before it was presented to the other MPs and then rewrote
the summary and conclusions late into the night. The chairman
read the final product carefully, and to my surprise endorsed it –
although he joked I was losing him his peerage in the process. The
conclusions were stark even behind the formal committee prose:

> We conclude that despite ten years of international assistance
> designed to bolster the Afghan state, the international community
> has not succeeded in materially extending the reach and influence
> of the central Afghan government or in improving governance more
> generally. The current full-scale and highly intensive ISAF counter-
> insurgency campaign is not succeeding. The conditions for a political
> settlement do not exist, and in the resulting political vacuum,
> regional powers, and Pakistan in particular, are forging ahead with
> their own agendas on reconciliation, not necessarily in the interests
> of Afghanistan or the wider region. In spite of substantial amounts
> of money being made available to train and develop the Afghan
> National Security Forces . . . serious questions remain as to the qual-
> ity of the force that will eventually emerge.

I was proud. It was the strongest statement I was aware of from
any NATO Parliament, certainly stronger than anything produced
by the Senate Foreign Relations Committee. I waited to see what

the response would be. There was essentially no response. The press hardly noticed, the House of Commons was indifferent to our impassioned speeches, and the Labour opposition continued to back the government's optimism about the surge, governance, political settlements, and police training. The government's formal reply to our report was bland, and untroubled: 'This multi-track approach is showing signs of success . . . the Afghan National Army has grown by 42 per cent in the past year . . . effective, inclusive and transparent governance is central to the goal of building a stable Afghanistan . . . making progress towards creating the right conditions for a political settlement. In Helmand,' it replied, 'district governors are now in place in eleven of the fourteen districts, up from none in 2001.' Yet I knew there had been fourteen district governors in fourteen districts in the spring of 2002.

The Conservative government, which I supported, was perpetuating the myths of a failing war, and lying to justify more deaths.

In October 2011, the Defence Secretary resigned because of questions around a close friend who had accompanied him on formal state visits while running a private business on the side. In his place, David Cameron appointed Philip Hammond, the Transport Secretary, who had no previous interest in defence or foreign affairs, had never even visited Afghanistan, and ten years into the war, had still not seen the need to learn basic elements of Afghan history and geography.

Different arguments were made for appointing such ministers who were not experts in their fields. The first was that the talent pool of serving members of Parliament was too small. The second was that people with specialist experience did not make good ministers. But neither of these arguments seemed to apply in this case. The Conservative benches included fifty women and men who had been in the military, including many long-serving regular soldiers, a full colonel, a man with a doctorate in defence policy, people who had taught defence strategy, former members of the Diplomatic Service and the intelligence services, and the SAS. And among the backbenchers was Malcolm Rifkind, who had already been a good Defence Secretary and Foreign Secretary under John Major, and Ben Wallace, a Scots Guards captain, who had the potential to be an excellent Defence Secretary.

The third and most popular argument was that amateurs did better as ministers. This was an assumption which still ran through many elements of British public life. It was, of course, true that experts often got things wrong, and that there was value in a fresh pair of eyes. But the idea that there was nothing to be gained from having been in the military, or served in a conflict zone, or read military history, or struggled with related problems, when Britain was engaged in a major conflict, was close to insane. Particularly when the Civil Service had been so hollowed out that there was often limited expertise beneath the ministers.

During the period when the UK appointed two successive Defence Secretaries who had never before taken any interest in defence, followed by a forty-one-year-old fireplace salesman who had never worked overseas, and had never even served as a minister in any department, the US Defense Secretaries ran from a senior CIA officer to a Harvard professor specialising in defence and security to a four-star general from the US Marine Corps. The US equivalents didn't have to learn the difference between a battalion and a brigade, be informed that control of borders mattered in a counter-insurgency campaign, or be told that an aircraft carrier without a carrier battle fleet was little more than an unwieldy oligarch's yacht. Successive British Defence Secretaries knew none of these things when they were appointed. It was difficult not to conclude that at some level, subconscious perhaps, Cameron and Osborne were often deliberately selecting Defence Secretaries and later Foreign Secretaries without any background or knowledge, to avoid any challenge to their own policy or position.

This did not mean Cameron's new Defence Secretary in 2011, Philip Hammond, was a dud – he had a quick, intelligent mind, a great capacity for work, toughness and clarity. But he was being made to live out the Edwardian fantasy that a first-class degree from Oxford was qualification enough for anything. He was being forced to stand in front of soldiers, about to deploy to a fierce insurgency, like a bright undergraduate, making the most of a few recently acquired nuggets of information, to assert himself with absolute confidence – in short, he was often required to bluff.

It seemed impertinent to send the new Defence Secretary my books or documentary on Afghanistan, but I asked to see him. I was given a time by his PPS, waited outside his office for half an hour, and then received a text saying he wouldn't make it. I tried again the following week. By this time, he had been put through an intense series of briefings by the MOD, in which he had been taught and perhaps forgotten the difference between Sykes–Picot and the Durand Line, and shown maps of the 120 forward operating bases. This time he was only ten minutes late. He invited me in, said he was short of time, and, pacing like an agitated lurcher from his desk to the door, asked me what I had to say.

I began by saying that the counter-insurgency strategy would fail, and that Britain was putting too much emphasis on its Helmand operations. 'Helmand contains only 3 per cent of the land mass, and 5 per cent of the population of Afghanistan—'

'6 per cent,' he snapped, fresh from his MOD briefings.

'5 per cent . . . 6 per cent? There hasn't been a census in Afghanistan for thirty years—'

He interrupted me, 'If you don't even know the population of Helmand, why should I listen to you at all?'

He never spoke to me about Afghanistan again. It suited him better to think that there was no point listening to someone whose figures differed from the Ministry of Defence's, than to explore whether I might have a useful alternative perspective. Perhaps, excluding outside voices was partly a way of not being over-whelmed with the amount he was having to learn about this new job.

The problem, I realised, however, was not simply one of information. It was probably rooted in his conception of his role. He believed that the overall strategy in Afghanistan was someone else's responsibility – not the Defence Secretary's but the Foreign Secretary's, perhaps. And when later he became Foreign Secretary, he would conclude it was not really the Foreign Secretary's responsibility, but the National Security Council's, perhaps. At any rate, it was never his job to listen to the kind of challenge I was posing or to determine whether what we were doing in Afghanistan was right or wrong.

PART TWO

6.

District Commissioner for Cumbria

(2010–2012)

'Forget the MPs, and spend your time in Cumbria,' said my father who had served in government for thirty-five years. 'Parliament is a talking shop, darling, full of windbags. The constituency is where you'll get the job satisfaction. Get things done. Be the district commissioner for Cumbria and bugger the whips.'

I was tempted to agree. The more inert, depressing and shallow Parliament and government seemed, the more I was drawn to the truth and potential of local communities. The level of community involvement in Cumbria was staggering – almost every single person in my local village of Bampton was involved in the theatre and village-hall committees, or the half-marathon, or the library, or the church. In Brough, a much poorer place, 530 out of 600 residents actively participated in the annual fair. We had the first community-owned pubs in the country, the only community-owned snowplough and ambulance, more community hospitals, hospices, volunteer mountain rescue teams and fire engines, the smallest schools, and more common land – over 100,000 acres – than anywhere else in Britain.

All of this was under threat. Professional managers in Manchester or London saw almost all these small local institutions as examples of inefficiency. Health specialists explained that closing our community hospitals and forcing patients to take long journeys to larger hospitals would 'improve patient outcomes'. Education specialists told us that our students would benefit from the closure of our small rural schools. Our local police stations, banks, auction marts and post offices were to be closed; so too were the volunteer fire engines in Penrith and Lazonby, the community ambulance in Alston, the community hospitals in Wigton and Brampton, and the magistrates' courts, which had operated in Appleby since the Norman Conquest.

The people making these decisions were generally based hundreds of miles from the constituency, and had little idea, I felt, of what it was like to be trapped behind a 3,000-foot snow-covered pass in Alston waiting for an ambulance from Lancaster. If they had been elderly – or going into labour – they too might have preferred a hospital which was not an hour's drive from their family.

I joined, and sometimes organised, campaigns to save assets such as the community hospitals. We failed with police stations, magistrates' courts, the peat works and post offices. But I was also part of the successful drives to save the volunteer fire stations in Penrith and Lazonby, the community ambulance, the Penrith cinema, the school in Alston, the community hospitals in Wigton and Brampton and the Longtown munitions depot. In every case, I made impassioned pleas to ministers, and in many cases led a crowd through a town with a megaphone. The real secret to these campaigns was not me, but people like Dawn Coates, a volunteer firefighter who had divided us into seventy different task groups for the campaign to save the Penrith cinema, writing letters, organising petitions, placing press stories, soliciting expert legal and professional opinions, and lobbying councillors of every political party.

More and more of my writing and speaking was now concerned with community action. Community action and localism appealed to me more than any other aspect of Conservative Party policy. I believed that community groups could probably deliver broadband to rural areas more effectively than central government. I was sure that on issues such as planning and landscape, Cumbrians – not the government in Whitehall – cared more, had more relevant information, and they would make better decisions. When I was being grand, I thought this was conservatism in the tradition of Edmund Burke. When I was trying to be loyal to my new leader, I thought it might be what David Cameron had dubbed the 'Big Society'.

David Cameron had floated the idea of the 'Big Society' shortly after the 2010 election campaign, in a speech focused on giving more powers to communities, local governments, volunteers, and charities. Since then he had continued to describe it as 'a step change in voluntary activity and philanthropy' and 'an idea whose time had come'. The concept had provoked flattery, hope, resentful fury, grand theories and moral outrage, logframes, satire, a Scotch mist of statistics, a litter of spoofs, and the most elevated paeans on human dignity. Much of the Conservative Party thought it trendy nonsense. And since it celebrated volunteering, at a time of austerity, the opposition saw the Big Society as just an alibi for horrifying cuts.

Yet it seemed to be as close as Cameron came to a political philosophy and, insofar as I understood it, I was enthusiastic. It seemed to link closely to why I was a Conservative and what I could do for Cumbria. When I learned that there was to be a new Localism Bill, I spoke passionately in Parliament at the second reading and approached the whips to be allowed to serve on the legislative committee. The minister responsible promised to champion my participation. I explained to the whips that nothing mattered more to my constituency, that I had studied all the preliminary papers, and that I really wanted to play a role in crafting this legislation.

I was not appointed. The whips had apparently been told to exclude anyone with an interest in a subject from a bill committee, for fear that they would ask awkward questions. They preferred non-specialist MPs, who spent the committees looking at their phones or catching up on their correspondence. For the same reason it seemed doctors were not allowed on the health legislation committee.

Hearing that there were to be national broadband pilots, I pushed for a meeting with Jeremy Hunt, the Secretary of State responsible, to convince him to include Cumbria. This was my first glimpse of the old Secretary of State offices left by a Labour government. Vast beige sofas and pine tables stood on cream carpets. At the far end a striped tapestry in saffron yellow, russet and turquoise had been hung beside a painting by the Turner Prize-winner Mark Wallinger, of an invisible man in a jockey cap.

Jeremy Hunt stood and greeted me in the same hall where, it appeared from photographs, he had greeted Arnold Schwarzenegger.

Tall and in starched shirt-sleeves, he seemed less a politician and more a Hollywood vision of a CEO. When I talked passionately about 'barriers of distance', and grandmothers with Parkinson's who could do consultations by video link, he was calm, courteous and thoughtful. To my astonishment, after a little argument, he agreed to look at adding to the existing list of three national pilots and making Cumbria the fourth.

But his civil servants, the Treasury, and the CEO of the new quango, Broadband UK, remained reluctant to accept this additional pilot. They claimed to lack detailed information on the current broadband infrastructure in Cumbria and asked me to provide – presumably with the resources of my constituency office – a full analysis of our needs, of the likely costs, and details of the broadband network, including maps of the British Telecom copper wire network in Cumbria, which the company claimed had been lost in the privatisation of the early 1980s. To answer these questions, I recruited 120 constituency broadband volunteers, who quartered the parishes, recording fibre-cabinets, testing speeds and not-spots, and then – with the help of a former Salomon Brothers bond trader who had retired to dedicate himself to public service and was volunteering in my office – combined their reports with open-source data to create interactive coverage maps. These were so much better than anything the government possessed that BT itself asked for copies.

When the support from civil servants in London continued to be tepid, I went to Number 10 to meet Steve Hilton, Cameron's director of strategy, a small man in a tight V-necked T-shirt and no shoes – the inventor, it was rumoured, of the idea of the Big Society. The room in which we met might have been his office, except it was empty, and he moved so restlessly around it that I could not be sure. The conversation spilled into the corridor. I followed him at pace. He threw comments over his shoulder, peered into a room of people, who nodded and returned to their screens. He seemed to be searching for something – although I couldn't tell whether it was a cat, an idea, or his shoes.

He told me rapidly that he wanted 'to blow up the Foreign Office', which he thought was useless, and get rid of the ambassadors. Did I agree? As I began to try to frame what I thought worked and what didn't work about the Foreign Office, he was on to a discussion about technology and the European Union. Almost everything I said seemed to excite him. He would nod furiously or express surprise and pause in apparent wonder at things I would have guessed he had already considered. Later, I saw him on the floor staring at a map, saying: 'Fuck me, look how big Scotland is. This is just fucking mad, man.'

'Steve,' I said, 'I think Cumbria is the place really to do something with the Big Society.'

'Okay . . .' he stood still for a moment, and looked at me.

I explained about our common land, and community finances, and community snowploughs and volunteers. I sketched out what we could do with community broadband. Steve kept his bright blue eyes fixed on me: even when, reverting to one of my more tenuous historical digressions, I told him how in the seventeenth century the farmers of Orton had formed a collective to buy all their farms from their feudal lord.

He asked how this model could apply to energy or housing. I explained Appleby's micro-hydro project on the Bongate Weir – with a new design which was safe for the salmon. I said that in Kirkby Stephen people had a plan to convert disused barns on the edges of villages into affordable housing. I talked about how from Morland to the Northern Fells parishes had developed ways of delivering broadband – from beaming radio signals from church towers, to digging and laying their own fibre-optic cables.

He asked what the government was doing. I took him as quickly as I could through my months of bureaucratic wranglings and disappointments. I explained that the Environment Agency, which controlled the rivers, had so far blocked all proposals on hydropower; that the district council was ignoring the community's planning ideas; and that the telecoms companies and the government were not prepared to work with the parishes on broadband. The large institutions all insisted that communities and parishes didn't have the right qualifications, insurance paperwork, management skills or processes: in short, that they were amateurs who couldn't do projects and shouldn't be allowed to try.

I mentioned a minister whom I hoped to work with on this.

He shook his head. 'I can't take him seriously because of his bad breath. I'm telling you,' he continued, 'I had to sit through a whole meeting with him.'

I demurred.

'No, he is just stupid – you should have his job – we should get you his job . . .' he trailed off, as though he would make me a minister that afternoon. He ended by promising that he would get Cumbria designated as a Big Society pilot, that he would tell the Civil Service to make these schemes work, and that he would get David Cameron to visit the project. He then disembarked me at the door and continued on his solitary circumnavigation of Downing Street.

Two weeks later, nothing had happened, so I phoned Hilton and explained I wasn't asking for money or new legislation but simply a senior civil servant to support me on the community schemes. This time he acted. Within two weeks, Cumbria had been made one of four national Big Society Vanguards, and I had been assigned a civil servant from the Department of Communities and Local Government, who was patient, charming, boyishly enthusiastic and willing to try almost everything.

Since no extra money was available, and MPs had no budgets, I had to hold fundraising dinners in London to pay for the travel of volunteers to Cumbria and to host a new website. When Eden District refused to discuss design in its new master plan, I paid for an architect to come up, hosted her in my cottage, and asked her to document the vernacular architecture, and create a pattern book for the Eden planners. I was getting things done but only because I had been able to mobilise outside money.

If I thought any of this activity would impress my local Conservative councillors, I was mistaken. They seemed as indifferent to victories in Whitehall and Cumbrian offices as they were to my campaigns for community hospitals, or my chairmanship of the

All-Party Parliamentary Group on Mountain Rescue. They didn't want me to spend my Cumbrian evenings eating with local farmers or addressing local charities, still less in village halls, with large tea urns and unreliable microphones. They wanted me at branch events – drinks and canapés for thirty people – where I might be able to raise £400 for the party. They didn't want me visiting schools and charities on a Saturday afternoon, they wanted me delivering leaflets. And they were not impressed when I pointed out that my work was attracting Labour and Lib Dem voters. In fact, they were slightly disturbed.

With the prime minister (or at least Steve Hilton) apparently behind us, however, things began to move. Suddenly the Environment Agency, instead of rejecting the community hydro scheme, worked a little harder to think how it could be made safe for salmon; the housing trust agreed to help a community land trust; the county council acknowledged that we could perhaps connect to the school fibre network without endangering children's safety; and the planners agreed to let Kirkby Stephen develop its own neighbourhood plan.

Meanwhile, I continued to hold my constituency advice surgeries between seven main towns, and thirteen smaller villages. My first summer surgery was held in a back room of the George Hotel in Penrith. At the tall bow windows at the front of the hotel, ladies took their tea and watched people walking between N. Arnison & Sons (a clothing shop founded in 1742) and James and John Graham (a bakery and grocery store, founded in 1793).

My first visitor was heavy, unshaven and pale. He was carrying two plastic shopping bags, filled with documents. His problem, he explained, sitting down, concerned a footpath past his house. 'You see it starts in 1987,' he rummaged in his bag and pulled out a faded photocopy of a property deed.

'But this does not seem to mention a footpath.'

'Exactly. So why are they saying there is a footpath?'

Other documents cascaded onto the table. He mentioned a lawyer that he had hired in 1990; a 1992 council ruling, a change in the law, and a complication with his mother. He had been defeated in court.

'Then I'm afraid you must appeal.'

He had. And appealed again when that appeal had failed. He had spent over £100,000 on legal fees, and all his savings, over nearly twenty-five years in this battle. He could no longer sleep. Now he wanted to know if I could back his taking it to the European Court. I said I would try and read through some of the documents – we could photocopy the most important, I did not want the originals.

Next was an older man with a narrow face, and quick eyes under a dark cloth cap. He disagreed with the service charges from his local housing association, and had refused to pay his portion for a new fire safety door. When they had threatened to evict him, he had organised a residents' committee. He wanted me, he said, to look at the 'bigger picture'. He accused the housing association of abusing their tenants, falsifying their records, and bribing politicians. He had researched the procedures of the House of Commons and concluded that it was within my power to launch an inquiry. But first he wanted me to attend a public demonstration, which was due to be held in a month's time, against two of my Conservative colleagues, who served on the board of the housing association. I promised only to meet other residents and to research the allegations. He said he would be back the following week.

Third was a dairy farmer whom I knew well. He liked to quiz me in a local Penrith dialect, which I was sure became stronger for my benefit, 'How are you?' being turned into 'Owz't ga'an?'

We talked about the ewes, which he like most farmers called 'yows', and a problem with gravel from flooding in a field by Newton Reigny and a disagreement with a water expert from the Environment Agency, whom we both knew. He gave me a bit of paper and suggested I put it in my pocket. Again, to send himself up, or tease me, he phrased this as 'I 'ope thou's garna put that in ye pocket?'

And then he looked at me curiously and suggested I needed a break. 'Tha wants f'ot git thasel a holiday. Do you like Penrith?'

'Yes, very much.'

'Do you like Wes-minster?'

'Not as much.'

He winked broadly, and left.

Next came a small, quietly spoken lady of about eighty in a tweed suit, who had been denied her dead husband's army pension. This case I took up immediately and, as I learned in a thank you note from her nine months later, she won.

My next visitor was angry about British arms sales to Saudi Arabia. No, he would not be allowing me to leave 'a little late' for my next meeting. He wanted the time and space to talk about forty years of corruption and abuse. He had done, he said, some research and he knew that I had visited Saudi Arabia and had been in the Foreign Office. He wondered whether I had personally profited from arms sales. I said I had not. He suggested that I was lying. When I lost my temper and showed him out of the office, he shouted triumphantly that he had covertly recorded our conversation and would expose me on the web.

By now the surgery had been going on for two hours, and I was aware that I was very late for an evening meeting thirty miles away. The seventh visitor was a woman with a loud laugh, and a light cashmere jumper, who greeted me in an upper-class voice. She was sorry to trouble me, she said. She was not used to this sort of thing. In fact, she was, though she preferred not to say it, very successful. Usually people did this sort of thing on her behalf. She had been a yacht captain, and had captained 'well let us just say you would have heard of them'. Anyway there had been a misunderstanding – 'I've never denied it was my fault.' She had been in prison briefly. She had paid the money she had 'borrowed' back. The prison sentence was preventing her piloting at the moment. Now she was talking more quickly. But actually, she should be able to restore the Monaco licence. And that wasn't what she wanted to talk to me about. The problem was her partner. Who had left.

And yes she didn't mind saying she had been depressed. She should never have represented herself in the first court. She had missed a deadline by forty-seven hours and the law had changed. But what she wanted to say, and she knew it was a little unusual, was she was aware that the Attorney General had a rarely exercised medieval power allowing him to overturn a court ruling and, although he had not exercised that power for some time, in this case, well she thought this was justified. Now her voice was breaking slightly, and she seemed at a loss. After a long silence, she said she thought she probably wouldn't try to harm herself, wouldn't actually kill herself. It was just her house – here were the papers – and it would all be fine. After she left, I contacted the Attorney General, the police and local mental health.

On the first short parliamentary recess in 2010, I was able to walk the Eden river, which formed the heart of my constituency, from its source to the sea. I walked from high volcanic hills, where the river water was poor in nutrients but alive with dancing flies, through mid-hills, glittering with mica and coral, which favoured the white-clawed crayfish, to the sandstone rift valley ninety miles long and twenty miles wide, in which each pillar of a bridge or a variation in the stream base created runs for the adult salmon, riffles for the fry, or pools for the parr. I finished on the fourth day in the salt marshes and tidal rip of the Solway Firth, where at weekends people fishing for salmon stood with nets made to a Viking design.

Then I went to the Appleby Horse Fair. A few thousand gypsies and travellers came, as they did every year, to this small market town. The gypsies claimed that they had been there since King Edward III had established the Appleby market day in the fourteenth century. Emails sent to my constituency account claimed the gypsies had moved like locusts, picking the valley clean of every last quad bike and lawnmower, and leaving a carpet of litter in the lay-bys. Men from Appleby were standing outside shops with home-made truncheons.

The chief inspector of police had deployed over a hundred officers, closed all the pubs, and in a search of the fairground had confiscated 135 weapons. He told me that Billy Welch, whom some called the Gypsy King, had threatened to march 2,000 of his followers into the town in protest. He thought Billy was bluffing. He questioned whether he was a real gypsy. Let alone their king.

'He owns nine houses in Birmingham,' reasoned the chief inspector. 'Other people in the community say he is not really their leader.'

In Iraq, I remembered, British officers had often questioned whether tribal sheikhs were genuine. It usually ended badly. I tried to suggest, as politely as I could, that neither the chief inspector nor I could claim to understand the exact influence of Billy Welch, but that it was dangerous to assume he had none. He ignored me; 2,000 gypsies appeared in the square.

I went up to the Fair Hill to meet with Billy. He sat by a campfire in the centre of a circle of caravans, on the top of an extinct volcano – smooth as a Neolithic barrow. He spoke in bursts of furious eloquence, scattering Roma words in his speech and invoking 650 years of gypsy history. Young shaven-headed men, who would have looked like football fans if their bare shoulders had not been almost touching the withers of white horses, galloped past to the Eden. 'This earth,' shouted Billy, 'is sacred to us – this is our Mecca.' Behind him, doves flew past Knock, and Dufton Pike.

'You,' he roared, 'I will talk to – but I am not talking to them.' He gestured to the officials who had climbed the hill with me. He said a hundred police was an insult. He agreed that he would back off, and that 'his people' would behave, if some of the town reopened. I told him I would do my best, and passed on the message to the police chief and the chief executive of the council. This was not Iraq, I had no legal power, whatever he implied or some of my constituents believed. But someone agreed with my argument and, through others' work not mine, some pubs were opened, and the town was calmer by the evening.

I received 20,000 emails in the first year, one for every three voters in the constituency. They asked me to block housing estates and wind turbines; to finance flood barriers; expedite single-farm payments; transform breast cancer services; ban heavy tractors from rural roads; and open train lines closed fifty years earlier. The emails implied that some of my constituents perceived me as a figure of immense power – personally responsible for quasi-judicial decisions, in control of local budgets and all the laws and regulations that affected local life – a colonial district officer. And yet, the same people seemed also to sense that I had no budget, that planning decisions rested with the local council, and that my powers were limited to voting for laws in Parliament. They wrote to me because they had already been let down by the courts, local councillors or police. They often asked me to do things that they didn't expect me to do – and perhaps in a different mood would not have wanted a Member of Parliament to have the power to do.

In all of this, there may have been traces of a memory of a time when my predecessors in this county seat, the Lowther MPs, had been knights of the shire, great landowners of immense wealth, justices of the peace, and commanders of the local militia. The confusion about the power of a local MP seemed typical of the whole muddle of the British constitution. Some seemed to treat me as rather like a bishop in the House of Lords – a relic of an authority whose power they doubted, and insofar as it existed, mistrusted. Others seemed to perceive me almost like a duke or high sheriff: a dignified, or undignified, phantom of a former power. For others perhaps the analogy was older and darker. Some seemed to come to my surgeries almost as though they were visiting a witch: going through the motions of ritually invoking my power and calling on my aid, but with embarrassment – even perhaps shame – that they had made the visit: and with little hope that it would work.

In almost every case, I wrote to the government on my constituents' behalf. In most cases I found myself agreeing with them. And mysteriously in about half the cases I seemed to be able to help constituents win their complaints with the government. I could not quite explain why an MP with no legal powers should be able to overturn these things, or what should happen to those many constituents who had experienced similar things but didn't find their way to their MP.

Half-flattered, and almost as confused as my constituents, I threw myself deeper into the task of bringing superfast broadband, better mobile signals, and better roads. In meetings with senior civil servants I challenged 'weighting' and 'rurality'. I tried to persuade ministers that as fellow Conservatives they should feel like me a particular obligation to traditional rural areas. I persuaded a dozen ministers to visit, marched them through farmyards and village halls, and challenged them to find mobile reception by Ullswater, or to get a constituent in a wheelchair to the other side of the Penrith station platform. Half agreed to stay in my cottage and eat my boiled eggs. The chancellor George Osborne, confronted with my attempt at frying a steak on an underpowered electric stove, shredded it into pieces, pushed it round his plate, and tasted none. He – unlike me – knew how to cook.

The greatest challenge was in broadband. We were the largest, most sparsely populated constituency in England. Our mountains blocked wireless signals. Our broadband relied on a daisy chain of copper wire telephone lines, which delivered only the ticking whirrs of dial-up speed. And there were too few people to interest the commercial companies, still less justify the cost of building a cell-tower or laying new lines. Some of the farmhouses were so far from the hubs that it would cost £100,000 per house, we were told, just to give them fibre.

Yet the benefits could be extraordinary. Thirty per cent of my constituents worked from home. People lived a long way from hospitals or schools. With faster broadband, patients could be seen by a skin specialist without ever leaving home. Children unable to stay for after-school activities could learn online. Grandmothers could talk to grandchildren in New Zealand, and businesses could trade directly with China. It would transform our economy. And as broadband enabled young families to live and work in villages, rural depopulation would slow and communities would remain alive. Nowhere needed broadband more than Penrith and the Border; nowhere felt less likely to get it.

I held a 200-person conference in the constituency, with a keynote speech from a junior minister who refused to stay to listen to any of the other speakers. BlackBerry, perhaps in a sign that they had already lost their focus on the bottom line, flew in a top executive from Canada to address us and paid for community broadband activists to come up from Lancaster and East Anglia, Yorkshire and

Cornwall. I fed them all and had some to stay. They mistrusted each other, almost as much as they mistrusted my cooking. Each had a different technological solution to broadband delivery: cellular for Mike; point-to-point microwave for Alan; pre-existing school, rail and emergency-service fibre for Paul; and fully community-owned broadband networks run up from Lancaster for Barry. But all agreed that with technical ingenuity and cunning use of existing infrastructure, we could do a lot in Cumbria for £40 million, which sounded like a great deal but was less than a third of what the government thought it would cost.

Back in Parliament, I secured and introduced a debate on data coverage, and won a majority requiring the government to meet a national target of mobile coverage of 92 per cent of the British landmass, and 98 per cent of the population, up from an existing target of 85 per cent. I pulled it off because backbench business committee debates were another of Cameron's constitutional innovations, which the whips didn't yet quite understand. The government was horrified because they believed the new targets would lose them billions in their next auction of the spectrum for mobile licences. A little later they decided that this constitutional convention could be ignored and they would pay no attention to this kind of vote in Parliament.

I then shepherded county council officials in and out of ministerial offices, and frogmarched senior executives from BT and the mobile companies around village halls on bleak Saturday afternoons. I pitched to George Osborne by making him listen to my lecture on the need for rural mobile at a secretive conference in Switzerland. Amused by my chutzpah in subjecting Henry Kissinger and Jeff Bezos to my obsession with Cumbrian mobile signal, he created a new £100 million Mobile Infrastructure Project Fund for rural areas. Eventually, we learned that by some creative repurposing of European match-funding, we had secured our £40 million for Cumbria – and I entered the next battles: to prevent the Labour council from directing all the money towards its voters on the West Coast, and to ensure that BT actually spent the money on expanding into rural areas, rather than picking up new customers in the city of Carlisle.

Our most dramatic achievement was in Mallerstang, a long valley of about a hundred people that ran up into the bleak Howgill ridges. Here, an official had informed Libby Bateman, a resident, that fibre broadband was impossible. Libby, thirty years old and five feet four, was in the habit of fighting for affordable housing and station footpaths around Kirkby Stephen, and winning. She proposed running fibre up the valley, ten miles from the fibre hub. The initial estimate for reaching these fifty-eight houses came in at £500,000.

But Libby analysed the cost of 'way leaves' and of laying fibre, the risk of not finding subscribers – and solved them one by one. She knocked on the doors of the fifty-eight houses in the valley and signed up fifty-six – taking contributions from all. She identified each farmer and absentee landowner and convinced them to let the cable go across their land without charging 'way leave'. Then she borrowed a mole-plough. And let me drive it. What sounded like a pink-nosed, black-velveted niffler turned out to be a small metal plough hitched to the back of a tractor. I ploughed a tiny, uneven, trench and someone much better qualified finished the job, laying fibre down the whole valley. Within two years she had convinced BT to connect it to their hub ten miles away. Through this, and a dozen other ruses, we increased speeds from less than half a MB to almost 10 MB per second for about 80 per cent of the constituency.

But in truth I felt I achieved far less for my constituents in many years than I achieved in Kabul in nine months. Civil servants remained charmingly non-committal, and the junior ministers, exaggerated in their enthusiasm, never went so far as to act. A Secretary of State eventually agreed on the fourth meeting to fund the dualling of the A66, and a special adviser finally confirmed the £2 million for a lift for Penrith station. But I never saw the dualling happen. After three more ministerial visits, two steel and glass lift towers were built awkwardly at one end of the neat Victorian station. Virgin trains erected a plaque in my honour – the only memorial that I ever secured to my work in the constituency. The name was illegible within two years, and the plaque fell off within three.

Nevertheless, the work I was doing on community projects

seemed uniquely significant: the only authentic element in the political pantomime. People who had every reason to distrust an
incomer from a very different background opened their homes and
enterprises to me, taught me, supported me, and often fed me. I felt
safe and at home in the constituency. And in return, I was beginning
to feel that I owed constituents an absolute duty of care, and a relationship of trust and confidentiality, and that as constituency MP,
I might have a place as meaningful as that of a doctor or even a
priest.

Shortly after being elected, I had been accompanied by a journalist
from the *Scottish Sun*. There had seemed little advantage in doing an
interview for a newspaper in a neighbouring nation, which none of
my constituents read, but he had been patiently asking for an interview for some months. I suggested he could join me at the
Langwathby Fair while I judged the fancy-dress competition and
admired the white-elephant stalls. Looking around, he suggested
that Cumbria was a soft, comfortable place, a version of the Home
Counties. He seemed to want to believe that everything south of
the border had it a bit easy. He underestimated, I replied, the toughness of the local farming culture.

'But you don't need to worry about austerity and spending cuts
here . . .' the journalist persisted.

I disagreed. There were, I insisted, many striking examples of
rural poverty. There were areas in Cumbria where people lacked
many things taken for granted in cities. We needed more investment and more public services. I repeated the observation of my
neighbour in the Lowther Valley, about areas in the North where
farmers, on very low incomes, were doing backbreaking work with
old tractors, and 'Some areas are pretty primitive,' I said, repeating
the comment I had heard months earlier from my farmer-neighbour.
'If you go up half an hour north of here, in the small farms around
Bewcastle you can find old farmers holding their trousers up with
twine.'

The journalist was a nice guy and he felt sorry for me but this was
irresistible. Eight weeks later, when I had largely forgotten about

the interview, I received a call from a journalist asking whether I would care to comment on the *Sunday Mirror* whose headline ran 'A new Tory MP has outraged constituents by calling them "primitives who hold up their trousers with string".' Their central picture portrayed me standing arms crossed, legs apart, at the head of an avenue, with my Scottish house behind me, in the full pose of a contemptuous aristocrat. Then the *Guardian* picked up the story and ran it in a poverty and social exclusion section claiming that I had called my constituents 'yokels'. (The twine story was true, but I have never in my life called anyone a yokel.) Then everyone else followed.

On the *Daily Mail* comment thread, people wrote:

Same old Tories with derogatory jibes about their constituents. This man would not have been out of place oppressing the natives in colonial Africa with his memsahib sipping Pimm's and smirking.

This is the Tory Party I remember from my childhood. The one that hates people and looks down its nose at them.

Typical of his party – laugh at the impoverished, disadvantaged and sick.

I felt that I had been running in the sun, and suddenly found myself continuing off a fatal cliff. The constituency seemed like the only place where I had made real personal friendships or won anything approaching trust or respect in politics. And now I was presented, or revealed, as a sneering hypocrite who was contemptuous of all the rural traditions and people whom I claimed to serve. I felt my comment had betrayed everything I valued about my vocation, that there was no point in continuing in Parliament, and that the shame could not be overcome. It seems ridiculous recording it now – but for the only time in my life I briefly considered killing myself.

Everyone in Parliament appeared to have read the articles. Some colleagues seemed not to want to meet my eyes. An older card boomed 'Good one, old boy, you get one of those, but only one.' I tried to reach out to Number 10 for some media advice but they didn't return my calls. The whips had no advice. I went out to try to apologise and explain and by doing so generated another two days of headlines ('Rory Stewart forced to apologise after yokel gaffe'), and comment threads: 'an apology will not make this arrogant man's thoughts go away, he should be removed from office, the sooner the better'. In a television interview, a BBC journalist asked me whether I didn't think I should resign, and I could barely string an answer together.

The reporting was grotesque. My love of my constituency was sincere. But I was unable to put any of this in proportion. Something – which the farmers laughed at – felt to me like a stain on my reputation so permanent, and too large, ever to be overlooked. I was half-aware that I was investing too much honour and meaning in political representation, and inflating my relationship with a constituency which spent far less time thinking or worrying about me. I was trying too hard to make something, which was secular, sacred. I ought to have been able to recognise that abuse on Twitter and the *Daily Mail* website was not an objective judgement on my value as a constituency MP. But it took me many years before I could contemplate the incident without shame. What I had done felt not just mortifying but mortal.

7

Team Player

(2012–2014)

In Parliament, the personality and prejudices of David Cameron continued to define the tone of British politics. 'Of course, you have no influence as a backbencher. Parliament is an utter waste of time,' a junior minister confided. 'The only people with any real power in this place are David Cameron and, because Cameron trusts him, George Osborne. All you can do is be loyal, impress the whips, vote as you are told, keep your nose clean as a junior minister, and one day hope to make it to Downing Street.'

I was not beginning to warm to Cameron, but I was beginning to sympathise a little more with the experience which had formed him. His working life had coincided almost perfectly with the great age of liberal democracy. The Berlin Wall had fallen a year after he had taken his first job in the Conservative Research Department, and over the following sixteen years, the number of democracies had increased, and poverty and violence decreased, worldwide. He had formed his views in the age of American hegemony and the humanitarian interventions in Bosnia and Kosovo: the age of free-market economics and globalisation, of the formation of the World Trade Organization and the high-water mark of Davos – in a planet apparently bending to the irresistible example of Western liberal democracies. He had been elected to Parliament under the reign of Tony Blair: the most successful political entrepreneur of a centrist, post-ideological age. Cameron's causes – gay marriage, international development – were the progressive causes of that age. And all of this was a refreshing improvement, at least from my point of view, to the opinions of some of the older Eurosceptic Conservative MPs whose political formation had occurred in the 1970s and 80s and who could hardly imagine a world beyond Reagan.

But this age was ending in 2005 – when Cameron became Conservative leader. That was the year in which the number of democracies ceased to increase, and in which the civil war in Iraq exposed the full catastrophe of the Iraq intervention. It was the last year in which the British economy was larger than the Chinese. Facebook had just been founded, Twitter was about to be launched. And I did not feel that he found it easy to adjust the views he had formed to this new context.

Cameron's world view had been formed in the era of Blair. He continued to embrace the economic model formed by Margaret Thatcher and largely preserved by Tony Blair. He did not question Britain's over-reliance on financial services before the financial crash of 2008. He had little to say about artificial intelligence, robotics, or nanotechnology. Despite his relative youth he had no feel for social media (he said that people who used Twitter were 'twats'). He continued to push Britain's decarbonisation – closing the last coal plants, and dramatically expanding renewable energy. But he failed to make industrial investments sufficient to benefit from the emerging green economy. He inherited a British battery industry which was larger than any in Europe, and talked often about the importance of electric vehicles, but it was Germany and Sweden, not Britain, which under his premiership were taking the lead in battery technology and production.

He continued to perceive Russia as the bankrupt, chastened fragments of the Soviet Union, and he further reduced Britain's strategic focus on the threat of conventional war in Europe. He celebrated China's accession to the World Trade Organization and emphasised it as an emerging market opportunity for Britain, rather than perceiving it as a potential threat. He spoke about the missions in Iraq and Afghanistan as though they were a version of the humanitarian interventions in Bosnia ten years earlier. Unable to see the growing evidence of the West's ignorance, impotence and illegitimacy, he tried to repeat such interventions elsewhere. Instead of seeing China's and Russia's backing for a UN resolution on Libya as a precious opportunity to shore up a fragile global order, he pushed well beyond their authorisation – destroying future cooperation.

And undeterred by how his intervention had triggered state collapse in Libya, he argued hard for an intervention in Syria.

But Cameron's most fundamental blind spot was over the way that these different elements (the humiliation of the West in Iraq, the rise of China, the financial crisis and the rise of social media) had created the space for an entirely different politics: the age of populism – which between 2014 and 2016, the year he left politics, produced Modi, the Law and Justice party in Poland, Donald Trump, and the loss of the Brexit referendum.

There were a few MPs – Ken Clarke, David Lidington, Hilary Benn and Oliver Letwin – who seemed more attentive to how rapidly the world was changing. But many committee meetings, parliamentary debates and even, I sensed, National Security Council meetings, seemed oblivious to the rapid transformation of the global order. Nor was this simply a party issue. Many of my Labour colleagues – discounting those who were active sympathisers with Russia – were even more insular, and wrong-footed by the accelerating pace of world events. The cracks in the ice-sheet of the world passed largely unnoticed in the overheated parliamentary chamber.

For the time being, however, Cameron's government continued to be an elective dictatorship, propped up by the quasi-secret service known as the whips. While most MPs spoke publicly and loudly, facing the opposition benches, the whips hid behind the Speaker's Chair, and their gaze was turned not to the opposition benches but inwards to their own, whispering and scribbling down examples of loyalty or insolence, helpfulness or foolishness, to report to their chief. The whips were, I was learning, paid through still active medieval sinecures, as comptrollers or vice chamberlains of Her Majesty's Household; prohibited from making speeches in Parliament or giving media interviews.

Some whips were large men, who sought to fill a room, exaggerated their regional accents, and raised their voices. Others adopted tailored suits and gentle voices, and insisted that they would never presume to threaten. The most effective seemed to be the women, who were straightforward, liked a cigarette on the terrace, and said they only wished people 'would show some appreciation for others, and do their job'. Whether sergeant major or gentleman assassin or blunt confidant, however, their central task was gathering intelligence, overt or covert, targeting, spreading propaganda, running their flock, compiling their lists, for their central aim: to make MPs always vote in favour of government legislation. Every time the bell went, they stood at the doors to the voting lobbies firmly indicating which door our party was passing through and intercepting anyone who had decided to vote in anything other than the government lobby.

MPs could in theory be exempted, 'slipped' from voting. But the whips took particular delight in refusing requests for anything they might envy, in my case permission to attend the Bilderberg conference and a royal visit to the constituency. Even quite practical constituency business left them unmoved. Sometimes, the whips tried to use moral arguments for particular bills, but this was a little risky, as the government had a tendency to change its mind on matters of principle. Generally, they simply pointed us at the relevant voting lobby and hinted at the consequences of rebellion through the way they spoke about other members. 'Brown is a twat.' 'How much more of ministers' time does Emily want?' 'Awful story that about Bobby, can't imagine how his kids are going to take it, lucky that he's got some savings.' 'Did you hear that Henry is up not only for a peerage but also to be an assistant secretary general at the UN?'

Many ambitious MPs went through their entire career without ever voting against the party – Michael Gove was an example. An independent-minded backbencher might choose after many conversations with the whips and ministers to vote against the whip perhaps once in a year, on an issue which mattered very profoundly to them or their constituents, and by doing so they were likely to damage their careers. Even the most rebellious MPs, famous for their obstreperousness, voted against the government in perhaps only five votes out of a hundred. All of which raised certain questions about the theory that MPs were independent legislators, carefully scrutinising laws.

*

I had been in Parliament a year when I finally secured a time for Jeremy Hunt, the Secretary of State responsible for broadband, to visit the constituency – a Tuesday morning, when there were late votes on the previous evening. I went into the tea room to try to get a 'slip' from the whips.

Nicholas Soames was sitting on the green leather Gothic oak chair at the second oval table on the left, which I suspected he had occupied for thirty-two years. His tie was funereally dark, and thick as a horse blanket, and he had removed his jacket to reveal the white skulls on his black braces, and to tackle a copy of the *Sun*. Perhaps his father and his grandfather, Sir Winston, had sat on the same chair when they were MPs. His great-grandfather I knew had not, because in March 1881 – when other statesmen were concerned with the withdrawal of British troops from Afghanistan – Lord Randolph Churchill had treated the House to fifteen minutes of persiflage, euphemism, litotes and faux-technicalities on why he abhorred the tea room, and wanted to seize a new one from the House of Lords. The dining preferences of Nicholas Soames's other direct ancestors, who had been, it seemed, in the House of Commons without a break since the thirteenth century, were unknown to me.

On the other side of the table sat the new MP for Sherwood, a constituency that no one thought he could win, but which he had taken by 200 votes. He was a Nottingham farmer and the son of a farmer. He had a big frame, an easy grin, a comfortable manner, and had been chairman of the National Federation of Young Farmers' Clubs. His ancestors had not dined in the House of Commons. There might be people who didn't like him, but I didn't know any. (I continue to like him, even though nine years later, as chief whip, he sacked me, and Nicholas Soames too, from the party by text message.)

Beyond both of them, lounging back so far in a low green armchair that his upper body was almost horizontal, was the 'pairing whip' who was responsible for deciding who was allowed to be slipped from votes. He had, I learned, been a teacher in one of the lesser-known public schools and then parliamentary private secretary to David Cameron. His detachable white collar was stiff and high around his neck. But he had left his pork-pie trilby and paisley silk scarf outside the room. When I sat down next to him, he stood up to leave. When I asked for a minute, he narrowed his small pale eyes and stared at me like an unblinking wolf. This whip had made his reputation as the palace whisperer to the last three party leaders, sending regular unpleasant reports on colleagues. Someone else had leaked these messages to the *Sunday Times*.

I was as polite as I could be. I explained how much effort we had put into broadband over the last three years. How we were one of the broadband pilots for the country. How it had taken a year to secure the visit from the Secretary of State. How all my constituency broadband activists were gathering to meet him. And I reminded him that I had written to him a week earlier to ask to be slipped from the Monday evening vote but had got no reply. Could I please be slipped?

'No,' he said without hesitation, and pulled his mouth into a thin-lipped grin – with the corners pulled so high in his cheek that they seemed almost to touch the points of his long white sideburns – and stood up to leave.

'Please. It will make so much difference in the constituency.'

'Take the train the next morning.'

'There isn't one that would get there in time for his visit.'

'Then take the overnight bus at midnight – and change in Preston – it's only 400 miles – you should be there by seven in the morning.' He left the room.

At seven o'clock that Monday evening, by which point I had been in the Commons for eleven hours, eaten seven pieces of toast, and had drunk eight or nine cups of coffee and black tea, I wandered again into the tea room. Nicholas Soames stretched flamboyantly and announced: 'I am going home, there are not going to be any votes tonight.' And wrapping himself in a vast tweed overcoat, headed towards the stairs.

'Can we go as well?' I asked, for there was just time to catch the last train to Penrith.

'Well, there's not going to be a division. They have withdrawn the amendments. Labour have all gone home.'

'So does that mean there definitely won't be a vote?' I asked earnestly.

'Talk to the whips.'

And the whip shouted across the room, 'Please stay until the adjournment.' Seven and eight and nine o'clock passed, as 300 of us shuffled between the restaurant and the smoking room, the tea room, the bar and the library. At ten, as Nicholas had predicted, there were no votes, the screens changed to 'Remaining Orders of the Day' and everyone lifted their satchels, shrugged on their overcoats, and started moving towards the Tube, while I began to ponder the night bus to Preston.

I made it in time for Jeremy Hunt's visit and sat eagerly with the community-broadband activists, working our way through plates of biscuits. Finally he walked in, I stood up to greet him, and he stopped and turned on his private secretary.

I went over and could hear him hissing that this was not in the programme, that he didn't have time for this, that he was late, and that they would have to leave. And before I could stop him, he had walked back out again, private secretary in tow, heading for his car. I returned alone to apologise to the broadband activists who – not seeming very concerned either way – moved to the plates of digestive biscuits.

Policies and the laws on which we were asked to vote descended via the whips from an Olympus hidden in clouds. And I had little idea on how policies were composed on that holy mountain. I knew from friends who had worked with the previous prime minister that Gordon Brown had relied on a large Number 10 delivery unit and many special advisers, and that he had followed tiny intricacies of policy, brooding like a vast spider with melancholy ferocity, late into the night. Cameron, however, had immediately got rid of the delivery unit, and most of the special advisers, and relied instead on a much smaller group, which he chaired with jaunty facility, resolving issues in office hours and moving smoothly on. The spider seemed to have been replaced with the chair of a 1980s stockbroking house – appropriately dressed, brisk on the agenda, not pretending to obsess over detail, conscious of other pressures on his time.

It was believed that the key decision-makers alongside Cameron and Osborne were two chiefs of staff: one, small with a lively mind, another improbably confident and good-looking; and with them a Conservative policy wonk; an ex-editor of the *Sun*; and the senior civil servant who had served every PM for the last fifteen years. Around them sat junior gods, who exercised occasional, if undefinable, influence: Nick Clegg, the leader of the Lib Dems (for this was supposed to be a coalition); Steve Hilton (Cameron's Rasputin); Lynton Crosby (the domineering Australian pollster); and two other members of the Cabinet. Some of these people gave the impression that if they left politics they would emigrate to Silicon Valley.

Cameron's circle shared liberal metropolitan values, but the policies they pursued often seemed at odds with those values. They had announced that they would cut immigration below 100,000, when they knew it couldn't be done. They claimed that Sadiq Khan, the ineffectual but eminently moderate Labour candidate to be mayor of London, had links to Muslim extremists. They briefed that the leading candidate to be president of the European Union was an incompetent drunk, even though they would later require his support. I presumed much of this was an awkward effort to flatter the right of the Conservative Party.

But I found the details of their spending cuts even less easy to understand. It was not that I was opposed to spending cuts. I agreed with Cameron and Osborne that if we continued spending and borrowing at the old rate we risked undermining confidence in our currency, our gilts and our economy. And I did not agree with the many who claimed that the cuts were motivated purely by sadism, or with those who argued that by continuing to increase public spending, Britain would generate so much growth that the deficit would disappear on its own.

But I was uneasy with the fervour with which Cameron and Osborne embraced spending reductions, and their insistence that Labour had grossly mismanaged the economy. And the particular ways in which Cameron cut confused and sometimes horrified me. Twenty-five per cent was cut from the prison budgets, and a third of the prison officers laid off, while the number of prisoners in the

overcrowded jails was allowed to increase. International development spending was doubled – heading to almost £12 billion annually,
paid for in part by deep cuts to welfare spending, and early childhood support.

Defence spending was cut – removing the last pretence of being
able to engage in a European land war, or sustain more than a few
thousand troops in the field. But Cameron still pushed ahead with
buying two aircraft carriers that we didn't need, had no carrier
groups to escort, and for which we could not afford any planes (his
solution to this conundrum was to build one aircraft carrier and
then immediately mothball it). Corporation tax was slashed, which
was relevant to large wealthy companies, but not National Insurance, which would have done more for employment and small
businesses. Still, I was not close enough to Downing Street to judge
why or how reluctantly he had made these decisions, or to be certain that the alternatives were as obvious as they seemed to me.

In the early summer of 2011, I went for a run over the fells facing my
cottage. On my route, past the whitewashed church, I was stopped
by a group at a table in the pub beer garden. They greeted me cheerfully, and asked me how I was enjoying my job. I said that I was
loving it, and felt a little ashamed at my dishonesty. My constituents
had chosen me, and presumably expected me to feel the privilege of
that rare position. Hadn't Churchill said that 'MP' were the proud-
est letters that anyone could carry after their name? And wasn't
being an MP necessary for our democracy? And as my mother liked
to say, if good people didn't go into politics . . . But inwardly, I was
reeling from the reality of the world I had entered.

Continuing on up the hill path, past the fell ponies, I was struck
by how much more fulfilment I had found with Turquoise Mountain, the charity in Kabul, than in Parliament. There, I could see
buildings which I was sure would have vanished without us; schools
and clinics which we had been able to define and implement in
every detail; and a place to which we had delivered healthcare, education, sewerage and electricity for the very first time. But in
Cumbria, communities had all these things already. I could help to

accelerate the arrival of broadband. But it would have arrived without me, and I was not managing the teams who were laying the fibres, merely trying to winkle out budgets and signatures in London.

I sensed that many of my colleagues were equally frustrated by their roles as backbench MPs. Ken Clarke had told me the previous week, after a One Nation dinner, that the problem with the new batch of MPs was that we all now wanted to be ministers. His words had stuck with me.

'When I joined,' he had said, 'there were Knights of the Shire, who were quite happy being backbenchers all their lives, who viewed it as a dignified part-time job and rather looked down on ministers. All that has changed. Everyone now wants to be a minister.' But only a very small number of us would even make it into the Cabinet. Perhaps that was why Parliament so often felt like a chamber of hungry ghosts, in which no one was at ease.

Some people, like my friend Richard Benyon, seemed to remain normal and unscarred, but he was rare and almost saintly. I felt myself becoming less intellectually inquisitive, coarser and less confident every single day. On the Tube the week before, my colleague David Willetts had looked down at me. 'Don't you understand?' he asked. 'You need to become a minister, and that means you need to demonstrate more public loyalty. It's a Mephistophelian bargain, loyalty in exchange for promotion.'

When the phone rang – which never rang, for almost no one had its number – I was in the kitchen. The Swaledale sheep were grazing on the floodplain beneath and I could see the farmer and his wife racing on their quadbike towards their flock. The call was from David Cameron. I had spoken to him perhaps three times since I entered Parliament and never on the phone. He apologised for interrupting my weekend. He was ringing to ask for my support to abolish the House of Lords, and replace it with an elected second chamber. I did not want to anger him, I needed to prove my loyalty if I were to be promoted, and although I was uneasy with his proposal, I could understand its appeal. The Lords – retired generals and ambassadors; business people; detective novelists; scientists; sports stars; hereditary aristocrats; bishops; judges; and many, far too many, retired politicians – could seem with their ermines and crowns a particularly egregious anachronism, much less easy to explain than an elected senate. Peerages were in hyperinflation. Queen Elizabeth I created eighteen lords in her forty-four-year reign. Tony Blair created 400 in a decade. And David Cameron seemed set to match him.

But there were still many impressive individuals in the Lords with genuine expertise, whom I was reluctant to replace with another group of politicians. And the power of even the less impressive members was limited. Because the body was unelected, they could only revise and delay legislation, not overrule the House of Commons. If Cameron created an elected second chamber, the new members would have much more legitimacy to challenge the authority of the House of Commons: risking, as with the US Senate and House of Representatives, legislative and budgetary gridlock. So I was opposed, in principle, to replacing the Lords with an elected second chamber.

But what had really convinced me that I could not support David Cameron on this measure, whatever the cost to my career, was the way that he seemed to be approaching the issue. He said that he was doing it because he had made a bargain with the Lib Dems. He would give them an elected House of Lords in return for their agreeing to reduce the number of MPs and redraw the electoral boundaries in a way which Cameron believed would guarantee a Conservative majority in the next election. In other countries, abolishing an upper chamber of Parliament required a special procedure, a two-thirds majority, a referendum, or a constitutional convention. But he was proposing to whip the abolition through in a simple vote on a summer afternoon, as though he were imposing VAT on Cornish pasties, and in order to gerrymander our electoral position.

So, while I would have liked to be in his good graces, I explained as politely as I could that I could not vote for the measure. I added that I had written to the chief whip almost a year earlier explaining my position and principles on this type of constitutional change.

And signed a joint letter, a week before the vote, with seventy colleagues. With the tone of a man who had not been expecting much from me, Cameron pleasantly wished me a good day and hung up, presumably to call another rebel.

The following week, Cameron invited us to discuss the Lords on a circle of sofas in his House of Commons office. He still had, I thought, a chance of winning some of us over. Most of us would have been thinking hard over the weekend. We were sympathetic to his more liberal conservatism and didn't want 'to let the side down'. And we almost all wanted him to make us ministers. But we were also prickly – a little charged with rebellion, our lines over-polished through too many conversations with colleagues and journalists. He would have to adjust his argument to his sense of our emotions, and characters. And he was not accustomed to persuading or debating fellow MPs in this way. His speciality was reaching efficient conclusions at the end of Cabinet meetings, or performing in Prime Minister's Questions for a TV audience. Perhaps as a result, his tone was more pleading than convincing.

'Come on,' he began, 'would it be so bad, really?' The proposal, he reminded us, was to do it in three stages. Perhaps if we won a majority and no longer had to deal with the Lib Dems we could back-track and leave the other two-thirds of the House of Lords in place.

I and two others emphasised first that however odd the place looked from the outside, many of the Lords, particularly the non-party members, were impressive people – drawing powerfully on their experience as judges, spymasters, senior diplomats and scientists. We named a few. It was clear from Cameron's expression that this argument did not work for him. He knew these individuals, and had little time for them, perhaps because many of them had been 'unhelpfully' critical of the interventions in Iraq and Afghanistan, at a time when he was trying to defend those invasions. He countered lightly with the example of his father-in-law, a good-humoured fox-hunting grandee whose ancestors had bought his title.

As the conversation continued, the gap between Cameron and the rest of us became starker. We were all from the same party but it was clear he didn't share our instincts about history, tradition, the constitution and the significance of this ancient chamber. In fact he struggled to understand where we were coming from. He might be a Conservative, but he was not that kind of Tory. Perhaps, despite these differences in perspective, Blair could still have charmed us with a burst of detail and energy. Margaret Thatcher might have swung the room with the force of conviction. But this would have required taking us more seriously. And that Cameron was also struggling to do. From his point of view, House of Lords reform was a fake problem: one that, he believed, none of us had cared about till a few weeks earlier. He felt that it was grotesque to turn the issue into a moral crusade and began to wonder 'what planet we were on'. And whether through tiredness, distraction, a habit of not consulting backbenchers, or a limited respect for our opinions, he began to sound patronising.

'What I am saying,' he tried again, 'is would the reform really be that bad? It could be done in stages. Why worry about the role of the House of Lords now? Let's fix how it's elected first. I'm personally convinced,' he said, 'that Lords reform will never get beyond stage one. Why not start the process but not quite finish it? Some elected; the others not. Is that really the end of the world?' We left, thinking he was a cynic. He concluded that we were simply 'anti-change, anti-coalition, anti-Cameron'.

After our meeting, the whips warned Cameron that he would lose the vote. He pressed ahead. On the evening of the second reading, the whips sought us out individually and tried to convince us that if we only voted with the government that evening, we could always hold our rebellion for a later stage of the bill. A few agreed to change their vote. The chief whip and the deputy chief whip sought me out, speaking with particular avuncular concern about the way I was blighting my career. One of David Cameron's inner circle said, 'Come on Rory, you don't really care about the constitution do you? It's boring and irrelevant.'

Five minutes before the vote, George Osborne approached me outside the lobby.

'Rory, I am going to promote you to be a minister in ten days' time.' He was drawing here on his reputation as the person Cameron listened to most closely. 'But if you walk through that door,' he said, indicating the 'no' lobby for the Lords Reform Bill, 'you will, I promise, not be promoted in the rest of this parliament. You will be a backbencher for at least five years.'

I walked through the door. The bill was heavily defeated. The House of Lords was not changed. The party did not get the electoral boundary changes which it wanted from the Lib Dems. Osborne was true to his word.

8.

Select Committee

By 2014, I had been a government backbencher for four years. I had held eight, ten, sometimes fourteen meetings a day: say 2,000 meetings a year; had attended hundreds of hours of debates in the chamber and in committee, visited each of the 200 hamlets and villages in my constituency, written 200 columns for the *Cumberland and Westmorland Herald*, received 100,000 emails and letters, answered 100,000. After much lobbying, I received from the government another promise to double the width of the A66 in twenty years' time, but the road remained not much wider than when the Roman legions built it as their expressway to Hadrian's Wall.

A year into my time in Parliament, I had married Shoshana, who had worked with me in the charity in Kabul. She now ran the charity and I envied her frequent trips to Afghanistan and the new office she had opened in Myanmar, and above all her colleagues: people we had built the charity with – eccentric, idealistic, irreverent – real friends. I didn't find much of that in Parliament.

Four years on the back benches had left me contemptuous of what I saw as the superficiality of the leadership. I had been appalled at the apparent pettiness, insecurity and envy of so many older MPs – the hearty obsequiousness to Cameron in the tea room. I had struggled to reconcile what I had witnessed with a Parliament whose reputation had been founded on Churchill's irrepressible insistence on awkward truths, or Gladstone's prophetic dignity. I felt that MPs – who had served the long apprenticeships of doorstep campaigns, who used Prime Minister's Questions to land little stories in their local papers, and exploited their media appearances to repeat party slogans – too often treated friends with the same half-truths and evasive geniality with which they approached their electors. I felt the very skills which helped them get elected and promoted undermined their ability to think clearly about what the country needed. I hated how politicians used the pompous grandeur of the Palace of Westminster to pretend to a power they did not have, and to take credit for things they had not done. I felt all this was at the heart of our failure of responsibility in Iraq and Afghanistan. And the grotesque inadequacy of so many of our domestic policies.

But now I realised that I had become part of the same phenomenon. With the exception of Afghanistan, the House of Lords, and a nervous abstention on mountain rescue, I had always gone along with the whips. I had spent a decade, before entering politics, writing and speaking about how to intervene abroad, but I had not defended a principled position on Syria. I had ceased to study legislation in detail. I mocked the pallid inconsistencies of so much of our policy, and winced at the careless machismo of so many cuts to government spending – but I didn't speak out publicly against those things. I didn't argue with my right-wing local councillors, or even call out their racism.

I tried to find reasons to defend government policy and to convince myself that the most positive statistics (I liked to emphasise how well we were doing in employment) were an honest picture of our economic performance. I argued vehemently that we were 'protecting education spending in real terms', although head teachers in my constituency had shown me how new burdens of pensions and regulations in fact meant less money. I crafted visits and press releases to ensure I was in the local paper once or twice every week of the year. I was jealous when colleagues were promoted and was desperately anxious at reshuffles. I felt every snide comment about me in a newspaper was potentially career-ending and slept badly, worrying about petty insults and my underwhelming performance. I talked about seriousness, but I had no clear economic policies of my own and no vision for fixing the things that worried me about Britain. In short, while I complained about my colleagues and talked them down, the real person whom I despised in all of this was myself.

In my dreams Parliament often appeared as an even grander palatial complex, with ceilings 200 feet high, devoid of people. Often I wandered down golden staircases through empty libraries, and cold autumnal cloisters, not knowing my way. In one dream I finally, came through a small side door, into a vast cathedral – with choristers in the distance and every wooden pew packed with MPs. Jacob Rees-Mogg was languorously stretching his legs over the marble floor, chatting loudly to a colleague, as a Minister of State clambered up into the pulpit. A doorkeeper in white surplice walked over towards me. It was clear from his polite expression that he understood why I might have mistakenly believed that this was a place I could enter, but he explained that – regretfully – I would have to leave.

In my waking hours, I often wondered whether I could stand down after a single term but it felt like a betrayal of the trust of my constituents. There seemed no alternative other than to continue.

Gradually, I saw another side of myself. A more furtive bureaucrat was emerging, who was beginning to 'hear hear' more loudly at prime-ministerial statements; who was assiduous at sitting with the senior Cabinet ministers at Wednesday lunch, and who lingered over the roast beef in the hope that Cameron might take the empty seat beside me. I had begun to send short texts, much considered and agonised over, to the inner team in Downing Street, praising the prime minister's latest initiatives. Texts which, even now, make my ears burn with embarrassment.

This tendency had reached its climax with the Syria vote in August 2013. The government wanted to bomb Syria in response to Assad's use of chemical weapons. I supported this. Obama had drawn a public red line over the use of chemical weapons. And what remained of US credibility in the Middle East after the debacle of Iraq and the rise of ISIS terrorism seemed closely tied to the ability to respond.

But I feared that Cameron would use the vote as an excuse for a much larger intervention, which would be a catastrophic repeat of the follies of state-building in Iraq and Afghanistan. I had already seen him request Parliament's permission for strikes to protect citizens in Benghazi and then use that vote for full regime change in Libya. So while I could defend voting for the letter of the motion on Syria, I could not support what I feared its spirit and use would be.

So I was relieved that my sister's wedding was in Devon on the day of the vote, and that the whips had slipped me. But when I returned from the church, I turned on my phone and found frantic texts from the prime minister's chief of staff saying that they feared they would lose by one vote and that they needed me. Rather than expressing my anxieties, I sprinted out just as the plates were being laid for the reception dinner, and leapt in a taxi for the three-hour drive to London. Cameron's chief of staff and I must have texted back and forth a dozen times on that journey. The prime minister himself, I was assured, had been told of the effort I was making. He was immensely grateful. He would not forget it. At one point – when I was stuck in traffic – there was a discussion about the party paying for a helicopter to collect me.

The taxi arrived in Parliament six minutes after Cameron lost the vote by thirteen votes. Obama used the defeat as a reason not to launch the air strikes. Assad, having crossed the red line, remained unpunished. It was a humiliation for the US, for Britain's waning international reputation – and for Cameron's personal credibility and leadership. Perhaps so much so that a Victorian leader would have been tempted to resign. I was left with a £300 taxi bill, little gratitude from the prime minister, a rather unimpressed sister, and no one except myself quite sure how I would have voted had I made it on time.

In June 2014, reasoning that Cameron would never promote me to be a minister, I stood to be chair of the Defence Select Committee. Like the chair of the Senate Armed Services Committee in the US, this was supposed to be an important position. My predecessor, who was stepping down to go to the House of Lords, was a senior member of the House and the party, and a former chief whip. My seven competitors, mostly long-serving MPs, included former ministers, almost all of whom had served for many years in the army. One was a full colonel with a DSO. I was relying on my lived experience in the Balkans, Afghanistan and Iraq and my writing about counter-insurgency and state-building, but I was not a professional soldier. David Cameron told a friend of mine that my move was pretentious. MPs, who had been irritated by my standing to be a simple member of the Foreign Affairs Committee, were now enraged.

All MPs were eligible to vote for the Defence chair, regardless of their party. I prepared 650 notes for colleagues, and with a team of volunteers delivered them to every office, the day that the old chair announced he was going. I followed up with texts to every MP's phone, and secured dozens of commitments before anyone was quite clear who my competitors might be. I made ruthless use of my books and BBC documentaries on Afghanistan and Iraq: and in the hustings, exploited the fluency that came from having given a hundred speeches on these subjects in the United States. And because my leading opponents, perhaps befitting the crustier end of the military men, were right-wing Eurosceptics who had expressed for years a bluff contempt for pacifist socialists, I was able to whip unexpected parts of the Lib Dem and Labour vote in behind me.

On election day, I came down the corridor to the room in which all MPs were casting their secret ballot for the chair. Michael Gove was standing with three of my competitors. He had his back to me and was saying: 'It's a quite extraordinary coincidence, I put you one, two and three on the ballot paper!'

A fourth competitor emerged from the voting room. 'And you,' he said with delight, 'were my next choice.'

I entered his field of vision. He glanced at me, seemed about to say something, and then bolted, disconcerted, his head down: like a hedgehog surprised.

I was elected. This was the first time a first-term MP had become a committee chair and I was the youngest chair, it seemed, on record. In our opening meeting, the man who had threatened to punch me after our disagreement on Iraq a few years earlier, and who was one of many members of the committee to have stood against me, presented an ultimatum. It demanded that I never speak again in public on defence, without the explicit permission of the rest of the committee. 'We will not have you,' he said, 'using the committee as a platform for your ego.' He also insisted I resign my part-time teaching position at London University. And claimed he had the whole committee behind him. I looked down the table. No one seemed to be standing up to disagree with him.

'We can't have you telling students things you haven't cleared with us,' barked another Conservative MP. A Labour friend on the committee seemed to be with them. After a tense hour of argument, I agreed to give up the teaching position but refused to concede my right to speak without their permission. After the meeting I tracked down the Labour MP in her office. I was hurt.

'Why are you doing this?' I asked.

'You know why, Rory.'

'No, I don't. Why?'

'You know, Rory.'

I didn't, don't, won't.

Over time, however, the committee seemed to readjust to my chairing, and we plodded solemnly around the world from NATO to the Middle East. And I was grateful to have one MP whom I admired, Richard Benyon, to sit next to on planes. As chair, I was now treated by journalists as an authority on defence, which I was not, and I was deferred to, rather than challenged, while I pontificated on geopolitics.

We put out a report pushing for the government to commit 2 per cent of GDP to defence spending: they had been reducing it. Then we managed to change a piece of legislation in favour of veterans (the defence minister was dismissive of my attempt to reason with her, and the amendment got through only because the whips somehow failed to notice it in time).

I next turned our attention to Syria and Russia. David Cameron had been proudly insisting that Syria was the UK's number one strategic priority and that we were the 'second largest' contributing nation to the operations. I pointed out repeatedly on television that the Royal Air Force were a very minor component under a US command that was ten times larger, and that our much-vaunted air missions against ISIS amounted to two flights a day.

Next, we published a whistleblower's claims that the Defence

Intelligence Service had been cut so much that the MOD had had no Crimea desk office when the Russian invasion began in 2014, and had been forced to strip out an officer from another geographical area. And at a time when talk was turning towards Asia and cyber, and money was being absorbed in aircraft carriers, we produced a third report pointing out that the UK had entirely eroded its capacity to fight a conventional war in Europe, and warned of the potential of Russian attacks on the Baltic States.

The Defence Secretary, Michael Fallon, approached me after a last vote to shout at me in the corridor about our Syria report. It was late at night, he had just come from dinner, and he was flushed and agitated. He stood too close to me and barked that I did not know what I was talking about. He said I was not seeing the secret reporting. I offered to look at it confidentially. He stormed off. Cameron was now apparently making grudging jokes about my ability to cause problems. But in truth, our reports were largely ignored, and the departmental replies remained a tissue of evasions and propaganda. We never convinced the Ministry of Defence to reinvest in conventional warfare capacity to balance Russia in Europe, or to increase defence intelligence. And although the government agreed to spend 2 per cent on defence, only my proud father believed this was entirely because of our campaign.

I had entered politics imagining I would be helping to form policies within the national debate. My leaflets in local campaigns implied I could get government money for highways. Constituents and journalists still questioned me as though I were responsible for national policy. But most of what I knew about the bigger issues still came through the newspapers, not Cabinet discussions, and if my influence on defence policy was minuscule, my influence on domestic policy was non-existent. The key decisions on austerity and the economy were ones on which I and my 200 backbench colleagues had hardly been informed, let alone consulted. When called in to constituency surgeries and television interviews to defend austerity, food banks and waiting times at the NHS, I could often only guess at the reason for the government's decisions.

It was only the Scottish referendum of 2014 – four years into my new profession – which finally gave me the chance to engage with an issue that was national and existential. Nothing mattered more to me than the question of Scotland. My attachment to Britain, which had made me a civil servant and a politician in the first place, was the fruit of my love for Scotland. My family home – my parents' and grandparents' house – was in Scotland. I had grown up helping my father paint the correct tartan on the plastic kilts of model Black Watch soldiers, and had spent the holidays clambering over uneven clumps of heather, muttering lines from Burns and Scott. I saw in my Scottish neighbours modesty, courage and quiet honour. I felt Scotland had a humility and toughness, practicality, equality and rawness that England often lacked; and that Scotland was what forgave England's hollowness. But none of this made me a Scottish Nationalist.

I saw Scottish independence as a defeat and a retreat, cutting us off from fellow countrymen with whom we shared so much, making us not only geographically but spiritually smaller. And making England worse too. The United Kingdom offered richer connections, relationships and opportunities than any one of the four nations could generate on its own. Splitting the country threatened centuries of common life, the most intricate interweaving of trade, institutions, and even family. And it would split me apart, leaving me in a Parliament without a country.

Cameron's campaign focused on trying to scare the Scots with the economic consequences of separation. I did not like this. It felt as though, threatened with a divorce, he was responding with 'If you leave me, you will be poorer,' rather than 'I love you.' I began to try, from my own marginal position, to explain why I thought we could be proud to be both Scottish and part of a United Kingdom – to emphasise the deep connections of soil, history and culture that knitted us together.

I made and presented a two-part BBC documentary, arguing that the communities on either side of the English–Scottish border were part of a single culture divided by an artificial line, first drawn by the alien colonial power of Rome. (This provoked a Scottish

Nationalist demonstration outside the BBC offices.) I did a 600-mile long walk along the Marches – the border lines – interviewing people on their sense of nationhood, and wrote a book, arguing that Cumbria, Northumbria and southern Scotland were part of a single historical 'middleland' culture, separate from both lowland England and highland Scotland. I took on Nicola Sturgeon, the Scottish Nationalist leader, in a BBC debate in Scotland. And put her through a brutal public questioning in front of the select committee on the costs of Scottish foreign and defence policy. I gave increasingly long, and my father remarked 'over the top', speeches in the House of Commons. One ended, to even my embarrassment, 'in the end what matters is not the [Roman] wall that divides us but the human ties that bind us in the name of love'.

Finally, I proposed the formation of a human chain of Scots, English, Welsh and Northern Irish holding beacons, stretching from one end of Hadrian's Wall to the other. When the permits, organisation, car parking and risks involved in a mass gathering on an archaeological site became ever more intimidating and expensive, I settled on inviting the same people to build a cairn of stones on the English–Scottish border, with rocks brought from their separate parts of the United Kingdom.

We were donated a field at Gretna Green, right on the border line. Two young men volunteered to help me by staying on site week in week out, increasingly shirtless in tight shorts, living out of a caravan, supporting the volunteers building the cairn, and curating it on Facebook. I enrolled actors, and writers, and explorers, and generals. I commissioned a poetry competition on 'Hands Across the Border'. A Belfast poet embraced the masonry:

Every one of us is a stone
dappled grey and edges age-worn rough
alone, we are solid enough
but together, we could make towers, mark paths

The public began to come, in ever larger numbers, carrying Cornish tin ore, Grampian granite, Welsh slate and Sussex flint, and on most of it they wrote messages of love to Scotland. Eventually we had laid over 100,000 individual stones, making a circular cairn thirty feet in diameter and nine feet high, which was photographed from the air and printed on the front page of *The Times* just before the vote.

All of this felt fundamental to why I had entered politics in the first place. We recoiled from the sharp edge of modern campaigning. We had no attack lines; no three-word slogan. But we were folding thought, speech, literature, personality, movement and the fingernail-breaking shifting of rocks, into politics. Meanwhile, Cameron ran the sort of campaign with which he too was comfortable. He raised a lot of money, commissioned a great deal of polling, and set up a cross-party campaign, led by a Labour activist, which was reinforced with celebrity endorsements, and earnest letters to *The Times* from experts. He took some awkward risks – hinting that the Queen was on his side. And belatedly – driven by desperate and passionate pleas from many, including me, and much more significantly Gordon Brown – he put a little emotion into a speech. But the centre of his campaign remained exploiting economic fears about exit. The Union side won 54 per cent to 46 per cent. A profound existential threat to the United Kingdom had been averted and the status quo preserved. So he felt vindicated and confident.

But politics was changing fast. The turnout in the Scottish referendum was 85 per cent – 20 per cent higher than in the previous general election – demonstrating a quite new level of political engagement. Incomes were stagnant, productivity had not recovered from the financial crisis in 2008. In Scotland and across the world, algorithms on Twitter and Facebook were already rewarding the most provocative voices, turbocharging fake news, deepening a daily habit of anger and bafflement. In March of the referendum year, Putin had formally annexed Crimea – the first violent change to a European border since the Second World War. Two months later, populism had arrived in India with the election of Narendra Modi. A month after that a few hundred ISIS fighters routed three divisions of the Iraqi army and seized the second largest city in Iraq and declared a caliphate. On four continents provocative, anarchic, charismatic leaders were gaining, spitting out half-invented facts, presenting themselves as the people in revolt against an unrepresentative elite. The age of populism had begun.

But Cameron and I – each in different ways – were still behaving as though Britain might be the exception to this global rule – each of us approaching referenda as though arguments on the economy, prudence or the common ground would win the day. This time, somehow, they did.

Our first son – Sasha – was born eight weeks after the Scottish referendum. Weekend travel to the constituency now involved a zip-stretching overstuffed bag of nappies, wet wipes, changing mat and milk pumper for use on the four-hour train rides, and a lot of standing between the carriages hoping he might stop crying and go to sleep. My constituency days were usually twelve or fourteen hours long, leaving Shoshana alone with Sasha in a freezing cottage, half a mile up the fellside, and three from the nearest village. I tried to cut short some of the weekend appointments to spend more time with the two of them. Parents helped to babysit. Sasha got an Afghan visa. And somehow Shoshana remained cheerful and never told me that my job was cramping her life. In fact, she seemed oddly proud of me. And this must have been an important part of what helped me to keep going in a job that I found so deeply frustrating.

I went on to speak – according to Hansard – 400 times in Parliament. And tried to speak much more than I was called. I had travelled to Syria, I think, more than anyone in the chamber but I could not get the Speaker to call me in a Syria debate. I had visited Ukraine straight after the Crimea invasion, and been on the front lines, and had crossed the southern border to enter Tripoli the day Gaddafi fell, but I struggled to speak in the Russian or Libyan debates. I was proud of my careful speech, limited by the Speaker to four minutes, on intervention; my hour-long speech on why we should remain in the European Court of Human Rights; and my speech on why Scotland should remain in the Union. But the only speech which seemed to achieve any public prominence was a ten-minute speech, delivered at ten at night in an adjournment debate, on the subject of hedgehogs. This was watched by six people in the chamber and over a million times on social media.

By the time Sasha was six months old, I had spent five years among my parliamentary colleagues. Perhaps a flock of politicians can never be a happy gathering. Still, it was surprising. Among us were nurses and doctors, soldiers, diplomats, solicitors and the rest. In the hospital, or the officers' mess, or embassy, or law firm, we must have often felt valued, secure in our work, been reasonably honest, and made friends. Such things were more difficult in Parliament.

Of course, we never failed to greet each other in the corridor, compliment a colleague on an article, send a handwritten note on a successful speech, mention how much we had enjoyed our holidays in their constituency. Occasionally we remembered their partner's name. And when – as seemed to happen once a fortnight – a colleague was exposed in a scandal and splashed across the newspapers, we sent supportive text messages. We continued to sit in the tea room chatting to MPs whose careers had been ruined by drunken indiscretion, or an off-colour joke, a poorly administered expense claim, a tax evasion, a pyramid scheme, or even their betrayal of national secrets. We attended award ceremonies hosted by MPs who had been suspended for corruption; some continued to drink with MPs accused, and later convicted, of assault and rape. But this extreme tolerance itself suggested that we were often not expecting the standards and trust we would from friends.

Instead of staying in Parliament after votes, I preferred to rush home to be with Shoshana and Sasha. I resented every wasted hour in the chamber, and was sad that we rarely got a chance to go out in London. Of course, I appreciated the qualities of some of my colleagues. I travelled for example to Iraq with the Henley MP, Nadhim Zahawi, just the two of us, and found him a joyful companion, with a quick eye for the comic, as easy and realistic with armed militia at checkpoints as he was with prime ministers. I admired Sajid Javid's courtesy, and the lightness of touch and sincerity of the MP Ben Gummer. But we didn't know what music each other listened to, or where we went on holiday. And somehow, when we walked out of our dining halls and had to parade in front of the whips, and be singled out for criticism or promotion, there were no Spartacus moments: we didn't seem quite to stick together. Frankness about the prime minister was a little dangerous. Too many of our private conversations seemed to get back to Number 10 and the whips. I loved the One Nation dining club, but I was not surprised when its secret proceedings appeared in the *Mail on Sunday*.

I began to feel that the longer I stayed in politics, the stupider and the less honourable I was becoming: the less I was listening to other people. I reflected a great deal, far too much, about my House of Lords vote. I did not conclude that I could have done anything else, when George Osborne had tried to bribe and threaten me. Indeed, I was pretty sure that most of my colleagues would have done the same. But why, if I had done the right thing, did I feel anxious about it? Had I not quite understood what it would mean to spend five years in my late thirties and early forties trapped as a backbencher in the House of Commons, while my peers engaged with policy and made decisions in ministerial departments?

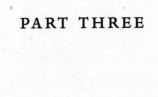

PART THREE

9.

Red Box

In the spring of 2015, Cameron summoned us to a 'retreat' in a conference hotel in his constituency in Oxfordshire. It was the parliamentary recess. Some MPs chose to stay away but most of us did what we were told and turned up. We rambled into the lecture hall bearing paper coffee cups and paper plates of Danish pastries and took our place in cinema seats. MPs whom I had only seen in dark suits and white shirts and blue ties were experimenting with the idea of casual clothes – one had a pair of pressed blue jeans, another a pink polo shirt. But only the prime minister's inner circle wore sneakers.

George Osborne came on the stage. He introduced Jim Messina, a thin man with an underpowered voice. He said that Messina had just won the second election for Barack Obama, through his use of Facebook and Twitter, and that he had been hired to win the same victory for us. The party, we were told, had raised tens of millions of pounds for our new campaign – buying consumer data and building a new software platform. We were to be the first generation of British politicians to enter the world of Big Data, AI and social media. Messina's data-scientists would micro-target exactly the right supporters in the key target constituencies, with the most efficient allocation of money and resources, and persuade them to vote through their phones. (The older MPs glanced at their phones as though unsure whether they had turned them off.)

In March 2015, Cameron called the election and I returned for six weeks of constituency campaigning. Every few months over the five years, I and the other backbenchers had been dragged into presentations on internal opinion polls, which were optimistically at odds with the national polling. But even the most loyal Conservative pollsters didn't suggest we could win an overall majority. That, Cameron insisted bitterly, would only have been possible by reducing the number of MPs and changing the boundaries – and we had lost that chance in the House of Lords rebellion. Instead, the general consensus was that both Labour and Conservatives would fall short of an overall majority and we would have to form another coalition with the Lib Dems.

I was sent down to campaign in Cheltenham, far from my own seat. The candidate Alex Chalk was busy with the party chairman Grant Shapps – who had emerged in shirtsleeves with a gleaming smile from a 'battle bus' packed with very young and overly anxious would-be MPs in tight T-shirts. I was sent to canvas some backstreets with a local councillor. Our sheet didn't direct us to every door, but instead to a seemingly random collection of doors in every street. Number 5 was followed by number 17.

This, the councillor explained, came from the consumer shopping data which the party had bought from the big supermarkets and other retailers. Our new software used this data to predict which numbers in the street were likely to vote Conservative.

'How does that work?'

'Well, I suppose, it is something like, if we know they bought Stilton, perhaps, as opposed to edamame, at Tesco's, they are more likely to vote Conservative . . . but Cheddar . . .' I was not sure if he was joking.

Still debating politically indicative dairy products, we turned up another path. If someone answered the door, the councillor explained, we were to interview them about policy and write down their mobile phone number. Someone else would then collect our canvas sheets, and enter the data in a computer. An algorithm would compare this to other data sets, adjust its parameters, and generate an ever more accurate, real-time picture, not only of how each individual would vote, but which issues in particular would motivate them on election day, generating tailored messages with just the right claims on the NHS or education or defence, and ping them to phones. This was apparently how Obama had won his election.

Except the first door to which the computer directed us had a

Labour poster in its window. The next target had been rented out as a student squat. We passed a house which the councillor said, morosely, contained Conservative voters, but which the software had failed to identify. It had taken me nine hours to get to Cheltenham from Cumbria. In three hours of campaigning we found only one potential Conservative voter. We reported this name to the campaign headquarters – now filled with Grant Shapps's young activists apparently readying for the post-battle bus party.

Elsewhere colleagues were gloomy. Campaigning back in Cumbria, I began to notice that if a house was filled with books, the occupants would not be voting Conservative. I was exchanging texts with many MPs. Each assumed that we would fail to win a majority because we had failed to be the kind of party which we each separately imagined. I, for example, felt that we had seemed too vindictive in our spending reductions, lamentable in our lack of support for the Civil Service and the BBC, had not sufficiently supported rural communities or delivered on the promise of the Big Society, and had conducted ourselves without dignity.

Kwasi Kwarteng, who was still a backbench MP, told me the problem was that we were not right-wing enough. He felt his voters were more sympathetic to the Eurosceptic party UKIP, which had taken 25 per cent of the vote in the 2014 European elections. He had applauded Cameron for refusing to approve a European bailout for Greece (Cameron's refusal horrified me) and he was pleased that Cameron had promised to hold a referendum on Europe. But Kwasi felt we had squandered the right-wing voter base. He was immersed in the history of local constituency elections, and he felt the national polls concealed how weak our position was at an individual constituency level. 'How many of the people who you are canvassing in Cumbria are genuinely enthusiastic about Cameron? Do you really think we will be able to hold a marginal like Carlisle?' I agreed. I had not felt much enthusiasm for Cameron in Carlisle.

Perhaps Kwasi and I found it difficult to believe in our government because it had given neither of us a job. But most journalists, and perhaps Cameron himself, also agreed that we could not win a majority and therefore would not be held to the promise of a referendum on Europe (the Lib Dems would throw the referendum out in the coalition agreement).

Only my friend John Hatt predicted that we would win. He had compiled a list of 232 'errors' of judgement made by David Cameron during his time in office – from economic policy, to his handling of Rupert Murdoch – and said that in any normal situation we deserved to be crushed. But he said that Cameron's offer to hold a referendum on Europe would be enough to win the election. We needed to put nothing else on our leaflets. None of this matched what we were told by the internal pollsters who assured us that Europe was number fifteen in the public's lists of priorities.

'I guarantee, and will give you an omniscient bet, that the pollsters are wrong on that,' said Hatt.

When the results came in, I had won a record majority. We increased the vote across Cumbria and indeed across the country. Our Lib Dem coalition partners were wiped out, dropping from fifty-seven seats to eight. Labour lost every seat in Scotland to the Scottish Nationalists – ending a century of domination in the North. The old two-and-a-half-party system seemed to be over. How much of this was due to Jim Messina and his digital campaign, and how much to the promise of a Brexit referendum, was unclear. Each MP attributed our success to our own ability, charisma and dedication to our seat. But political scientists insisted that it had been a national swing and the character of the individual MP made very little difference to the vote.

Cameron read this victory as a firm endorsement of his particular style of politics, and it emboldened him to feel he could win the Brexit referendum, just as he had won the Scottish referendum and the election. First, however, he was faced with filling empty Lib Dem seats in his government. He therefore set out to, in his words, 'harvest the crop of talent from the seeds sown over the past decade or more'. I, of course, hoped he would promote me and some of my friends, harness from among the backbench MPs Damian Hinds's toughness, calmness and modesty; Nadhim Zahawi's practical if piratical management skills; Gavin Barwell's patient eye for the incongruous; Charlotte Leslie's empathy.

But these were not the people who Cameron had been fast-tracking for the last five years to the Cabinet, or whom he meant when he said he was building a 'modern, compassionate, Conservative Party and ending the idea that the Tories aren't open to talent, to women, to minorities'. He meant nine people in particular. Not people on whose advice he relied, or whose judgement he particularly trusted: for that he still relied on his inner circle, and his Old Etonians. Not people who spoke particularly well in the House of Commons; some did, some didn't. Not people with particular strengths in running departments: some of them were competent, others incurious, uncritical and inept. He meant the 'team players'. Or so at least it appeared to my jaundiced eye.

'I divide the world,' Cameron liked to say, 'between team players and wankers: don't be a wanker.' A team player was someone who parroted the party line with fervour, never rebelled, and was never abashed. His younger promotions – Priti Patel, Liz Truss, and Matt Hancock – took this to a vertigo-inducing extreme. The older women, such as Amber Rudd and Anna Soubry, with adult children and long careers before Parliament, were blunter, even funny, about some issues in private. But in public all these high-fliers from my intake were fanatically supportive of David Cameron.

Did he worry about what they really believed about him, or the European Union? Did he speculate on how willing they would be, if one of his rivals such as Boris Johnson took over, to shift their allegiance, champion a completely different position, and deny that any contradiction had occurred? Did he ask himself whether the younger ones would be more idealistic and loyal to Cameron conservatism, or whether the older ones would prove more steady? Was he worried about who exactly Priti Patel or Liz Truss were, how well they governed, or what exactly they believed? I doubted it. But by promoting these people consistently, Cameron had created the future leadership candidates for the Conservative Party. And probably made at least one of them a future prime minister.

★

I had been encouraged to keep my phone on in case Downing Street called with a promotion. I did so for three nights, was woken by calls from the States and Afghanistan, and finally, increasingly certain that I would not be promoted, turned it off. I woke at 8.20 on a Tuesday morning to find four missed calls from Cameron's chief of staff. And texts: 'Where are you?', 'Call me'.

I called. 'So sorry, my phone was off.'

'Not a very good time to keep your phone off is it? The prime minister wants to see you in twenty minutes.'

I put on a white shirt, dark blue suit and sober spotted tie. At South Ken station, I picked up a cappuccino. A British diplomat, whom I knew from Iraq, was on the District Line platform and wished me luck. Transferring the paper cup, to shake her hand, I squeezed too hard on the cup and cappuccino foam exploded down the right breast of my navy suit, and my right trouser leg. She convinced me that I didn't have time to go home to change. I dabbed it with a thin disintegrating napkin. As I walked through the gates into Downing Street, the flashes exploded from the cameramen, and I strode past, with one hand raised, my lip jutting out like Mussolini's, and my body angled towards the wall, in the hope of concealing the shreds of paper and beige foam on the crotch of my damp suit.

For the first time, the door of Number 10 was opened before I reached it by the policeman who had been watching me on a camera. I sat in a waiting room. Officials whom I knew walked past, smiling congratulations. After five years of waiting for my first job, I was not sure what Cameron would choose to use me for. Perhaps because of the work I had done on broadband, a job on digital infrastructure? Or perhaps having run a heritage charity, I would be appointed to the Ministry of Culture? Big Society minister? Or maybe as a Scot and a Unionist campaigner I would be put in the Scottish Office?

Colleagues who had seen on Twitter that I had been called to Downing Street began to text advice. They said that Cameron would try to promote me because he wanted me inside the tent, not attacking him from the outside. I should not undervalue my position: I should refuse anything that wasn't a senior job, and remain as chair of the Defence Committee. The chair of the Culture Committee had been put directly into the Cabinet.

Finally, I was called into the Cabinet Room. I had never seen it before. A dining table more than thirty feet long, laid with green baize, ran the length of the room, lined with thirty red leather chairs. The walls were a pale yellow, and mostly bare. Two glass bookcases on my right held almanacs and registers. There were a couple of small old-fashioned clocks. It looked like the dining room of a 1970s country house hotel. David Cameron sat at one end of the table, facing the door, with his chief of staff beside him.

'Hello Rory,' he said. 'I understand you want a chance to do something different.' He sounded a little distracted. 'I would like you to be', he said, glancing down, 'the parliamentary under-secretary in the Department of Environment, Food and Rural Affairs, dealing . . . with issues like . . . farming.'

'Actually, probably more with the environment,' said the chief of staff.

It was the most junior position in perhaps the most junior department in government. But my chance had come to stop simply being a commentator, get off the back benches, and start governing. I thanked him warmly. David Cameron made a non-committal noise. I glanced at the chief of staff, wondering if there would be a second to discuss what was expected of me in this role, but he raised his eyebrows and nodded towards the door, so I thanked the prime minister again, got to my feet and walked out, with no indication of why he had appointed me, or what he wanted me to do.

Outside the door of Number 10, a black government car was waiting. Journalists were waving and shouting questions. The car shielded my stained trousers from the cameras. We drove down Whitehall, round the awkwardly sized bronze fetishes of dead politicians, each out of scale with its neighbour, and then south along the Thames to a granite block, carved with giant images of men with haunted faces, in scientific coats, holding laboratory instruments. This, the driver said, was the former headquarters of Imperial Chemical Industries (ICI), the manufacturer of insecticides, fertilisers, explosives and poison gas weapons, known for its exploding factories and chemical spills. Now it was DEFRA – the Department of the Environment, Food and Rural Affairs, charged with regulating insecticides, and chemical spills.

Two men and three women were waiting on the steps. They said, 'Welcome, Minister,' and guided me past a staircase glittering with chrome balustrades, to an elevator with walls of blue art deco glass and burnished steel marked 'Ministers Only'. We emerged in a tight flock onto a boardroom corridor, lined with black and white pictures of former ministers of agriculture. On the facing wall was a set of posters celebrating Britain's greatness: Wallace and Gromit appeared under the headline 'Creativity is Great'. Another poster, 'Innovation is Great', depicted a dark robotic hand, that seemed to represent Britain as Darth Vader, reaching for the throat of the world. I was introduced to two women, whose tasks included serving afternoon tea to ministers.

Passing through an outer office, apparently for my private secretaries, and a waiting room with leather sofas and an eighteenth-century landscape on the walls, I arrived at my new office. Long windows showed sunlight on the Thames and fresh green leaves on the plane trees on the Embankment. Across the river I could see the red-brick castle of the archbishop's palace. Prominently displayed on the long dining table was a cherry-red, lead-lined briefcase, packed with manila folders. On its front was a royal cipher and the gold title 'Parliamentary Undersecretary for the Environment and Rural Affairs'. This was my 'red box'. Whether the lead lining was there to sink the secret papers, or protect me from a bullet, was unclear. But its design was identical to the one used by Gladstone, and, at £1,000 a box, it served, I was told, to sustain the British traditional craft industry.

Three women (Jo, Liz and Suzie) and one man (Tom) asked if they could sit down at the table. 'We are your private office, Minister,' they said, in the tone of a concierge team at an expensive hotel. They explained that the department consisted of three ministers – Liz Truss was the Secretary of State and my boss. The Minister of State, the second most senior minister, had been given the portfolio for 'food' – which meant farming. I, as the parliamentary undersecretary, had been allocated the 'environment and rural affairs' brief.

'Would you like a coffee, Minister?' Given that the last one was on my trousers, I gratefully accepted.

Jo got up from the table in quest of a cappuccino from Pret. Liz pushed over my diary for the next two weeks. Suzie handed me one of the red briefing folders, also marked with a gold royal cipher. Its neat sections, each marked by a coloured label, had just been pulled together for a minister, of whose identity they had been completely unaware twenty minutes earlier. I glimpsed in Tom's hand what seemed to be my speeches from Hansard – presumably he had been reading them in the hope of getting some clues on my beliefs.

The folder told me that I was now responsible for the nation's forestry, all the rivers, the national parks, and the country's nature and biodiversity, flooding, chemicals, air quality, billions of pounds of annual environmental payments, and much more. I felt an excitement I had not felt since establishing Turquoise Mountain in Kabul ten years earlier.

I paused, looking at the four junior officials who formed my inner team: each with neat clothes, neat smiles and even neater files: as crisp as the lime-wood carving on the walls. They were all I guessed in their twenties – Tom looked as though he had only just left university.

'The big question,' I said, 'is what shall we change? How will we make the world a better place?'

They didn't reply.

'Not me. All of us together. What should we do?'

Still they didn't reply.

I requested a flip chart, and Jo returned quickly with one, whose three unsteady white metal legs seemed more suitable to an industrial estate in Slough than the art deco office. Asking them to call out my various roles, I began recording in different colours my responsibilities. I wrote 'environmental payments and flood money (£3 billion a year), forestry (150,000 acres)', and wrote 'ACTION?' next to each. I proposed that I should make an immediate visit to the headquarters of the Environment Agency and asked them to arrange an emergency flood exercise, for I feared that a flood might come before I knew what I was doing. I requested roundtables on chemicals, air quality and international conservation. I sketched out a job description, so that I would know what exactly to request in my first meeting with the Secretary of State. They remained silent.

I stopped. 'Of course, I'm sorry. I don't have any idea what I am talking about. I've only been here fifteen minutes. You are the experts . . . come on, argue back. Tell me I'm talking nonsense. We'll change things together. What would you like to change?'

Now the senior of the three spoke, in a tone that oozed restrained competence. 'We will definitely think about that, Minister, and come back to you.'

I took a moment, stretched and walked to the other end of the vast office. I had heard that it was Labour who had spent millions of pounds restoring this building – right down to the glass mosaic in the ministerial lift. Now, it seemed the Conservatives wanted to sell it for apartments. I opened a cupboard: it contained glasses and half-empty bottles of liquor: tequila and Aperol. I turned and grinned at the team.

'Legacy of a Labour minister?' They smiled politely back. I opened the drawer of the elaborately carved Edwardian desk, which sat in a scalloped alcove. It was empty apart from a comb.

'Whose comb is this?'

'Our apologies, Minister, we should have removed it.'

'Whose comb was it?'

'Minister Rogerson's, Minister.'

'Who?'

'Dan Rogerson, your predecessor.'

I had to open Google on my phone to remind myself who he had been. I was reminded of a quiet man, younger than me, who had spent an afternoon in Cumbria, listening to me pitch different ways in which this department could invest more in Penrith and the Border. He had seemed a little confused by my approach and we had received no investment.

'What is he doing now?'

'We are not sure, Minister.'

'Is he no longer a minister?'

'He is no longer an MP.'

Returning to Wikipedia, I discovered to my embarrassment that Dan – who I had assumed was an obscure Conservative colleague on the front benches, elected on some earlier intake – had in fact been a Liberal Democrat, who had been given the ministerial role as part of the coalition agreement, and having run the environment and rural affairs portfolio for a year and a half, had lost his seat to the Conservative candidate. 'Could you at least tell me what Dan Rogerson was trying to achieve before he left?'

'Yes Minister. We will prepare a note.' I asked for his mobile number. They said they would try to get it, but they didn't sound confident. A month earlier, they had been anticipating every nuance of Minister Rogerson's diary, supporting him on shifts twenty-four hours a day, seven days a week. But it was already clear that there would be no pretence of a handover – no explanation of my predecessor's strategy, and uncompleted initiatives. The arrival of a new minister was Groundhog Day. Dan Rogerson was not a ghost haunting my office, he was an absence, whose former existence was suggested only by the black plastic comb.

I was beginning to question whether ministers had any significance or presence at all, when my friend the Conservative MP Richard Benyon knocked on the door. Richard, Dan Rogerson's predecessor, was fifty-four and looked twenty years younger, with an open handsome face. I asked the private office to leave and Richard helped me work steadily through the portfolio. He had ingenious ideas about canals, and shrewd suggestions about my new team. The tea ladies who, it seemed, worshipped him, kept us nourished with cake, served on a set of bone china, apparently salvaged from some even grander ministerial office. I was astonished that Cameron had demoted someone so committed and knowledgeable about his brief. But Richard would not join me in criticising Cameron. He seemed to view every Conservative leader with an adjutant's loyalty: never presuming to judge whether the eccentricities of his commanding officer reflected wisdom or shell shock.

Then I was summoned to meet my new Secretary of State. I

thanked Richard and walked down the corridor lined with photographs and posters to her office, where I was told that she was in a meeting, and that I was to wait with her secretaries.

After what seemed a long time, her inner door swung open. Liz Truss stood very close to me in the doorway, blocking my way.

'Yes, Rory?'

'Hello, Secretary of State.'

'Yes, Rory?' she said again, and she suddenly swung away, letting me into another absurdly grand space with floral carvings running over the pale wooden walls: this I suspected had been the boardroom of the Liberal MP and minister Alfred Mond, who had financed this building, while my room had once been his private office.

Liz was younger than me. We had entered Parliament together and David Cameron had made her a Cabinet minister within four years – when she was thirty-eight. I was told that she had been promoted faster than anyone because she was a 'strong media performer'. Intrigued by this, I had watched a number of her interviews. In none of them had she reflected, apologised, explained, empathised, or attempted to persuade. Nor did she ever, except in the rarest cases, answer a question. Instead, she approached interviews as broadcasts: opportunities to repeat the party attack line, never giving ground, or varying her tone. I wondered how Cameron had developed any views on her skills as a minister: her ability to inspire civil servants, or be patient with difficult briefs.

'The problem with you, Rory,' Liz said to me, conversationally, 'is you try to be interesting in Parliament and the media. Never be interesting.' And yet, she was herself unusual. She was known for submitting her civil servants to a barrage of questions about mental arithmetic, and popular books on economics. And although her speeches were generally confined to the blandest opinions – she liked to emphasise her fondness for British cheese, for example – she delivered these banalities in the tone of someone challenging an entire establishment consensus.

Off the public stage, she delighted in winding up colleagues. In my case – because she saw me as a foreign policy specialist – this involved saying: 'I cannot see why you waste your time with foreign policy. I cannot imagine a job I would less like than to be Foreign Secretary, I think the Foreign Office is a waste of time.' Everything she did, I was concluding, had the flavour of a provocation.

'We will,' she said, sitting me down very close to her, 'become the most open, transparent department in the government. And the most efficient. I want you to write a ten-point plan for the national parks.'

'Yes, Secretary of State,' I said, addressing her with the formality I reserved for generals. 'I will get straight out to visit the parks, then we will get the heads of the national parks down. I will have a plan ready for you within four weeks.'

'You have three days, Rory,' she said with such exaggerated firmness that I wondered if she were joking. 'We need to get it into the *Telegraph* on Friday.'

I looked at her and concluded she was not joking.

'But Secretary of State, if you could just give us a couple of weeks, we might really have a chance to—'

'Come on Rory, I can write it myself already. Do you want me to give you some clues? Point one, connect young people with nature; point two, apprenticeships; point three, health and well-being . . . Make it eight points, if you can't find ten. But ten is better.' And again she smiled, as though she were testing me.

The details, it seemed, mattered hardly at all, nor did their implementation, for this was only a press release, masquerading as a plan. She showed me a picture she had just posted on Instagram. Liz Truss was the leading exponent of Instagram in Parliament. She seemed to be using images of herself in different costumes to suggest a pattern of progress, just as she used provocative policy statements to create an impression of forcefulness.

I explained that I wanted to review our flood plans around the country, recruit a brigadier from the army as my crisis deputy, and get straight on to the ground if a flood happened.

She said that she thought that sounded fine.

I said I was concerned by the Met Office flood forecast maps, which appeared to represent the probability of a flood with no indication of its severity. 'Frankly I don't understand the forecasts,' I said. 'I would have thought that unlikely but severe floods are much more of a problem than milder frequent floods.'

'Well I understand the forecasts, Rory,' she said with a grin which emphasised her confidence in her intellect, stripped some of the provocation from her tone, and seemed to signal agreement.

'And,' I said, 'I have taken the liberty of writing a job description for myself. I would like the CEOs of all the arm's-length agencies to report directly to me every Monday morning.'

She took the job description I had drafted, and glanced at it and said that too was fine. 'Anything else?'

'No, thank you, Secretary of State.'

'Very good, Rory,' she said laughing. 'Now let me tell you what I want you to do. We're going to begin by cutting the department,' she said, with great relish. 'I want you to cut 25 per cent in your part of the department.'

My rural affairs team, I had learned, was down to six people. It was impossible to find even £100,000 for a new waste strategy. I stared at her.

'Don't worry, Rory. I have a mentor who is a very successful businessman who says all businesses can always be cut by 20 per cent. I want 20 per cent staff cuts too. We need to make better use of technology. We can put back offices together.'

'But, Secretary of State, this scale of savings—'

'You can do it.'

'But the rural affairs section of the department already hardly exists. It is down to half a dozen people. If you cut it further how can we claim to be the Department of Environment, Food and Rural Affairs?'

'I don't believe in rural affairs, Rory. I think there is no relevant difference between rural and urban populations.'

David Cameron, I was beginning to realise, had put in charge of environment, food and rural affairs a Secretary of State who openly rejected the idea of rural affairs and who had little interest in landscape, farmers or the environment. I was beginning to wonder whether he could have given her any role she was less suited to – apart perhaps from making her Foreign Secretary. Still, I could also sense why Cameron was mesmerised by her. Her genius lay in exaggerated simplicity. Governing might be about critical thinking; but the new style of politics, of which she was a leading exponent, was not. If critical thinking required humility, this politics demanded absolute confidence: in place of reality, it offered untethered hope; instead of accuracy, vagueness. While critical thinking required scepticism, open-mindedness and an instinct for complexity, the new politics demanded loyalty, partisanship and slogans: not truth and reason but power and manipulation. If Liz Truss worried about the consequences of any of this for the way that government would work, she didn't reveal it.

'And data, Rory. DEFRA is the most data-rich department in Whitehall, with much of it – millions and millions of files – worth billions of pounds. Think of the possibilities: 8,000 sets of data, we will use LIDAR data,' she said. I nodded although I could only guess that this was an acronym for some type of imaging system. 'It can pinpoint which places have the best soil and microclimates to grow grapes for English sparkling wine, isn't that right?' she challenged her private secretary.

'That may be more an idea for the Copernicus Satellite System, Secretary of State.'

'We will work with games companies and do hackathons,' she continued unabashed. 'You can lead a hackathon, Rory. And we're going to win the government Red Tape Challenge.'

'Secretary of State, could we talk about some of this?'

'Tell me if you want a lift with me in the ministerial car to the votes tonight.'

'I will . . .'

'Hashtag OpenDefra,' she said, smiling again as she showed me the door.

10

Particulate Matter

Perhaps, I reflected, Truss's overdeveloped traits of simplification, and her allergy to caution and detail, were simply a response to the impossible, absurd demands of the jobs which we had been given: a way of sustaining momentum in the face of vertigo. I could feel this impossibility in my own portfolio. I seemed to have not one but a dozen jobs. Responsibility for the nation's flooding, air quality, national parks, wildlife and nature, recycling, environmental subsidies, public forest estate, chemical spills and water supply seemed to be only part of my portfolio. As new roles emerged ('in charge of the national litter strategy', 'responsible for the Areas of Outstanding Natural Beauty') I continued to list them in bright red and green marker pens on the limp sheets on the office flip chart.

My first briefing from civil servants was on our poisonous air. A subject on which my predecessor Alfred Mond MP – who was closely involved in the production of poison gas in the First World War – may have had more expertise. I, by contrast, was shockingly ignorant. A broad-smiling, civil servant in a large floral print announced that 56,000 people in the United Kingdom were dying prematurely because of nitrogen dioxide emissions from the very diesel cars which we, the government, had subsidised for years (on the grounds that they emitted less carbon). Our air pollution was breaching EU standards. She unrolled a map of air pollution across Britain. I looked at the red halo around Leeds.

'That looks bad.'

'It could be worse. Luckily our air-monitoring sensors are on the edge of the city. The figures would probably be much worse in the city centre.'

'Why do we not put monitors in the city centre?' I asked.

'We are not required to by the legislation.'

She passed me another sheet of paper, which explained that air pollution was costing the economy more than £2 billion a year.

'How much would it cost to end air pollution?' I asked.

'A few hundred million pounds would address most of the excess emissions.'

'And that one-time payment would save billions every year going forward?'

'Yes Minister.'

'Well then that is what we are going to do.' I looked around the table. I sensed behind the patient encouraging smiles the years they had already invested in the air-pollution strategy: the briefings of previous ministers, the days spent rewriting presentations to accommodate the different prejudices of Treasury officials and politicians, lawyers and scientists; and the continual disappointments. I was looking only at the tip of a vast submarine structure, which had been patiently constructed long before my appearance, redeveloped again and again, and would be rewritten again for my successor.

I asked for more briefings. At first, I had understood that our problem was a failure to comply with EU standards. But in the second briefing, the officials explained that the EU standards themselves were pathetically weak. Years of negotiations between EU civil servants and the automobile manufacturers, focusing on sulphur dioxide, nitrogen dioxide and particulate matter (which seemed to be a general word for sooty gunk, graded into different sizes), had resulted in an agreement called the Euro 6 standards for diesel cars. But the standards applied only in laboratories. The car companies installed special devices to reduce emissions for the lab tests, and then removed those devices when they put the cars on the road: so that Euro 6 diesel cars emitted seven times their official limit for nitrogen oxides on the streets. The US, discovering this, had fined Volkswagen billions for its illegal emissions. But neither we, nor any other European country, had taken action. It seemed that I might have a chance to address some of this, for I was now a member of the EU Environment Council.

Two weeks later, I travelled with my private office to Strasbourg, entered the hotel by the back doors to avoid a demonstration from French farmers, sat in the barely furnished rooms of Britain's diplomatic mission, and was then led down to a vast underground conference centre, where I was sat at the central circular table alongside my fellow EU ministers. Behind us circles of diplomats, civil servants and commission officials, each with their own folders and half-drunk cups of coffee before them, spread out towards the dim edges of the room.

Listening to the representatives of twenty-seven member states read their preprepared statements in different languages, I felt like a delegate at an intergalactic conference. We all stayed solidly through the session, except the French environment minister, Ségolène Royal, who stayed only for her own presentations. Called, I looked around the room at my fellow ministers, their heads framed by simultaneous-translation headphones, at the chair and at the prominent clock ticking down the four minutes which I had been allocated for my speech. I spoke, without notes, of our shameful failure and called for radical action, trying to catch the eye of the chair and the other ministers as I did so. Many seemed to be nodding their heads.

Over the break for Chablis and gravadlax, I continued my sales pitch with a young Danish minister. Then our ambassador took me to meet the senior civil servant in the European Commission responsible for the policy. The official gave me only a little of his time. Apparently a junior British minister did not rank very high in his priorities. But he said that he shared my outrage, and that the estimate of 400,000 premature deaths annually in Europe was too low. The actual figure – if the monitors had not been deliberately put in less polluted places – was probably closer to 750,000 deaths a year. He agreed that we should measure how much the vehicles actually emitted on the roads, rather than simply in the laboratories, and said the commission would be proposing what he called 'a real-world driving test'. But when I returned to the council chamber the real world seemed more elusive.

As the conference came towards its end, I heard some of my fellow ministers say that they were willing to agree a 'conformity factor' of 1.5. Henceforth cars would be allowed to emit only 50 per cent more poisonous gases on the roads than in the laboratories. This was at least progress, in a world in which they were currently emitting seven times the limit. I turned excitedly to the ambassador behind me. She shook her head. Coming round to join me, she whispered that this would apply only to new vehicles, yet to be manufactured, not to the trucks and cars which were currently killing hundreds of thousands. Angela Merkel, I was told, had blocked anything else because of pressure from German car manufacturers.

'But don't worry,' she added, 'there is nothing to prevent you from setting more stringent requirements in Britain.'

I returned to office life in London. In a small gesture I had stopped using the departmental car and had instead started using a minicab firm with a fleet of hybrid cars. Every morning, I was dropped by the twenty-foot silveroid nickel doors with their astronomical telescope, pert as a 45-calibre naval gun, and walked into the art deco palace. A Pret cappuccino was waiting on my desk. I carried it out onto the balcony and glanced down at the Thames and up at the facade above me, on which was carved a chemist in a lab coat, trapped in the giant hand of a builder. The builder was making a chain, which was bound around his own neck and wrists. It was difficult not to perceive all this decoration as a profound satire on Alfred Mond's own work as a minister and a businessman.

Mond had been elected MP for Chester in 1906 and then Swansea from 1910 and during the First World War, while simultaneously directing nickel companies, a bank, a newspaper, and trying to 'rationalise the chemical manufacture of the entire world'. He had combined serving as a minister in charge of government procurement with winning the government contracts to manufacture most of the high explosives that smashed Flanders into barbed-wire-flecked, corpse-embedded, suppurating mud. All this energy, ambition and conflict of interest seemed embedded in the haunted faces carved above my deep balcony and was entirely out of proportion to anything within the scope of those of us whose plastic combs now rattled in his old desk.

Inviting George Osborne to my house and, catching him alone for a moment in a corner, I suggested that if he gave me £300 million from the Treasury, we could save billions on air pollution annually. My idea, drawn from the air-quality team, was to subsidise low-emission buses, and combine it with higher taxes on polluting vehicles. He laughed. The savings, he said, were hypothetical based on calculations about how much a life was worth. The Treasury would not get any real money back.

'But surely it would at least be popular – good for us politically to clean the air?'

He laughed again.

'Come on George, why are we not leading on the environment?'

'Because,' he said, 'we are the Conservative Party.' He was, I hoped, joking. But there was certainly never any money from the Treasury.

Next, I tried to muster support in an interdepartmental committee on transport. On what looked like a Chippendale chair, in front of a red velvet throne, in a gilded fragment of a royal palace, I suggested that we could fund the transition to cleaner air by fining companies like Volkswagen for breaking the emissions standards. A fellow minister snapped back that there was no scientific basis for my claim that tens of thousands were dying. I offered to set up briefings for him. He declined. The transport minister said a fine was impossible for legal reasons. I checked with our lawyers, who said this was untrue. The Department of Transport now changed their objection to say that it was impossible for 'commercial reasons'.

I hoped the health minister, whose £150 billion budget was bearing much of the burden of lung and heart disease caused by air pollution, might be prepared to 'spend to save'. But, he explained, half-gleefully, every department in government was trying to convince him that their priorities would ultimately save the NHS budget. The savings, he felt, never materialised. And besides there was no spare cash.

Technocratic arguments got me nowhere. Neither did a bald moral appeal to save 52,000 lives. In Number 10, Cameron's new environmental adviser – a thoughtful ex-journalist, early in her term – still seemed hopeful of helping me. But on our second meeting she confessed that no one seemed to want to listen to her either.

Finally, Cameron's senior policy chief asked me in to his office and told me to drop my campaign. A CEO of one of the large automobile companies had called, had said that the entire British car industry depended on making diesel cars, and that my push would cost the country tens of thousands of jobs. The prime minister had decided we would not be pushing for stricter emissions standards than the rest of the EU.

I had more success with plastic bags. The plastic-bag tax had been blocked for seven years, apparently because the *Daily Mail* and a single right-wing adviser in Number 10 thought it 'unconservative'. Liz Truss, perhaps mindful of the Tory right, was reluctant to be too closely associated with the issue. But she was willing for me to pursue it. And it was an obvious measure. A 5p levy on each plastic bag would cost nothing, massively reduce the number of plastic bags, and raise hundreds of millions for charities. I was given permission to take the legislation through Parliament. It went through with no opposition.

The *Daily Mail* made a limp attempt at a headline, 'Plastic Bags Chaos', covering the first day of my new policy. But the number of plastic bags reduced by over a billion in less than a year: an 85 per cent reduction. Streets were cleaner, and beaches, and rivers, and the sea. Nothing I had ever done in government had such impact. I tried to follow up with a tax on takeaway cups. This, however, was immediately slapped down by Liz Truss, who issued a formal statement to the papers, saying that she was overruling my initiative. 'Stop', she warned again, in a furious call on a weekend, 'being interesting.'

Back in Cumbria John Hatt, who had done so much to help me get elected, and had put up with my complaints about five years on the back benches, seemed delighted that I had finally in his words 'got power'. He wanted me to describe how my portfolio fitted together. So I tried for the first time to summarise my daily work.

'I've told you a little about air pollution and plastic bags,' I explained, 'but I am also the water minister, which means having dinners with the heads of the privatised water companies, visiting a super-sewer under the Thames, debating the design of treatment stations, and encouraging a new twenty-five-year strategy for UK water supply.'

'Okay. What else?'

'I am also the minister for rural affairs, under which I have come up with the idea of a Borders development zone – investing in the rural economy on both sides of the English–Scottish border. And I think or hope some money is coming. But it is apparently impossible to find even £150,000 to support my national litter strategy. Another role is I suppose as minister for international conservation.'

'Aha! And what does that mean?'

'It means I have spent much of the last few weeks,' I explained, 'on Cecil.' Cecil was a lion who had been filmed being killed in Zimbabwe by a Minnesotan hunter. Social media had been outraged. 'I have given speeches in Parliament on Cecil, met activists in my office, funded research on Cecil, and spoken at an Oxford conference on Cecil.'

'And what are you doing for Cecil?'

'Well, I am being encouraged to ban the imports of lion trophies into Britain in order to stop more Cecils being killed.'

'Well that seemed pretty obvious.'

'Except the academic research suggests that the income from trophy-hunting incentivises African governments to protect lion reserves, which would otherwise be turned into farms. The bigger issue is that we – the British – are deluded in thinking that Britain banning trophies imports will save wild lions. The UK only imports ten trophies annually and, of these, nine are from lions bred in captivity on South African farms.'

'How do you feel, about the other parts of the job,' John persisted, 'now that you have real power? It's a drug, isn't it, power? I bet you're glad now you didn't give up on being an MP.'

I stood and poked the fire, glanced out of the window and grimaced.

'I don't know,' I said. 'It doesn't feel like what I mean by power. I felt far more powerful running a small NGO in Kabul.'

'But you are changing far more lives now – one stroke of a pen on plastic bags has changed the behaviour of millions.'

'Maybe. But it doesn't feel like that. It feels very distant and theoretical. In Kabul, we delivered the first water supply, the first sanitation, the first electricity for people who had never had these things before. Every week, we seemed to be erecting a new building. It was fast. I was on the ground, shaping, managing. Not signing paper in an office. I was confident that I was changing lives.'

'But that was tiny, Rory. You were only working with a few hundred people. Now you can change the lives of millions.'

'Only by a tiny amount, if at all.'

'Give it time. I think you will come to feel the addiction of power.'

Angry now, I snapped. 'You bloody do it, then, if you think it is so satisfying.' And seeing I had hurt him, immediately regretted it.

At least, I conceded, I did love being the minister for national parks. I lived inside the Lake District National Park – a living landscape filled with farms and hamlets – and loved it. I visited most of the parks in the country and, on long walks beside them, I warmed to the quirky, confident, energetic CEOs. I gave them a budget, and was able to push through the expansion of a park boundary in Cumbria. But generally, these women and men were splendidly independent of ministerial control: choosing to favour small farmers in Yorkshire or battle with them in Cumbria; rewild in the Lakes, or focus on Roman heritage in Northumberland. They had real power over their own small patches, and a confidence and joy in their job which I saw in few civil servants. And they stayed in the roles for decades. I felt I would prefer to be the CEO of a national park than an MP.

Liz Truss called me in again.

'Rory. I have decided to cut the budget of the national parks by 20 per cent.'

'Please don't, Secretary of State. Their budgets are tiny – it will save you no money, and seriously damage them.'

'Okay,' she smiled, '5 per cent then.'

'Please don't. You will just get attacked for the cuts and it won't make us any money.'

'Okay, Rory, for you then,' she said, 'I won't cut them at all.' And pirouetted out of the door.

The best way to try to protect my part of the department from the impulses of the Secretary of State was, I decided, never to allow any decision to reach her desk without passing me first. I persuaded civil servants to tell me whenever she requested a briefing, and insisted on accompanying them into all meetings with her. This meant, I now often spent much of the day in her office at her meeting table, trying to guide the conversation and answer her challenges. She could be startlingly rude to me in front of civil servants, mocking what she portrayed as my antique prejudices and my lack of ambition, but she also seemed to enjoy my presence and came to treat me as something more like a chief of staff, as opposed to a junior minister.

She commissioned me, for example, to write a twenty-five-year plan for the environment. Now, every time I saw her in the lift she asked 'How is the plan?' and I, awkwardly eager to serve my boss, provided vigorous updates. I held seminars, commissioned studies from civil servants, called in academics. Here was my chance to help the government to be the 'first government to leave nature in a better state than we had found it in'. It took me a month to discover that I was not the only person she had asked to write the plan. She had also given the same commission to the director of Nature – a civil servant – and also, separately to the special advisers in her extended ministerial office. I suggested we combine and present together.

We brought our merged plan to her. She didn't seem pleased to discover we had combined our activities. She preferred competition.

'No,' she said. 'This is not what I want. Have another go.'

After she left, we tried to guess what she had disliked. Perhaps she wanted more graphs and images. We presented again two weeks later.

'This is worse than the last draft,' she said.

'Yes, Secretary of State.'

On the third rejection, I spoke up, 'Secretary of State, can you tell us what exactly you don't like about the plan? Is it, for example, that you would like different areas included, or excluded; or that you don't like the style of the presentation; or the ambitions? Could you give us just one example of something you liked or didn't like?'

'Rory,' she said, flashing the smirk which closed meetings, 'I will know when I see it and I think everyone else here understands perfectly well what I want.' The civil servants nodded energetically. After the meeting, I asked them what they thought she wanted. They apologised.

Every week, she continued to ask for rapid and radical action, on some new part of the portfolio which had caught her eye. In all my previous roles I had felt that it was I who was the entrepreneur in a hurry, taking risks that others thought would not pay off, but Liz Truss made me feel like a cautious bureaucrat. My attempts to urge caution seemed to simply encourage her radicalism. She was, as Shoshana pointed out one evening, out-Rorying Rory. She was in the white water. I was shouting from the bank.

My ninety-three-year-old father was suffering from nosebleeds which would not stop. I travelled up to Scotland and sat with him on his bed. It was a warm bright August day and he talked about the young oaks we had planted together. He had supported my work as the constituency MP, and he had liked my speeches as the Defence chair, pushing to spend 2 per cent on defence, but he was a little doubtful about my DEFRA job. I said I enjoyed it. I added, perhaps a little defensively, that I was proud of modern Britain.

'You really enjoy your job . . . that's very good darling.' His eyes searched mine.

'Yes, and I really admire the people,' I insisted. 'The chief executives who I work with in the national parks, for example – their freedom and energy. I love visiting them.'

'You're really getting into your job. I'm so pleased.' He squeezed my hand. But I sensed he found it difficult to believe.

Those were almost the last words he spoke. I was with him when he died half an hour later.

Back in London, Liz Truss asked me how my weekend had been.

I explained that my father had died. She paused for a moment, nodded and asked when the twenty-five-year environment plan would be ready.

The role, however, that concerned me most was my responsibility for flooding. It had been eight years since the last major flood, in which millions of households had lost power and water, and people had been killed. Determined to be ready for the next one, I persuaded the Ministry of Defence to loan me a Royal Marines brigadier and gave him the task of reviewing our flood-preparedness plans, and inspecting different branches of the emergency services around the country. I also insisted on an early exercise on flood response. I imagined a full-day simulation in a control centre. The Environment Agency instead gave me an afternoon, standing in a lane near Slough, watching three engineers blow up inflatable flood barriers.

When I said I would visit the US to study the lessons from Hurricane Katrina, my private office replied that there was no budget available for travel. I appealed. The permanent secretary insisted that although I was responsible for a £1.8 billion flooding budget, the department could not justify an economy flight. This was apparently an instruction from Liz Truss. So I offered to pay for the flight myself and came back with more ideas on how to improve the crisis centre and use satellite data for planning.

For the first six months in my new job there were no floods, and officials pointed out that since catastrophic floods had happened only five times in a century, the likelihood was that I would not be in office when a major flood occurred. When, however, the Met Office issued a weather warning for Cumbria in November 2015, I ignored the team, who suggested I wait a few days to see what would happen, and headed immediately to Appleby. The rain stopped, the waters remained below the banks. I peered at the tranquil river and returned to London. Then it started to rain again.

A couple of weeks later, when I was with Sasha at a first birthday party in London, the Met Office issued another weather warning. I apologised to my hosts, left Sasha, and raced to Euston station again. As we left the station, I received a call from a senior civil servant saying that I was breaking protocol. Ministers should not arrive too soon at flood events. I might hamper the operational response and the first defenders. It was better to wait two or three days.

I restrained myself from saying that I had been in enough crises abroad to know how to support an operational response. Instead, I said that the public saw me as the minister responsible for flooding and that they would expect me to be on the ground. Communities would be more sympathetic to ministers who had their feet wet, than to ministers who arrived after the water subsided. And I said that Liz Truss had agreed at the start of my tenure that I could get on the ground immediately. The rain closed the train line behind me, and I did not hear from the official again.

Two Environment Agency staff, Keith and Andy, were waiting for me in the Penrith operations centre. They explained that 341 mm of rain had fallen in the first twenty-four hours – the highest rainfall ever recorded in the United Kingdom – 61,000 houses in Lancaster had lost power, and the epicentre of the flooding was my own constituency. They dressed me in an Environment Agency coat and a hi-vis jacket and suggested I jump in the car with them.

The next three days were a water-odyssey. We crept through the deep water into Pooley Bridge shortly after sunrise to find that the bridge had been completely swept away. Stunned residents stood on the higher ground, as men in hi-vis jackets clustered around the severed stumps of the bridge. The rain was still falling. At Appleby, we looked across the boiling water, but were unable to talk to the people who were marooned on the far bank, and could not get across the fragile medieval crossing. Arriving at the peaceful village of St Michael's in Lancashire, we saw helicopters lifting people who had been cut off for two nights. On the main road into Carlisle before first light, rescue boats were floating slowly down the streets.

We waded into front rooms filled with water above the level of the mantelshelves, a swirling mess of photo albums and furniture. We watched rescue boats lifting families from top-storey windows, we saw the bloated corpses of sheep strewn across field edges, and other agricultural holdings wrecked with a thick layer of gravel. We tried to comfort business owners, who were staring in horror at the destruction of their stockrooms and getting no response from the insurance agencies. My notebook began to fill with names and emails and requests from residents.

In each place, Keith focused on his Environment Agency teams, checking their updates, fixing requests for equipment, or simply putting an arm around an engineer's cold shoulders on a flood defence. Andy sat with communities, listening to their accounts of the exploding catastrophe, and enduring the anger of people who had been flooded five years earlier and who had now been flooded again.

I saw my role as taking some of the pressure of dealing with the teams of journalists who had been sent to ask why we had allowed the flooding to happen, and who would take the blame. I spent hours on the edge of floodwater, in my hi-vis jacket and boots, a coffee cup from a burger van in one hand and a mobile telephone in the other, explaining what was happening to television stations. Generally, I seemed to be able to handle the interviews because I knew more of the details than the journalists. And I felt I was useful in convincing ministerial colleagues in London to send more support north.

But I also screwed up. On the first morning, I told the BBC that we had spent £1.8 billion on flood defences in the last five years but had never seen such rainfall. 'Rivers here, which haven't flooded in this way for seventy-five years, are fifteen feet up. The flood defences are working,' I concluded, 'the problem is that the water came over the top.' This clip ran happily on *Have I Got News For You* as the week's finest example of political idiocy.

Each morning over the next week, I continued to follow the Environment Agency teams on their rounds, visiting as many villages as I could, and dealing on my phone with the hundreds of requests for sandbags, evacuation and compensation, which were coming into the constituency office. We called on the Cumbrian police ops room to learn how they were deploying officers, and protecting them. (One of their officers had been swept to his death trying to help in the previous flood.) We sat with tough, witty, competent mountain rescue teams as they rested in their drysuits between long cold hours in inflatable rafts. And I sat with Andy in the flood control centre in Penrith, as he monitored the warnings coming in from sensors on a dozen rivers.

In the afternoons, I dialled into the Civil Contingencies Committee meetings, which were now chaired by Cabinet ministers in London. Traditionally, flooding ministers were expected to be in London for such meetings, but I argued that my voice would carry more weight if I remained near the water. And to my surprise the whips for once gave me a slip. Being in Cumbria allowed me to point out that despite the optimistic presentation on Appleby, neither I nor anyone else had actually managed to reach the community. And that Glenridding was not 'fine' – in fact a wall of rubble was coming down the hillside towards the lake-front – and that this was the second time the village had flooded in four days. I explained that we had only been able to reach Glenridding on foot, where we had found a farmer dragging the debris out of the beck, and a very quiet middle-aged couple sitting with dignity by the roadside looking down at their drawing room in which books and photo albums moved in circles on the flood.

To my delight and astonishment, ministers in London generally responded quickly to our push for immediate cash support for communities. Hotlines were established. The prime minister came up to visit. But some parts of the system remained suspicious of my role. The Lancaster police, for example, refused to allow me into their flood coordination meetings, and were unimpressed with my statement that I was the flooding minister, who the public held responsible for this mess. Or that the prime minister had just appointed me his flood envoy for Cumbria and Lancashire. It required a written authorisation from the police minister to force them to include me on their flood response calls.

The rain hardly stopped over the next fortnight. And almost exactly two weeks after the first flood, the rivers burst their banks again in Appleby, Keswick and Kendal. Glenridding was flooded for the third time. Shoshana and I had been planning a holiday in Costa Rica with her parents: the first real holiday since Sasha had been born. But we agreed that Shoshana and Sasha should go without me. It was four months since my father's death, so I had only my mother to invite down to share a mini Christmas pudding with me in the cottage. She looked well, utterly unphased by the plunging temperature in the kitchen or my barely functioning stove.

By the night of Christmas Day, every river in Lancashire had peaked at its highest level since records began, and the following day, the Yorkshire rivers were flooding. I had spent many of the calls over the previous weeks asking for military help and being rebuffed. But now the departments agreed to deploy soldiers to fill sandbags in the villages on the upper stretches of the Yorkshire rivers. I apologised to my mother and set off across the Pennine ridge towards them.

Arriving in York with the Environment Agency team I discovered that the Foss barrier control room, which had protected the city centre since 1987, was itself flooded, and the pumps were failing. The river Foss was now backing up. If we left the barrier down, 1,800 houses would flood. If we lifted it, 600 would. We lifted the barrier. Liz Truss came to join us. I found myself, to my surprise, happy to have her. She asked tough questions, was willing to wade into the water, did not interfere with the decisions from the Environment Agency, and was good at reassuring David Cameron that we knew what we were doing. We arrived together in Tadcaster just after the bridge collapsed, and then continued up the higher rivers of Yorkshire, finding and thanking military, police, fire and rescue, Environment Agency and volunteers in almost every village.

Finally, the rain stopped, and the floodwaters began to fall. I had gained immense admiration for the emergency services, a new understanding of the impact of flooding on communities, and had made some new friendships. But what exactly had it meant to be the flooding minister through this month? The media and the public often addressed me as though I were a general commanding the flood response, but I was not. I had done TV interviews, run community meetings, extracted a bit more money from the centre, challenged some of the more optimistic stories in London, and occasionally put the human in front of what the computer seemed to be saying. I had thanked and commiserated, and bought some time and space for the professionals to do their jobs. Just occasionally, I made part of a decision. But I was generally distanced from the response – more of an observer than a responder. Much of the time, it seemed that a minister in a crisis was less of a chief executive and more of a press spokesman, a coffee-server, a source of money, and a mascot.

It now remained to focus on the clean-up and the plans to prevent future floods. The Environment Agency was careful to sound deferential to their minister but given a choice between my views and computer models, the engineers rightly favoured the mathematical models. And yet, politics never quite vanished. Many of the communities, which had been flooded three times in ten years, had been told, on the basis of the computer modelling, that they were not entitled to extra flood defences because they were still only technically at a 'one in a hundred years' flood risk. The attempts of climate modellers to explain that being flooded three times in ten years meant that you were unlucky, but not that you were at more risk, did not go down well. I managed to secure an extra £40 million for these villages from the Environment Agency budget, and was attacked by Labour and in the *Guardian* for allocating money 'for political reasons'.

I became deeply involved in trying to fix the problems which materialised at every bend in the river Derwent above Keswick. It made sense to lower the water levels in the reservoir at the top of the river. But the private water company, which controlled it, said that they were legally required to keep the water levels high to prevent drought. (Challenging this claim required many calls to lawyers and the chief executive of the water company. They lowered it, but not by much.)

Again, a mile further on, I tried to support the Environment Agency's ambitions for natural flood management by planting oaks, which were better for slowing the flow of water than scrub. But I found that the rewilding movement wanted to use the same land for natural regeneration, which would not produce oaks for decades, and the fields were tied into long-term EU schemes in which even the slightest deviation in land use was punished. No oaks were planted. I found that the bridge which acted as a dam near Keswick was a historic listed monument which could not be touched. It took a long time to persuade the council to pay for the pumps. And although many residents were pleased that we were going to install higher flood walls in Keswick, many of the tourism businesses were enraged because they blocked the view.

Often, communities and journalists assumed there was some scientific way of resolving these dilemmas, if only I 'listened to the science'. But the new computer models – with all their data, based on years of collection, and their ever more sophisticated formulae – struggled to predict extreme situations, when the underground streams switched watersheds, and rivers leapt into new banks dragging down a fresh chaos of rock and gravel. And no computer could tell me how much financial support to provide to Cumbrians who had been flooded three times in ten years, as opposed to communities in Hull, who had not been flooded in decades, but which the data suggested would be flooded soon. Still less how to balance environmental priorities, with heritage protection, droughts and the view in Keswick.

I encouraged the Environment Agency to have more meetings with communities. Andy Brown's team went on to hold more than 400 over the next two years. In the end a flood plan appeared under my name complete with my picture and signature. £40 million extra was spent on a motley mosaic of walls and natural schemes and river improvements that angered many, satisfied few, and convinced none. And the probability data still suggested that the protection would not be tested for another hundred years. For all this I took public responsibility. But I was often only perpetuating the illusion of democratic control over a portfolio which was more art form than science, and whose detail and complexity was far beyond the reach of even the most diligent and attentive minister.

I had greater hopes of direct impact in my role as minister for forestry. The UK had only half the forest cover of most comparable European countries, and our forestry was dominated by Sitka spruce, a tree originally from Alaska, traditionally planted in dark straight-edged blocks across upland Britain, in a way which damaged precious peatland and supported very little in the way of wildlife. The largest forest in England, planted in this way, consisted of 150 million trees.

I had long dreamt of planting 500 million more native trees in Britain: from oaks to hawthorn, spread thinly and evenly across the whole country, creating a more mixed traditional landscape in the lowlands. This seemed far better for biodiversity than planting dense blocks of forestry in the uplands, because the forest edge was much more productive for wildlife than the heart of dense forests, and the lowlands were richer in biodiversity than the uplands. A single oak could host 1,000 separate species. And I felt it would be beautiful.

The plastic-bag tax had been many people's idea, but this was my own, and I tried to work through the details myself. Five hundred million trees would mean twenty-five trees per hectare across the UK. A young oak sapling cost less than 20p, and a single person working steadily, could plant over 1,000 a day, with simple turns of a spade. Even with protective tubing and staking the total cost was about £1 a tree.

Since we were handing out over £3 billion a year in single-farm subsidy payments to farmers, I suggested that the subsidy payments should be conditional on farmers planting five native trees for every hectare of their land, every year, for five years. They could choose any native tree – even birch or field maple or cherry or hazel or willow. They could group them in orchards, or along stream banks, or plant them as standard trees along hedges and fence lines. On an average-sized farm, it would be three days' work for a single person over the five years. And the result would be half a billion extra trees at minimal cost. And we would have created something of staggering beauty and environmental value.

My small team of civil servants who specialised in trees suggested my idea was probably logistically impossible, or even illegal, and certainly unacceptable to the National Farmers Union. But the strongest opposition, to my surprise, came not from the farmers, who seemed reasonably relaxed, but from the environmental NGOs, who told me they would not trust farmers to choose which tree to plant and where. Any national scheme, the NGOs argued, required the closest supervision to ensure only 'the right trees in the right places'. When I tried to argue that such micro-management would make the entire project unaffordable, guaranteeing that the half a billion trees would never be planted, they shrugged and refused to countenance a compromise. I was still trying to establish whether I was simply being naïve and impractical, when all my schemes were derailed by David Cameron's referendum on membership of the European Union.

The referendum campaign had begun while I was up to my knees in floodwater and grimacing over new drafts of the twenty-five-year environment plan. Our department, like all others, had been instructed not to do any planning for Brexit. But almost all the money in our department came in the form of European Union agricultural and environmental subsidies. All the water, air quality and chemical regulations which I had been overseeing were EU regulations; and the financial future of British farming depended on remaining part of the EU customs union. I, therefore, and all the civil servants, were very concerned about what would happen if Britain voted to leave.

Cameron, however, was confident that this would not happen. His approach reminded me of his approach to international affairs. With Brexit, as with Afghanistan, he seemed to think that the way to resolve deep divisions in society was to force people to come to a binary decision. And just as he had felt that he could resolve the Afghanistan–Pakistan tensions by inviting their presidents to have breakfast together at Chequers, he also seemed to believe that watching a football match with Angela Merkel might encourage her to make dramatic concessions over the European Union.

His campaign reminded me of his Scotland campaign. Yet again, there was generous funding, and pollsters and optimistic presentations, and at the heart of it a smooth-looking cross-party group, led in this case by the son of a Labour Cabinet minister. Yet again, Cameron seemed to focus on economic costs, not culture or identity. In this case, however, he allowed his ministers to vote and campaign in any way they wanted. He was certain that Michael Gove, whom he seemed to simultaneously praise for his intellect, and patronise for his earnestness, would back Remain out of personal friendship and loyalty – even though he had fired Gove from his post as Education Secretary. He was also optimistic that Boris Johnson – newly returned to Parliament while concurrently serving as mayor of London – would back Remain.

But Michael Gove and Boris Johnson came out for Brexit. In a joint article for the *Sun*, they promised that after Brexit: 'The NHS will be stronger, class sizes will be smaller, taxes lower . . . wages will be higher, fuel bills will be lower.' It was an astonishing claim for a project that most economists thought was likely to lead to reduced government revenue, falling wages and rising prices, more cuts and tax rises. In a separate article in the *Telegraph* on 26 June 2016, Boris Johnson claimed 'British people will still be able to go and work in the EU, to live, to travel, to study, to buy homes and settle down. There will continue to be free trade and access to the EU single market.'

Liz Truss stayed with Remain and Cameron. 'Michael Gove begged me to come with him,' she said to me. 'But it seems to me a massive distraction. If we vote to leave we will just waste the next six years discussing Brexit when we could be doing much more important things.' But she wasn't given many opportunities to express this view. The ministers and MPs who endorsed Brexit were freed by Cameron to give daily interviews – often with pugnacious and skilful impact. But ministers who backed Remain were controlled by a grid and rarely allowed out in public. Instead, carefully scheduled series of letters by grand figures, from professors to actors, were sent to all the papers solemnly predicting economic catastrophe and telling the British public what to do. My mother claimed that the patronising tone of these letters was convincing her to vote for Brexit.

In the middle of the campaign, I flew to a grand meeting in Rome: a legacy of my life as a Harvard professor, more than a reflection of my position as the most junior minister in the British government. There, I listened to the aristocracy of the European Union – Jean-Claude Trichet, the former head of the European Central Bank, Mario Monti, the former prime minister of Italy, and the newly ennobled Belgian former president of the European Council, Count Herman Van Rompuy – dismissing what they called 'British populism'. I recoiled from the implication that this audience of elder statesmen with beautifully cut manes of white hair somehow knew best. When the chairman of Goldman Sachs challenged me to predict the result, I snapped that the Leave campaign would win 52 per cent to 48 per cent. He kept the paper napkin on which I had written my bet, and later credited me with prescience. But, in truth, I had made the bet to provoke him and the others in the room.

In the streets in Penrith and the Border, however, I was beginning to sense that most of my constituents at least were in favour of what was becoming known as Brexit. If I could have brought myself also to declare for Brexit, I realised I would win quiet nods of approval from elderly colonels, reassure sceptical officers of my association who had not backed my selection, and silence the few ultra-nationalists who called me a traitor. All of them would have enjoyed hearing me mock the European Council meetings on air pollution. In Parliament I might have found common cause with a whole right-wing faction of the party, the very faction that I would need if I were ever to run for the leadership – for absurdly somehow even in this most junior of junior positions, I was already occasionally asking myself if I could be the successor to Cameron's successor.

Rishi Sunak, with whom I shared a table in the House of Commons library, chose to endorse Brexit. There was something bold and surprising in such a move, from a man who always seemed the epitome of caution and sensible ambition: the kind of unexpected move that Machiavellian politicians made to win. He was adored by his northern constituency and by much of the party for doing so. But he asked me a couple of times whether I thought Cameron would forgive him. I said he wouldn't. Rishi seemed anxious, and unsure whether I was teasing him.

I declared for Remain. Why? Partly because I was very aware of how many problems it would cause for farmers in my constituency, many of whom were already on the breadline. I would have added that the environmental problems with which I had been struggling did not stop at borders: we breathed the same air and smoke as Scandinavia; and our fish did not stop at the invisible lines of our territorial waters. Brexit would damage the City of London, on which so much of our economy depended. Departing seemed reckless, inconsiderate and discourteous to a club which we had once fought hard to join. But, presumably like many other voters, I found it difficult to disentangle these formal arguments from instincts, hardly conscious, hardly examined, which made me feel closer to the Remainers than to the Brexiteers.

I didn't get to express or explore any of these things in public. The only public event which the special advisers in Downing Street allowed me to address was on the subject of the importance of the European Union to environmental policy; and it was to a group of students at Sussex University.

II

Plenipotentiary Powers

I was in an Edinburgh hotel room when it became clear, at four-thirty in the morning, that Brexit had won and that British politics had been torn apart, as though by an earthquake. For more than a quarter of a century, the main political parties had operated on tight predictable assumptions. Elections were fought in the centre ground. The change from Major to Blair or Brown to Cameron was far slighter than party members liked to pretend. The limbs of the British state were hedged around with regulations, precedents and checks – the scope of ministers often reduced, like a bound Gulliver, to a wink or a wiggle of a finger.

We had been a member of the European Community from the time of my birth. Contemporary Britain and contemporary Europe had evolved together. Every part of our state – laws, regulations, trade agreements, industries and immigration rules – had been developed to fit. Some parts of our economy hardly made sense on their own. Cumbrian sheep farmers relied on European rules to exclude cheaper foreign lamb. Our car factories relied on parts crossing and recrossing the Channel seven times in the manufacture of a car. Millions of our workers were in Britain as European not British citizens. And the Good Friday Agreement, which had brought peace to Northern Ireland, relied on both the United Kingdom and the Republic of Ireland being members of the European Union with no border between them.

But this close vote tore all these certainties apart. It was a rejection of all the party leaders who had campaigned for Remain – and of everyone else who agreed with them: the BBC, the Civil Service, the diplomats, every leading economist, and the vast majority of Members of Parliament, including myself. It was a revolt of the public. And under instructions from Cameron, not a single department had been allowed to do any contingency planning for what this might mean.

I did not sleep that night, nor, I guessed, did most of my colleagues. When I arrived at the Royal Highland Show the next morning to represent my department, I found that the visit and all media interviews had been cancelled. We got the earliest flight we could back to London. While we were on the plane, Cameron announced his resignation as prime minister. Turning on my phone on landing, I found messages from three different leadership teams. Michael Gove wanted to convince me to support Boris Johnson, who had been back in Parliament for a year. I rang Michael to remind him that he had once told me Boris Johnson was chaotic and unsuitable.

'I have changed my mind, Rory. Boris Johnson would be an excellent prime minister. We need a Brexiteer. And we need you. You are a man of remarkable talent. We are not making use of your talents: it is like leaving the Duke of Wellington in the ballroom during the Battle of Waterloo.'

Boris called me in to meet him in his tiny room. His arms waved suddenly, a smile broke across his face and then seemed to vanish. He gestured to all the seats in the room, apparently inviting me to settle. 'You mustn't believe a word I am about to say,' he confided, 'but I can see you in my Cabinet, flying around Europe, sprinkling a bit of British eau de cologne.' Then he sat back gazing at me – as I tried to balance my amusement and shock at his ability to both promise me and not promise me a job at the same time.

When I returned to the constituency to inspect the new flood repairs at Glenridding, more calls came in. 'As a friend,' said one MP, putting a heavy emphasis on the word 'friend', 'I would advise you to endorse Theresa May as soon as possible.' Two hours later I got a call from another. 'Look, as a friend I would advise you to endorse Theresa May as soon as possible.' There was a noise in the background. I guessed my 'friends' were being watched, performing these scripts for a group of Theresa May's whips. I said I would like to speak to her first. 'Look, as a *friend* I suggest you just endorse her now.'

Back in Parliament, I waited in Theresa May's outer office. Her special adviser pulled off one pair of shoes and pushed another pair beneath her desk, which I guessed from their startling colours, belonged to her boss. Then I was ushered in. The room was as high-ceilinged, expansive and joyously wallpapered as the library of a Victorian duke. The angular figure of the Home Secretary rose to greet me on improbably high heels, and motioned me to a chair.

I remembered only two conversations with Theresa May, although we had been in Parliament together for six years. There was the half an hour when she had asked me to brief her in the tea room on Afghan narcotic strategy (she had been attentive, but I thought unconvinced by my suggestion that there was little that Britain could do to reduce opium production); and the visit to my constituency for a fundraising dinner where I had taken her around the tables of guests. On that occasion, she had seemed very tired. I had suggested that she had done enough, and was rewarded with a sudden, natural and unexpected smile of thanks, which had stayed with me.

Now, enthroned in the splendour of the Home Secretary's rooms, she had some of a monarch's stiff authority. Her first question was whether we should cut international aid. I only understood why she was asking me about international aid much later. I said we shouldn't: that after Brexit we should be focused on demonstrating that we were still committed to the world. She nodded. But when I looked at her again, I wasn't certain that she agreed. I then gave her three minutes on the reforms which I thought were needed in the Foreign Office. Then she saw me out. Unlike Boris Johnson she did not even hint that I might have any role in her government. I had got a sense of someone who – unusually for a politician – retained a private personality: someone who might be capable of being hurt and capable of being serious: who might lapse from quiet to startling revelation.

After the meeting, I sat in the library and wrote Theresa May a long note on the problems in British foreign policy. I proposed moving my family to Brussels and working full-time on the Brexit negotiations, as Ted Heath had done for Macmillan. I thought the Europeans might feel more comfortable negotiating with me than with a Brexiteer. I should have realised that she was more concerned with who the Brexiteers would be comfortable with.

That evening, Gove rang again, pressing me to turn up on the Thursday morning for Boris's launch event. Thursday came. I didn't write the op-ed endorsing Boris, which Boris's team had been pressing me to write, nor did I go to the launch. An hour before the launch event, Gove gave his own press conference, announcing that he now felt Boris was entirely unsuitable to be prime minister and that he would be standing himself. Gove had not warned me of his decision, but he had clearly warned others, for many announced they were abandoning Boris Johnson and joining him. I saw Boris's brother Jo Johnson in Central Lobby. Often, he downplayed the connection to Boris. And he had supported Remain. But this crisis brought out his passionate religion of family. 'Boris is a greater man than any of them,' he said angrily. He made it sound as though Johnson were five times Gove's size. Johnson's campaign collapsed; then Gove's; then Andrea Leadsom's; and Theresa May became prime minister without having to convince the party members. I had not yet committed to any candidate.

The change of prime ministers was so slick and sudden that I barely had time to reflect on what we had lost and what we had gained. Both Cameron and May were modernisers, closer to the One Nation liberal centre where I felt most at home, than they were to the Tory right. But the change in tone was stark. Cameron's breeziness was replaced with May's introverted earnestness. George Osborne was fired, brutally. So was Michael Gove. Other Cameron favourites such as Liz Truss and Matt Hancock lost their departments and were demoted. The Cabinet was redesigned to include a much broader coalition including prominent Brexiteers.

I was a little taken aback by how quickly David Cameron had resigned. I was coming belatedly to see his qualities, and to recognise that he had been the last representative of the old Blairite liberal order in British politics with all the flaws and strengths which that implied. Compared to Boris Johnson, who had almost become prime minister, Cameron had been diligent, truthful, and respectful of Parliament, courts and the opposition, and embraced a pluralist, socially liberal conservatism. He had transformed the diversity of the Conservative parliamentary party – putting eight MPs from ethnic-minority backgrounds on track to be Secretaries of State, when there had been none under the previous government. He had brought through the first legislation for gay marriage. He had doubled the amount that Britain spent on international development assistance. He had been happy to combine with other political parties in his campaign against Scottish independence. He was respectful towards the permanent Civil Service. He did not attempt to stir identity politics or culture wars. He was in rhetoric and substance a pluralist.

At the time, however, I did not regret his departure. Partly, I had not liked the way he approached foreign policy: he hadn't challenged the global financial system before 2008, or questioned Obama's approach to Afghanistan. I felt he had failed to prepare for a military threat from Russia, and mishandled Libya and Syria, and misjudged his charm offensive on China. But perhaps my views were coloured by the fact that he hadn't seemed to warm to me personally or make much use of me in his six years in government. In any case, I was drawn to Theresa May's more introverted, earnest and serious style. And for all her shyness, she seemed more comfortable with me than Cameron had ever been.

Theresa May called me when I was trying to persuade Sasha to eat Lebanese hummus. She sounded on the phone like a game-show host revealing the jackpot prize. 'I would like you Rory to be [pause] Minister [pause] of State [pause] in the Department [pause] of [pause for more excited rising voice] International Development.'

I took a taxi back to DEFRA to say goodbye to my old private office. They had already packed boxes of my books on climate, flooding, urban trees and African conservation. I had fantasised about spending five years as environment minister. I had lasted twelve months. Liz Truss, who had been sent from being number one in DEFRA to number two in the Treasury, was packing down the corridor.

This velocity of ministerial reshuffles might be stimulating for MPs, but it made little sense for good administration. Ministers could only be drawn from a tiny pool of MPs, who knew little about their briefs. It was hardly likely that the best of us would master such vast, complex departments within a year. And yet even under Cameron, who prided himself on limiting reshuffles, the average ministerial tenure had been less than two years.

I reached out to Thérèse Coffey, my successor, to offer a handover. She had a reputation for being smart, understated and reliable. She had a doctorate on 'Structural and reactivity studies of Bis(imido) complexes of molybdenum'. She said she might come back to me later to learn what I had been trying to do for the environment. But she never did.

I found my new department located in another abandoned temple – this time much older than Alfred Mond's shrine to the Imperial Chemical Industries. The Old Admiralty had been purpose-built as the headquarters of the British Navy in 1703. Its courtyard walls were topped with leaping dolphins, the ceilings decorated with plaster anchors, and the internal walls hung with paintings of wooden battle-ships on calmer and choppier seas. In the boardroom across from my office there was a weather gauge, which I was told had been used, though the dates didn't seem to match, by the fleeing James II to check the winds for his escape to France. Entering, I passed the black chairs, padded and enclosed as sedentary coffins, on which captains in knee britches had once sat, hoping to be given a ship.

Humanitarian specialists, in branded polo shirts and cargo pants, crowded around food-security graphs near a bust of Nelson. The room in which Nelson's body had been laid was hosting a gender seminar. Officials opened the same mahogany doors for me which their predecessors in powdered wigs had opened for Admiral Byng. The office was no longer composing despatches for the Ushant blockade, but debating climate and Ebola; not capturing pirates, but providing Somali pirates with alternative livelihoods. The Old Admiralty had been turned into the Department for International Development.

There was something fitting about this context: for the Department for International Development had inherited the Royal Navy's disproportionate weight in Britain's overseas presence. Its annual budget was £13 billion (or $20 billion), more than ten times the core budget of the British Foreign Office and more than the operating budget of the modern navy. In DEFRA I had struggled to find £100,000 for a national litter strategy. There, as in most departments, almost all the money was committed to civil servants' salaries, running costs and payment schemes. But this was not true at the Department for International Development (DfID).

Only a tiny proportion of DfID's budget was committed – billions of pounds remained at the discretion of ministers, free to be spent on almost any project in the developing world. The Treasury could not reduce the budget or assign it to other ministries, because it was protected by law. DfID ministers mingled on easy terms with heads of state. Its mid-level officials dominated discussions at the World Bank. Its very existence was enshrined in an Act of Parliament. It was the largest and most dramatic remaining symbol of Britain's claim to be a global power.

I would be able to travel to extraordinary places, hand out British largesse, avoiding responsibility for the daily domestic crises that defined the life of a flooding minister, and unusually, as the minister for the Middle East and Asia, I had been given responsibility for development in a region I knew. I had set up and run development projects in four of the countries in my new portfolio, and served in embassies in three more. I knew many of the heads of state personally and spoke a little of the languages in six of the countries in which we had projects. More importantly, I was now in direct control of programmes I had been analysing and often criticising for fifteen years. I could see, therefore, why Theresa May had felt she was doing me such a favour with the promotion and why so many colleagues sent me messages of congratulation, often repeating how good it was to 'finally see a round peg in a round hole'.

But I was less certain about this promotion. I had come to admire the engineers in the Environment Agency, and to enjoy my debates with the chief executives of the national parks. I had lost my opportunity to help small family sheep farms and to bring some balance between food, nature and tradition in the British landscape. I had not succeeded in improving air quality in cities, or planting trees. And I was back to a world which I had joined politics to leave.

I had become an MP precisely because I had lost faith in the idea of foreigners trying to reshape other people's countries. I had been looking instead for a role in which I could feel legitimately local, and engage with the competing voices of my hyper-articulate fellow citizens. DEFRA had given me that opportunity. My focus on forestry, national parks, land management and even flooding had fitted neatly with the concerns of my Cumbrian constituents. Now I had been sent to a department distant from their everyday concerns, abstract and technocratic in its culture, absorbed in the contested question of Britain's international influence. But I noticed that I had not turned the promotion down.

My first call was on my new Secretary of State. I found her in the attic box, which her austere predecessor had used as an office. Unusually in a world of frequent reshuffles, there had been only two DfID Secretaries of State in the previous six years. The first, Andrew Mitchell, had majored on 'targets and an internal market in results' before he was tempted to become chief whip. His successor, an accountant, had insisted on approving every business case worth over £5 million, in a department that spent more than 2,500 times that amount annually.

Now Theresa May, as part of her strategy of keeping rival factions within the Conservative Cabinet, had appointed the Brexiteer Priti Patel. This was an even more paradoxical appointment than Cameron's appointment of Liz Truss to the Department of Environment, Food and Rural Affairs, because Priti had called in the past for this department to be abolished and merged with the Department of Trade and had frequently called for its budget to be slashed. She had brought with her a special adviser who had written about the 'unaccountable, bureaucratic and wasteful industry that has grown up around spending taxpayers' money on international aid'. And yet, she had now apparently agreed, as the price of her promotion, to defend the aid budget and the department.

As I came onto the attic floor, Priti saw me through the glass wall and stepped out to embrace me. Her smile was broad: the right side of her face slightly more carefree, even cheeky; the left side, more square-jawed and serious. Sitting down, she brushed her skirt, and clasped her hands. Through the glass walls, beyond a Union Jack flag and a white porcelain statue of the elephant god Ganesh, I could see people moving fast between desks. A red box was being filled. Her private secretary was trying to placate a senior civil servant, while examining an online diary.

'There is,' she began, 'quite frankly . . . shock-ing-ly . . . from my personal point of view . . . not enough about value for money in this de-part-ment.' She enunciated every syllable, in a voice that was half-Hertfordshire, half-Essex. Among the word-flurries, her body remained preternaturally still. 'I think it's fair to say . . . that value for money is non-ne-go-tia-ble. It's o-ver-whel-ming.' I wondered if the phrase 'value for money' was her way of reconciling herself to serving in a department so alien to her instincts and experience. Her smile lapsed, she swallowed. 'We need to roll the pitch.' I suggested that I could help her by reviewing all the country strategies. Her eyes narrowed, and she nodded vigorously 'We need to get stuck in, which I do every single day: dealing with people.'

When I tried to engage her in a particular example, however, of the trade-offs of working in Myanmar and Bangladesh, I lost her attention. 'Look Rory, I want you to roll the pitch. Okay? In the end this is about . . . I think it's fair to say . . . ac-count-a-bi-li-ty.' Then she stood again – she was seven inches shorter than me and I was not tall – hugged me and ushered me back out through the glass doors.

Of the eight civil servants who came to brief me for my next meeting, I knew four. It was a stark reminder of how much I had been reinserted into my former pre-political life. One had been a colleague when we worked together in an embassy, one had been my boss when I was employed to implement a DfID programme in southern Iraq. I had huddled with a third under mortar fire in Nasiriyah in Iraq and danced with a fourth in Kabul.

The woman at the end of the table was the most senior, and I had known her both when we were undergraduates, and when we had served at the same time in Iraq and Afghanistan. She began 'We thought we would brief you, Minister of State, on our current priorities.' Her opening, delivered in a crisp confident voice, half-Balliol and half-Belfast, did not acknowledge our pre-existing friendship but sought instead to establish the proper distance between a director general and a Minister of State. (My new title of Minister of State was a promotion one rank up from my previous position and involved a pay rise and more senior civil servants in my private office, but if it had any greater constitutional significance than being a parliamentary undersecretary then I remained unaware of it.) A large folder was pushed across the desk: beige card, I noticed, rather than the red and gold favoured in DEFRA. 'I will let Rachel begin on her part.'

Rachel began. As I listened, I realised that, even though I knew most of these civil servants, I was looking at a group very different from the development workers who had shared an embassy with me in Jakarta, a generation earlier. Then, British development had been dominated by men who prided themselves on being able to find weevils in rice paddies in Sumatra. Now I was looking at a much more diverse elite who had gone to the best universities, and passed out top of the Civil Service exam. As Rachel continued to talk about logical frameworks, randomised control studies and multilateral trust funds, I sensed the emergence of a new culture which, like Nelson's navy – in whose shrine we were based – was now proud, demanding, singular, deeply imbued and occasionally thin-skinned.

'We are often blamed, Minister of State,' interjected the director general, 'for projects that are not ours, but are in fact implemented by the Foreign Office.' I guessed that she was referring to a small grant for tropical-fish research in the Caribbean, which had generated the tabloid headline 'funding Nemo'. 'We are in fact the most scrutinised part of the UK government.' Another official pushed across a diagram with boxes labelled IDC, IAC, NAO and the phrase 'intense contestability'. I sympathised with their desire to pre-empt any criticism from their new ministers. But I was also irritated. It seemed to be a presentation designed to win over our new sceptical Secretary of State. Friends were addressing me as a potential enemy: not someone whom many of them had known and worked alongside for fifteen years. This made me argumentative.

'I agree,' I began. 'We are probably the best development agency in the world, but we still need to justify ourselves to voters: 70 per cent of voters think we are spending too much on international aid—'

'Ah Minister,' my friend of twenty-five years interjected in her warmest and most reassuring voice, 'but I don't know whether you have seen the research, if you actually ask them how we are spending on aid, they believe we are spending ten times more than we do.'

I had seen the research and I would have preferred her not to assume I hadn't.

'It's not just the public. I was talking to an official from the Foreign Office yesterday. Their cuts mean that they have been reduced since 1995 from twenty-six to two diplomats left in Zambia, while our budgets are soaring'.

The FCO is not eligible for our funding, we are bound by the terms of the International Development Act and the Development Assistance Committee rules—'

'I know all of this,' I said, speaking more sharply, and not liking myself for doing so. 'I think we have to at least acknowledge the context here,' I tried again. 'We have just been given an extra £1.5 billion this year, which is most of the prison budget of England, at a time when prison staff are being laid off.'

'The total amount, Minister, is calculated by the Treasury, based on a 0.7 per cent commitment introduced by the prime minister. And the prime minister is very clear—'

We all knew that our budget was £13 billion because the government had signed up, fifty years late, to a 1969 calculation that, if the developed world gave 1 per cent of its GDP, it would generate 5 per cent growth in the developing world. The 1 per cent was then shaved to 0.7 per cent for political reasons. The global economy had changed utterly since 1969. No economist still believed that you could calculate a fixed sum which, if transferred, would guarantee growth in the developing world. But the formula had stuck. Cameron and Osborne had enshrined this 0.7 per cent in law, more than doubling spending on international aid during the six years of austerity, from £5.7 billion to £13 billion. This was ten times the amount needed to avoid all their cuts to policing – enough in a decade to build every single hospital in the UK from scratch. It was opposed by 70 per cent of the British public and the majority of Conservative MPs. And we were not beginning to win these opponents over.

'Please . . .' I interrupted.

'We have the most transparent spending and procurement processes in government.'

I took a deep breath. I had spent a long time thinking about this problem. I felt that in the attempt to defend international aid we were failing to be honest about the mess, corruption and half-failures that defined even our best programmes in the poorest countries. By insisting so piously and implausibly on our flawlessness we risked losing the trust of the public, and ultimately perhaps our budget and department.

I tried to suggest a compromise. We could defend our work but still concede that we had done some projects which the *Daily Mail* had been right to mock. We could recommit to improving the quality of what we did, with better-informed staff on the ground. 'There is also the problem of the press,' I said. 'I don't want to waste time on the decision to fund the Ethiopian Spice Girls . . .'

'Minister, we have done detailed studies on the cost-effectiveness and impact of that programme, and in terms of women's empowerment . . .'

'It may be a good project but perhaps better suited to a philanthropist than a taxpayer.'

'No one can question the quality of our delivery.'

'Look, I'm on your side but that is not totally true is it?' I said, more tetchily. 'I love DfID but the most serious think tank in Afghanistan has conducted detailed fieldwork studies to demonstrate that the 3,500 teachers that we believed that we had funded in Ghor simply didn't exist.'

'We spend more than £1 billion annually on research into development . . .'

When they left, I walked to the long window, and looked out over the Robert Adam screen onto Whitehall. I was aware that everything I was saying was driving a wedge between me and old acquaintances in that room, alienating people whom I wanted to win over, allying me in their mind with superstition, self-interest, shabby outcomes and populism. I was sounding like a journalist, a voter, or a politician, when, as the first minister who was a former colleague, and who had worked with many of them before entering politics, they would have expected me to be their ally. Or was this part of the problem?

I called the most senior of the officials back in for a further meeting that afternoon. I suggested I could help by reviewing the country strategies for the Middle East and Asia. My friend, whom I had known for twenty-five years, and worked with in Iraq and Afghanistan, interrupted, 'There is no need Rory – sorry, Minister of State. The strategies have been agreed already with the Secretary of State.'

I explained that the Secretary of State wanted me to review the strategies. 'I would also like to speak on a regular schedule to the heads of each country office.'

'May I ask why?'

'I would like to know what they are doing,' I replied.

'Why?'

Now I looked at her in astonishment. 'Because I am responsible for these programmes.'

'So you can do press interviews and answer questions in Parliament?' she persisted.

'I am the minister.' By now there was a tremor in both our voices, as though all the nerves in our chests were tingling.

'I think,' she said, her body rigid, 'you can understand why we might be worried that you could be using this department as your own ego trip.'

I stared at her. She stared back. I did not trust myself to speak. I knew that we had long had different conceptions of development, and of government. And two different forms of pride. But this was more than bluntness. Perhaps I had encouraged her to talk to me like this by presenting myself, not as minister, but as a colleague and friend. I felt my role demanded at least a pretence of politeness. But at the same time I was grateful for her response, for it had revealed more about how a senior civil servant viewed a minister than I might have picked up in a year. It was clear that she felt that all ministers – including me – were a necessary evil: people whom she had to serve, but whom she was not required to respect. And if I viewed myself as the CEO, running my part of the British development, she, and many of her colleagues, preferred to see me simply as a parliamentary spokesman.

Trapped as usual by the whips in Parliament for votes, I could not visit our development programmes for weeks. Instead I had to content myself with video conferences with each of the country offices. When the summer recess came, however, I was able to use the holidays to visit Afghanistan, Nepal, Bangladesh and Myanmar. In each case I was accompanied on the planes by two or three civil servants. A private secretary kept hold of my passport and ticket as though I were, again, an eight-year-old flying home from Malaysia to prep school in Oxford, and when I was seated in my business-class seat, came forward with a hundred pages of briefing notes – itinerary, country briefing papers, diplomatic telegrams, and profiles of every person I was due to meet – trimmed with delicate semi-transparent section markers.

Halfway through the flight my private secretary would leave the seat beside me to be replaced by a more senior civil servant, who would brief me on 'policy'. Landing, we were met at the plane doors by the ambassador, taken immediately through a VIP lounge to the ambassadorial car, with no noticeable passport inspection, and the luggage somehow retrieved without us. 'Minister,' the ambassador would always begin, as he or she sat beside me on the back seat of the Range Rover, 'the schedule is very much up in the air at the moment. They always leave things to the last minute. But we are very much hoping for a meeting with the head of state.'

I stayed in residency guest rooms, bathed in residency baths previously used by the Queen, swam in residency pools and sat at mahogany tables gazing at white menu cards with gold coats of arms, which proclaimed 'dinner in honour of the Minister of State, Rory Stewart'. Very occasionally I was taken with great drama to meet intelligence officers, who met me in locked soundproof rooms and talked mysteriously about next to nothing.

In each place, to the delight of the ambassador, I was eventually invited to meet the head of state. We rode together to the state house in the ambassador's limousine. I was handed bullet points, which I was supposed to recite, without seeming to recite, on prisoners, human rights and requests for British trade. I was asked to tell one president to stop persecuting the opposition and hold fair elections. Another to eliminate corruption. A third to release political prisoners.

At the presidential palace, the carpets were almost always red, the guards in giant generals' caps, attentive, and festooned with braid. The head of state and I would sit kitty-corner, with our national flags behind us, holding a fixed grin for the official photographer, while men with trays waited to deliver the official coffee and Fanta cans. The prime minister of Bangladesh was the aunt of a British MP and wanted to talk about the MP's baby in London.

The embassy was particularly optimistic about British influence in Myanmar. At home, a former ambassador to Myanmar had said to me, 'It is I think the single British foreign policy success of the last twenty years: in twenty years, only Burma.' The diplomats were pleased that the Nobel Peace Prizewinner Aung San Suu Kyi was prepared to meet me, although disappointed that she wanted no officials present. They asked me to convince her to stop the rapes and massacres committed by the Burmese army in Rakhine.

We met in her private sitting room in the capital, Naypyidaw. The Lady sat very straight at the front edge of her chair, hands folded on her tight skirt of embroidered cotton, hair held back with a spray of jasmine flowers, her face serene. Positioned at irregular, and I thought perhaps sacred, intervals around the floor were bowls and figures, in gold-leafed teak, and lacquer. I knew her a little from before politics, so we talked about Oxford and her son, and my son. I praised the progress that was being made with the support of

DfID in tax collection. In deference to my friend John Hatt in Cumbria, I reminded her of the endangered Irrawaddy river dolphins. Finally, I turned to the atrocities in Rakhine. Aware that I must have been the hundredth minister or head of state who had tried to raise Rakhine with her, I began gently. She explained that the Rohingya who had been killed were not 'really Burmese', they were immigrants from Bangladesh.

I pushed on, citing an example of a recent killing. She replied, as softly as though she were speaking from the heart of a meditative trance. The 'atrocity' had been invented: the 'Burmese' passports that the dead Rohingya had been carrying were fake. I had expected her to pay lip service to the rights of the Rohingya, promise to investigate, and produce the hypocritical platitudes that I had heard from Suharto's ministers, twenty years earlier, discussing West Papua or East Timor. But she did not seem prepared even to say the appropriate things. I tried a third time, suggesting perhaps she might visit the Rakhine, to see for herself what was happening.

She ignored my suggestion, and instead placed the blame on British Bengal and migrant labourers. Then gracefully, but with a sense of exhaustion on her narrow face and in her large eyes, she turned the conversation back to Scottish nationalism, on which we agreed, before wishing me well, and taking me politely to the door.

In Kabul, my one-mile journey from the airport to the embassy and presidential quarter was done by helicopter. We then transferred to armoured vehicles to drive slowly under the ashlar gateway of the old royal palace. It was here that two of the Afghan presidents had been killed. I had known the new president – Ashraf Ghani, an ex-professor at the Johns Hopkins School of Advanced International Studies, and senior official at the World Bank – for fifteen years, originally when I had been a diplomat, and he briefly, through the UN, my boss; then when I was running the NGO, as fellow enthusiasts for the heritage of Kabul (his wife accused me of poaching her carpenters), and later still as adversaries in the debate on Western intervention in Afghanistan. I had been on the side of the West having very modest ambitions, he on the side of the West deploying tens of billions of dollars to radically restructure the

Afghan state. Fifteen years had convinced me that his optimism was oppressive, and had convinced him that my pessimism was patronising.

On this occasion, I tried to raise anxieties about the Taliban and corruption, and challenge the work on police and military training. He talked about modalities, Max Weber, accountability, and trust fund management, and offered precise statistical calculations on the anticipated return on a railway linking Central Asia to India, and concluded that almost no one supported the Taliban. Thus with great politeness we continued an argument we had been having for a decade. Some cameras came in, and I handed him a cheque for £400 million of British development assistance. After the event, the Afghan media interspersed his effusive thanks to me with a speech during his election campaign four years earlier, in which, angered by my criticisms of his state-building fantasies, he had called me a 'bach-e-khar', a son of a donkey. This was less polite than it sounded.

As our armoured vehicle pulled away, the ambassador suggested the meeting had been an endorsement for his proposal to put £70 million into training the Afghan police. Here, I was sure in my opposition. I had watched General Caldwell sink almost $12 billion into training the Afghan army and police while I was still living in Kabul. I had studied the reports and visited the embarrassingly poor police training facilities in Helmand. Every piece of evidence suggested our money would be far better spent on health and education than on trying to improve the corrupt, drugged-up, illiterate, vicious and ever-deserting Afghan police. But the ambassador was proud of having ridden shaggy ponies with the mujahideen in the 1990s, and still hoped to fix the failed state.

Our flustered and energetic argument went on for an hour. Suspicious of how the ambassador might try to circumvent my veto, I got in touch with the Development Secretary and the Foreign Secretary. Each confirmed the decision was mine. Two months later, however, the ambassador managed to get the proposal into a meeting of the National Security Council, to which I was not invited, and in which it was signed off. No paper trace of my objection appeared to remain

('Our apologies, Minister, there seems to be a problem accessing files during the reorganisation'). I was infuriated by what I felt was deliberate disobedience from the Civil Service. But again I was glimpsing only a fraction of this absurdity. For the idea of training the police had originally been David Cameron's – part of his confident 'exit strategy'. And three Defence Secretaries, three Foreign Secretaries, and a new prime minister had left this idea untouched like rotting fruit in the bowl of national security policy.

Frustrated by the pantomime engagements with grand policy and heads of state, I tried to compensate by spending as much time as I could with more junior staff in the field. These trips were a relief. Gail Marzetti, our country director in Nepal, for example, took me to visit efficient emergency relief programmes in the earthquake areas, and her team took me to the lowlands, where we sat beneath whirring fans on the floor of an old school, listening to trafficked women, and discussing the improvements that could be made to support them at border crossings. Watching her team rattle on motorbikes along unpaved roads to villages affected by landslides, I became convinced that if Gail had been allowed to spend ten years in the country, and had designed her own programmes without interference from London, she would have achieved twice as much for half the cost.

The department, however, saw my real job as being far from the field, approving business cases in London. Almost every afternoon, my red box in the Old Admiralty was filled with sixty pages on programmes worth tens or even hundreds of millions of pounds annually: making the case for working with UNICEF on refugee education in Lebanon; describing grants to trust funds for global vaccination; cash transfers to Bangladeshi women; or training for political parties in Pakistan. Many of the grants seemed to be given to a plethora of acronyms – TMEA, FSDA and PIDG – established by DfID and headquartered in Nairobi. How was I supposed to decide in my office in London whether the Ethiopian programme should be £100 million or £200 million, or whether to prioritise Nigeria instead? Even with our vast budgets, the scale of need was always twenty times larger than anything we could meet. Choices felt wilful and arbitrary. And vetoing a business case was a demoralising insult to the teams that had spent up to a year preparing it.

The one business case which I was determined to veto was presented to me by three officials, who I suspected had been given the task as part of their career development. The leader, a quiet woman, apparently in her early twenties, began: 'This is largely a formality, Minister. It is about providing support to Syria.'

I flipped through the paperwork. It seemed to propose funding municipal councils in north-west Syria.

'Are these not the enclaves controlled by jihadi factions?' I asked.

'I think, Minister, there are many different groups in these areas.'

'So we are not funding jihadis?'

'No, Minister,' she said with absolute confidence.

'How do we know?'

'We have due diligence and monitoring and evaluation teams in each context, Minister,' she said. It sounded as though she were reciting a catechism.

'Have any of you ever visited these areas of Syria?'

She glanced around the table. 'No, Minister.'

'Do we have any staff currently in Syria?'

'No, Minister, but . . .'

Desperate to stop a repeat of the follies which I had witnessed elsewhere, I tried to give my sense of those areas of Syria. I described the municipal councils that I had seen taken over by jihadi groups in southern Iraq: the windowless buildings, pockmarked with shrapnel, and the exhausted civil servants, cowed by swaggering militias in black clothes, with Kalashnikovs bound tight to their chests.

'I suspect,' I said, 'that we all know that the generator we have just bought for the hospital is the same generator which the doctor stole from the hospital the week before.'

They looked at me in silence.

'I am vetoing this programme.'

'Yes, Minister.'

Except the next day a much more senior group of civil servants came to tell me that it was not actually within my power to veto the programme. They seemed to be explaining that my signature was enough to approve this business case, but not to block it.

'The decision is above our pay grades, Minister.' But none of them could tell me whose decision it was. So, I set off to try to find the Wizard of Oz who was in control. A clue pointed to the British Syrian Embassy in exile in Turkey, and I won, after a battle with the whips, a slip that allowed me to fly to Turkey and meet with them. But although the ambassador admitted that he favoured the decision, he denied that it was he who ultimately controlled it, and pointed me to US Special Forces Command instead. Our liaison officer with US Special Forces was on a secret trip to north-west Syria and it took calls to three generals to persuade him to meet me for a covert cappuccino on his return. He assured me that the decision had nothing to do with Special Operations.

The Foreign Office director, and the MI6 chief – the senior civil servants responsible for Syria – also denied responsibility. They implied that the decision rested with Brett McGurk, the US presidential envoy for Iraq and Syria. I knew Brett from Iraq, eleven years earlier. Officials told me he was at the wrong level for me to meet in London, so I flew to Washington and saw him there instead. Brett said that the US had no idea what was happening in the north-west, and that it was very likely that jihadis were profiting from our money, and implied I was probably wise to close the programme.

Next, I was told that the policy emanated from the 'small group', a meeting of senior civil servants in London. I was not allowed to attend the group, because it was 'officials only', so I procured the attendance list and went to see every member of the small group individually. Then I took my case to the ministers on the National Security Council to whom the small group reported. The relevant ministers seemed a little bewildered to discover that they had made a policy decision about funding jihadi-controlled councils in Syria, and said they were happy to trust my judgement. But still the money kept flowing to the municipal councils. Finally, perhaps three months into my campaign, officials told me that only the PM could stop the funding flow.

I asked my DfID private office to draft a letter explaining my concerns to the prime minister. The draft they produced didn't challenge the policy – presumably because some official had told them not to convey my message. So I rewrote it. They took it to 'lightly edit'. This edit again removed my argument. So I wrote my own letter and booked a meeting with the prime minister's foreign affairs adviser. The foreign affairs adviser had been in DfID. I should have realised how close he was to the senior official in DfID who seemed to be one of the mysterious figures fighting me over this issue.

'A little bee tells me,' he said, 'that there is in fact a different draft of this letter.' He took the tone of a headmaster resolving a playground spat. I said that this letter was my view as the responsible minister, and that I had cleared it with my own Secretary of State. I asked if he would take it to the prime minister. I tried for the next two months to find out whether it had reached her, and got nothing back.

When I complained to ministers in other departments, they were surprised. One of them intoned solemnly 'It is a Rolls-Royce Civil Service. I never had any problems at all with my department.' The implication was that I was not a very good minister. But I wondered – perhaps unfairly – whether all my colleagues were interested in the details of their portfolios in the way that I was interested in funding Afghan policing, or in Syrian jihadi councils, and whether some colleagues particularly in the Foreign Office were more concerned with seeing heads of state than with changing the details of country programmes.

Two months later still, the director responsible for the Middle East came into my office. 'I'm afraid I am here to brief you on a problem, Minister. It appears that one of the individuals whom we fund in north-west Syria has been videoed on a stage at an event organised and sponsored by al-Qaeda. We have prepared press lines but our advice, Minister, would be to terminate the funding to this kind of project in Syria.' There was no acknowledgement of my campaign, but the funding somehow ceased.

12

2017 Election

'You spend too much time in your department,' my friend Nick, a fellow minister, observed from over a newspaper in the tea room. 'I try to spend as little time as possible in the department. We are politicians not administrators.'

He was more right than I liked to acknowledge. I was still obliged as an MP to spend much of my time in Parliament, not only voting, but standing at the despatch box to provide semi-plausible answers on human rights in Cambodia, and to take through the legislation to allocate another £2 billion to the Commonwealth Development Corporation. I had to appear on TV programmes, and I accepted dozens of invitations to speak and stay in colleagues' constituencies: trips on which I subjected small groups of local councillors and their partners, in golf-club dining rooms, to impassioned rants on the future of the Russian–Chinese world order, laced with demographic statistics, insights into semiconductors, and the long decline of humanitarian interventions. I suspected they enjoyed Jacob Rees-Mogg's pantomime evocation of a resplendent Victorian England more.

I continued to delight in my work in Cumbria: seeing staff and volunteers in hospices, visiting villages who were supporting affordable housing, calling on remote farms, trying to help communities cut off by snow or support individuals in advice surgeries. Every weekend in the constituency restored my faith. But I was much less happy in Parliament, which increasingly reminded me of a boarding school, stripped by scarlet fever of most of the responsible adults and all the nicer and kinder pupils.

There were still a handful of MPs whom I admired. But Parliament was too often dominated by aged backbenchers, grumbling about Number 10 and their salaries. And that was before I considered the more troubling minority: the paid-up apologists for Russia; the MPs being investigated for corruption, harassment and rape; and some of my fellow Etonians, who traded off old-fashioned manners, while shedding much of the honour or duty, which once half-justified some of our class. And as always, I was unsettled by how similar I was to all these people: with my own versions of snobbery, obsessions, envy and anxiety about promotions: never missing a seat at Prime Minister's Questions – or the roast beef afterwards – or failing to skip a day of departmental business to please the whips, by setting off with forty colleagues to deliver Conservative leaflets in a target seat.

The lurches from meetings with the UN secretary general and heads of state abroad, to concealing my feelings about colleagues at home, and anxious attempts to impress the prime minister in Parliament, left me feeling seasick. I tried to explain some of this to Nick.

'But then,' Nick drawled, with all the authority of a boy three years older than myself, 'you need to learn to fit in. You are not a senior civil servant. Or a development expert. You are a politician. You have only become a minister, and will only remain a minister, through the three Ps.'

'The what?'

'Parliament, party and politicking.' He returned to his paper.

Theresa May had inherited from David Cameron a twelve-seat majority, and three years to run in office. A year or more remained before a Brexit treaty could be expected. But she felt a larger majority would give her more authority in Brussels and over Parliament, and she had a lead in the opinion polls, which seemed to offer her a 200-seat majority and five years in office. So, in 2017, a year into her government, and my time in DfID, she chose to go double or quits and call an election. The decision seemed at first bold and splendid. When I campaigned for her on Cumbrian doorsteps, I encountered a respect and admiration for her which I had never experienced with David Cameron. Other colleagues reported the same from Norfolk to the Midlands.

During a political campaign, departments went into what was still called, in a bizarre legacy of imperial cultural appropriation, 'purdah' – as though the civil servants were junior wives retreating behind a desert-thinned goat-hair screen. This meant I was not even permitted to step into the DfID office. So I spent six weeks almost entirely in Cumbria. I was more confident of holding my seat in what was my third election, so I focused on leading teams to hold a recently won Cumbrian seat, and tried to help colleagues win two more. This took me far into the old Catholic and Methodist mining towns of west Cumbria that were for the first time, because of Brexit, considering voting for the Conservatives.

As Theresa May's opponent, the members of the Labour Party had selected Jeremy Corbyn, a backbench MP for over thirty years, who had never been even the most junior of ministers. I knew him as a slender figure, with a neat white beard, rarely without a blazing red tie and a jacket which did not match his trousers. He had beautiful large ears. We saw each other in debates on Iraq and Afghanistan: although in his case his opposition to the interventions derived from his general theories on Western imperialism, and his prior commitments to Palestine and Venezuela and Cuba. The Labour front bench often laughed when he spoke, and this made me more sympathetic to him.

In 2015 Corbyn had been put up as the token candidate for the far left of the Labour Party, taking his turn from other colleagues who had gone through this ritual over the years. But to universal astonishment he had been elected by the members, affronting decades of assumptions about how politics worked. He had done none of the things that ambitious MPs were supposed to do to succeed. As my colleagues were quick to point out, he seemed to find it difficult to avoid association with terrorist-sympathisers and anti-Semites. But Labour under Jeremy Corbyn also found a freshness and energy I had not encountered in my first five years in Parliament.

Party membership tripled – making Labour suddenly by far the largest political party in the country. While the 'big beasts' of the Conservative Party could hardly expect to attract 400 people for a political rally, Jeremy Corbyn could mobilise thousands – and his supporters were young, diverse and passionate. Corbyn embraced the idea that the financial crash of 2008 had been the categorical refutation of the capitalist model, and proclaimed the necessity of a different economic system. His supporters viewed his calls for heavy taxes on the wealthy, and for the renationalisation of industry, not as a return to the 1970s but as a vision of a new utopia. The old Tory town of Brampton in my constituency, where there had never been a Labour campaign, suddenly acquired two stands manned by young Labour activists.

Theresa May, by contrast, offered no revolution. She hoped to do more for the marginalised and poor, but not through reinventing the economic model. Nevertheless the statement of her Conservative philosophy in the new manifesto was brave, elegantly put, and intriguing:

> We do not believe in untrammelled free markets. We reject the cult of selfish individualism. We abhor social division, injustice, unfairness and inequality. We see rigid dogma and ideology not just as needless but dangerous. True conservatism means a commitment to country and community; a belief not just in society but in the good that government can do; a respect for the local and national institutions that bind us together . . . We respect the fact that society is a contract between the generations: a partnership between those who are living, those who have lived before us, and those who are yet to be born.

Theresa May's boldest proposal was a property tax to pay for adult social care: addressing not just the scandalous neglect of the poor elderly, but also the central inequality of British life – the decades of rising house prices, which had left the 60 per cent who owned homes far wealthier than those who didn't. This proposal delighted me. The conditions of the elderly poor whom I had seen in my own constituency and who received care visits of fifteen minutes a day, seemed the single most shameful element of British life. Seventy years of different governments had not fixed it. May chose the more transparent and courageous course of trailing the policy in her manifesto. Whatever kind of economic radicalism the country wanted, it was not this. The catastrophe was immediate. Jeremy Corbyn, whose idealism at this juncture gave way to political cunning, branded it 'a death tax'. Older voters, instead of being reassured that their care would henceforth be covered, perceived a raid on the precious wealth embedded in the lottery that was their home.

When May had called the snap election for 8 June, surveys indicated she would win a majority of 144 seats. Within three days of the announcement on social care her lead over Labour had halved from 20 to 9 percentage points, suggesting a forty-seat majority. On election day Theresa May still took one of the largest Conservative vote shares on record. But Jeremy Corbyn also managed to increase the Labour vote to a record. And, although Theresa May secured 2 million more votes than David Cameron, through the odd maths of a first-past-the-post system, she lost his majority.

British politics had shifted in a way that had caught more than the polling companies off balance. Corbyn had shown the possibilities for a form of nostalgic populism, which had no real precedent in British political life, and which would soon suggest new possibilities for the Tory right (although their nostalgia seemed more for the Victorians, while his was for the socialism of the 1970s). A desperately needed reform to social care had proved unable to cross the lowest political hurdle. Theresa May's form of Brexit had not been endorsed. And the hopes for her social reforms and for her premiership itself had been ended. The long shadow of the financial crisis, years of stagnant wages and public mistrust had given space for populism. And the path had been laid for Boris Johnson. But, as I discovered at the very first dinner of the One Nation dining club in the new parliament, my colleagues experienced this moment not so much as a historical shift, or even a moment for reflection, but as the chance to move against Theresa May.

We were still on our elaborate starter when Andrew Mitchell asked permission to speak from the chair. Seven years had now passed since I had first sat next to him at the One Nation. Five since he had been tempted to move from a job he had loved as International Development Secretary to be chief whip. In 2012 a one-minute altercation with a police officer at the Downing Street gates, who said that Andrew had called him 'a pleb', had destroyed his career. His descriptions of what followed were deeply shocking. He had received 1,000 hostile emails in a single weekend. One policeman at least had lied about the encounter. Eighteen journalists had camped outside his house. His ninety-two-year-old mother-in-law was forced to hide in the house while someone shouted through the letter box. He lost more than a stone in three weeks, was spat at outside Tube stations and felt like a hunted animal. He had tried to sue and lost his libel action and £2 million. His physical and mental health suffered. It took him, he calculated, three years to recover. Even in this brutal profession, few MPs had been through so much abuse.

'There is of course,' he now began, 'sympathy and residual loyalty for Theresa May, but there must also be a recognition that we cannot go on like this.' Some people looked at Andrew. Others at their plates. 'Theresa May,' he continued, 'is weak, has lost all authority.' He said 'with a heavy heart' that he had concluded that 'she could not command the confidence of the House or run a government'. She was no longer a One Nation prime minister, he said. 'She should resign immediately.' And then he waited for us to reveal ourselves.

I was proud to support Theresa May. I wanted her to remain as prime minister and far preferred her to the alternative candidates such as Boris Johnson. A minister beside me spoke up calmly and clearly in her defence, disagreeing with Andrew. I nodded. Nicholas Soames growled about loyalty. Theresa May's deputy prime minister said he felt he should be excused from the conversation.

Then another MP from my intake chipped in, 'There is a big, big problem with Theresa May. She cannot fight the next election. I think she has to go sooner rather than later.' It was a polished statement and I wondered whether she had coordinated her statement with Andrew Mitchell. Another Cabinet minister looked very uncomfortable. Although such discussions at the One Nation were supposed to be secret, the entire conversation was immediately leaked to the *Mail on Sunday*.

Not long afterwards, Grant Shapps fell into step with me in the voting lobby. We often met this way because we were both in the short line for those at the end of the alphabet. In the past, he had often asked me why I was ranked at twenty or sixteen to one in the betting odds for next Conservative prime minister, and never seemed satisfied when I joked that it must be my mother betting on me. He seemed to assume that I had some trick. On this occasion he asked me what I thought of the prime minister's performance.

Relieved to have a chance to stand by Theresa May, after the One Nation, I said that I thought she was honourable and the best prime minister we were likely to find.

He nodded warmly, 'And what do you think of Boris Johnson?'

I said I thought Boris Johnson was a chaotic and tricky confidence artist, entirely unfit to be prime minister.

'Don't you think he did a good job as mayor of London?'

'Only by making it a purely ceremonial role.'

'I see,' he replied, and giving his name to the clerk at the voting desk, passed smoothly on behind the Speaker's Chair.

A few days later, a newspaper article appeared revealing that Grant had recruited a tight group of chief agents for Boris Johnson, and was sending them out to cultivate targets, testing their loyalty, probing for weak points. His favourite technique was said to be pretending to support Theresa May. The papers called this, in dramatic tones, a 'false-flag operation'.

PART FOUR

13.

'A Balliol man in Africa'

I had first met Boris Johnson outside the sandbagged shipping container in which I lived in Iraq in 2005, when I was still working as an administrator and he was a backbench MP. He was wearing blue body armour, and he had not looked overweight then: his white-blond hair was short and clean, his cheeks were pink. When he reached me, he held out a hand and, glancing up suddenly from under heavy slanting brows, caught my eye, and revealed, in a grin, a row of small uneven teeth. Not a word had passed, but it was a glance that suggested we were already sharing a joke, perhaps about something he oughtn't to have done, and about which I would be unkind to be angry, the anxious half-grin of a toddler who has been caught splashing bathwater. Then he had sat beside me on a concrete blast wall in the sun, with the giant generators roaring, and his pale hair moving in the sand-dry wind. When I suggested I tell him a little bit about what was going wrong in Iraq, he kept his large head down, staring at the sand.

Until this meeting with Boris Johnson, the only politicians I had got to know had been Indonesian, Montenegrin, Afghan and Iraqi. I didn't then know any British Members of Parliament. Perhaps if I had known how many hours of their lives were spent with people a bit like me, complaining about the slides at the water park in his constituency, or China's actions in Tibet, I would have guessed how boring he must have found the encounter. How irritating it must have been for him, a supporter of the Iraq War, to listen to a diplomat analyse the Islamist protection rackets at the local hospital, forcing him to look at mistakes which he felt were not his fault; and to engage with details which he didn't want to understand.

He continued to hold his big head down, sunk in his shoulders, making an occasional motion of his short, thick neck that might have been a nod, and smiling. And when I had finished, he told a story about his recent meeting with an Iraqi officer, who had boasted of 'working with chemicals' in Saddam's Revolutionary Guard, and glanced up at me, perhaps to check whether I found it as funny as he did.

This was the first time I had met Boris, but I knew that, like me, he had spent part of his childhood abroad and had been sent to Eton and Balliol. People who had taught him, taught me too. And one of them had told me that he admired the Greeks and Romans, liked to talk about Achilles, and had a bust of Pericles in his office. I, too, had been to a prep school, where over a supper of fish paste on white sliced bread, in a brick low-ceilinged strip-lighted 1970s dining hall, we listened admiringly to the story of Regulus, who offered himself to the Carthaginians to be tortured to death. I too had admired Achilles, who wanted to 'die young and far from home, to be the best among the best, now and in perpetuity'. I had once dreamt of modelling myself on a classical hero, a Victorian image of a gentle-man, austere, with a prickly sense of honour: keen to work, perhaps even die, for one's country. And I wondered whether we might not, after all, have something in common. But I knew almost nothing about him.

I didn't know then, for example, that he had recently been shamed for unfairly claiming that drunken Liverpool football fans were responsible for the deadly crush at Hillsborough stadium in 1989; that his mistress had lost their child, that his wife had found out, and thrown him out; and that all of this had played out across the tabloids. And that he had been fired from the shadow Cabinet for lying. He had seemed serene, cheerful and cheeky. Not resilient, so much as indestructible.

I had described the role of the terrorist Abu Musab al-Zarqawi, the founder of ISIS, the interference from Iran, and the mistakes of the British army in Iraq. I had thought I was raising fundamental questions about the policies of a Labour government that he opposed, and about a war that had cost billions and hundreds of

British lives. But Boris didn't ask many questions. David Cameron, later in Kabul, came across like a host at a pheasant shoot, rented only for the day, courteously presiding, without any particular desire to know much about the detail of the soil on which he was standing, or about the professionals whose job it was to drive the game. Boris in Iraq had presented himself as a dishevelled, but engaging, guest.

His conclusions had appeared a week later in a *Spectator* article. In it, he had diluted all the earnest hours which I and American colleagues had spent convincing tribes, Iranian agents and Baathists to support the Parliament, to a single sentence. We had reminded him, he said, of 'exhausted adults inviting their apathetic children to use an Early Learning Centre climbing frame'. No fact, or argument, or authority, shook his sense that Iraq would be okay, and that people like myself who dwelled on the grimmer details were world-weary, and defeated.

I noticed that he had allowed *Spectator* readers to enjoy his fantasies, because he hinted that he might not quite believe them himself. He had described the British military in Iraq as both a charade and a triumph, as though he was watching not a trillion-dollar occupation, but the Life Guards in their polished breastplates, trotting down the Mall. His mock-heroic nostalgia had managed to be both self-satisfied and self-deprecating. Scenes which seemed to demand the prose of the First World War were presented in the tone of the Owl and the Pussy Cat.

Cameron later arrived at his lines on Afghanistan through more attention to polling and focus groups, and a greater commitment to what the campaign managers called 'message discipline'. Johnson laced his patriotic boosterism with moments of clowning, and arrived at his mock-heroic message almost instinctively. But he appeared no more interested in an open dialogue about our problems in these places. Instead, everything seemed curated for the British media, which didn't demand detailed analysis, while he continued apparently to perceive, or at least present, himself as authentic, idly and incuriously real.

Boris had used his article to praise, in particular, the Iraqi military training school which he had just visited. 'If you want to make your heart burst with patriotic pride,' he wrote, 'then I recommend that you go to . . . the "Sandhurst of the desert", and here you will see the beginnings of a new Iraqi army . . . created by the British.' This doomed endeavour, in which British soldiers without a word of Arabic were 'teaching' reluctant Iraqi army recruits without a word of English, brought out Boris's featureless undefined Britishness, to which he gave expression in comic tears. 'It was,' he said, 'a large compound built by – choke, gulp – us, the British, in 1924.' He hadn't seemed particularly troubled later when the divisions of the Iraqi army, officered by men trained in the 'Sandhurst of the desert', were routed by a few hundred ISIS fighters in pick-up trucks, losing a third of Iraq overnight.

Three years after our meeting in Iraq, Boris was elected as mayor of London and promised he would definitely not stand to be an MP again. 'Why would I? Why would I want some beery whip telling me do this, do that? Why would I want to be told by the whips to go and vote at 10 p.m.? Even if I was a Secretary of State why would I want some Cabinet committee telling me what I can or can't do?'

But, perhaps on the same grounds that no one should ever tell him what to do, he had blithely broken this promise and had re-entered Parliament in 2015, just as I was being sent to DEFRA. David Cameron had not made him a minister, although Boris was by now the most famous politician and the only true celebrity in British politics. One of the whips told me confidently that Boris Johnson would never amount to anything. 'I was his whip when he was here last time. His schtick may work on *Have I Got News For You* but it doesn't work in the chamber. My advice to him is to be less Boris-like. But he didn't take my advice. And look where he is now.' A year later he had belatedly embraced the cause of Brexit, delighted the Conservative right and become a decisive factor in winning the referendum.

Theresa May had then decided that she could no longer afford to exclude him from the cabinet, and made him Foreign Secretary immediately after the referendum in 2016, when I was sent to DfID.

When I convinced Theresa May to make me a Foreign Office minister, after the 2017 election, he became my boss.

I found my new boss in an armchair marooned in the vast gold and scarlet office of the Foreign Secretary, overlooking St James's Park. Among the clutter of imperial regalia was a bicycle cap and Tube map from his time as London mayor. His small eyes darted to the door as I entered, but his body did not move. The room that surrounded him was far larger than that of the prime minister. It was the room of Lord Curzon, and Sir Edward Grey, Lord Balfour and Lord Rosebery. His childhood dream of being World King seemed to be getting under way. But as he crouched ponderously in his armchair, glancing towards the door, he seemed to be not so much occupying the office as haunting it, and being haunted by it.

His hair seemed to have become less tidy, and his cheeks redder since I had first met him in Iraq, as though he was turning into an eighteenth-century squire, fond of long nights at the piquet table at White's. This air of roguish solidity, however, was undermined by the furtive cunning of his eyes, which made it seem as though an alien creature had possessed his reassuring body, and was squinting out of the sockets. Sitting with him, alert and upright, was the senior civil servant, the permanent secretary Simon McDonald, who carried himself with the smile of a man who was not sure that he had a boss.

I had suggested that Theresa May make me a minister in the Foreign Office, as well as a DfID minister, so that I could think systematically about combining our different diplomatic, security and development projects. I hoped that this would avoid some of the departmental squabbles I had experienced over Syria and improve our development work too, for politics was almost everything in development, and all that we were doing in Afghanistan or Myanmar would be derailed by a Taliban takeover or a military coup. My proposal was not to merge DfID and the Foreign Office, which had quite different expertise, but to create a joint regional minister, with responsibility for the work in both departments. This meant I would now have two bosses: Priti Patel in development and Boris Johnson in the Foreign Office.

The chief whip Gavin Williamson called me back to say the prime minister agreed.

'But only,' he said in a pantomime snarl, 'if you guarantee to get contracts for my constituents in those countries.' This line fitted his reputation as a whip who liked to be known as the baby-faced assassin. But it seemed slightly half-hearted as a threat or request – as though he felt he needed to demonstrate he was not a pushover, without quite having his heart in the debate. He concluded by saying I should confirm the details of my appointment with the Foreign Secretary, Boris Johnson. I presumed that Theresa May intended me to continue to focus on the Middle East and Asia in both departments.

'Good morning Foreign Secretary,' I said now, taking the sofa opposite him. 'As I think you know I have been the DfID Middle East and Asia minister for the last year, and now the prime minister has asked me to be a minister here in the Foreign Office as well.'

Boris Johnson looked at me. 'How about Africa?'

I laughed. 'Foreign Secretary, I have spent the last twenty years, working on the Middle East and Asia. I speak three Asian languages. I have been the DfID Middle East and Asia minister, I know the programmes and most of the people. I can see in real detail how to bring the departments together. I can hit the ground running. If I am made the Foreign Office Middle East or Asia minister, I can change things for you.'

'Africa,' he boomed. 'A Balliol man in Africa.'

'I know absolutely nothing about Africa.'

'Come on Rory, what is the capital of Uganda?'

'I have no idea.'

'You're just saying that . . .' He paused for me to answer, and then when I didn't respond, 'It's Kampala.'

Later that afternoon, Boris called me again, 'I have spoken to Priti, she suggests you can do Asia and the Middle East for DfID, and Africa for the Foreign Office.' I explained why that ruined the entire point of being a joint minister.

An hour later, he rang again. 'You can do Afghanistan and Pakistan for both departments, instead of Africa. You'll find Afghanistan fascinating.'

'Boris, I have lived in Afghanistan, I have spent most of the last ten years working on Afghanistan, you don't need to tell me . . . Okay I will do Africa . . .'

'You'll love it, Rory: a Balliol man in Africa.'

A few weeks later, at a Conservative Party event I was approached by a close aide of a wealthy Russian, Evgeny Lebedev. She said he would like me to come to stay for the weekend at his castle in Italy. A celebrity was coming who had made her name modelling topless in the *Sun*.

I said, as politely as I could, that this was a joke. 'I've just become a foreign minister. There's no way I can possibly go . . . the man's father was an officer in the KGB.'

'Oh, don't worry about that,' she replied, 'Boris Johnson is coming, and he is Foreign Secretary.'

He went. I did not.

My new ministerial office, my third, was in the grandest of all the abandoned temples of the British Empire. Every day, I walked past the Sicilian marble of the Durbar Court, beneath the statues of viceroys on the Gurkha Staircase, around the fireplace representing Britannia and the riches of the East Indies, to an office whose two cherubs, perched twenty feet in the air, bore the gold letters 'India'. My office had been that of the Secretary of State for India. Mine was the desk from which Lord Salisbury and Lord Randolph Churchill had presumed to rule the Raj, and the foreign policy of another dozen countries from Afghanistan to Ethiopia. A Mughal domed ceiling, plastered in gold leaf, soared above my head. The two curved doors were doubled so that two maharajahs could enter simultaneously with no problem of precedence. The office had remained that of the minister for India and Asia, until Boris had moved me to Africa.

I had not exaggerated when I told Boris that I knew nothing about Africa. My only exposure to the continent had been on short holidays. Yet I had been given control not only of the Foreign Office in Africa, but also of the entire annual £4 billion of DfID spend on the continent, and – so Boris Johnson insisted – 'full plenipotentiary powers' for dealing with forty-five countries scarred by colonialism and Cold War proxy wars, artificial borders, the decline of the UN, the rise of China, climate change, and the poorest and most rapidly growing population on earth.

Two weeks after my appointment, I found myself at the despatch box in Parliament being called on to speak about peacekeeping in Côte d'Ivoire. An MP then asked what I was doing 'to resolve the political impasse in Burundi'. I drawled that 'We call on the Burundian president to respect the Arusha accords and to give proper space to the former Tanzanian prime minister in leading the peace talks', and intoned that 'the only long-term solution is a political solution to a humanitarian crisis'. I also called 'on all parties in Cameroon to refrain from violence, respect the constitution and address the root causes of the dispute'.

What I did not say was that I would be unable to name the former Tanzanian prime minister, or list the six countries with a border with Cameroon, or define the root causes of the disputes. And I feared that some of the MPs asking questions knew little more than I did about Africa. The person asking about Burundi seemed curiously unfocused on the fact that we didn't even have an embassy in Burundi.

I pushed to get to Africa as soon as possible. My first significant trip was to South Sudan, an area the size of Spain and Portugal, containing 200 separate ethnic groups and over sixty languages, which had been consumed by fifty years of civil wars, stoked in different eras by the CIA, Mossad, Ethiopia, the Cubans, Gaddafi, Uganda and others. In 2005, when I was still in Iraq meeting Boris Johnson, the US Congress – inspired by Christians, officials concerned about terrorism, and George Clooney, who was focused on a potential genocide – had voted to give $300 million for South Sudan, and championed a peace agreement between North and South. In 2011, when I was struggling with broadband and the Big Society in

Cumbria, the US had backed a referendum in which 99 per cent of South Sudanese voted successfully for independence.

In the five years before my visit, billions of dollars, thousands of international development advisers and over 10,000 peacekeepers had been deployed to support the world's 'youngest nation'. It was a last echo of Iraq and Afghanistan. Some of my friends moved from Kabul to Juba and danced in rickety hotels with failing generators and duty-free whisky; Lebanese entrepreneurs packed the crowded flights; local stalls sold T-shirts emblazoned with logos of high-school lacrosse teams; and there was optimism based on the roll-out of cell-phone coverage. But the outcome had been in its own way as depressing as Iraq or Afghanistan.

In 2012, when I was immersed in the internal Conservative quarrels about House of Lords reform, the South Sudanese invaded Sudan, and bankrupted themselves in the process. In 2013, the president declared war on the vice president, killing thousands of civilians from the latter's Nuer ethnic group in a single night. About a quarter of the population fled the country and 350,000 people lost their lives between 2012 and my visit in 2017. The US Secretary of State made regular calls to the satellite phones of rival leaders. But the South Sudanese president, Salva Kiir, had told a blatant lie to President Obama in their first meeting and when former President Bush also rang to plead for peace, Salva Kiir had hung up on him, although he continued to wear his gift of a Stetson hat.

My friend Mark Green, the administrator of USAID, had just visited, and told Salva Kiir that, unless he stopped the violence, the US would withdraw all development aid. 'Go ahead,' President Kiir had apparently replied, 'I don't mind, if you want to starve people, it's up to you. It makes no difference to me.'

What was I to do? South Sudan was a particular area of British focus in the UN. It was my responsibility to chair the meetings on South Sudan in the UN General Assembly in New York, with the secretary general sitting solemnly beside me. We were part of a special peace 'troika' with the US and Norway. The UK had, I was told, 'its largest single peacekeeping mission' on the ground in South Sudan. When I arrived, however, I found that the British diplomatic and development presence on the ground consisted of little more than a small guarded plot in Juba and that our peacekeepers amounted to a couple of hundred Royal Engineers trapped within the inner wire of a UN compound. Our soldiers were restricted to the inner base by a cautious London, and were not even allowed to dig ditches for the refugee camp that surrounded their base, let alone do military patrols. When I suggested that the humanitarian adviser should be spending at least 50 per cent of his time in the field, people laughed.

I had read that much of the killing in South Sudan centred on raids for oxen, that much of the wealth of the warlords was collected in the form of oxen, that many of the child-soldiers were recruited to protect oxen, and that among the Nuer, boys continued to be named after the patterns on their ox, composed poems to it, shouted its name as a battle cry, decorated it with tassels and, if they died, expected their ox to be sacrificed at their grave. None of the British staff, however, had much to say about the details of rural Nuer culture.

Neither they, nor indeed any of the 12,000 peacekeepers and policemen who had been posted to South Sudan from sixty nations, had spent a single night in a rural house, or could complete a sentence in Dinka, Nuer, Azande or Bande. And the international development strategy – written jointly between the donor nations – resembled a fading mission statement found in a new space colony, whose occupants had all been killed in an alien attack. In 400 pages I found only one reference to 'clan', but 125 to 'accountable' and 'accountability', and 141 to 'sustainable' and 'sustainability'. 'Gun' appeared twice, 'governance' 180 times. But the words 'Nuer' and 'oxen', didn't appear at all.

On my second day in South Sudan, I travelled north to Malakal, and encountered a city which had been recaptured twelve times by rival militias. On either side of the boulevard, the houses lay in weeds, their roofs stripped, every stick of furniture gone. The single market in a truck park held sacks of sorghum, cassava, groundnuts and plastic toys, but hardly a customer. Six years earlier, the population of Malakal was 150,000 people. Now there were at most 6,000.

The local mayor asked me to rebuild the same government building which the US had funded in 2005, the Japanese had rebuilt in 2013, and the South Sudanese government forces had razed to the ground in 2015.

I returned to a tight, prefabricated DfID office in Juba, its walls plastered with maps marked with areas of conflict and famine, and tried to work out what we might do better. I liked the head of the DfID office – an ex-soldier in crumpled clothes with a tired face and a rueful smile – whose days seemed to be spent trying to keep her staff safe and motivated in the gaps between two-hour UN coordination meetings, and an email inbox full of the latest corporate initiatives from London.

She gave me a far more blunt and realistic account of the problems than anything that I had read in her formal strategy (which was still filled with fantastic references to 'eliminating corruption' and building 'technologically advanced education management systems'). She said that education projects were going better in the southern provinces, with the Catholic Church, and that it was possible to get food aid through, if you accepted some of it being stolen en route by the militia. But when I suggested we get rid of the jargon and write a new strategy focused on these more modest objectives, she laughed.

'Aren't you being a bit naïve, Rory, not about South Sudanese politics, but about British politics? Do you really think we could justify the lives that might be lost, or this money we are spending, if we tell London that all we will be able to achieve is get some food through, a quarter of which is then stolen by the militia?'

In my first few months, I travelled to Ethiopia, Somalia, Uganda, Tanzania, Kenya, Rwanda, the Democratic Republic of the Congo, Nigeria, Botswana, Zambia and Zimbabwe, and in every country I was astonished by the speed and depth of the erosion of the Foreign Office's position in Africa. When I had joined the Foreign Office in 1995, there had been twenty-six UK-based British diplomats in Zambia. By the time I returned to Zambia as Africa minister only two remained: an ambassador and a secretary. Germany had over a hundred personnel in Zambia in their development agency alone.

My lack of knowledge about Africa – as an amateur, unqualified, part-time minister, the product of Britain's insistence on only choosing ministers from the very limited pool of serving Members of Parliament – was supposed to be compensated for by the strengths of the professional Civil Service, but the high commissions had been closed in Commonwealth countries such as Lesotho and Swaziland, and the high commissioner in Botswana was unable to secure a meeting with the once pro-British president, in part because we had cut all aid and almost all our staff.

We now collected very little political intelligence on the continent. Compared to France, we had very few soldiers in Africa. Our forward deployment of troops in Nigeria to help combat the jihadist group Boko Haram amounted to seven people, including three officers, whom the Nigerian major general refused to meet, and when they finally insisted, they told me he handed them a wrench and asked them to fix his car. We pontificated from our position on the Security Council about the crisis in the Central African Republic but we had no diplomats there. Perhaps as a result, many of our descriptions of Africa in London often had the air of fairy stories, and the diplomatic telegrams sent from our embassies increasingly contained platitudinous evasions proclaiming 'wins for global Britain': as though Britain were shifting continents.

I gave my first formal speech to our ambassadors in Africa in one of the flamboyantly decorated conference rooms of the Foreign Office: the rows of smartly dressed ambassadors gazing up at dark red walls, topped with golden pediments, plaster medallions and other ornamentation of empire. I dedicated it to the theme of humility. Abroad, and perhaps at home, I said, we seemed to be papering-over emptiness with abstract jargon and gimcrack strategies: using hysterical optimism to cloak despair. I wondered whether we could not achieve more by recognising our constraints, and our modest – but real – strengths. We might not be able to bring peace to South Sudan, but we could support good clinics in Ethiopia, and better schools in Lebanon, and help save Somali babies from starvation. And in some countries the British high commissioner still had some influence. If we could do less than we pretended, we could do more than we feared.

A hand shot up from an immaculate white cuff, and a handsome diplomat in a beautiful suit asked, 'Minister, are you not aware that we have been asked to write this new style of telegram by the Foreign Secretary? Do you not feel that your entire criticism, of Potemkin villages and charade foreign policies, would be better addressed to Boris Johnson?' Thirty other ambassadors laughed.

Discomfited, I ploughed on. I said it was vital to preserve the tradition of telling uncomfortable truths in diplomatic telegrams: to admit where we didn't have influence, to avoid taking credit for others' actions.

'Well,' said our high commissioner in South Africa, 'I can assure you we have next to no influence in South Africa.' And everyone laughed again.

Meanwhile, far from our marble halls and hardly acknowledged in our breathless telegrams, 400 million Africans continued to live in destitution and despair. Visiting Mathare – a slum in Nairobi with mud lanes, viscous with raw sewage – I met young men who slept on the hard benches of bars after nights working in illegal alcohol stills, and women who tried to keep six children alive with one meal every two days.

In my previous role in the Middle East and Asia, I had found DfID projects which I admired – solar plants in Jordan producing electricity at 2.3 cents per kilowatt hour, cash transfer programmes in Bangladesh which seemed to be transforming the savings and incomes of poor women. But such programmes were often in middle-income countries. In Africa, where the poverty was most entrenched, many of our projects seemed grotesquely ineffective. The water and sanitation programme which was supposed to encourage girls to attend school during their menstrual cycle sounded impressive in the briefing in London. But arriving in rural Zambia, I found four white UN-branded land cruisers and a group of international engineers, who explained that the $40,000 we had allocated for the project had paid for two latrines at a cost of perhaps $1,000, and five red plastic buckets. This, I was told, was an example of 'appropriate technology'. 'No need for maintaining pipes, Minister,' said a UN engineer, who was implementing the project on our behalf, 'the students can fill the buckets at the well.'

'But why didn't we just give a twentieth of this amount to the teacher and ask him to buy all the latrines and buckets?'

'He might have stolen the money.' I restrained myself from suggesting the UN had stolen the money instead.

Again, I had been briefed that our work in Malawi had allowed hundreds of thousands more girls to be educated at a cost of less than $85 per student per year. But I then discovered that after seven years in school, almost 80 per cent of those Malawian girls were unable to read or write. Half the students had no classrooms, there were no textbooks, not even chalk for the blackboards. The average class-size across the country was one teacher to 130 children. And yet DfID continued to boast about the programme because it met a manifesto commitment to 'educate 100 million girls'.

In Ethiopia I found excellent medical records, keen young community health volunteers, and many patients, but in Nigeria, I entered the clinic through an arch that proclaimed it was a gift of the British people and found human excrement on the floor. There was an electric fan, but no electricity within ten miles: no sheets on the beds, no medicines on the shelves, and no patients mad enough to enter the clinic. I was astonished that officials had chosen to drive me so far to see such projects. And I was even more troubled that no one seemed to want to respond to these discrepancies by either proposing we do more in Ethiopia (on the grounds that we would be more successful) or in Nigeria (on the grounds that it needed it more).

Every Monday morning, back in London, I clattered down the tiled corridor to see Boris Johnson. Here, in a room that could have held a hundred, Boris Johnson liked to assemble his Ministers of State and tell us that that we were 'a crack ministerial team'. He referred to the Europe minister, Alan Duncan, whom he didn't like, and who didn't like him, as a 'Mount Rushmore of wisdom'. He compared us to Periclean statesmen, or Titans, or figures in Horatian odes. Once, I made the mistake of trying my own classical reference. But he had little interest in trading classical references. His were designed only to give him, through Horace, a chance to ponder whether journalists were, or were not, more important than politicians. And to sprinkle some eau de cologne on meetings.

Every week, he would turn to small cards on which he had written a list of global problems. It was almost always the same list. 'Right,' he would say, 'I want this to be a year of achievements. These are my priorities – what are my priorities?' He glanced down at the cards. 'We will sort out the relationship between India and Pakistan. Let's sort out the relationship between Saudi and Iran . . .' And then he would look up and bark, 'The pluckiness of global Britain,' before returning to his cards again, 'I'm worried about Saudi Arabia. And North Korea. We must stop them getting a bomb.' The list appeared to be lifted from the first five pages of that week's *Economist*.

Since he never raised Africa, I developed a habit of preparing a short statement for each meeting on Africa, generally emphasising the grotesque gap between the need and British capacity – including my own limited capacity. This was not appealing to him.

He was looking, he said, for 'wins'. 'And Libya,' he suddenly added, 'that's a bite-size problem. A good British-size problem, Rory. We should sort out Libya.'

After the meeting I stayed behind. I explained that Libya was another minister's brief. He had only given me sub-Saharan Africa. And it was worth remembering that we didn't have a resident embassy in Libya. That, if we wanted to do something, we might be better working with the Italians and the UN. But if I expected him to engage or ask a couple of questions about the details, I was to be disappointed.

'Come on Rory,' he replied, 'you can do it. Libya!' There was a dynamic hand gesture. 'Now Rory I hear you have not always been absolutely positive about everything that Britain is achieving around the world. You must be more optimistic. We need fewer doomsters and gloomsters. It's about time we talked ourselves up a bit. Think of morale.'

I said stubbornly that we needed honest reporting too. I heard myself saying piously that 'truthful telegrams are the foundation stone of good diplomatic work'.

'Now Rory,' he continued, shrugging his shoulders to ease them, and putting a less friendly edge into his tone, 'I know something about this, I captained a rugby team. You have to motivate people. Come on, you don't win a rugby match by analysing the strengths of the other side. You tell your side they are the greatest team in the world.'

I muttered something about diplomacy and development not being an eighty-minute rugby match and he waved me out.

14

The People's Political Consultative Conference

The stakes in British international development were high. Politicians including Boris Johnson were becoming more openly contemptuous of the aid budget. Other government departments were trying every ruse to grab our money – even the navy wanted to spend aid money on frigates because the ships 'might be used for humanitarian evacuation from hurricane-hit Caribbean islands'. The *Daily Mail* and the right wing of the Conservative Party were coming for us. There was a growing risk that DfID would be abolished, and the budget hacked, impacting the lives of tens of millions of the poorest people in the world.

I felt our best defence was to improve our development programmes. We could have been buying much cheaper buckets in Zambia, running better clinics in Nigeria and better schools in Malawi. But in order to do so, we needed to transform the way that we worked. There was no shortage of money – I had over £4 billion of discretionary spend a year. But there was a shortage of staff with deep country expertise, compounded by heavily centralised programmes, rigid manifesto commitments, inflexible business cases and a staffing structure which kept all power in London and gave very little scope to people in the field.

The first step I thought was to have far more staff in remote areas, willing to listen to women and men in rural communities, and with the linguistic and cultural knowledge to understand their challenges. I proposed that these teams should be predominantly local, supported by a few internationals who had learnt local languages, and who were incentivised to spend serious time in the most impoverished areas. Trying to make this specific, I suggested that 'in Malawi this might mean people who spoke Chewa, Yao or

Tonga, and who spent significant time in areas from Nsanje to Machinga'.

But my previous jobs had taught me that I was unlikely to make any of this stick unless I could embed my ideas in a formal strategy, endorsed by the people at the very top of government, so I called on the National Security adviser whom I knew well from before entering Parliament. He was a former intelligence officer with the confident smile and handshake of a man who spent a lot of time in the gym. He had, it seemed, some respect for me left over from my time in Afghanistan and he appeared inclined to trust my instincts on what we needed to do on Africa. He paired me with a senior DfID civil servant and told me that together we could write the National Security strategy for Africa.

But it was very difficult to agree even the first principles within the department. Many of my colleagues, particularly in DfID, disagreed with my push for more staff with more local expertise. They believed that the answer was to go in precisely the other direction: fewer staff running larger, more carefully planned strategic programmes from London, based on randomised control tests. They felt there was hardly any point in DfID staff spending time in the field, or learning the local language or studying the culture: 'Come on, Minister, really? Men in safari jackets and long shorts puffing around inspecting rural clinics?'

They were perhaps half-right. My obsession with improving knowledge and quality in our existing projects was blinding me to a simpler and more radical solution. While trying to transform our expertise on the ground, I was ignoring the problems that all outsiders – local or foreign – would face in assessing the particular needs of the extreme poor in remote areas. I should have seen the potential in stepping aside entirely, and simply giving the extreme poor cash to spend as they wished. But I did not think the British public was ready simply to deliver aid through unconditional cash transfers. So I remained stubbornly focused on improving the quality and design of our existing programmes.

★

Meanwhile, my role as a joint Foreign Office and DfID minister brought me to African countries for many meetings with heads of state. The bullet points provided to me by ambassadors before the meetings instructed me to persuade the Ugandan president to bring peace to South Sudan, the Rwandan president to focus on human rights, and the Tanzanian president to change his policy towards international mining companies. Perhaps such approaches had worked better in the 1990s – when the number of democracies in Africa was soaring, when Western intervention had brought peace to Liberia and Sierra Leone, and many leaders seemed happy to remodel their constitutions and economic systems on the West. But I doubted it, and in any case that age had passed.

In 2005, five years before I entered Parliament, the British economy had been larger than the Chinese economy. Just twelve years later, the Chinese economy was already four times larger than the British economy, 100,000 Chinese citizens were in Zimbabwe, and China now provided twice as much investment and finance to Africa as all Western countries combined. And it was not only China. Many countries were flirting with Russian mercenaries. The ports in the horn of Africa were owned by UAE, and their fight with Qatar seemed to be settling, or at least unsettling, the fate of Somalia.

I got the first clear sense of our relative position when I attended President Uhuru Kenyatta's inauguration in Nairobi. As the most senior non-African minister to attend, I was led up to the front row of the stadium, next to the presidential box, and sat straight-backed trying not to wince into the sun as dancers poured out and giant flags were unfurled. Then I was tapped urgently on the shoulder by an official.

'I'm sorry could you please leave this seat and move some rows back? We need it for a VIP.'

I stumbled up and backwards. An elderly Chinese man moved slowly down the front row towards my former seat. This wasn't a member of the Politburo, or the head of the Foreign Ministry, or the chair of the Foreign Affairs Committee (I had known the latter for twenty years).

'Who is he?' I asked the Kenyan official.

'I don't know.'

The Kenyan president worked his way along the front row and shook hands with the Chinese official. He did not reach my new position in the back row. Later, I discovered that I, as the British Minister of State, had been demoted in favour of one of the twenty-four vice chairmen of a largely powerless advisory body called the People's Political Consultative Conference.

Britain still retained some influence in countries such as Kenya, but it was not helped by the startling fecklessness of Boris Johnson. I had issued a letter, for example, also signed by the American government condemning interference in the Kenyan elections. (Gunmen had attacked the deputy chief justice's car just before the court was due to rule on the legality of the election.) Amina Mohamed, the foreign minister of the victorious president, called me in a rage. I took the call with six diplomats crouched around other telephones listening in. She said I was implying that the president had ordered the assassination attempt, and that this false libel was undermining the stability of her country and challenging the sovereignty of an independent state. She said it would be the end of bilateral relations, and she demanded we withdraw the statement, before she expelled our high commissioner.

I held the Foreign Office line, emphasising our desire for good relations with Kenya, while repeating again and again that the attack on the deputy chief justice was unconscionable. The team – which during the call seemed to have expanded to almost twenty people listening to every word – congratulated me. Hanging up, I felt I had achieved some minor success.

Not long after our conversation, however, the foreign minister tweeted that the British Foreign Secretary had sent his warm 'congratulations' on the election. We rushed down the corridor.

'Cripes,' said Boris, 'I am so sorry. She caught me on my mobile as I was going into a meeting. So I thought I should be friendly . . .'

On other occasions, I simply felt ridiculous. My encounter with President Kabila of the Democratic Republic of the Congo, for example, was eagerly anticipated by the Africa directorate. Kabila was a reclusive figure, reluctant to receive senior foreign visitors and rumoured to spend his days playing video games. The country he had ruled for sixteen years was one of the largest, most corrupt and poorest on earth. The time for another election was well past. And nobody expected him to hold one anytime soon.

The police escort led us fast along the potholed highway from Kinshasa, and then turned at a checkpoint onto a road as glittering and smooth as obsidian, flowing up and down the rolling slopes of a primary forest. Few, I was told, had had the privilege of being invited to Kabila's country seat. We passed more checkpoints, a bridge with Chinese workers, an artificial waterfall, and finally emerged in front of a one-storey building.

Concrete light boxes stood in the car park, among balding palm trees. The walls were a peeling coral red. French windows, some broken, led into a dusty dining hall, furnished with some panes of glass in cardboard boxes and a hundred white plastic stacking chairs. It looked like an abandoned motel in South Carolina. I was led to a cracked veranda and seated on a swivelling high-backed black leather office chair on wheels. Facing me was a wicker seat, one leg sinking into an untidy lawn.

Kabila emerged after only twenty minutes. It seemed as though he had been sitting at one of the French windows watching me. The posters in town showed him clean-shaven in an Italian silk tie and tightly tailored blue jacket. But now he was in an open-necked shirt and a safari suit, and he had grown a white beard which made him look like an ageing kung-fu master.

Again, I had my talking points and, despite the implausibility of the whole interaction, I sketched out some potential 'milestones' for an election, including international observers and dates for registration. He replied in a gentle voice that I was not to worry. He would hold the elections. He would respect the constitution. Then he put his head back, laughed, stroked his beard, and said, 'So how about Brexit?' And spent the next half an hour mocking me about Brexit. Which was perhaps why he had consented to the meeting in the first place.

★

It was the fall of Robert Mugabe, however, which defined my time as Africa minister. My predecessors had helped to negotiate the agreement in 1980 which had brought Mugabe into power and ended White Rule in Rhodesia. At first, Mugabe, one of the great icons of the national liberation movements in Africa, had seemed a voice of moderation and compromise. But three years after independence, he had killed 20,000 people in an operation that was known in Shona as Gukurahundi – 'the early rain that washes away the chaff'. Farms had been occupied and expropriated, the economy had collapsed, inflation had reached millions of per cent. Elections had been stolen by force. Zimbabwe, which had once been one of the most prosperous countries in Africa, had become one of the very poorest. And Mugabe had kept ruling into his nineties.

The decline of Zimbabwe was felt so strongly in Britain that I remembered people in 2003 asking why the UK had intervened in Iraq and not in Zimbabwe. No British minister had visited Zimbabwe in fifteen years. But the hope still remained that when the elderly Mugabe went, it would be possible to unlock the true potential of Zimbabwe's resources and well-educated population and make it again one of the most successful countries in Africa. Opposition leaders, business people, and academics insisted in seven separate meetings that Britain could use its leverage to bring democratic and economic reforms.

When Mugabe was toppled in a coup d'état, I learned it in a tweet from the BBC in the early hours of the morning. No one from the Foreign Office had thought to inform me. Guessing, however, that meetings must be already happening, I told my private secretary to find out where, and jumped in a cab to King Charles Street. The winter sun had still not risen when she met me in the courtyard, and swiped me through three security doors. In an underground room off the crisis centre, I found a dozen officials well into a meeting. The Africa director looked up, did a quick double-take, and then without a word gave up his seat at the head of the table, and everyone shuffled to their right.

Our ambassador to Zimbabwe, perhaps not entirely aware that I was even in the room, kept speaking down the video link. She described the military trucks in the streets, and ran through what the evacuation plans would be. She said that it seemed the veteran Zimbabwean power-broker Emmerson Mnangagwa would be taking over, and she implied we should endorse him, and above all not alienate him by describing what had happened as a coup d'état.

All this – although she was too polite quite to say it on the video conference – felt like a coup by her. The ambassador had made an immense effort to get to know Emmerson Mnangagwa. She had been criticised for doing so by White farmers, and human rights activists who associated him with land confiscations and torture. She had been criticised for it by the opposition who felt she was too close to the regime, and she had been criticised by me as well. But if, as seemed likely, Mnangagwa became president, she was the only ambassador who had really built a relationship with him.

Even I knew that this was a bad moment to start a debate about Emmerson 'the crocodile' Mnangagwa. But then in the Foreign Office it never seemed to be the right moment to start a debate. So I asked what conditions we were setting Mnangagwa before supporting him. She paused. Everyone around the table stared at me as though they could not quite work out what I was suggesting.

'For example,' I said, 'it seems important the opposition are given a fair shot at the elections.'

'The opposition cannot win the elections,' interrupted the ambassador.

'Even more reason why Mnangagwa should be willing to give them a fair shot.'

'Morgan Tsvangirai is finished – he cannot win the elections.'

For a moment, I was tempted to start an argument about that too – and try to make the case for the old man, whom I liked – but I let that go. Instead, I repeated that the very weakness of the opposition meant that Mnangagwa had no reason to avoid fair elections.

'We should set clear requirements – a dozen requirements? Does that seem right?' Someone nodded, and then looking at the other immobile faces, stopped nodding. 'I don't know how many. But conditions anyway.'

'What kind of conditions?' asked the ambassador. The meeting seemed increasingly to consist simply of me and her.

'First, letting expatriate Zimbabweans vote . . .'

'Mnangagwa will never allow that . . .'

'Second, clearing up the voter registration. Third, international observers. Look, could someone try to work up a list? And then in return we need carrots and sticks – the carrots I think are using our position at the IMF to authorise an emergency loan to stabilise the economy; we could bring investment, and we could increase development aid. Could someone reach out to our director at the IMF and see whether that is plausible? And perhaps to the US.'

This encounter was reported back to Sir Simon McDonald, the permanent secretary in the Foreign Office. Zimbabwe was not something he spent much time thinking about. But insofar as he did, he did not think it was a priority – certainly not compared to getting the Treasury to invest more in our embassies in Asia and for that matter the Middle East. (He was an Arabist.) He told his friends, who then told me, that I was an idealist, and that he didn't like junior ministers trying to create policy. The ambassador followed up with her own messages to London, formal and informal, arguing that I was undermining the opportunity to reset a more positive relationship between Britain and Zimbabwe through Mnangagwa.

I had convinced Boris Johnson to agree to my flying immediately to Zimbabwe. But the Foreign Secretary's endorsement being apparently insufficient, I grabbed the prime minister herself in the voting lobby to secure permission to board the plane. My first night in Harare began with a dinner. The ambassador had invited a group of Zimbabwean civil society activists who were so positive about Mnangagwa that I ended up, in a coarse breach of diplomatic protocol, betting a pastor $50 that Mnangagwa would not hold fair elections.

After dinner, the ambassador said I risked wrecking the relationship she had built with Mnangagwa. She did not like my emphasising, even in private, that he had been imprisoned for murder as a child, or that he had run Mugabe's secret service. She did not think there was much point in pushing him to reform. I replied that I felt she was prizing our access, more than our influence. She looked, however, at my first draft of election conditions, and accompanied me to present them to the US and EU ambassadors in Harare and then to my meeting with the new president.

I was the first foreign minister from any country to meet Mnangagwa after his inauguration. This great hope of new civilian government strode in surrounded by generals in uniform. He talked to me fondly of his days in a terrorist training camp in Angola and his friendships with some of the great Marxist revolutionaries of the 1970s. He asked me to take his best wishes to Kabila in Congo, whom he said he had known as a boy. I tried to be as clear and specific as I could about improvements to the elections – including allowing expatriate Zimbabweans to vote. And he – thirty years older than me, and a veteran of forty years of liberation politics – simply smiled.

A few weeks later, I was reshuffled out of the Foreign Office, and Mnangagwa was able to secure international financial support without implementing any fundamental economic or democratic reforms. He ran an election on his own terms and won. Zimbabwe collapsed back into inflation, instability and one-party brutality. Our ambassador was promoted. It was difficult to know whether my attempts to push for improvements in the elections had simply been, as Simon McDonald continued to say, 'idealistic and naïve'. Or whether the problem was that the British system hadn't wanted to try.

Such experiences only further convinced me that I needed to focus less on fighting current foreign policy, and more on changing the culture of the Foreign Office and DfID. I felt that building this new and larger cadre of African specialists, with a deeper focus on local politics and context, would not be a threat to anyone today, while it would allow us, in a generation's time, to run better development programmes and make better decisions on African politics. So I swapped my focus from the short term to the very long term and tried to put some of my £4 billion bilateral budget, and my authority derived from writing the National Security Strategy for Africa, behind this plan.

At first, it seemed too easy. I booked a meeting with the Foreign Secretary and turned up with a flip chart in his Commons office. Four very senior civil servants sat around the room, listening while I took him through my new proposals.

'Splendid,' Boris said when I had finished, 'go forth and multiply. You have full plenipotentiary powers.'

I went as carefully as I could through the document again, clarifying, for example, that he was content that I was proposing opening new embassies, and employing another 440 staff, and training them to specialise in African politics and languages.

'Splendid! Go for it, Rory!'

'Do you really support all the strategy?'

'*Cent pour cent . . .*'

'Well,' I said to the permanent secretary outside the room, 'it looks like I have finally done it.'

'Well, Minister—'

'But the Foreign Secretary has given his full endorsement for the project,' I persisted.

'Well, Minister, it would certainly have been unhelpful if he had opposed it, but the fact that he has said that he agrees with it . . .' The civil servant explained that Boris Johnson liked to agree with the last person he had spoken to – even if this contradicted the last instructions he had given – and therefore civil servants could not be expected to act on his apparent endorsement.

I, therefore, focused on the longer path of trying to embed all of these ideas in the National Security Strategy for Africa. I continued to work on the strategy for seven months, partly with Lindy Cameron, the director general, who had been assigned as my pair, and partly with a DfID director, George Turkington, who debated much of the content with me on unpressurised aircraft flying between Virunga and Kasaï in the Democratic Republic of the Congo. Seven months of work with a Civil Service team meant that my ideas were now buried beneath Civil Service jargon (I found our ideas on girls' education, for example, lumped under a 'shift on demographic transition' among four other 'shifts' and three 'enablers').

But the strategy still included a transformation of the British presence in the Sahel, opening new embassies in Niger and Chad, and increased funding, staff and troop presence throughout the region. Across Africa as a whole, I and my DfID co-author proposed almost doubling our existing numbers, and opening five new embassies. This larger Africa cadre would give us the flexibility to provide language training, emphasise political expertise, and provide more thoughtful and flexible integration with other parts of government. And, provided no one cut the legal commitment to spend 0.7 per cent on international aid, these cadres of experts would be reinforced with at least £4 billion of annual spend in Africa. Britain would again have a hope of pursuing a credible Africa strategy, justifying its role in the UN Security Council, and providing some balance, alongside the US, to the growing Chinese domination of African resources and African governments.

I took the ideas individually to all the senior members of the National Security Council in advance of the final meeting, and called on every relevant director general and director. I tried to excite Simon McDonald in the Foreign Office with the potential of free resources, and to reassure DfID that the scheme would still leave them with 99 per cent of their budget untouched. I did not have to fight with Treasury or Number 10 because I was funding it with flexible DfID money. At the beginning of 2018, this Africa strategy was presented to the National Security Council, and to my astonishment, approved.

As a minister I had often struggled to change the smallest programmes. In DEFRA I had not succeeded in securing £150,000 for my litter strategy. But this time we had apparently created a new well-funded organisation in Africa, which would survive our departure. The secret, it seemed, had not been to try to argue about a particular policy, still less try to match my knowledge of a country like Afghanistan against the advice of civil servants. Instead we had concentrated on changing structures. Seven months of writing a document in the correct jargon, pushing it through the proper channels, reassuring the right people, had resulted in a formal National Security strategy which, once approved, assumed an influence that all my previous initiatives had lacked. Over the next few weeks, a dozen separate sub-departments adjusted their plans – budgets were agreed, new departmental objectives were set and monitored, engineers and architects and security advisers flew out to inspect new embassy sites in the Sahel, language teachers were recruited, job descriptions were posted, an African investment conference was launched in London, Theresa May was flown to South Africa, troops were deployed to the Sahel.

Back in my office, I climbed a twenty-foot ladder to stick up, in celebration, the new gilded signs, which I had commissioned in Afghanistan. They said 'Africa' and fitted precisely over the plaques saying 'India', held by the cherubs beneath the globe-domed ceiling. I brushed aside my private office's concerns as to what English Heritage might say about this intervention in a historic room. I was still struggling with the Blu Tack when my private secretary shouted up that Downing Street had called. I was to be reshuffled that afternoon to another department. I clambered down and begged them to leave the Africa signs in place for my successor.

My meeting with Theresa May in the Cabinet Room lasted two minutes. She congratulated me on the Africa strategy and told me that she wanted me to be a Minister of State in the Ministry of Justice – which was responsible for courts and prisons. I accepted, partly out of loyalty to her, and partly because she seemed so tired, and I did not have the heart to argue with her. I was rewarded with a wan smile, perhaps reflecting the fact that many other ministers that day had refused their new appointments. I was left, however, with no idea why she was moving me, or what her ambitions might be for the Ministry of Justice.

Returning to pack my things in my office in the old Admiralty, I found most of my father's Chinese porcelain, which he had collected piece by piece in the 1960s, still on a shelf. It was perhaps very valuable. His set of yellow Kang Hsi imperial bowls were dusty. My father had broken one; I washed them carefully. In drying one, I broke another – it cracked like an egg. I felt the crack for weeks after. I also noticed that, leaving home in the dim morning light, I had put on my blue trousers with my black jacket. So I reached for my only tailor-made suit, which I had kept in the outer office. The trousers had a dozen gaping holes. They had been eaten by moths.

Then I noticed my father's green Chinese vases were missing. They had, it seemed, been stolen over Christmas. Despite all the cameras and security guards. Everyone shrugged. It was probably the cleaners, they thought. A lot of things had apparently been stolen. And no, the department had no insurance. My private secretary brought in a cardboard box to help me pack. In the bottom I saw my Africa signs – he had climbed the twenty-foot ladder to take them down.

PART FIVE

15

Unlearning Helplessness

Every department in which I had served had represented a different era of British government. In DfID the black and white chequered hall, flanked by leather captain's chairs, and the bust of Nelson, had commemorated eighteenth-century Britain, emerging to challenge the French superpower through blue-coated circumnavigators and chart-makers, remembered in pub signs. In the Foreign Office, the granite columns, red from Peterhead and grey from Aberdeen, sustained the gilded ceilings of the victorious Victorian Empire. In DEFRA, I had travelled up in a chrome and nickel lift into the early-twentieth-century palace of an MP and armaments manufacturer, who had done well out of the First World War.

But my new department, the Ministry of Justice, came from the Britain of my childhood, a brutalist tower designed by Basil Spence, whose fourteen floors of dark rough concrete were topped with glittering aerials. The windows were slits, set in sloping concrete shelves, like a stack of pillboxes, designed to prevent incoming fire. The giant letters 'Ministry of Justice' were unnecessary, the Soviet framing was clear enough. A junior official waved from the fringes of a reception, modelled on an airport check-in desk. I was given a pass, queued to go through the glass tubes, and moved on into what had once been a concrete car park, now converted into an atrium, faced by a canteen and coffee bar.

Only the posters on the low wall, depicting staff from different parts of the ministry, suggested it was 2018 not 1978. Each poster had, beneath a photograph and a short life story, a multicoloured hexagon containing the words 'Together we listen, collaborate and contribute, acting together for our common purpose,' and a banner saying, 'Has your team used the Values Climate tool? Visit the intranet to find out more . . .' A crowd was waiting at a bank of lifts. The poster beside the lift depicted the 'Diversity and Inclusion Manager, National Probation Service Midlands', a woman with a warm smile, a polo neck, and giant blue glasses. A speech bubble beside her said, 'I thought returning to work as a transgender woman would be the most frightening experience imaginable. It turned out to be the most life-affirming.' People tapped electronic keys. Letters flashed on a keypad, then appeared above different banks of lifts. A lift arrived. And then another. But apparently the letters were wrong. The lifts departed empty. The crowd swelled.

'These are intelligent lifts,' someone observed. Finally, the official with me, embarrassed by the delay, stepped forward and typed a code into the lift keypad. The letter above the lift vanished, a door opened, and a voice from a loudspeaker announced shrilly to the waiting crowd that 'This lift is no longer available, the minister has taken control.'

The official catching my expression suggested that perhaps we shouldn't do this again.

The lift opened on what her hushed voice described as 'the ninth floor'. I found my new staff seated not in a ministerial outer room but in a corridor. My new office was a cramped low-ceilinged space behind a glass partition, just large enough to contain a desk and a two-seater sofa with a window overlooking the Tube station. An unconvincing pot plant and an empty Ikea bookshelf had been arranged along the glass wall, presumably for privacy.

The texts from colleagues on my phone were less enthusiastic than they had been for my DfID and Foreign Office promotions. Someone suggested the chief whip was trying to destroy me by giving me responsibility for prison riots. But I was not too downhearted. It seemed more plausible to me that in the lurching uncertainty of Theresa May's minority government, with various Secretaries of State refusing to leave, I was only one of many ministerial dominoes tipping in improbable directions.

My new private office team – my fifth in two and a half years – handed me a blue ring binder containing the briefing from the permanent secretary, the senior civil servant in the department. It informed me that over 7,500 staff had decided the new values for the Ministry of Justice. These were to be 'purpose, humanity, openness, together'. I didn't ask whether the last word was an adverb or an adjective. I did ask where the permanent secretary was. I was pointed to a tall, bearded man in a blue cashmere suit, soft shirt and electric tie, now striding down the corridor away from me.

'There will not be any use of a ministerial car in this department,' my senior private secretary explained, 'the permanent secretary will expect you to take public transport. There will not be any newspapers. The permanent secretary will expect you to get your own.'

'Where is his office?'

Beyond the corridor in which my staff were crammed, I was pointed to the permanent secretary's waiting room, his outer room for his secretaries, and then his great corner office, with windows on two sides. Behind a big desk and facing a large seating area was a white wall hung with a portrait, composed of metal, bolted on a blackboard. 'The permanent secretary is something of an authority on contemporary art,' said my new private secretary. 'It might be advisable to congratulate him on some of the pieces from his own collection.' Newspapers were scattered across a low coffee table in the permanent secretary's outer room. I walked out of my office, and picked up a *Guardian* and a *Financial Times*.

The permanent secretary's assistant private secretary said, 'These newspapers are the permanent secretary's, I'm afraid.'

I smiled, said, 'I imagined so,' and carried them back to my own room.

So far, I pointed out, no one had mentioned the substance of the job. 'I think it is up to you, Minister of State, to choose which portfolio you want. Traditionally the Minister of State has focused on courts; but you could,' the official said doubtfully, 'choose to focus on prisons.'

I called the previous Minister of State, Dominic Raab. 'Take courts,' he said. 'There is nothing you can do in prisons, and no good news, because there is no money.' I called the previous prisons minister. 'Who have you upset?' he said, laughing with all the glee of a young MP, still enjoying the political game. 'You have to ask yourself why you were given the job. Basically,' he said with relish, 'it's a . . . grenade. You'd better get ready for' – here he put on a voice of mock officialdom – 'the "episodes of concerted indiscipline": the riots. Almost no prisons minister has ever been promoted,' he reassured me. 'Prisons ministers get fired.'

I found it difficult to be excited by the administration of courts. I told the team I would be prisons minister. Immediately, my private office, which wanted to focus on courts, excused themselves, and moved down the corridor to sit outside another minister's office. In the place of my precisely formal private secretary, I was given a young prison officer: scrawny like me, perhaps thirty, with a light beard, and a flat, northern accent. He had just been dealing with an escaped prisoner.

'It beggars belief, Minister,' he snarled. 'He just climbed the prison wall and none of the prison officers even tried to grab his legs as he pulled himself over.' I sensed I was going to like my new private secretary.

The first ministerial meeting in my new department was held in the Secretary of State's office. My new boss David Gauke, the Lord Chancellor and Secretary of State for Justice, was seated at the centre of the table. Like me, he was only a few hours in the job. I knew him by reputation as a seven-year Treasury minister and trusted lieutenant of George Osborne, who had slowly and unspectacularly climbed the ministerial rungs. His nickname-phrase 'uncork the Gauke' implied that he was a cautious, unshowy batsman perfect for defending a tricky crease. But I noticed as he greeted me that there was an unexpected warmth and richness to his voice, followed by an ironic, cavalier lift to one heavy eyebrow, hinting at a warmth and irreverence unusual in our rickety political world.

Also already present was another junior minister, the local GP for his constituency, an able cricketer, a long-term party member and councillor. He smiled as I came in and motioned to a seat beside him. We had both stood for the Bracknell constituency, where he had defeated me and we had remained close since.

He was the ideal of a square-jawed representative – Dan Dare as Conservative MP. While we waited for the others to arrive, we talked about how other colleagues from our intake had fared in the reshuffles. Fluent Chinese-speakers, decorated colonels, physicians, lawyers and many successful businessmen, qualified it seemed for Cabinet, had been left permanently on the back benches by both Cameron and May. Cameron, he observed, had overlooked him in four reshuffles.

'I wonder,' he joked, 'whether my problem is that I am neither an Old Etonian nor a woman?' And he pointed out that when Theresa May had finally made him a minister, she had sent him, a doctor, to the Ministry of Justice, and sent a lawyer in his place to the Department of Health. 'And this department,' he whispered, in a tone that seemed to magnificently blend the jocular and the bleak, 'is defined by learned helplessness.'

Finally the permanent secretary arrived, flanked by ten civil servants. He began the meeting by leaning forward, as though to share a secret. 'Can I be *honest*?' he asked. 'I am simply going to be *open* about the distance we have yet to travel.' We – the ministers on the other side of the table – nodded. The permanent secretary stroked his tie. Its stripes of burgundy, electric blue and lemon yellow gave him the appearance of a Channel 4 news presenter. 'The department,' he confided, 'is working together to embed our organisational *values* and ensure they underpin our strategic decisions through *collaborative working* and through rock-solid commitments to *make progress against goals.*'

David Gauke listened. When the flood of corporate language briefly subsided, he asked what we were planning to do about the billion-pound hole in our finances. The problem had begun, I gathered, in 2010 – when Cameron and Osborne had decided that the department's budget would be cut by 25 per cent. There had been some valiant attempts to save money. The first Conservative Secretary of State in 2010 had fired a third of all prison officers and privatised the maintenance of prisons. The second Secretary of State had privatised the Probation Service. The third, Michael Gove, had decided to sell off the London prisons, which stood on prime city-centre real estate. Liz Truss, the fourth, had rented out floors in our office building, got rid of more managers, and promised to reduce costs across prisons and courts with new technology.

But none of this had been enough, in part because Cameron had not followed through on his promise to cut the prison population. Each year, the Treasury had demanded more radical cuts to meet the target. A catastrophe was now spreading across the department, which I had only glimpsed through newspaper headlines – courts cut to the bone, cuts to legal aid, which had driven lawyers to strike, a Probation Service losing control of dangerous ex-offenders, and prisons, which were ever more filthy, drug-ridden and violent. And yet all the cuts and damage so far had still been insufficient to meet the department's budgetary target. It had required an emergency bailout every year.

During the same period, the budget in my previous department – DfID – had almost doubled to £13 billion a year. Only the day before I had blithely approved giving £210 million to a World Bank project for education in Ethiopia. Now, I was in a department where we were having to rent out the bottom three floors of our building in the hope of making £7 million extra a year.

'Do you mind if I am reasonably *frank*?' asked the permanent secretary. We didn't. 'It's always been a challenge to live within our budget – *frankly*.' The permanent secretary continued. 'We've been bearing down on costs, and made lots of efficiencies . . . And I'm proud of that. We've played our part in fiscal consolidation . . . So I make no apologies for that . . .'

When David Gauke asked the question about the billion-pound hole in the budget for a second time, the finance director replied. The permanent secretary was an Oxford-educated barrister; the finance director had left school and joined the Civil Service at fifteen. He was as large, however, as the permanent secretary, his smile more radiant, and as he spoke, he brushed back a peak of unruly white hair that seemed to lift with energy.

'We have used some capital,' he said, 'which means longer-term *investment* money.' David Gauke nodded, while I marvelled at his patience. 'We switched that capital,' the finance director confided breathlessly, 'into *shorter-term resource* in order to help us handle the financial situation.'

By this he seemed to mean that both the £2 billion, which Michael Gove had allocated for building six new prisons, and the £1 billion which Liz Truss had won from the Treasury for the digital transformation of courts, had already been blown on current spending. The money for new prisons and technology no longer existed.

Gauke, glancing down at some careful notes he had made in the margins of the accounts, asked about the privatisation of the maintenance contracts.

'Yes well, frankly, Secretary of State, the maintenance contracts leave something to be desired. There is a maintenance backlog. The companies now say they shouldn't have bid to do all the £170 million of work that the government used to do for £42 million . . .'

I would have been tempted at this point to ask how the ministry had convinced themselves this contract was going to work in the first place. But David simply asked, 'What happens when we ask them to honour the contract?'

'Carillion will declare bankruptcy.'

'How long have we got?'

'About five days.'

'And then what?' he continued calmly.

The permanent secretary produced something between a smile and a wince – a non-answer that hinted that we were five days from inheriting responsibility for filthy prisons, no maintenance staff, and a clean-up task which would cost £100 million more a year than we had budgeted. Gauke's left eyebrow rose and fell.

Last to speak was Michael Spurr, the chief executive of the Prison and Probation Service. The other civil servants were large florid men, who had made their names as high-fliers outside the Ministry of Justice; Michael, I had learned, was a thirty-year prison man, short and slender, his grey hair neatly combed, his face red and marked by deep frown lines. He had begun as a prison officer on the landings, and governed some of the tougher jails, before taking the top job seven years earlier. His presentation was as blunt and bleak as the others had been shimmeringly evasive. 'We have prison places for 65,000 prisoners, but we have locked up 85,000. Cells, which the Victorians intended to house one, now hold two.'

The permanent secretary interrupted him with another gleam of bureaucratic optimism, 'Which is why we are working to reduce the prison population, send fewer people to prison, release them earlier—'

'Except,' Michael Spurr interrupted, 'that will not work – 16,000 of the inmates are sex offenders. Three-quarters are in for violent crimes. The public don't want them on the streets. Which is why we needed new prisons. And now the money, which has been promised for new prisons, has been taken away.' There was likely, he predicted, to be a prison officers' strike soon. And, when the strike came, we would only be able to keep the prisons running for twenty-four or forty-eight hours.

Since all this was now my portfolio, I asked the obvious question, 'What happens after forty-eight hours?'

He shrugged.

The permanent secretary took back control. 'Behaviour change doesn't happen overnight. We need to constantly review what is and what isn't working, so that we can keep improving . . .'

'Sorry. What does that mean?' I persisted.

'How are we responding?' The permanent secretary dropped his smile, furrowed his brow, leaned on his crossed arms, and deepened his earnest voice. 'Beyond active listening and empathy, you mean, important though those qualities are? Well,' he raised his hands, 'to do any of it well, we must have a plurality of voices and talents in decision-making and leadership roles.'

David Gauke brought the meeting to an end. I asked to see the chief executive of the Prison Service in my office to begin preparation for the strikes. At the door, my friend the junior minister muttered again 'learned helplessness'.

Number 10 and successive Secretaries of State had imposed the eight years of savage cuts and ill-considered reforms on this ministry. The imprecise and evasive liturgy of the civil servants was an attempt to justify decisions they had not made and which they would not have made – after they had been forced to become complicit – in a horrifying deterioration of their ministry.

I asked to visit my first prison. I was reminded that there was no ministerial car so I took an Uber instead. I knew Brixton in terms of a stall with fresh eggs run by a man from Ethiopia, Nour's Cash & Carry, and the hair-implant store (the proprietor bought the hair on annual trips to Ulan Bator), but I had never spotted the prison. I found the yellow wall behind the Windmill Community Park ('spring and autumn bat walks, Santa in the windmill . . .').

Wikipedia, to which I turned to compensate for the thin departmental briefing folder, told me Brixton prison had been built in 1820, when the area was just emerging from undrained marshes into a patchwork of strawberry gardens. The windmill had long stopped turning; the church had been built and abandoned; the Lambeth Council skyscraper had been demolished: only Brixton prison it seemed had remained, its fundamental function of incarceration unchanged. Ten generations and perhaps half a million people had passed through its cells.

I knew far less about prisons than I had known about the environment, international development or even policy in Africa. Apart from a very brief time teaching drama in Oxford prison as a student, I had barely stepped into a prison. I had not the slightest idea how many prisons were in the country, nor tell a 'Cat A facility' from a 'Cat C trainer', or even understand the import of words such as 'remand', 'recall', and 'licence'. I hadn't spoken to a prisoner or a prison officer in twenty years, and I had never met someone who worked in probation. But thanks to the genius of the British ministerial system, I was now responsible for all the prisons, prisoners, ex-offenders, prison officers, probation officers, and sentencing policy in England and Wales.

At least, it seems the problems I faced were not entirely new. Brixton prison, so a parliamentary archive site accessed through Google informed me, had already been heavily overcrowded in 1829 and facing problems with reoffending, suicide, brutality and overuse of solitary confinement. The solution back then had been to replace the governor and ease the overcrowding. Things had improved and then collapsed again. The cycles of decline, improvement and decline seemed to have got shorter. The 2001 inspection found horror. Things were better in 2004. Terrible again in 2008. Improved in 2014. Worse in 2017. At every crisis, for two centuries, the authorities had reduced the numbers of prisoners, addressed a maintenance backlog, published an action plan, and replaced the governor. This was, it seemed to me, a standard rhythm: as intricate, but perhaps predictable, as the ebb and flow of spots on the surface of the sun.

I stepped out of the Uber and stood looking up at the soot- and mould-stained entrance. A Union Jack fluttered above, a CCTV camera pointed blankly downwards. No one was on the forecourt to greet me. I entered reception, checking that my shoes were at least polished, and my back straight. A microphone behind a thick glass partition told me to hand over my phone and sit on the bench. Five minutes later, one set of gates slid back, another was unlocked, and a secretary led me across a yard to what had been the house of the drunken Victorian sadist, Governor John Green.

The governor was the first I had ever met. He was a bald, strong man in a tight modern suit, with pointy shoes, who told me he had been in the army. 'When I came here it was a disgrace,' he began, as he made me a mug of Nescafé, 'overcrowded, drug-filled, unsafe. Partly because my predecessor was trying to do too much. So I've got back to the basics: I've cut the numbers, and sorted the maintenance.' We were again, he implied, on one of the upward lines in the oscillating waves of Brixton's fortunes.

Across the yard, at the first gate, he pulled the keys from the black leather pouch on his belt: locked, unlocked, locked again, and checked his locking. A second gate led to a steel door, and a corridor whose buttercup-yellow paint all but hid the outline of the bricks. The walls were plastered with posters containing sexual health advice, biblical quotes, and the new phrases, presumably encouraged by the permanent secretary ('together we listen, collaborate and contribute, acting together for our common purpose'). Deeply set in the walls were the cell doors, each painted sky blue. A cast-iron staircase of the same colour led to upper storeys, fronted by cast-iron balconies. Wire nets had been strung between each landing, the governor explained, to prevent the prisoners from throwing themselves off. No prisoners were visible.

The governor led me first down a flight of stairs to what he called the 'segregation unit', and what I had already learned was sometimes called in other prisons the 'care and separation unit'. This was what the Victorians – with more honesty – had called 'solitary punishment'. Two prison officers, in a uniform of white shirts and black trousers, with keys prominently displayed on their belts, stood near the entrance. Voices from unseen men barked and echoed off the steel and tiles: delivering questions, insults and observations at no one in particular. Then the prisoners seemed to sense our presence. A chant began, 'Who's come to see us?', reinforced with a rhythmic banging. Through all this the prison officers stood unmoving. I asked one how long the shouting would last.

'They never stop,' he said.

The man behind the final door on the left was screaming. I asked about him. The governor replied: 'It's very unfortunate. He was convicted for two years. But in fact he has had to remain for twenty because of his attitude to the prison staff.'

The governor didn't suggest we open the doors, or talk to the prisoners. Instead, I was led across another yard, in which had once stood the first treadmill in the world: a giant rotating staircase, on which prisoners walked in silence for ten hours a day 'grinding the air'. The treadmill had been removed. On the other side of the yard, we entered another wing. Here thirty or forty prisoners wandered along the narrow landing towards us. They wore pale-blue T-shirts, with baggy grey tracksuit bottoms. Most had shaved their heads. Some wore Muslim prayer caps. Some were impressively muscular and tall, but many were scrawny and underweight. I glimpsed, in a side room, two prison officers having a cup of tea. They glanced at me but didn't greet me.

One prisoner grinned, revealing a toothless mouth: 'I've seen you on TV.' Two chuckled, 'It's the suits,' I heard mock-cockney cheeriness, ''Ello Guvnor!', 'How ya doin' sir?' Pressing in closer, the prisoners pulled scraps of paper from their pockets, shouted questions about their paroles, and asked for my signature. 'Too many drugs,' one man whispered urgently in my ear, 'seriously these prison officers want their heads examining.' I couldn't guess who these prisoners were: why the fit young black men were in prison; whether the pale, toothless faces belonged to heroin addicts; whether the quiet middle-aged men were sex offenders.

One prisoner tapped me hard on the shoulder, as I turned round, another grabbed hold of my hand. I pulled my hand away. Another prisoner seemed to want to embrace me. I was beginning to feel a little uncomfortable, surrounded by thirty prisoners, without a prison officer nearby. I pushed one prisoner gently back, and then another more firmly, and stepped sideways to climb the staircase to the upper landing. They did not follow me. Instead they stayed below gently repeating, 'Hey Rory – hey man – hey, have a good day,' till I was out of sight.

I was a week into this new job, when the chief inspector of prisons delivered his report on Liverpool prison. Two-thirds of prisoners had told his inspectors that it was 'easy' or 'very easy' to obtain drugs in prison. One prisoner with complex mental health needs had been found 'left for weeks in a dark and damp cell with no furniture other than a bed, broken windows, exposed wires and a filthy blocked lavatory'. There were violent assaults on prisoners and prison officers daily. The chief inspector said his team of experienced ex-officers 'could not recall having seen worse living conditions'. They issued for the first time an 'urgent notification' demanding immediate improvement.

Against the advice of the department, who wanted me to stay in London for ministerial work, I took the train to see what had gone wrong in Liverpool. The expectation seemed to be that I should go alone. In every other department in which I had served, officials had accompanied ministers on visits, partly as a way of getting them alone and influencing decisions. Ambassadors had sat with me in airport transit lounges at four in the morning just to register a request for new staffing. But no one seemed interested in accompanying a prisons minister. No one came from the prison to meet me at the station. I was beginning to sense that no one in the system saw much point in prisons ministers.

The taxi dropped me at a large car park. Behind a blank grey corrugated shed, the size of an aircraft hangar, was what seemed to be an early Norman tower – presumably constructed by a Victorian architect delighted to have a chance to make a medieval castle at public expense. I queued, handed over my phone, and was asked to wait on the visitors' bench. The governor of Liverpool was waiting beyond security. She was five feet tall, had flowing hair, a broad smile, a heavy scarlet brooch, and two large hooped earrings. She had just taken over the prison, she explained, and was trying to clean up what she had inherited.

The first cell she showed me was damp to touch and smell. The lavatory was filthy. Jagged edges of glass stuck out from the window frame, blocked ineffectually with a stained rag that might once have been a T-shirt. In the next cell, the windows and lights were smashed. In the third the bowl of the lavatory was leaking and the emergency call bells for summoning the prison staff had been disconnected. It looked as though the building had been abandoned for twenty years. But, in fact, she explained, this was an improvement on how they had looked a month earlier, during the inspection, when there had still been prisoners in these cells.

'The prisoners broke the windows, because they got too hot, because they wanted to throw things out, or take things in,' the governor explained.

Like Brixton, Liverpool had often been in a bad way, under both Labour and Conservative governments. In 2001, an inspection at the time of the Tony Blair government had uncovered cockroach infestations, and inmates able to shower and change their clothes only once a week. Under Gordon Brown, there had been no improvement in drugs, bullying and violence. A new governor had arrived in 2016: a broad-shouldered man, one of only two governors to be still on active service with the anti-riot squad. A hard man, apparently, for a hard job. But he had not managed either, and had been moved on to a prestigious job in headquarters.

I had read a recent letter from Anthony Paine, a prisoner in Liverpool, to his mother. It had been printed in a newspaper: the letters were formed neatly but without punctuation: 'phone the plod for me tell them you what the video evidence on who was in my cell No Body is doing any Fink to help me plz mum tell the police am not takeing me meds now and I Not eating Food help me.'

Anthony had been sent to Liverpool prison for 'affray and endangering the public' after climbing on a roof. Two weeks before his release date, he had tried to press the call button, which was broken, and then spent the day kicking the door to try to attract attention. Then he had hanged himself.

The new governor, my companion, seemed to be from a different mould to traditional prison governors. She had been a psychologist before she joined the Prison Service. Most of her career had been spent in women's prisons, or resettlement prisons, not in this type of place.

'I sometimes,' she explained as we left the wing and crossed the yard, 'have to be pretty clear and masculine in my communication and leadership.' She smiled up at me, 'And not give too much scope for discussion.' I pointed to the sandwich boxes scattered across the grass, and a pile of rubbish outside a cell.

'The prisoners get most of their meals in their cells in boxes,' she explained. 'When they are done, they throw the trash out of the window.'

'Why can't they put them in a bin?'

'Exactly – or a black bin liner anyway, because we can't have bins for security reasons. We have got 1,000 prisoners here with nothing to do. All we have to do is get them out, picking up the trash. I like to put the more, shall we say, "respected" prisoners on the job. Someone with influence in the jail. Pretty soon, he gets fed up with picking up the trash and he stops people throwing it out of the window.'

She had increased fourfold the prisoner cleaning rota, and was pleased to have been allowed to close over a hundred of the worst cells. We walked down some more landings, talking to prisoners and prison officers, and finished in the staffroom where six prison officers were having a cup of tea.

'This is one of the best prisons in the country. We get on very well with the prisoners, ask them,' suggested a prison officer. I wondered if the prisoners saw the relationship quite as the officers did. She had been on the staff for fifteen years 'I don't know what the inspector is going on about.'

'Cleanliness?' I suggested. 'The garbage and rats?'

'That particular pile was just too big for us to deal with, you'd need a specialist, we're not trained or equipped to move that amount of garbage.'

'But presumably it started smaller, like that pile, on the landing out there . . .'

'We didn't drop that rubbish, did we?' a second woman challenged me. 'Do you think it's us that drops the garbage?'

Another interrupted, 'We have Liverpool gangsters who we have to segregate on wards by gang. You wouldn't want to be running this jail, I tell you . . .'

'Off their head on spice – coming in by drones,' said another prison officer. Drones were an obsession in the Prison Service. I had already received two briefings on how drugs, phones and concealed weapons were being flown into prisons on drones. It seemed to be happening continuously across the prison estate.

'What can we do about drones?' I asked.

'Nothing. There's nothing you can do about drones.' This had seemed to be the view in the ministry as well. Apparently everything from electronic jammers to lasers had been tried and had failed.

'We are decent human beings,' the first woman continued, 'we are friends with each other – we go on holiday together.'

It was tempting to conclude that everyone had just given up. But during our tour of the landings, I had been struck by how resilient many of the prison officers seemed to be in the face of an almost impossible job. I had met a prison officer whose jaw had been broken by a prisoner, and another who had just opened a cell door to see a body swinging from a noose. I had seen one of them run to assistance in a fight. I had also seen them sitting on prisoners' beds, listening to difficult life stories. Even the bravado in the staffroom came from people with deep experience and competence and a pride in their uniformed service.

'They are feeling guilty.' the governor said as she walked me back to the gate. 'It's common in prisons. Without continual efforts there is inevitably desensitisation, a moral hardening. It is a form of learned helplessness.'

16.

Barking at Drones

Anthony Paine's letter before his suicide in Liverpool implied that, like most prisoners in the system, he struggled with literacy. I didn't know about his childhood. But the statistics suggested that 30 per cent of prisoners had been in care as children; 40 per cent had been excluded from school, compared to 2 per cent of the general population; 50 per cent had a reading age of less than eleven. More than half had addiction or mental health problems, or both.

We were locking these vulnerable adults in cramped and filthy cells, in some cases for twenty-three hours a day. Little wonder the suicide rate in most prisons was more than six times that of the general population, or that 127 prisoners had killed themselves under our care in the previous twelve months. Little wonder the violence was beyond imagining, and increasing. Five years earlier there had been 10,000 assaults a year in prisons. That number had now risen to more than 30,000 assaults a year, among 80,000 prisoners. And the new drugs coming in through drones seemed to be making all of this worse.

Confronted with prisoners and prisons, I was beginning to feel some of the shock that I felt walking through a slum in Nairobi, intensified with shame at the fact that this was Britain. Despite our complacent boasts of liberal progress, government after government had left prisoners in conditions that seemed more dangerous and squalid than prisoners had experienced in the same jails in Victorian Britain. And I realised that in nearly eight years as an MP, I had hardly thought about prisons.

I was already trying to work out if there were lessons we could take from Brixton and Liverpool and apply them to other prisons. Perhaps we could be using more influential prisoners to pick up the

garbage, and fix the windows, and prevent the prisoners from breaking them again. I asked my private office to organise a meeting of
prison charities and criminologists to gather more ideas. They clustered around the small meeting table which had now replaced the
old desk and pot plant in my cramped ministerial office. One participant praised a governor who allowed his prisoners not to wear
uniform, and to address him by his first name. Everyone seemed to
attribute the terrifying rise in violence to the new psychoactive
drugs that were flooding prisons. And everyone seemed to prefer to
talk about structural reform of the welfare state and criminological
theories on reoffending, rather than about how to control violence
or reduce piles of garbage in prison, or how to restore the pride and
morale of the uniformed staff on the landings. Perhaps such things
were not considered sufficiently academic.

'We should be talking here about child poverty,' began an ex-
governor. 'The government budget should be directed towards
early-years education, not prisons.'

If the violence was driven by drugs, then I had to work out how to
stop the drugs coming in. There were, I reasoned, only two ways of
getting drugs into prison: through the gate or over the wall. Netting
over the yards and proper windows could prevent drugs being
thrown in. Proper searching could stop drugs being carried through
the gates. In the US and Sweden, where there was proper searching,
I had discovered, the drug rates in prisons were far lower.

But when I shared these suggestions with the ministry drugs
team, they were wearily dismissive. 'If you stop drugs coming in
one way, they will come in another,' they said. One said, 'You don't
want to be like your predecessors, fantasising about how to stop
drugs coming in on drones.' My predecessor, it seemed, had suggested flying eagles at the drones. Liz Truss had stood at the despatch
box and said, 'I was at HMP Pentonville last week. They've now got
patrol dogs who are barking which helps to deter drones.' This, I
was told, provoked an MP to shout 'You are barking.'

If this had been Afghanistan, filled with happy talk, I would have
commended the brutal honesty and realism. But this group seemed

absurdly pessimistic about what they could do in a guarded compound in our own country. I suggested installing body-scanners and
searching everyone including prison officers. Again, I was told that
I was not the first minister to make this suggestion. But all my predecessors had been convinced in the end that this was the wrong
way to go.

When I continued to insist on scanners, I was told the Prison
Officers Association would not accept their officers being searched.
But I knew that a 20 kg bag of drugs had just been found under a
bed in prison. This had clearly not been carried in on a drone, it had
been carried in by a prison officer. I suggested we had to search officers, and that it would be impossible for the union to refuse, without
looking corrupt.

In the next meeting, they did not raise the unions again, but they
told me that scanners were impossible because of human rights law.
In the third, the problem was a health risk. Finally it was the expense
of buying them and redesigning the reception areas to accommodate them. But in the end, I managed to establish that scanners
could be compatible with human rights law and health. This was
not surprising. After all, they were used daily in airports.

I was unsure why the civil servants were so determined to oppose
me. Did they believe that the whole system was so porous and corrupt that technology was irrelevant? Did they resent a minister
pushing an option which they had not proposed? Or was resistance
just a habit?

I asked all the MPs who had served as prisons ministers over the
previous ten years to meet me in a windowless room beneath Parliament. To my surprise, all except one came. The first, the son of a
general and an ex-officer of the Hussars, was already lounging in
the chair nearest the door, with his long legs stretched out in front
of him. The second to enter hinged his six-feet-five frame over the
table. Both were public school-educated army officers. They had
little else in common. The hussar was gay and was campaigning to
abolish prayers in the House of Commons. The taller man had
voted against gay marriage, insisting that 'it is directly against what

Jesus said'. The flamboyantly liberal hussar favoured Brexit; the Christian, Remain.

The third was fifteen years younger than them, about a foot shorter, had lived with his mother in Ghana till the age of sixteen, had been a banker at Goldman Sachs and Britain's Young Entrepreneur of the Year. The fourth, the only Labour prisons minister left in Parliament, was the son of a forklift driver, who had worked in the charitable sector for a decade, focused on physical disability and solvent abuse, and had been in Parliament for twenty-five years. Each of them had been prisons minister for two years.

The hussar began: 'Well I was very liberal with prisoners,' he began, stretching his grin, well above the nostrils, like the lips of the Joker. 'I encouraged comedy workshops and fancy dress parties . . . Perhaps you shouldn't follow my lead, because the powers that be didn't like it and I lost my job. And I may not be', he said joking about his own well-publicised use of poppers at parties, 'perhaps the best person to advise you on drugs.'

The Christian spoke next. He had recently backed a campaign to have the sayings of Jesus emblazoned on seventy-five buses around the capital. The quotes included 'Let he who is without sin cast the first stone'. His tone now was secular and sepulchral. 'You have 80,000 prisoners under your care, but almost 200,000 on probation. You must focus on rehabilitation.'

The Entrepreneur of the Year interjected, 'I think you need an honest analytical assessment of what the challenge is, and then an action plan to address it. You've got to be quite technocratic. Innovate.' He spoke about electronic monitoring, organisational redesign, and the management of contracts.

I sensed stances, liberal progressive, Christian and a McKinsey management style. But they seemed oddly unfocused on the conditions within the prisons – the filth and violence, which had risen relentlessly through almost all their tenures. I warmed most to the Labour minister whose only advice was to visit at least one prison a week.

Outside the room, one of the Conservative ministers took me aside. 'The key question for you,' he said, 'is whether the journalists will see you as tough on crime or soft. You have to be tough. There is no option.' Then he brightened up. 'There are great media opportunities around drones. The media loves stories about drones.'

'Fixing windows?'

'No, technology: laser-gun the drones! They love that stuff.'

No one from the Prison Service would have been surprised that I had not got much from ministers. Their advice was consistent, and concise: listen to Michael Spurr. He was the earnest, sombre chief executive of the Prison Service, who had given such a bleak presentation in the first departmental meeting. He alone exercised, it was said, the ultimate control over which governor got which prison, who was promoted, who got resources, where numbers went up and down, which prisons were prioritised. His network of allies extended into every prison and kept him informed of everything. He was admired for his head for figures, and his prison craft, He was a Christian lay preacher. He had 'given his life to prisons'. He was, I heard from nine different people, 'a man of integrity'. Others talked about his 'empathy', his 'lack of spite' and his 'lack of ego'.

Violent assaults in prisons had tripled during his time as chief executive, till there were over twenty-five assaults against prison officers every day, and far more against prisoners, but no one seemed to feel this was his fault. Instead, he was considered to be doing his best with an impossible situation. Michael Spurr, I was told breathlessly, 'had often considered resigning, but he hasn't because he is a loyal public servant and despite all his efforts to build a management team, there is no one who could replace him'.

I tried to build a relationship with Spurr by asking him for lessons on the Prison Service. But this was not a success. Because of the need to vote, our lessons took place in the Pugin Room, forcing him to lift his quiet voice over the booming of MPs, and describe his plans for new prison categories, beneath a chandelier which floated above our heads in coronet upon crown of Victorian brass tracery, garnished with sinuous serpentines, shaped like forty bishops' mitres. He brushed aside my questions on broken windows. He refused when I asked for an exercise on prison strikes. He agreed to consider my request to spend a night in a cell, but I could already sense he would never deliver. I gathered that he felt – with some reason – that all the problems in his prisons had been caused by politicians. And that he was determined to keep me as far away from his prisons as he could.

Two weeks into my new job, he and I were both called in front of the Justice Select Committee to defend the conditions in Liverpool prison. The eleven Members of Parliament on the committee met in one of the new rooms in Portcullis House: around a pale horse-shoe table under a barrel-vaulted roof of rough white-grey concrete; in front of a half-abstract tapestry of the British countryside.

The chair – a small, veteran Conservative barrister in a three-piece chalk-stripe suit – opened by reminding us that Liverpool prison had been troubling in the 2013 inspection; worse in the 2015 inspection; and catastrophic in 2017. The inspection reports had apparently not led to any improvement. Michael Spurr explained that this decline was the result of political decisions, austerity and staff shortages. After twenty-three questions, Alex Chalk, a barrister, took over: a man whom I knew as an unusually courteous and gentle MP. But his tone was much sharper than I expected.

'If I may say so,' he snapped at Spurr, 'you are making the same reheated excuses. The fact is that in Liverpool there were 549 staff against a benchmark of 466 staff. The report makes it crystal clear that this is not, perhaps unusually, an issue of staffing; it is an issue of leadership. The question is, is it just the governor or is it you?' He paused. There was silence. 'Who,' he continued, 'is responsible?'

'I think there is responsibility at local level,' said Spurr soberly. 'There is responsibility at organisational level. I would need to check those figures. I am not suggesting—'

Now the chair interrupted, 'It is in the report.'

'Those are not officer figures,' said Spurr solidly.

'I am sorry; are you challenging the figures in the report, Mr Spurr?'

'No, I am not challenging the figures . . . I am saying that is the total number of staff in the establishment . . . the point is about benchmark figures and where they are at the minute . . . I am not saying that Liverpool was short of officers . . .'

Next up was another lawyer, Victoria Prentis. The daughter of an MP, a traditional Conservative, a lover of the countryside, a Remainer. Not a troublemaker: 'We have heard that the previous governor thought he was running quite a good prison in Liverpool. What evidence do you have that he understands the true reality of the situation, and that he has been trained or supported to change his behaviour, to make sure that this situation does not continue?'

Spurr looked up briefly and then down at the desk again. 'We are obviously reflecting deeply on what happened at Liverpool, as you are in this committee.' But he was not going to let anyone criticise a leader he had appointed. 'I want to reassert this point: he is an experienced and extremely able governor.'

'So why didn't he notice what was going on?' she asked.

'He was dealing with it through 2017 . . . It was not, "Oh, we hadn't seen it was happening." He was dealing with it, but I accept—'

'But vandalism doubled . . . so he was not dealing with it very well.'

Silence. Spurr was not going to dignify this with an answer.

'Mr Spurr, are you telling us that you cannot cope?'

'No, I am not saying that we cannot cope,' he said wearily. 'I am giving you the context of a system under pressure, where people have done exactly that; they have coped and they have kept a lot of things working. In some areas, they have improved actually.'

But where exactly was anything improving? He declined to say. The chair could not think of any improvement. 'Not resolving it as fast as you could implies some progress, but actually it was getting worse. How much of a grip did you and your senior team have on this, Mr Spurr?'

Then the Labour ex-prisons minister, who had told me to visit a prison a week, noted that Spurr had finally removed the prison governor, but he asked whether he would still have done this if the prisons inspector had not returned and exposed the horror in the prison.

'Well, the inspector did return,' retorted Spurr.

In the Foreign Affairs and Defence committees we often failed to pick up on damaging admissions by witnesses, and tended to grand-stand rather than cross-examine. But here, I was watching MPs, who were mostly professional lawyers, using their skills to pose crisp, well-planned questions about a field they understood. And I didn't like Michael Spurr's defensiveness.

Finally, the committee turned to me. I said that I had been shocked by what I had seen in Liverpool. That it was clear that the last governor had been out of his depth. And that I had been impressed by the new governor. I thought that her approach, beginning with cleaning the yards and fixing the cells, seemed a good one.

A Labour lawyer asked me whose fault it ultimately was.

I reflected for a moment and then said that it was my fault. That if I was not able in the next twelve months to achieve some improve-ments in making these prisons cleaner, with more fixed broken windows and fewer drugs, I was not doing my job. I felt Spurr stiffen beside me.

'But how is a minister to transform the prison system?' I asked Michael Gove, the previous Secretary of State for Justice. We had agreed to meet for a cup of tea in the Pugin Room, and he had come quickly between the two standing candelabras, under the stained glass, pushing aside the brass door grilles, trotting across the thick carpet, and slipping neatly between the chair and the tiny Gothic oak table, apologising fulsomely for being one minute late. No, he would not have a cup of tea.

'Congratulations,' he said, in his light Aberdeen accent, 'on becoming Minister of State for Prisons.' His eyebrows came together in a light frown, and he darted a quick look at me, as though to see if I was not in fact disappointed at having been moved from the Foreign Office.

'Thank you,' I replied, 'I'm very excited.'

His eyebrows rose briefly, questioning, then settled, 'You are very lucky. This is the very best job in government.' I suspected that I was not the only minister to whom he said the same. 'How may I help?'

Three years had passed since he had told everyone he was not supporting me for the Defence Committee, two years since he had been merrily blocking many of my proposals in DEFRA through the ministerial write-around process (he had had an inexplicable objection to my litter strategy), and eighteen months since he had told me I was the Duke of Wellington and tried to get me to endorse Boris Johnson's leadership campaign, before announcing that Boris was unsuitable to be prime minister.

Sometimes he carried himself like a schoolboy, today he was in the role of headmaster, gazing at me benignly through heavy-framed glasses, nodding his head slightly, as I tried to lay out my initial conclusions. I explained that I had been struck by the contrast between Liverpool prison, which was run by the government, and another prison a mile and a half down the road, which was run by a private company. I had been suspicious of private prisons but this jail seemed to have a confidence and competence which was lacking in the public prison. On the landings, the officers smiled, and were keen to talk. The cells were clean, and each prisoner had a computer monitor. Across a yard, amidst a shimmering blaze of sparks, and under the struts of a large hangar, prisoners were welding and cutting metal to make canisters and recycling bins. The prisoners moved with confidence, absorbed in their task.

When I had asked the director of the private prison why there was no litter in the yards he had been surprised.

'What do you mean?'

'How do you stop them throwing garbage out of the windows?'

'You don't need to. All UK prison windows are sealed, and the ventilation comes from a metal grille.'

'But what happens when they break the windows?'

'They don't. If a prisoner broke his window he would lose his privileges.'

This private prison had the same number of inmates as the public prison, with the same mix of offenders, also drawn from the same Liverpool gangs. So why did it seem in a better shape? I had wondered whether it was benefitting from a larger budget. But the private prison was run with a slightly smaller budget and fewer prison officers than Liverpool prison. Yet it had much better inspection reports on cleanliness, education and prisoner engagement, and much less violence and drug use.

I had also asked the director about drones bringing in drugs.

'We don't have any drones,' he said.

'Why not?'

'How could we? As I said, prison windows have to be sealed. A prisoner would have to be allowed to break the window glass, and put his hand out of the window to take the drugs from the drone. If you fix the windows, you don't have drones.'

The ministry often talked as though filthy, violent, drug-ridden prisons were an inevitable result of austerity, and that nothing could be done to stop them getting worse. But this visit had suggested to me that good governors could still make a difference. By insisting on basic minimum standards, they could make prisons much safer, cleaner and less drug-ridden, and restore the morale of their over-whelmed staff. My fear, however, was that the Prison Service was beginning to lose its confidence, hope and sense of what it once stood for.

'You seem to be saying,' Gove observed quickly, pushing aside a bulbous china teapot marked with a fading gold portcullis, and momentarily tempted by a silver-plated bowl of ready-salted crisps, 'that the Prison Service is a uniformed service that does not have the sense of autonomy or confident expertise that you would asso-ciate with a uniformed service.' He didn't tell me whether or not he agreed. 'But, of course,' he added with excessive courtesy, presum-ably aware that I had only spent a few months in the army, 'that reflects your own uniformed service.'

He smiled at an MP who was seated behind us with some con-stituents, including a nine-year-old who was looking disconsolately at a showy tower of stale scones. As I continued to talk about the lack of decency in prisons, he became more animated. 'Any judge-ments I make are tentative and provisional,' he suggested, before rattling off confident statistics. 'Prisons are not playing their part in rehabilitating offenders – as they should . . . As you know better than I, Rory, 45 per cent of adult prisoners reoffend within one year of release. For those prisoners serving shorter sentences, those of less than twelve months, the figure rises to 58 per cent . . . We must not "define deviancy down".' I was too taken with the alliteration in the phrase to ask what this meant. He proposed 'operational independence and autonomy for governors' and new targets: 'targets on amount of time out of cell, targets on purposeful activity, targets on reoffending'. And having finished his oration, he leant forward, pleased and keen, transformed in an instant from a head teacher into a brilliant schoolboy indulging a reasonably intelligent master.

But much as I admired Michael Gove's ambition and commitment, I disagreed with his solutions. He was still placing his faith in autonomy for prison governors and new targets: it seemed to reflect his approach as Education Secretary, in more autonomy for head teachers and new targets in schools. But I thought targets were the wrong way to think about prisons. A target was an aspiration: you might hit one and fall short on another, whereas cleanliness and safety in prison was a basic, non-negotiable, minimum standard. It was not simply one target to be balanced against other 'nice to haves'. As my favourite Cumbrian hotelier liked to say, 'Chocolates on pillows can't excuse filthy sheets.' I felt that the prisons were drowning under dozens of different targets, scores of different eye-catching initiatives. I sensed that governors already had too much autonomy over how much they prioritised cleanliness or safety standards, just as they had too much choice over what kind of clothing prisoners wore, and how they addressed the staff.

Naval captains did not get to choose what colour to paint their ship, or whether their ratings wore blue. They were judged on how well they fought within a uniform system. Prisoners, who often moved between many establishments over the course of a sentence would benefit, I felt, from a much more standardised reliable system. And I suspected that a focus on getting the basics right might also be the key to rebuilding the morale and confidence of the prison officers themselves.

Behind us at the bar, a Conservative MP was loudly asking the waiter, with exuberant hilarity, about his family in Turkey. 'Yes, I think, the usual, would be the answer. Perhaps with some of those delicious crisps! *Teşekkür ederim,*' he bellowed. '*Allah razı OLSUN.*'

Three older Brexit supporting MPs were hunched over one of the tiny tables in the corner of the room plotting, I assumed, Theresa May's downfall and their own elevation. Red garter chains and gold rose bushes clambered across the black wallpaper behind them.

Now, Michael changed verbal register and, as he spoke, his right hand moved to underscore each point, neatly revealing an expanse of Jermyn Street cuff which, with his thick green silk tie, made him look for the moment less like a schoolmaster and more like a banker before the tech boom. But his tone was not 2005 JP Morgan, it was Victorian evangelist. 'Prisoners,' he said, 'have grown up in circumstances of the greatest deprivation of all – moral deprivation – without the resources to reinforce virtue. They come from violent homes, and disrupted and difficult schooling.' Then he handed over a sheet of paper covered with ideas.

One of his many detractors might have laughed at his hyperarticulate alliteration and chalked the whole session down to Machiavellian alliance-building. But I was impressed by the intensity of Gove's focus on prisons. He was the only minister I had encountered in five portfolios who was prepared to attempt anything resembling a proper handover. He suggested contacts. He followed up over the next three days with the telephone numbers of people to call. And when I saw one of them I was struck by just how passionate she was, how well informed, and how deeply loyal she was to Michael Gove, how impressed by his intellect and commitment.

He and I disagreed profoundly, however, about how prisons should be run. And I could see in this disagreement one of the reasons why civil servants resisted energetic ministers. Some prisons ministers – who seemed to lack clear ideas and actions – could be reshuffled annually with little effect on the system. But too much clarity and energy from ministers such as Gove or perhaps me – who were reshuffled every year – meant reverses and re-reversals which could only leave a shaky system, spinning and churning water in our wake. And yet still I felt I was right, and I was determined to bring change.

★

By June 2018, I had been prisons minister for almost six months, and had visited perhaps twenty-five prisons in different parts of the country. I had become used to the gate security and the ritual of the keys and the locking and unlocking at the gates. I had met a gypsy, who was serving life for having killed someone in a bare-knuckle match, and who was now visited by a desperate mother weekly. I talked to a bearded giant in a special cell for convicted terrorists, who didn't want to exchange memories of the Middle East, and sat with a middle-aged man with the manner and voice of a child who had been incarcerated, released, caught and locked up again, nine times in a year.

Almost everywhere I went, the garbage still lay deep in the yards, the violence statistics were shocking and getting worse, and the prisoners on the landings seemed often unsettled, or frightened, unclear of what they were expected to do, or what the prison system was expected to do for them.

And yet, I sensed that the problem didn't lie with the uniformed officers. I had not seen any role in public service with responsibilities so raw or so immediate. No uniformed service, from the army to the fire brigade, was so full-on, so intimate, so much on active duty every hour of the day. Their interactions with prisoners required prison officers to switch continually between the roles of counsellors, policemen and teachers. On each visit, I made time to meet the uniformed staff without a manager present, and I found that many of them – despite the horror that surrounded them – were very proud of the difference they had made to individual prisoners' lives. I was ashamed that the public still didn't understand what they did; and I was determined to do more to champion the uniformed officers inside the ministry. But the whole service seemed to be suffering from a lack of direction, clear expectations and leadership.

In June I took two days out of my diary to travel up to Yorkshire for the annual Prison Officer of the Year Awards. Before dinner Michael Spurr and I had a ninety-minute conversation on the porch. I said that I noticed that the awards, which I was handing out in my dinner jacket, seemed to be going to 'Sport and Education', to

'Change and Innovation', and 'Partnership Working'. But few to the uniformed officers: the core and backbone of the prisons. I also described the visit I had just asked to make to the prison officer training college. I had found the training course to be very short, and little attempt to build morale. I complained that we had abolished the passing-out parade and even removed the tiny budget for coffees and sandwiches for families on the graduation day. I told Spurr that I wanted to do more to demonstrate we cared about protecting officers in an environment of soaring prison violence. Some prison officers had been stabbed. Many of them had asked me if they could be issued with stab vests. I said I would like us, at least, to do that.

This was not the way to approach Spurr. I had touched on issues to which he was sensitive and which seemed to challenge the values he had set for the service.

'This is not,' he said, about the proposal for stab vests, 'the US with a militarised service, and guys with shotguns looking down the landings.'

I stopped talking, and tried to give him time to tell me why he felt as he did. And to his credit he was prepared to try to explain. He described how it had felt when he joined the service in the 1980s; when prisoners were required to look down and bow their heads whenever a prison officer went past; when corrupt unions had run prisons, while the governors cowered in their offices. He described his very difficult struggles in his early career to challenge bullying in prisons and to fire prison officers for abuse. He talked passionately about how important it was to help prisoners turn their lives around. And that was why his messaging to the service put so much emphasis on relationships, change and understanding prisoners. Why he seemed to praise and promote people who talked a softer language.

When he had finished, I tried to praise what he was trying to do, but also to ask whether there wasn't some way of preserving what he had achieved, while still restoring some basic standards. Our prisons were in a mind-blowingly awful state – and yes, I added quickly, that was in large part the fault of ministers and austerity.

But even now that the cuts had ceased, and more money and staff were returning, prisons were still getting filthier, more drug-ridden, violent and out of control by the day. Could we not ask governors to set certain clear, properly enforced rules on how prisoners should dress and behave? Use regular cell-inspections, cleaning parties and searching at the gate, to make prisons cleaner and reduce drugs? Take firm action against prisoners who assaulted prison officers, without permitting bullying by prison officers? Insist on more control, in other words, without permitting brutality? Prisoners, many of whom came from chaotic backgrounds, might benefit from a more predictable, structured environment. Surely prisoners felt terrified.

He said he saw what I was talking about. And of course, there was always a balance to be struck. But he told me that when I talked about how prisons were 'out of control' I often sounded to him and others as though I cared only about control. A prison, he said, was about much more than that. He wanted to create prisons in which prisoners 'use their time not do their time'. In this awkward situation, reprimanding a minister, he sounded defiantly stern. Aware that every criticism I made of our prisons was a criticism of a system he had been managing for eight years, I nodded vigorously, and said how much admiration there was for him in the service.

Later, Spurr told a management meeting that he felt the hour and a half we had spent together had been important. He was finally, he felt, getting through to me. And I felt the same. But our sounds of agreement did not mean that either of us had changed our minds.

17.

Backstop

It was now the summer of 2018. A year had passed since Theresa May had lost both her majority and her authority in the 2017 election. Six months since I had become prisons minister. Theresa May had survived. Grant Shapps's spreadsheet of rebels remained small. May had, with the help of her whip, the self-styled 'baby-faced assassin' Gavin Williamson, persuaded the Democratic Unionist Party (DUP) to vote with the government in exchange for £1 billion of investment. The Tory Party in all its different shades – One Nation centrists, lovers of pageantry, libertarian free-marketeers, Catholic Conservatives, advocates for gay marriages – were still largely voting in a single bloc. Legislation was being passed.

But there were many signs of the subterranean conflicts bubbling beneath the surface of the Conservative and Unionist parties. In a dozen fora, which I did not visit – from think tanks in Westminster's Tufton Street, to blogs and websites, and meetings with right-wing newspapers, and dining clubs in Parliament – new factions were coalescing around more uncompromising visions of Brexit.

I picked up in brief exchanges with Kwasi Kwarteng, for example, that he was part of a group that saw Brexit as an opportunity for a more radical Reaganite economics. Dominic Cummings, the former aide to Michael Gove who had led the Vote Leave campaign, seemed in his blog posts to be inspiring a group which was thinking less in terms of Singaporean taxes or Victorian philanthropy and more in terms of Eisenhower's United States – of matching its economic growth, its vast defence spending, its research and technology companies (they talked less about its inequality, and lack of welfare provision). Steve Baker, the leader of the European Research Group of hard-Brexit Tory MPs, even seemed to see in Brexit the promise of creating a more godly society, inspired by the Book of Kings.

Elements of all these different aspirations had been contained in the great Conservative coalition for decades, and had been managed through careful compromises between leader and whips, and through Cabinets in which prime ministers sought to contain senior figures from every part of the party. But the seismic tremor of Brexit had cracked something deep beneath the Conservative crust.

The first draft of the Brexit deal was presented to the Cabinet in the Elizabethan splendour of a wood-panelled room at Chequers on 6 July 2018, two years after the Brexit vote. Theresa May had kept the negotiations very secret. Her Brexit Secretary paraded around with his papers in a metal briefcase, which looked designed for a nuclear button. I, and 90 per cent of my colleagues, had not been informed about even the bare outline of the deal. We learned the contents, with the rest of the public, from the newspapers. The media told us that May's deal involved an end to open European immigration, the existing jurisdiction of the European Court, and annual payments to the European Union. The UK would leave all the political institutions of the EU, from the Commission to the Parliament, and there would be no further talk of involvement in a European army.

But the deal would leave the UK in something very close to a customs union with the European Union. This compromise, known as the 'backstop' – because it was in theory a temporary measure – would keep the open borders in Ireland which were seen as the key to peace there, and allow British companies to continue to trade with minimal friction with the European markets. But remaining in the customs union also meant Britain could not make independent trade deals with other countries, and would have to align with many European standards. This was to prevent Britain from signing new deals, importing cheaper products, and then allowing them to slip into Europe, undercutting European producers. To people like me, remaining in the customs union was not a damaging concession. Preserving good trade with Europe and its existing partners was safer than gambling that the US, India, or China would suddenly offer Britain something much better.

But many of the harder Brexiteers in Parliament hated the idea of remaining in the customs union. They were excited by the vision of buccaneering Britain making its own trade deals. They felt that it was possible to manage a customs border between Northern Ireland and the Republic, without any impact on security in Northern Ireland, and they wanted more freedom to diverge from EU regulations. The Brexit Secretary resigned from the Cabinet in protest at the backstop. Boris Johnson was tempted to do the same. He had found his two years as Foreign Secretary humiliating. A man who enjoyed the improbable, the incongruous and the comically overstated had been trapped in a department whose religion was tact and caution. He had not enjoyed measuring and managing British diplomatic influence, which often felt to him as infinitesimal, unpredictable and elusive as a Higgs boson. Perhaps only being an abbot of a Trappist monastery would have suited him less.

And he didn't think Theresa May needed to compromise. Boris wanted Britain to be able to trade freely with the world, set its own import duties and regulations, *and* have an open border, strong trade with Europe and peace in Ireland. His personality and entire career centred on having his cake and eating it. Even if this meant making agreements and breaking them later. He was not interested in 'beery whips' telling him he couldn't have it both ways. And he saw the harder Brexiteers as a useful core for his campaign to become prime minister. So, after a characteristic three-day dither, he resigned and clambered on board the hard-Brexit wagon. His recent comparison of Theresa May's speeches to the 'lapidary codes of Hammurabi or Moses' was forgotten. He announced that the backstop meant that the UK was headed 'for the status of a colony'. He then sat in the Foreign Secretary's house for days, saving money on a flat, while his successor, Jeremy Hunt, waited to move in.

The day after Boris resigned, I was standing in Steve Pattinson's low-ceilinged sandstone milking parlour in the constituency surrounded by the half-sweet smell of grass and milk and manure. Steve was the governor of a local school which had only fifteen pupils, including his own two children. The shed in which we were standing, on 120 acres of sour, flat, clay north of Hadrian's Wall, was hardly large enough to handle his sixty cows. It cost, Steve said, 18p to produce a litre of milk. He then sold it at 26p a litre to his processor who sold the product to the continent. If Britain crashed into a no-deal Brexit, his processor would face European tariffs on milk at 40 per cent.

'There would be no milk exports.' He paused. 'The processor would cease collecting milk. But my cows need to be milked. I only have enough storage for twenty-four hours and my cows are producing thousands of litres each a year. I would have to get rid of the milk while the price would be plummeting . . . 16p, 14p . . . below the cost of production. Then I would have to sell the cows.'

Steve was thinking about his loan from the Cumberland Building Society. And his interest payments. The farm would then have to be sold. 'Not for a farm. Perhaps for a second home, perhaps to the Forestry Commission.'

Steve's whole life, his land, his herd that he had bred, would be gone. He was focused on what would happen to his son, now nine, who had been given his own cow to look after to get a feel for the business.

I had campaigned for and voted Remain in large part because I was very conscious of how badly Brexit might affect small farmers in my constituency. But like every other MP I had promised repeatedly during the campaign to respect the referendum, whatever the result. I was prepared to accept control over immigration, and departure from the European political institutions, because it seemed that the overwhelming number of Brexit voters had expected to take control of immigration and leave those institutions. But I knew no-deal was a fraud, and I wanted to preserve a stable situation in Northern Ireland and free trade with Europe. So I was increasingly convinced by Theresa May's compromise – not least because it would offer more protection for people in my constituency.

But in Parliament Brexit was becoming more surreally detached from the daily reality of a Cumbrian business than the development strategy for South Sudan. In Westminster dozens of Conservative

MPs were now talking about rejecting the Chequers agreement entirely and leaving the EU 'without a deal if necessary'. Their arguments were rarely practical. Two of them compared their opposition to Theresa May's deal to their dead fathers' role in the fight against Nazi Germany; Boris Johnson drew analogies with the fight against colonisation; and Steve Baker – a lay-preacher who had also resigned as a junior minister – was wondering how to balance Romans 13:1–5, which underpinned his Brexit policy, against Hebrews 7:18ff and musing whether his radical scepticism of the welfare state would have been shared by St Thomas Aquinas. But to Steve Pattinson the rejection of Theresa May's deal for a no-deal Brexit would mean the loss of his farm.

Shortly before my visit to Wormwood Scrubs in autumn 2018, Winston, a prisoner in solitary, had been left for forty-eight hours without food or medical attention, and – contrary to all protocol – was not checked for hours. He had hanged himself at least four hours before they found him. I asked for and was given permission to spend a full day-shift shadowing a prison officer at Wormwood Scrubs. My guide was firm and friendly with prisoners and proud of her job. But when I joined a therapy session, I found a counsellor trying to guilt-trip a prisoner into not killing himself ('How do you think your children would feel?' she asked), and when I followed another prison officer into a cell, I discovered that he did not seem to know how to conduct a cell inspection.

The prisoner officer said he had received only a brief training course, much of it conducted online. He had been in the service for a matter of months and had been put in charge of a landing of seventy prisoners. He agreed with my suggestion that he should be partnered with a more senior officer. But the rank of supervisory officers who had previously mentored junior staff on their landings had been abolished to save costs.

When I called senior managers in to discuss these problems, they responded with jargon and acronyms: the Violence Reduction tool, the Offender Manager in Custody (OMIC) tool, the Gang Index, the Promoting Risk Intervention by Situational Management (PRISM) tool, the Safer Custody meeting, and the Assessment,

Care in Custody and Teamwork (ACCT) process that was supposed to stop suicide (except it seemed in Nottingham, where fifty people were on ACCT, and seven had killed themselves). Too many managers seemed to want to talk about identity change, 'Strong, integrated, service delivery between partners' and rehabilitative leadership, while their prison officers lacked basic skills and their prisoners lacked blankets and toilet paper.

On my next visit to a London prison, I was talking to the governor on the ground floor of one of the large wings, when a man strode towards us shouting 'Fuck . . . Fuck . . . Fuck . . .' Two prison officers were trailing in his wake. Through the suicide netting, I could see that every trail and balcony was packed with hundreds of prisoners staring down. The governor ignored him and kept talking. When the man reached us, he stuck his head between me and the governor, and shouted, 'Fuck the governor.'

The governor tried to continue the conversation with me as though the prisoner were not there.

'Did you not hear me?' said the man, pushing his face right up against the governor's. 'I said fuck the governor.'

Still the governor kept talking to me.

The man threw his arms in the air, and strode off again down the landing, shouting 'Fuck . . . Fuck . . . Fuck,' with the two prison officers behind him.

'Sorry about that,' said the governor. 'It's Billy – he had a bad time at the GP's surgery this morning.'

Hundreds of eyes were trained on us, watching the scene.

The governor, it seemed, felt he was showing understanding and compassion. I felt his inability to reprimand or control the prisoner undermined the authority of all the prison officers, and made the prison a more dangerous place.

Such experiences had convinced me that we needed to rethink training at every level of the Prison Service. Basic training for a soldier was far longer than for a prison officer although a prison officer's role was more complex. A colonel in the army would have received almost three years of training over twenty years before taking command, whereas a governor would have received only a few weeks. We needed much more training and a much clearer vision of what it meant to be an excellent prison officer, and run a good prison. My model here was Nils Öberg, the head of the Swedish prison service, whom I tried, unsuccessfully, to bring in to run the British Prison Service. Whereas in Britain the world seemed to divide between people who talked about compassion and people who talked about discipline, Öberg led a culture which understood how to combine both. He made Swedish officers treat prisoners as human beings, with compassion, but he was not ashamed to invest in scanners and CCTV and barbed wire, or to insist that prison officers, not prisoners, were in control of jails. And partly as a result his drug rates were 1 per cent, when ours were 30, and his reoffending rates far better. But the governors were not interested in my telling them how to do their jobs.

When I asked Spurr to reinstate the coffee and tea and passing-out parade for families at the prison officers' training college, he agreed. But when I asked him to reinstate the old grade of senior supervisory officers, he resisted. The downgrading of the role and salaries of the SOs had been one of his key cost-saving measures of the previous year. Nor did he agree on the need for longer training courses. He was relaxed about my request for a checklist for cell inspections, moving in sequence around the room. But I was troubled that the Prison Service had removed them in the first place. And I found it difficult to imagine that any training course or rubric or checklist would be enough to fix the problems, which I had now seen in forty different prisons.

My prison visits continued, and the Brexit story went quiet again. In the two months since Boris Johnson's resignation a strange peace had settled over the Conservative Party. There had been no more resignations. Boris was often to be seen brooding outside his tiny office, saying that his resignation was the worst decision he had ever made, presumably because he could see no way back from it to re-enter the Cabinet or become prime minister. The prime minister was again absorbed in the secretive negotiations with the French politician Michel Barnier in Brussels, during which the White Paper was said to be evolving into a Withdrawal Agreement. Cabinet ministers told me when I sat with them in the Commons that Cabinet meetings had become short bland affairs.

I was due to go to the States to see Shoshana's parents when the Prison Officers' Association, perhaps aware of my holiday plans, declared that they were going on strike. I apologised again to my children and my in-laws, and the family went without me. An inspection of Bedford prison had uncovered more horrifying violence, and the union said that prisons were now too dangerous for them to work in. They said they would walk out of every prison leaving only a few managers, who were not in the union, to manage 80,000 prisoners.

Michael Spurr explained all this in a tone of despair. He said he would try to negotiate with the union leaders but he could not guarantee anything. He may have been more confident than he sounded, for he was a highly experienced union negotiator. But I was worried. David Gauke moved a motion in court to declare the strike action illegal and threatened to seize the union's funds. I gave a series of interviews saying that while I acknowledged the scale of violence, and sympathised with the staff, we were trying to fix the violence, and the strike endangered everyone. I then asked the union heads to meet me in a Pret A Manger near Parliament Square. An hour after our first meeting one of those present gave an interview insisting that ministers were refusing to meet them. In the following meeting, I doubled down on the threat of legal action. But I also explained that I had submitted a draft bill to double the sentences for assaults on prison officers; that I would be authorising stab vests, and extending a pilot project to issue pepper spray to prison officers. The union lead said that if I could guarantee to bring these measures forward, he would call off the strike. I agreed and shook hands on it. The prison officers returned to work the following morning.

I took legislation through Parliament to double the sentence for violent assaults on prison officers. And authorised all prison officers to be trained in the use of pepper spray. The senior management in the Prison Service, prison charities and lawyers opposed me, arguing that issuing pepper spray to prison officers 'carried a high risk of its being used in a discriminatory fashion against minorities and disadvantaged prisoners'. Perhaps they were right, but I was also confident that we could manage this risk and demonstrate that we were serious about discipline and the protection of prison officers, and I was learning that I didn't need to argue every point in a seminar. My public promise to the unions, and the support from my boss, David Gauke, was enough.

There was no more talk of strikes. Michael Spurr was, however, very angry that I had negotiated directly with the unions and changed the policy on protective equipment. He said it set a bad precedent and it could have gone dangerously wrong.

18.

Resignation

I was beginning to sense, over five roles across four departments, that civil servants often preferred ministers to be dignified mouthpieces, who defended the department competently and fluently, without challenging operational policy. They viewed us, Michael Gove liked to say, as child emperors, to be indulged, praised and manipulated like a five-year-old in dragon robes. The deference to ministers in all departments was extravagant. Teams of private secretaries and diary secretaries worked night and day and through weekends to accommodate our travel requests; to move a red box hundreds of miles to our houses, and to get us a cappuccino or a plate of sushi. And we had constitutional power. We could introduce new laws in Parliament, cut budgets, lay off prison officers, and privatise. In short, ministers could make the lives of civil servants hell, and often did.

But changing day-to-day practice, I was learning, was a very different matter – in the Prison Service as much as in international development. Michael Spurr or indeed any civil servant had to accept ministers changing the law, or cutting budgets, but they didn't want a minister involved in operations. They were even happy in theory with the minister setting the destination, but they wanted the routines of the ship of state, its trim and its daily navigation, to be controlled by civil servants alone. This was for good reason. Ministers were amateur outsiders on very short tours, whose successors could introduce completely different agendas. What possible knowledge or qualifications did we have to engage in the operational details? How could we even think of anything that had not already been tried by officers and officials with decades of experience?

And yet it was at the operational level that so many of the worst problems in British government lay. Not in the 'what' but the 'how'.

This was why too many of our international development programmes were wasteful and poorly delivered, and why too many of
our embassies were unfocused, understaffed and underwhelming.
And nothing I ever saw in public life was as shameful as the conditions in which prisoners lived and prison officers worked. In each
previous department, from DEFRA through DfID to the Foreign
Office, I had tried to introduce change by being on top of the detail
and working almost as a civil servant among civil servants. But this
approach had not got me very far. Now, I decided to do something
different.

I went to see David Gauke. He sat me on the sofa opposite him
and his private secretary sat beside him, pen dramatically poised
over a red folder. Gauke's office was almost as large as the permanent secretary's, and resembled, with its sloping brutalist windows,
the control room of an aircraft carrier. It struck me anew that
his firm quizzical eyebrows would have sat well beneath an admiral's cap.

I was beginning to understand how tough Gauke could be when
he believed in a decision. Early on, he had asked me to take legislation through reducing compensation payments to people with
lifelong injuries. More recently, he had told me to offer lower salary
rises to prison officers than the public sector pay review body had
recommended. On both occasions, I had pushed to be more generous. But he insisted we needed to save to spend on improving
prisons, and I had done what I was told. The public outcry that I had
feared had not happened, and his firmness had saved the Treasury
hundreds of millions of pounds.

I had no idea, however, how this veteran Conservative politician
would react to my latest idea. I was not proposing introducing new
legislation. I wasn't privatising or nationalising. My project was not
recommended by the opinion polls. It might even alienate right-wing
voters. And it wasn't likely to interest the media. Or be noticed by the
prime minister. All of this would, I thought, have made my previous
bosses – Liz Truss, Priti Patel, or Boris Johnson – view the project as a
waste of time. Worse, it would probably be very unpopular with
Michael Spurr and the Ministry of Justice, and David's private

secretary would have a good chance of killing any suggestion I made as soon as I left the room and they were alone again.

Still, nine months had also taught me how clear, kind and even-tempered Gauke could remain in the face of strikes and bankruptcy. And how practical. So I simply said that the situation in the prisons was shameful beyond belief. I talked about the cluster of suicides in Nottingham, the despair among the prisoners I had met in Bedford, the filth in Liverpool. I reminded him that one of our prisoners had just been beheaded by another on the exercise ground. And I told him that I thought that the problem was that the whole system had lost its belief in itself. And that I thought we could rebuild it.

I wanted to start, I explained, in the ten prisons with the worst drugs or violence figures. I said I would like to set up a war room, and bring in my own team focused on improving basic standards in those prisons.

'What would you do?'

'We will start by fixing the windows – that will prevent prisoners taking drugs from drones and throwing garbage into the yards. Then I would like to install a body-scanner at each prison . . .' I went on to share my ideas on establishing new training courses and standards for prison officers, and rolling out checklists.

'Checklists?'

'They removed the checklists for cell inspections. They used to work like this,' I got to my feet and opened the door of his room, and recited 'lock . . . skin,' I tapped the wood, which unlike a prison door lacked a metal skin, 'day light', I gestured to the switch and then worked down imaginary items below it, 'night light, call bell . . .'

His eyebrows rose and fell. Then he asked to see what I had in writing. I passed over a couple of pages and sat still as he read them. Occasionally I caught the eye of his private secretary whose smile seemed to combine both loyalty to his boss and sympathy for the petitioner. Finally Gauke began asking questions about my prioritisation and my theory of change, then he leant back, said he was interested and that he would respond the following day.

The next morning, he called me in again to tell me he would give me a budget of £10 million – £1 million per prison – enough to cover the purchase of the scanners and the repairs to the windows. Then he instructed the ministry to get behind me. But thereafter, unlike Boris, he didn't announce that I had 'plenipotentiary powers' and take no further interest. Instead, he asked me to brief him in weekly meetings with officials present and made sure to look carefully into each idea before approving it. That way he let the ministry and the Prison Service know that when I asked them to do something, he was behind it too.

Almost immediately, I heard that I had been given a space down the corridor from my office which could be converted into an operations room. A gentle, thoughtful and intelligent ex-prison governor was assigned to work alongside me and he started recruiting a team for what was now called 'the Ten Prisons Project'. I was also given permission – as with flooding – to import a brigadier to help me. The brigadier whom I had targeted this time was Kevin Beaton, a large, grinning, moustachioed, rugby-playing soldier, first introduced to me by Nicholas Soames, when he was trying to set up a staff college for managers in the National Health Service. Kevin had begun as an infantry officer, before qualifying as a doctor, rejoining the army medical corps, winning an OBE during the civil war in Sierra Leone, and leading the UK military medical response to Ebola in Sierra Leone. He seemed a good person to help us run the war room, define support and training to governors, and improve standards among junior staff.

But even David Gauke's support brought only a limited sense of urgency. A military assistant who contacted the Ministry of Justice to confirm the brigadier's appointment somehow got the impression from Michael Spurr's office that we no longer required the brigadier's services. I had to track down the minister for the armed forces, and get him to promise to make it happen. Weeks went by. I tried again.

One scanner arrived and was put in Leeds prison. I went immediately up with Emma, my new private secretary, and asked to be put in the scanner. I was not aware until I saw the expressions that the scanner showed me entirely naked on the screen to my private secretary, the governor and the surrounding staff.

The other nine scanners were, however, apparently stuck in

China and not expected for another four months. Meanwhile, the latest figures in our new ops room showed that the ten prisons, which I had promised to turn around, were getting worse by the day. In particular, violence continued to rise fast.

I was beginning to conclude that in order to get things moving, I was going to have to be very directly involved in a system which saw ministers as non-executive board members, not chief executives. That meant shedding my tone as a civil servant and leaning much harder into my role as a politician. I would have to take my power not only from my Secretary of State but from the outside as well: harness the media; the public; and sound bites; create a momentum and urgency which didn't exist inside the department and, by embracing the bewitching, flimsy, uncertain potentials of modern politics, make them see me as a leader. Above all I needed a deadline which people would take seriously.

My interview on *BBC Breakfast* began quietly. I mentioned the ten-prisons project. The interviewer pointed out that it didn't seem to be going well. I had been in office for nine months and violence was in fact rising. I insisted that he would see me turn this around.

'It's a rare politician,' cut in the interviewer, 'who says "judge me on results". I mean, are you seriously suggesting I'll speak to you in twelve months' time, and we'll look at those statistics from those ten prisons and, if they're the same, or worse, you're going to quit?'

I paused and then said, 'Yes.'

This resignation threat suddenly became front-page news. Every TV station and newspaper loved the simplicity and drama and reported this in a way they had refused to report my predecessors' stories on drones. Having spent eight years insisting on nuance, detail, understatement and grounded reality, I had finally embraced the power of a sound bite.

I justified it as a rational management technique, but there was something more going on with this bet. I felt the excitement of dragging myself out of the suffocating swamp of government and finding my own voice again, and my own role, while also embracing the risk of a very public humiliation.

The Prison Officers' Association issued an immediate statement, explaining why my project was doomed: 'Well, that's another new prisons minister in post shortly, then, because the safety statistics keep telling us that violence is higher than ever and continues to rise. Prison officers are now being assaulted at a rate of twenty-four per day and investing £10 million in just ten prisons in an attempt to win back control and reduce violence is merely a pipe dream.'

The new clarity and stakes from the resignation gave urgency to the weekly meetings. I was beginning to set a battle rhythm, and in our new ops room, officials were wary and excited. Each week began with a presentation on what was happening in each of the ten prisons. The team focused on comparative data – drilling down into discrepancies. They discovered, for example, that 40 per cent of the violence in Wormwood Scrubs in one month happened between 1.00 and 1.40 in the afternoon in the dining hall. There, it seemed, a 'violence' issue was potentially a lunch-queue-management issue.

But when, in October, the Ministry of Defence finally assigned me the brigadier and I gave him my first briefing, I could hardly tell him that things were moving in the right direction. Our data still showed every one of the ten prisons crowded well beyond its capacity, and compulsory drug tests were showing more than 50 per cent of the prisoners on drugs. Our visits revealed cells covered in graffiti, windows still broken and stuffed with rags, and barrier reefs of garbage in the yards. The number of assaults – which we measured weekly – was continuing to rise steeply.

The senior management in the Prison Service kept their distance from the project. Neither Michael Spurr nor his deputy would accept my invitations to visit the ops room, or even listen to our presentations. I sensed that they found it profoundly offensive that I – as an outsider – was presuming to claim I had a formula to reduce violence. They made it clear that if they had believed my approach would work, they could have funded it – because even in our cash-strapped department there were programmes, such as our surveillance projects, which could have been cut to find £10 million.

But they hadn't, because they disagreed and disapproved of such an approach. And they seemed vindicated.

There had been 1,200 assaults on prisoners in our ten prisons in the second and third quarters of the year (an 8 per cent rise in a month and a 27 per cent rise in a year). There had been 380 assaults on staff (a 19 per cent rise in a month, and a 41 per cent rise in a year). In four of our prisons violence had increased by between 70 and 100 per cent. This was not an abstract set of numbers but a moral catastrophe – represented in bloodstains, broken jaws, gouged eyes and even death, set against a background of squalor and misery. And I was apparently failing to turn it around.

In the autumn I invited the governors of the ten priority prisons to my house in Scotland. They arrived late. First three Yorkshire governors emerged, unbending their massive frames from the back of a tiny Crieff taxi. The next taxi delivered two women from London who glanced quickly down at the Perthshire mud before greeting me.

I put every chair in the sitting room, propped a flimsy screen on the piano, and asked each governor to present on how they were going to commit to the standards around violence which I had begun to set. But only the representative from Hull prison said he wanted to focus on reducing violence. The representative from the East London prison didn't. She said she still preferred her old objective of 'developing relationships'. Humber prison was happy to commit to fixing windows. The fourth governor wanted 'a positive, pro-social attitude promoted by all', and the fifth a 'pro-active and preventative approach'. Which might or might not have been a different thing.

Over roast lamb at lunch, I tried to move the conversation on from an abstract debate around 'violence' to concrete examples of how we felt a landing should be run. I described the prisoner shouting 'Fuck the governor' in the governor's face. The Yorkshire governors didn't like that.

'Should never happen.'

Each Yorkshire governor had a separate account of how their prison officers would have intercepted the prisoner, and talked him round, and restrained him if the talking had failed. The London governors on the other hand seemed embarrassed by my question and the Yorkshire responses. They thought it focused too much on discipline and control.

In the field in front of the house, I had planted some trees. They had not got far in eight years of pale Scottish sun: beech and oak, spreading slowly and solidly out of plastic tubes. We walked in a pack around the edge of the field, inspecting them. The governor of Leeds shuffled alongside me, slower than I expected for such an active man, his head pushed forward, explaining why my pond was a disgrace, and describing the ornamental koi carp pond, which he had built at home and at Leeds prison.

He had been a cricketer and footballer before taking up rugby at the age of forty. He said he had started a gardening project at the prison, with a prize. 'One of the prisoners said, "Thank you Governor, this has meant I can stand barefoot on grass for the first time in fifteen years!"' This large man was visibly moved by this simple story. 'My prisoners are looking after chickens, snowy owls, eagle owls, hawks and bees – and living walls, wildflower meadows, poly-tunnels and fruit trees – in containers.' He was on track to be the longest-serving governor of Leeds prison since 1929.

After we had examined the pond-liner, he explained his approach to clean cells.

'I begin every morning by inspecting seventeen cells myself. My deputy does another seventeen. It is pretty difficult after that,' he growled, 'for people to bullshit me. If I ask why the call bell on the top left of the third floor in C wing is broken and they say, "It's on the work sheet," I say "Indeed, it is. But it's been on that for six weeks and the bell is still unfixed."'

In the afternoon session, the brigadier got to his feet. His tweed jacket was stiff and new, his brown brogues gleamed with many layers of polish. He had the moustache and huge chest of a sergeant from the parachute regiment, and the spectacles of a doctor. When he called us 'boys and girls,' one of the female governors winced. 'It's the morale factor that matters: often far more than resources,' he said. He talked more than I would have liked about Agincourt and Napoleon. 'Moral forces are to physical as three to one,' he said, 'and I am going to guess that is as true in a prison as in an army.' But it was hard not to be impressed by his images of the Ebola hospitals he had built as a military doctor in Sierra Leone. And the Yorkshire governors seemed to respond warmly when he described our plan to set up a Standards Coaching Team to improve the ten prisons, 'an elite unit, the best of the best from the Prison Service, travelling round training up the new recruits'.

Then a governor presented on how he prevented broken windows. 'Take away the televisions. If you vandalise your cell, you lose your TV. And check. Clear rules and clear sanctions – no exceptions. Pull the officers up hard: "Why is the man still on privileges when he has vandalised his cell?"'

Finally the ministry lead for the ten-prisons project spoke. Until then he had seemed the type who preferred discussing desistance theory with American professors at Irish universities. But on his feet, he gave an easy smile. He reminded us of the latest record figures for violence in our ten prisons, and how steep the task would be, if I were to avoid resigning. He said, 'Our insistence on challenging all violence might be part of the problem, it is provoking a backlash from prisoners.'

'Only in the short term,' growled one of the Yorkshire governors. 'Give it time.'

The ministry lead shrugged and turned to me. 'We have a choice now on how we measure this violence. How much of a rod we want to create for our own back.' Unspoken was the idea that we could make things easier by reducing the populations in these prisons – pushing the problem elsewhere – or even bringing in older sex offenders who were less likely to be violent.

I looked at the governors, all of whom were watching me. I said that we should not reduce or change the populations at all. We should make it as fair as we could, so every journalist and every prison officer who looked at our figures would feel we had set a real test. And so that if we succeeded, we could have a proper model for the system. I said I was beginning for the first time in government to rediscover some faith. To feel that we had practical ideas that might actually make a difference in real lives, lift someone out of living in a squalid cell; prevent someone else's jaw from being broken.

'Don't worry,' the Yorkshire governors said in unison as they folded their impressive frames into another tiny car to head back to the train station, 'we won't let you resign.'

19

Loving Strict

My daily route to Parliament took me from the Ministry of Justice past the Foreign Office. I had once revered the Foreign Office building and been proud to work within it. Now its glittering blocks of Belgian and Sicilian marble, within which Britain's international reputation flickered like an unreliable generator, felt to me like a Potemkin facade. I was relieved to be working within the concrete walls of the Ministry of Justice. When, just over a year into my job there, the prime minister's chief of staff offered me the chance to return as the Middle East minister in DfID and the Foreign Office, I refused.

Prisons, as my Christian predecessor had insisted, were only one part of my ministerial job. I was also responsible for probation and reducing reoffending outside prisons. This was a disaster, for as Michael Gove had pointed out, 45 per cent of adult prisoners re-offended within one year of release, while for those prisoners serving short sentences, the figure was 58 per cent. In other words, half of our prisoners left prison and committed a crime again. It was not impossible to reduce the chance of someone reoffending, if you provided good support, housing, employment, and counselling to prisoners after release. The government kept publishing papers, which showed this, but it seemed to be incapable of doing it.

Chris Grayling, the former Secretary of State for Justice, had tried to reduce reoffending, through the use of the private sector in 2012. He had privatised half the Probation Service, and issued contracts to private sector companies and charities, who promised to be innovative and apply the latest evidence-based approaches to managing former prisoners. In order to focus their minds he promised that the government would pay them hundreds of millions of pounds if they reduced reoffending rates. And fine them if they allowed reoffending to increase.

Grayling set very few rules on how they should deliver on this version of a 'social impact bond', since he felt the incentives and the results were all that was required. On paper this seemed radical and even plausible. Charities and businesses, freed of government constraints, had been given a strong financial incentive to innovate and tap the best global practice in reducing reoffending: protecting the public; transforming lives; and saving the vast sums of money spent on incarceration.

Except by the time I took responsibility for probation, it had all gone wrong. The companies had not succeeded in reducing reoffending. In fact reoffending had increased. The more the rates had increased, the more the companies owed the government. Desperate to save money, they had laid off the probation staff, whom they had inherited, and cut back ever more on their services to offenders. And because the contracts had been left deliberately unspecified, to encourage innovation, there was no way of forcing the companies even to meet offenders. The reoffending rate rose further. The companies owed the government tens of millions. At which point, instead of paying us, they were threatening to declare bankruptcy, abandoning tens of thousands of ex-offenders in the community. Abstract theorising and ill-considered ideology best left in a twenty-page report in a think tank, had blown up the system.

A very impressive senior member of the Prison Service – who had made a difference as governor of Brixton and was now running probation with calm and clarity – said bluntly that our best option would be to reverse the privatisation and renationalise the whole system, while squeezing as much from the companies as we possibly could. But, she feared that it might be politically impossible. As she reminded me, the privatisation had been allowed to continue by Michael Gove and Liz Truss, who represented the free-market right in Theresa May's unstable Brexit Cabinet. The whole idea of renationalising a privatised sector was a profoundly un-Thatcherite thing to do. The very act would imply that three serving Cabinet ministers had been negligent. They doubted it was even worth suggesting to the Secretary of State.

I said she was underestimating David Gauke. We took the proposal to him together. He asked difficult questions calmly, challenged numbers, weighed the chances of recovering money from the private companies against the risks of tipping them off before they had paid us, and clarified costs we had not fully articulated. Then, concluding that we were right to propose renationalising, he assumed the full weight of answering to fellow Cabinet ministers and the party for the decision. He could have done nothing, and kept warm relationships with the Conservative right. Or having made the decision, he might have publicised it, and won real credit with the centre and the left by reversing a toxic privatisation. He did neither. He renationalised discreetly – never naming what he had done – emphasising the small private elements that remained. And as often with David Gauke, this meant he brought significant change, and improvement, but won little public credit.

None of this, however, overcame the risks of reoffending that probation managers had to manage on a daily basis. Anxious that I had been spending too much time in prisons, I began to visit more probation offices around the country. If the caricature of a room of prison officers sometimes had echoes of a 1950s police squad room, the caricature of a probation office was of a 1970s teachers' common room complete with paisley shirts and copies of the *Guardian*. Whatever their fashion choices, however, the role of a prison officer and a probation officer seemed equally impossible.

In one office, thirty miles outside London, I was introduced to a woman two years out of university who was managing an elderly offender recently released from a long sentence for abducting and raping young boys. I asked her whether she was worried. She cited numerous studies which suggested that he was unlikely to reoffend, and that the courses which he had done in prison would convince him not to abuse again.

I acknowledged that he had served the sentence imposed by the judge, and that we could hardly afford to keep people indefinitely in our overcrowded prisons. But I found it difficult to believe that we could predict the man's future behaviour on the basis of general studies. She said that she was pretty sure that he was no longer a predatory threat, and that it was fine for her to manage him through fortnightly meetings. And at least while I was the minister, she seemed vindicated – he didn't reoffend.

Towards the end of 2018, however, an eighty-three-year-old wrote to me from Wolverhampton requesting a meeting. I asked about the case. The Probation Service explained that in her case probation officers had made a difficult judgement call, sometime earlier, which had gone tragically wrong. It was not, they said, the probation officers' fault. No disciplinary action had been taken. But it was of course 'very sad'. I asked for more details.

We had, it seemed, released a man called Leroy Campbell from prison, where he had been serving his third sentence for rape. In one of his weekly meetings with his probation officer, after release, he had told her that he 'felt like raping again'. A couple of weeks later he had told another probation officer that he felt the urges getting stronger. When asked to evaluate the urges on a scale of one to ten, he had suggested six out of ten. The officer, who had just come off a course on sex-offender behaviour, concluded that Campbell's honesty about his urges was a good sign: it showed that he was coming to terms with his condition.

Another manager met Campbell. Hearing from him that his life was more stable, that he was living with his sister and said he no longer felt like raping, the manager concluded no action needed to be taken. No one it seemed had reported this up the chain. And although the probation officers had the power to recall Campbell to prison, they hadn't. Shortly after this conversation, Campbell climbed through the window of a house in the West Midlands and raped and killed one of the occupants.

I reached out to friends who were psychiatrists. They said that when Campbell said he felt like raping again it should have been treated as an imminent threat and he should have been recalled to prison at once. I called retired probation officers. They agreed. I went through the reports and action. The more I looked at the case, the more indefensible it seemed. I told the civil servants that this had not simply been an unlucky judgement call. That in my view the probation officers were at fault and should be suspended. I asked to see the woman who had written to me.

She came to my office with her remaining daughter and her son-in-law. She sat quite still, well back in the chair. The light was behind her, emphasising her silhouette, her neatly curled white hair, held severely back, the set of her shoulders, and her strong hands, folded over her chest. As she spoke she looked directly at me, watching my face.

'*Your* colleagues let him out of prison. *Your* probation officers failed to recall him to prison. Let me explain what that meant you did. My daughter, Lisa, was a nurse. This man climbed through our window, after Lisa had got back from her day shift,' she said slowly and clearly. 'Then he grabbed Lisa and he raped her. Then he killed her.' Her eyes, fixed unflinchingly on mine, challenged me to imagine the scene. 'I am eighty-three. Before he left he set fire to the house, and wrapped the Hoover hose around my neck and tried to rape and kill me too.'

Nothing I had seen in Iraq or Afghanistan had prepared me for what it took to look this woman in the eye, or to take responsibility for what our collective failure to manage and recall a prisoner had meant for her life.

In the third aspect of my role, as minister for sentencing, I tried to abolish short prison sentences entirely. Almost half our prisoners were in our overcrowded prisons on short sentences, typically given for crimes like shoplifting. The average stay in Durham prison, I had been told, was ten days. I found it difficult to forget the prisoner in Bedford prison, who said that he had been in the prison nine separate times in a year. Short sentences had particularly perverse impacts. They were long enough to disrupt someone's life: lose their accommodation, and their job (if they had one), and quadruple their suicide risk. But the sentences were far too short to give the prison any chance for work on rehabilitation, addiction treatment or education. Short-sentence prisoners drove much of the violence in prison. Most importantly, research had established that sending offenders to prison for short sentences made them more, not less, likely to reoffend. In other words, short sentences increased, not reduced, the risk to the public. Abolishing short sentences would, I believed, radically reduce our prison population and leave calmer, better-ordered prisons, and less offending outside.

I began by trying to end the practice of sending people to prison for not paying their council tax or TV licences. Rishi Sunak was the junior minister whose department was responsible for sending people who owed council tax to jail. He had been a minister for only six months. We often talked in the library. I thought we both enjoyed our conversations, and that on this he would be helpful.

He entered the underground committee room fast, flashing a tense smile, and took a seat at the head of the table. Two of his officials, in his wake, hurried to draw up chairs beside him. His tight suit and shirt emphasised the taut restlessness of his body. He opened a red ministerial folder, and nodded to me to begin.

I explained as well as I could how squalid our overcrowded prisons could be. And because he had a reputation for numbers, I added that a place in prison cost more than studying at Eton or Winchester. 'I suppose, Rishi, I am basically saying that it's ludicrous. And we can do something useful. People shouldn't be going to prison for not paying their council tax or TV licence.'

But we found ourselves almost immediately trapped in an argument about exactly how many people were in prison for not paying their council tax bill. He had read his briefing carefully, had every figure ready, and his departmental data did not agree with ours.

I took a breath. 'Look, the point is that one would be too many. Can we please just step back from this for a second? How can it make sense to do something as extreme as sending someone to prison for not paying their council tax?'

'I can think of many reasons.'

'Prisons are horrifying places,' I persisted, 'violent, filthy and overcrowded. They make people more criminal.'

'That,' he retorted, 'is hardly our department's fault.' The hour ended with our relationship bruised, and Rishi Sunak unconvinced.

Having failed to get his department to voluntarily alter their policy, the only remaining option was to introduce primary legislation. I proposed a law to ensure that people convicted of crimes with a maximum sentence of six months could not be put in prison at all: failure to pay a council tax bill would no longer be an imprisonable offence. It was a policy I knew that Labour could not take through for fear of being considered soft on crime. Only a Conservative government, I argued, really had the political capital to be liberal on this issue.

David Gauke looked carefully into the academic studies and was convinced that abolishing the sentences would reduce crime and save money. And so with his thoughtful policy adviser and, his tough, unintimidated American–Turkish press adviser, he explained the policy to Number 10, won consent from the prime minister and the chancellor, warned them to expect media attacks, and sent me out to make the announcement.

I was rewarded with the entire front page of the *Daily Mail*, under the headline 'Minister gives Green Light to Criminals', complete with quotes from a colleague who described my proposals as 'ludicrous' and 'allowing child rapists to roam the streets'. Magistrates were angry because I was removing their powers to imprison offenders. One MP delivered a flowery, T. S. Eliot-laced invective against me in Westminster Hall; another snapped at me in the lobby. Theresa May's polling team came hurriedly to warn me that 'being tough on crime' was the government's only remaining lead in the opinion polls, and to beg us to reconsider. But David didn't flinch. We moved on to commission a White Paper. I gave another speech in Parliament. We took more negative headlines. And then the press stories ceased, and it seemed that we had emerged into calmer seas. All we needed now to abolish short sentences was the time to take the legislation through Parliament.

Meanwhile the prison inspectors continued to report cockroaches and rats; thousands of assaults; blocked toilets; filthy yards, and prison officers sleeping on duty, having disabled the cell call bells so they could not be disturbed. People were being battered every day under ministry posters that pronounced 'we have a zero tolerance attitude to violence'. The brigadier and I, however, still remained convinced that the prison officers were part of a fundamentally decent uniformed service, which lacked only the right kind of training, leadership and support. And that we could demonstrate this in the ten prisons.

Towards the end of the year we published an advertisement calling for the best senior prison officers to join a new Standards Coaching Team, designed to go into our key prisons, partner, train, and model behaviour on the wings. The day the notice went out, a prison officer in the Ministry of Justice lunch queue heard a civil servant say that I and the brigadier were naïve: prisons could not be turned around in this way. The prison officer told the civil servant he was wrong, and walked straight upstairs to the brigadier's office to volunteer.

The brigadier picked fifty candidates and then worked with the training college to design an intense course, focused on character and leadership. He told the course that their task would be to 'inspire the youngsters', and demonstrate how to run safe and orderly landings. Determined to show that this was an elite group, the brigadier insisted on 'binning' the five worst performers from the course. Then he deployed the trained team in small groups to the ten prisons.

The Yorkshire prisons seemed to welcome the standard coaching teams – not least because they reinforced their traditional emphasis on cleanliness, regular cell inspections and consistent standards. And I felt I could see improvements in all these categories in the Yorkshire prisons, even though the violence statistics remained stubbornly high. Wormwood Scrubs in London also showed some improvement, although it was more mixed. I had asked for the number of dog teams to be increased from two to nine, and the dogs were beginning to find more packages containing phones and drugs. The Standards Coaching Team had improved cell inspections. The governor was making sure prisoners had the kettles and bedding to which they were entitled. But in the textile workshops a Sikh prisoner told me he only felt safe 'about three-quarters of the time'. And I was not sure how long the improvements could last. An older prison officer said, 'Running Wormwood Scrubs is like pulling on an elastic band, eventually you tire and it reverts to horror.'

Our second priority prison in London confused me. Its governor was three years younger than me. She had entered in an accelerated graduate trainee scheme, and unlike the Yorkshire governors had not spent decades as a uniformed officer, walking the landings. While the governor of Leeds wore a waistcoat and a lavender tie fixed with a Windsor knot and a glittering tiepin, she patrolled the prison in a T-shirt and called her prisoners 'my boys'. She was intelligent and idealistic, but she continued to question my ideas on prison management.

A prison charity invited us both to speak in the heavily ornamented hall of a city livery company. An ex-prisoner in a smart white shirt, buttoned to the neck, introduced us both. He said, 'If it wasn't for the charity, I'd probably be back inside, eating off a greasy blue plate and sleeping with cockroaches. Now I'm working as an exhibition host.' I praised the charity. Then I introduced the ten-prisons project. I explained that we were aiming to reduce violence partly through checklists and getting the basics right. When the London governor stood up to make her speech after me, she began, 'I disagree with the minister. Managing prisons isn't about processes. It's about love.' The room applauded.

After the event, I suggested it might be better if we didn't contradict each other on a public stage. Our argument went on that evening, and then over three more visits to her prison. We seemed to be trapping each other into caricatures – she felt I was using too many analogies from the military, and I, that she was talking a great deal about therapy.

Hoping to resolve these arguments, I asked Ed Vainker, the young head of a school of 900 pupils in West London to speak to the governors of the ten prisons on a video conference. Ed's face was pale and drawn, his suit loose on his shoulders. On the screen, at least, he looked exhausted. He was running a school with one of the highest percentages of pupils with special needs and poverty in the country.

His students shared the backgrounds and challenges of many of our prisoners.

'To work with them,' he said, 'requires love: home visits, relationships with families, and a strong mental health service.' The London governor nodded enthusiastically. 'But it also,' he continued, 'requires standards, expectations, and discipline: clear and consistently enforced rules on behaviour, on clothing, on punctuality. People from chaotic backgrounds benefit from structure.' I nodded enthusiastically. When I pressed him on whether the governor should have allowed the man to shout in his face, he said quite simply, 'No. Of course not.' Although he had barely set foot in a prison in his life, he was definite: 'One person's bad behaviour should not undermine the atmosphere and potential of an entire group. Ignoring bad behaviour is not kindness, it's abrogation of responsibility and a lack of respect.'

His approach to education in the most challenging environment had already delivered some of the best academic results in the country. 'There's a misconception that places are either rigorous or they're sort of nurturing and cuddly and that you make a choice. You should be both. You should be "loving strict".'

On my next visit to the London prison, I began to sense that the governor and I agreed more in practice than we did in theory. She still didn't want to talk about 'process' but I noticed she was frank and tough on staff corruption. She still teased me about my obsession with broken windows, but she had established large maintenance teams, which kept the cells and outdoor areas clean. And she was doing many things in the prison which were not being done elsewhere. She had set up scaffolding training, for example, which was leading to jobs on release, she had good systems for dealing with gang activity, and I particularly admired her regular think-tank meetings with prisoners, where she took their feedback on what was going wrong.

The phrase 'loving strict' from the headmaster began to give us a concept which could pull us to a common ground. She had hated my saying we should run a prison 'at least as well as a good Travelodge'. But she was willing to acknowledge that prisoners needed to rely on professional responses, on getting their toilet paper and blankets on time. She still refused to set targets on violence – 'I deliberately steer away from hard targets' – but she was determined to create a safer prison.

Although she questioned my insistence on more gate procedures as a way of reducing drugs, she implemented our processes, and added some of her own, insisting that her prison officers could only each take in one clear plastic bag, run through an X-ray scanner, to ensure there was no issue of staff smuggling drugs. And she came to me at the end of three months to say our insistence on better searching had made a difference: drug-taking in her prison had reduced by 50 per cent in that period.

I sensed that the time we spent arguing and walking the landings had changed my perspective too. I was beginning to concede I needed to talk much more generously about things other than order and discipline: that soulless control in a prison was only slightly better than well-meaning chaos, and that I needed to put as much emphasis on deep empathy as on good process.

It was Hull prison, however, that seemed the best embodiment of our emerging vision. Rick Stuart, the governor, had a tanned face, broad hands and an air of practicality, fringed with thoughtfulness, like a land agent who was fond of reading. Hull was tough, old and overcrowded. But Rick Stuart had avoided the staff turnover of other prisons, and built one of the most experienced teams in the country. The yards were clean, the segregation cells were used only for short periods, and prisoners were generally out of their cells in high-quality classes.

He had written a new motto on every banner in the prison: 'A prison safe for prisoners, safe for prison officers, safe for families.' And he had achieved one of the lowest drugs and violence rates in any local prison in the country. He centred the prison around traditions – the war memorial and trophy cabinet. But he was also quick to embrace new training and new scanners. And as I travelled around the other nine prisons in the group, I began to promote Hull as our model.

★

Nine months after my promise to resign, we received our third-quarter figures for the ten prisons. And found that violence was finally coming down. Hundreds of people – governors with their very different backgrounds, cultures and priorities, the prison officers, the brigadier, the Standards Coaching Team and the civil servants in London – had concentrated on improving these ten prisons for three-quarters of a year. They had not used the traditional methods of reducing prison populations, importing more 'pliable' prisoner groups or increasing staffing numbers. We had increased budgets a little but, as the unions acknowledged, this increase was small compared to overall expenditure.

The biggest difference between these prisons before and after was our focus on getting a few basics right. We had concentrated on challenging violence, fixing windows, installing scanners, improving search procedures at gates, conducting better cell inspections, ensuring prisoners received the kit to which they were entitled, cleaning public areas, and setting clearer expectations on safety and decency. We had learned to harness the different experiences of Yorkshire and London governors, without smoothing out the contradictions. We had given both less and more trust to prison officers – searching them for drugs at the gate, but also allowing them to carry defensive sprays. We had focused on making life better for prisoners, but we had also set more demanding standards of behaviour. We had held opposing principles in tension – being, as the headmaster had said, 'loving strict'.

Nothing had at first seemed less suited to my life and background than making me prisons minister. But I had come to love this job in a way that I had never come to love being a Foreign Office or development minister. Most of my time had been spent in the Victorian inner-city jails from Cardiff, through Leeds to York. And although I visited some of the prisons enough to see the same officers or even prisoners three times, I was always a visiting minister able only occasionally to glimpse the reality of what might be going on beneath the dry summary of offences in the discipline ledgers, and behind the layer after layer of paint on the cell walls.

I never lost my sense of how disheartened I would have felt as a prisoner to spend twenty hours a day locked with a stranger, defecating in front of them on an open toilet, sharing their body odour and anxieties in an over-heated cell. I remembered the sound of screaming from the segregation cell in Brixton, the muscles on the favoured inmates who Chelmsford used to help police the landings, the gangs separated onto different landings in Liverpool, the sullen aggression from the Islamist groups in Belmarsh, and the pleas from elderly educated sex-offenders in Dartmoor. I never lost my sense of how frightened I would have been to be pushed onto an over-crowded landing when the violent assaults were rising every week. I never lost my admiration for the governors – whether in suits or T-shirts – who pushed themselves into this turbulent ocean every morning and managed to balance pride in their work, respect for the inmates and running a secure facility, while retaining their compassion and humour.

Those months spent in ministry offices, on iron railings in narrow Victorian blocs, with victims of crime, probation officers, judges and prisoners, were both a shameful indictment of the squalid ineptitude of British government, and a revelation of extraordinary, sometimes almost beautiful qualities in prison officers and prisoners. It was the first role in government that I had really loved.

And then there were the results. None of what we had done had been an academic trial, and we had not compared these prisons with randomised control groups. So we could not prove how much of the improvement in violence was down to our approach. But regardless of who or what should take the credit, something had changed. The violence rate had increased every quarter for five years, until December 2018 – from 10,000 to 30,000 assaults a year. In April 2019, it had reduced by 17 per cent on average across all the ten prisons. In eight of the ten, the curve had not just been flattened but it was coming down, by more than 25 per cent.

I had fulfilled my promise and I wouldn't have to resign. More importantly, these prisons had gone from being shamefully unstable,

filthy and dangerous to becoming slightly more decent environ-
ments. The quantity of drugs had reduced, the number of prisoners
and prison officers being attacked and injured had decreased, and,
despite all the problems, the landings were calmer, more orderly,
more decent: safer, as Rick, the governor of Hull prison, liked to say,
'for prisoners, for prison officers and for families'.

PART SIX

20.

The Vanishing Middle

(November 2018–April 2019)

On the afternoon of Wednesday 14 November 2018, when I was still in the middle of the arguments over prisons, a friend called. He had just come from the Cabinet meeting in which Theresa May had presented her final 'Withdrawal Agreement' with the EU. I took his call on a run in Hyde Park, passing the swan-boats on the Serpentine, and about to turn onto Rotten Row.

Michael Gove, a leading Brexiteer, had, my friend said, supported the proposal in Cabinet. But prominent voices in the Remain campaign – Liz Truss, the Chief Secretary to the Treasury, and Jeremy Hunt, the new Foreign Secretary – had turned angrily against the proposal, claiming it conceded too much to the EU. So had Gavin Williamson, who had been a particular favourite of both David Cameron and Theresa May. The arguments in Cabinet had gone on for five hours.

'Did these people not understand the deal before?'

'I've no idea,' my friend replied. 'Liz, Jeremy and Gavin are Remainers. They have spent two years agreeing the outline and hearing why this is the best deal Europe will offer. And now they are going to trash it. And start leaking . . .'

I felt privileged to have been given a glimpse into this Cabinet argument, but I discovered the following morning that every newspaper had also received a detailed account of almost every word spoken – generally from the perspective of Liz Truss and Gavin Williamson.

The following morning the Withdrawal Agreement was released to the general public and to more junior ministers, such as me. I ploughed through the 585 pages, following the web of references into other agreements, directives and EU regulations, which seemed to add up to another 1,000 pages. Then I phoned academics and civil servants, to make sure I had understood the pile of paper on my desk. It felt like trying to read the Koran or the Book of Revelation without the help of a theologian.

The more I focused on the document, the more impressed I was with the achievement of Theresa May and her team. My instinct, immediately after the referendum, had been to take a pre-existing customs union deal from the EU and implement it quickly before Britain split over the issue. Theresa May had succeeded in getting a more thoughtful compromise than I had feared possible. Her deal honoured, I felt, the priorities of the majority of Brexit voters (by putting controls on European immigration and leaving the political structures of the EU), while also doing all it could to limit damage to the UK economy (by keeping close regulatory alignment on trade), and protecting peace in Northern Ireland (through the 'backstop' which avoided customs borders between Britain, Northern Ireland and the EU). It would leave Britain closely aligned with Europe, diplomatically and economically, without being part of EU government structures.

On the way back from breakfast at Brixton prison the next day, I received a text from the chief whip asking me to start defending the deal to the media, on the lawn in front of Parliament. It didn't occur to me to wonder how many people had turned him down before me. I found the lawn packed with perhaps 400 cameramen, technicians, producers and journalists: some in tents, some on stages, and a few with tea urns. The less well-resourced shivered by the gate. A crowd was already on the pavements, waving banners, and shouting slogans, which I could not understand. I walked through the gate towards the tents. As I did so, my phone rang. A special adviser from Number 10 had spotted me on the edge of a camera shot.

'What are you doing, Rory?'

'I was asked—'

'You are not on the grid. Get out of there.'

I hung up and looked around. The grid was the government-approved schedule for media appearances. I could see other MPs, whom I knew to be enemies of the deal, beginning to approach the cameras. There was no government minister in sight. Defying Number 10 was potentially career-ending, but I felt that the chief whip was right, and that if we didn't start defending the deal immediately, it was dead, so I walked up to the first media station I could find – an Arab station at the gate – and began talking. I then moved on to the tents of Sky News, LBC and the BBC.

Over the next two hours, I answered questions from a dozen different channels. None of my interviewers seemed to have read the Withdrawal Agreement, but almost every interview began and concluded with the assumption that the deal was a disaster. Often the channels made me debate Conservative colleagues on the Brexit right. Most of the Brexiteers were clutching copies of the Withdrawal Agreement, with Post-it notes prominently displayed halfway through: implying, implausibly, that they had mastered the whole text.

The core of their complaint was about the backstop, which because it would require aligning with some EU regulations, they dubbed 'vassalage'. They all insisted that they could secure 'a better deal', that 'no-deal was better than this deal', and that 'Theresa May had to go'. It sounded as though they had agreed their lines long before anyone had had a chance to read the Withdrawal Agreement. In response, I tried to explain the strengths of Theresa May's compromise, and to expose some of my colleagues' faux-archaic nostalgia; their polite appeals to darker prejudices; their lack of thought about the economic impact of Brexit on the poor; and their wilful blindness to the EU's interests.

Just as I was concluding that the main threat to the deal came from hard Brexiteers, however, I found myself under attack from Remainers as well. The giant TV screens on College Green opposite Parliament now showed Tony Blair laying into what he dubbed a 'terrible' deal, and insisting that Theresa May had been humiliated by the European negotiators. Blair apparently believed that by trashing the deal he could keep Britain in the European Union, and he was untroubled by the legitimacy he was giving to the complaints of the Tory right. The deal wasn't 'a compromise', he said, but 'a capitulation'. 'Remainers like me,' he thundered, 'and Leavers like Boris Johnson are now in an unholy alliance: we agree this . . . is not the best of a bad job but the worst of all worlds.'

I, by contrast, believed that this deal was the best hope of healing a divided country. The fact that neither Tony Blair nor Jacob Rees-Mogg was happy with this deal made me feel we might have found the right compromise. As I went from podcasts to TV interviews and radio phone-ins, I found myself increasingly angry. I was shedding the role of a departmental manager and becoming a participant in a knife-fight about national identity. To my surprise, I lost the queasiness about confrontational politics, which I had felt during the Scottish referendum. I could see the point of political argument now.

My language simplified, and I developed slogans. 'This is a good, pragmatic, realistic deal, achieved against formidable odds,' I insisted on BBC's *Newsnight*. 'The alternative is a no-deal no-plan Brexit,' I told the BBC news channel. 'MPs would be taking a huge risk with our economy if they rejected it,' I growled at Nick Robinson. To Adam Boulton at Sky, I maintained, 'Another referendum would solve nothing – the only sensible prospect is to unite around the prime minister's plan.'

Thousands of Twitter messages began flowing to my phone: 'TRAITOR is the word I would use for you', 'RESIGN YOU TRAITOR TO DEMOCRACY'. A Remainer wrote to me, 'We will never ever forgive or forget – it's an agreement with bigotry and racism at its heart.' A Brexiteer wrote, 'The deal is enslavement . . . This is not compromise it is surrender and servitude. The Surrender Act and your part in its creation will never be forgotten. This sort of propaganda is usually attributed to the Nazi, Joseph Goebbels. I would suggest you resign and hold a by-election but you, sir, would have neither the honour nor the balls to do so.' The 'sir' seemed intended to imbue the insult with eighteenth-century panache.

But I still could not believe that the British public was violently divided between people who thought a second referendum realistic, and those who believed in the benefits of a hard or no-deal Brexit. In one of the radio interviews, I suggested there might be a fringe of 10 per cent at either end. But this was a nation famed for its moderation and compromise since the Glorious Revolution. On about my twelfth interview I said, '80 per cent of the population support the deal.' The interviewer seized on this statistic immediately. I tried to apologise but it was too late to clarify that I should have said 'I think 80 per cent of the population would support the deal, if they were given a chance to understand it.' Remainers and hard Brexiteers both triumphantly shared the evidence that I was a liar as well as a traitor.

While I was doing interviews, the Brexit Secretary Dominic Raab resigned from the Cabinet along with the Secretary of State for Work and Pensions Esther McVey. Later, the prime minister's chief of staff called to thank me for my loyalty and to apologise that I hadn't been put in the Cabinet in their place. I said I was not simply defending the deal for a promotion: I believed in it. The idea that I was genuinely enthusiastic about the Withdrawal Agreement seemed to confuse him for a moment. He returned to the more reassuring idea that I was showing loyalty, and suggested I would get the next slot that opened in Cabinet.

It appeared likely that Michael Gove, who was under great pressure from his former Brexit allies, would be the next to resign. This seemed a bad idea to me because if such a prominent Brexiteer walked out, Theresa May's Cabinet would collapse. I sent Michael an effusive message, praising him and encouraging him to stay in the Cabinet. He did so. Though presumably not because of my text.

For a few days the party seemed to regain its balance. The European Research Group (ERG) – the gathering of MPs most committed to a hard Brexit – announced via the languorous Edwardian drawl of Jacob Rees-Mogg that they were toppling Theresa May, but proved unable to muster sufficient numbers.

The second-referendum campaign, however, was just getting going. Four days after the publication of the Withdrawal Agreement, two men and one woman came separately to see me in the House of Commons coffee shop. I had grown up reading the first man's thoughtful, determined, account of living with dissidents in Central

Europe. I had seen first-hand the conflict-resolution work of the second in Iraq. And I revered the third, a handsome painter, fisherman and journalist, for his character, his novels, and for his generosity.

I sat with them in the cold glass-roofed atrium, cradling a cappuccino. Each in turn told me that they could not accept the result of the referendum. Their arguments were already as hard, crisp and intricate as ivory chess pieces. The Brexit campaigners had lied, they said. Brexit voters had not understood what they were voting for. One added it was an illegal process shaped by Russian money. All three insisted that the referendum was 'only advisory' and those voting in favour were not a majority of adults in the country, because not everyone had voted. For all these reasons, they insisted, the result was not binding, and we should remain in the European Union.

I did not know how to reconcile their theories with our other democratic events – including my own election to Parliament. There was hardly an MP who had been elected by the majority of the adults in their constituency, taking into account turnout, and if we came even a single vote ahead in the final result, we were still considered the legitimate winner. We often faced accusations of electoral lies, voters' ignorance, illegal processes and foreign money too, but elections could only be overturned by the courts – not simply rejected by the losing side. Our parliamentary system depended on realism about voters and elections, and good faith from the losers. But these formal-sounding arguments were also a cloak for an emotional stand-off, an irreconcilable difference on whether we should be managing Brexit to avoid its worst impacts, or just rejecting it entirely.

I argued that I had voted Remain, not least because of the damage Brexit would do to my own constituency. I agreed that it had been a mistake to hold the referendum in the first place – not least because of the divisions it had created. But every MP from every party had promised during the referendum campaign to respect the result, regardless of who won. There had been a very high turnout and Brexit had won by over a million votes. This was why I had become almost the only MP to fight hard in the media for Theresa May's Brexit deal.

They replied that it was incomprehensible that I, whom they had 'previously considered intelligent', could take this line. The conflict-resolution expert suggested that I had sadly become a coward, and a careerist, bending to the whips. I became heated, and said that all their complicated constitutional arguments were just alibis for the fact that they hated the result: if the vote had gone their way, they would have accepted the smallest majority and the most contested process. My conversation with the painter and journalist degenerated into a shouting match in which I roared that his attitude to Brexit voters was a form of elitism, and his willingness to overturn a democratic event because he didn't like the outcome, a form of populism. Painful arguments between friends were now, I sensed, breaking out in every household across Britain.

For eight and a half years, the government had been an elective dictatorship run by the prime minister, and Parliament an elderly, smelly Labrador, asleep by the fire. Once a year, perhaps, someone would step so hard on our tail that we would snap, and in doing so stop the redesigning of the House of Lords, or the Syria bombing; but generally we were entirely passive. We, the Conservative MPs, voted loyally for the government day in day out, late into the night.

But Brexit had transformed the conventions of British politics. The generally loyal, if grumpy, mass of Conservative MPs had been turned into warring Brexiteers and Remainers. As soon as the Withdrawal Agreement was published, the first volleys were fired in an artillery battle of obscure parliamentary procedures: motions, amendments, bills, humble addresses, and threats of prorogation – tactics which in some cases had not been employed in this way for centuries. Just before we broke for the Christmas recess, 117 Brexit-minded Conservative MPs voted to remove Theresa May, but 200 of us continued to back her. In January, the same group combined with Labour to defeat her Withdrawal Agreement in the House of Commons by 230 votes. (The ERG marketed this as 'the largest government loss since 1265'.)

But many of the MPs who were voting against Theresa May had still not read the Withdrawal Agreement. The same was true of many of those who were voting for her, as well. I asked an ex-minister in the tea room why she had voted against the deal.

'To be honest,' she said, 'I don't like it.'

'So what change could we make to it, to make you vote for it?' I asked.

'I can't answer that question because I don't understand it.'

I worked on a member of the ERG through whispered arguments in the library.

'Please, compromise with us,' I begged. 'If we don't get a deal, we are going to plunge off a cliff edge with no-deal. With literally nothing in place for our largest trading partner.'

'That's not our fault,' she replied. 'We are trying hard. But we have principles. We've offered solutions. If we crash out it will be because of your stubbornness, not ours.'

'What concessions can we offer which might convince you to vote for the deal?'

'I don't know,' she said. 'But there are better deals.'

'Which deals?'

'Look, Rory, if you want a detailed argument speak to John Redwood, not me.' John Redwood, a fellow of All Souls as well as an MP, seemed to have become the intellectual conscience of the ERG.

'Please could you just meet us halfway?'

'No,' the politician concluded grandly, 'I am not doing politics.'

I was now in the media almost every day, as one of the only defenders of Theresa May's deal. A colleague began to compare me to Saddam Hussein's hapless press spokesman Muhammad Saeed al-Sahhaf, better known as 'Comical Ali'. But I felt increasingly passionate about the deal – and increasingly troubled by what would happen to the economy and Northern Ireland if we failed to get it through. Other colleagues were equally fervent for a second referendum, or a no-deal Brexit. The House of Commons – so lamentable and inert a few months earlier – was packed, and the speeches increasingly passionate.

But authority was leaching away from all of us. The referendum, by giving a direct say to the general public, had made Parliament a low-lying island in a rough and rising sea. And many of the people, having 'spoken', began to perceive parliamentary debates and votes as just different forms of obfuscation, delay and betrayal. As January 2019 became February, the *ex cathedra* pronouncements of Tony Blair, the inventive parliamentary manoeuvres of the ERG and the bewildered complaints of the EU negotiators were being intensified by the vortex of radio phone-ins and Twitter storms.

Think tanks began to back Conservative MPs in sketching out their own alternatives to the Withdrawal Agreement: Max Fac, the Sanghera Scheme, the Malthouse Compromise and the Brady Amendment. The most radical proposal was for no-deal with the European Union. This sounded like a straightforward Anglo-Saxon thing but it was simply an absence, which pretended to be a presence; the negation of a deal, masked as a type of deal, a proposal that would drop the UK into the worst trading conditions available. Only a few specialists really understood the content of these proposals. But many more championed them loudly. Brexit began to take on some of the significance that I imagined the doctrine of the Trinity held for the people of late antiquity. As with the debates in the homoousian–Arian controversy, or indeed those in Lilliput about which end of an egg to crack, the key was not so much the detailed theology of the backstop itself, but the ability of politicians to convince their supporters to feel that this issue was worth fighting over. They sought to make a technical dispute tribal; to make their clan hate both the backstop and the supporters of the backstop, without ever being able to fully explain it.

Meanwhile, second-referendum campaigners were portraying their opponents in terms that seemed increasingly identical to those used by the other side. The hard Brexiteers argued that 'the real people' were being blocked by politicians, who had conspired with the Treasury and the European superstate to produce dishonest doomsday predictions. At the same time, in the hard Remain story, Brexiteers were portrayed as an unrepresentative coalition of the racist and the uneducated; the marginalised and the elderly, duped by an elite who had stolen the referendum with lies on the sides of buses, big data and Russian money.

The Brexit leader, Nigel Farage, referred to the BBC as the 'Brussels Broadcasting Corporation', while a Remain leader, Andrew Adonis, called it the 'Brexit Broadcasting Corporation'. Both factions claimed that the attempt of people like me to chart a moderate compromise between them was a formula for the worst of all worlds. Both supported democratic votes, elections, Parliament and the courts only when these institutions produced the results they wanted. And, when they didn't, both sides were willing to abuse parliamentary procedure and bypass public votes in the name of 'the people'.

An opinion poll showed that only half of Brexiteers or Remainers were now happy to even talk to someone from the other camp, and only a quarter were happy for their child to marry 'out'. A Conservative donor whom I had considered a friend, emailed: 'Rory – hello – your views on Brexit are – like so many bubble-inhabiting, superficial Remainers – ill informed; you have turned traitor to your party . . . egocentric and arrogant. It's a great shame that someone previously so self-aware and realistic should have now turned his life into such a giant ego trip.'

When I made the arguments for Theresa May's deal in my own constituency, I seemed to convince most of the members of the association. But I had to repeat the same speech to them six weeks later and answer all the same questions. Another month, and they had reverted again to hating a Withdrawal Agreement, which none of them had yet read.

Back in London, I was holding my four-year-old's hand when an old lady tottered down the aisle towards me at the end of a church service. I smiled encouragingly at her, expecting to introduce my son, and she said loudly, with a voice inflected by listening to the pulpit, 'You should be ashamed to be alive.' Waiting for a Tube, I was approached by a man who smiled, and when I returned his smile, shouted 'Brexiteer c**t,' and walked away with a flushed and warped grin of triumph. Such encounters lingered like the sting of a slap on the face, and I brooded over them for days.

*

On 13 March, David Gauke abstained on a rebel amendment in order to try to block a no-deal Brexit. The Brexit wing of the Conservative Party erupted in anger, insisting that David Gauke had to be fired from the Cabinet, because by abstaining on a three-line whip he had broken the principle of government collective responsibility. The chief whip tracked me down behind the Speaker's Chair, and told me that the Queen had agreed to my appointment as Lord Chancellor in David's place. It was an extraordinary promotion to the most ancient office of state, but I felt guilty towards David. Not least because I had been strongly tempted to abstain with him. David, however, was graceful and encouraging. 'You did the right thing. We need your voice in the Cabinet to continue the fight.' In the Cabinet meeting the following morning, a group of ministers threatened to resign if David was fired, and Theresa May backed down. David remained as Lord Chancellor and my immediate boss. I was relieved. He was the one person I truly admired in the Cabinet.

Theresa May brought her Withdrawal Agreement back for a third and final time on 29 March 2019. This time, by promising to resign as prime minister if the deal was passed, she won back the majority of the Brexiteers, including Jacob Rees-Mogg and Boris Johnson. Only twenty-eight – buoyed by watching Hollywood's *300* – held out, calling themselves 'the Spartans'. There were hopes that Labour might now support the deal, since it was far closer to their theoretical position than a hard or no-deal Brexit. But the Labour leader Jeremy Corbyn, and his new Brexit Secretary Keir Starmer, remained determined never to 'vote with the Tories', and imposed a three-line whip against the deal for the third time.

To win, Theresa May needed to bring over twenty-nine more MPs from about eighty potential allies among the DUP, Remainers and Labour MPs more sympathetic to her deal. She failed to secure any. In a continuation of Tony Blair's 'unholy partnership', nine Remain-supporting Conservative colleagues solemnly walked into the lobbies alongside the hard Brexiteers, and killed the Withdrawal Agreement with the support of the Labour Party.

★

As it became clear that the government – having failed three times in Parliament – could not present the deal again, Parliament itself took control of the process, holding indicative votes to see if the MPs could form a majority for some other form of deal. Like almost everyone else I had fallen into a faction, with our own solution. Our group had been meeting for weeks in Nicholas Soames's vast Commons office, among his pile of papers and Churchillian memorabilia. We thought of ourselves as trying to get a moderate Brexit done – avoiding a border with Ireland, retaining close economic ties to Europe, and delivering on the demand for control over immigration. For many others, of course, we were traitors.

I believed the simplest way to achieve our vision, in the absence of the Withdrawal Agreement, was to remain in the European customs union. After all, the backstop had been a form of customs union. I, therefore, drafted a simple amendment with a friend and persuaded Ken Clarke to put his name to it. I then spoke to Keir Starmer and Corbyn's director of strategy and communications, Seumas Milne, to confirm Labour support, winning the promise of their 230 votes. I now needed only thirty-six of the 250 conservative colleagues who had just voted for the prime minister's very similar deal. I began to seek out as many as I could, one by one. Here, I felt, was our last chance to avoid a hard Brexit. I brought to the cause all the slogans, emotions and arguments I had honed over four months in television studios, and fifty public meetings.

But I soon discovered that by redescribing the deal as the customs union, I was winning Labour members at the cost of alienating almost all Conservatives. Conservative colleagues who had been prepared to vote for Theresa May's backstop were not prepared to vote for it when it was made explicit. An older minister stopped me in the lobby and barked that I was breaking collective responsibility by whipping for my amendment, and then showed me with delight the WhatsApp messages he was sending whipping against it. The majority of the Whips' Office were also whipping against me, using the very phrase 'customs union' as a totemic curse, and terrifying MPs with what their constituents would say, if they voted for such a thing. Most strikingly, an hour before the vote, and two and a half years after the referendum, two ministers asked me to tell them what a customs union was.

Little of this mattered if I could win over the DUP of Northern Ireland. My amendment avoided a border in the Irish Sea and the risk of a political collapse in Northern Ireland. I fell in step with the dapper Ian Paisley Jr, who betrayed no particular impatience at hearing my argument, which had been made to him and his colleagues a dozen times before. I said that I hoped he was not falling into the trap of believing Boris's promises not to create a border in the Irish Sea. He smiled broadly and said not to worry: they all knew Boris well. And yet, all ten of the DUP MPs, perhaps because they mistrusted any idea of 'compromise', would continue to vote the customs union down.

With the vote now very close, I fell back on desperate pleas to Conservative Remainers, some of whom were close friends. But three of those who favoured Remain were still determined to vote against any and every deal in the belief that this would win them a second referendum. Only one was even prepared to abstain. I was able to convince a Labour MP who had previously thought a customs union 'too soft'. But to my fury, I lost two Labour MPs who had been prepared to vote for the Withdrawal Agreement the night before; and two Conservatives, who had been prepared to vote for the customs union three days earlier, now said they had changed their minds.

Nevertheless, my numbers still worked – just. Ten minutes before the division, it was clear that if everyone who had promised to vote for us did, we would win a vote for a customs union, although it would come down to a single vote.

The vote was called. I stood inside the lobby, watching dozens of my colleagues voting against me, and almost the entire Labour Party voting for me. The numbers seemed to be moving in our direction. Then I found a close friend, still outside the lobby. And to my astonishment he seemed to be dithering about voting for our amendment.

'Tom,' I said, almost shouting, 'this is our very last chance to stop a hard Brexit. If we lose this, we are done.'

'I don't think it is, Rory. There will be other chances to block a hard Brexit.'

'No. Tom, I have been in the middle of this fight now for five months. This is the last chance. If we lose this, we're done.'

'I disagree,' he said and to my horror proceeded, not to abstain but to vote against the amendment. Meanwhile, George, another junior minister, who had promised to vote for it, never appeared. He claimed later to have fallen asleep in the library.

We lost only by Tom's vote and George's abstention. It was 1 April 2019. April Fool's Day.

Nothing had changed and everything had changed. The maths of Parliament remained the same. Most Conservative MPs had voted for Theresa May's backstop and most Labour MPs for the customs union. A new prime minister, with a more collegial approach, still had a strong chance of getting some version of a moderate Brexit through.

But the twenty-eight hard Brexiteers in the ERG were certain that they had won. Their next plan was to elect a new prime minister committed to a hard Brexit and to complete the transformation of the Conservative Party into a populist party of the right. It still seemed difficult to believe that they could pull this off – since their numbers had been reduced in the final vote on the Withdrawal Agreement to only twenty-eight out of 300 Conservative MPs. But many of those who had sat in Theresa May's Cabinet and voted three times for the deal, were suddenly beginning to sound strangely like the hardliners in the ERG.

21

Secretary of State

All my media appearances, frantic lobbying attempts, parliamentary manoeuvres and conspiracies in light-filled rooms were taking place as I continued to work as a Cumbrian MP and a prisons minister. They were happening in the margins of visits to Perth prison; to the Cook County Jail in Chicago; and fifteen weekend advice surgeries in Cumbria, where I visited half a dozen primary schools; milked cows; inspected cheese factories, and gluten-free biscuit facilities; fought against cuts to the fire service; and negotiated with the Highways Agency to accelerate the dualling of the A66.

In April 2019 I had a new electronic tag fitted to my ankle in the Ministry of Justice to test a technology which was supposed to allow the safe release of prisoners. It would, I was told, track every metre of my journey from London to Cumbria. It tracked me to Portcullis House. There, in the rough concrete bunker that served as a meeting room, I met two MPs. The first, a seventy-one-year-old with rich brown hair and a blazing Labour red blouse, had been a Merseyside councillor for forty years. The second, in a Special Forces Club tie, was a young Conservative colonel, representing a wealthy seat south of London.

The Labour MP told me of her four-year-old constituent, Violet-Grace, who had been killed by a man driving at 83 mph in a 30 mph zone. The offender had been sentenced to nine years. She wanted a new law called 'Violet-Grace's Law', which would sentence him to life imprisonment. The Conservative MP told me of his six-year-old constituent, Tony, who had been beaten so badly by his father that he had lost the use of his legs. The offender had been sentenced to ten years. He also wanted a new law called 'Tony's Law', which would sentence him to life imprisonment.

Both were newer to Parliament than me – one addressing me as a Labour leader might a council executive, the other as a colonel might his adjutant. I tried to acknowledge the horror for the victims, the distress of these families and the pressure of fierce constituency campaigns. But I also tried to explain why the law made a distinction between deliberate murder, unintentional manslaughter and grievous bodily harm, and the pressures that longer sentences were imposing on our overcrowded prisons.

But the MPs were not there to hear my or the department's side of the story. I had been through the same story before with six other MPs each campaigning for a tragic case, branded with the Christian names of the victim. These MPs had already made commitments to families and constituents, contributed to the crowd-funding campaigns, and presented petitions long before they came to see me. The meetings were only preludes to press releases in local newspapers. And they would keep pushing until they found a minister willing to put these laws on the statute book.

The colonel had just taken his press photo with me when my private secretary re-entered, and whispered that Gavin Williamson had just been fired as Defence Secretary for leaking from the National Security Council, and that I was wanted in Number 10 to be promoted.

After almost nine years in Parliament, I was to be given full responsibility for a whole department, and a seat at the Cabinet table. And with violence finally down in prisons, I felt I was free to take a new role. As I hurried out of a side door of the House of Commons, across Whitehall, emerging briefly into a cold damp afternoon, I tried to look as smart and soldierly as possible. I was led up to the yellow drawing room in Number 10. Time passed. My cup of tea got cold, waiting for some milk which never arrived. I admired the eighteenth-century furniture. I remembered my previous meeting in this room in which President Nana of Ghana had inverted the normal relationship between an African and British leader. ('So, Prime Minister,' Nana had drawled, 'I wondered – having talked to my friends in Europe – whether there is anything we can do to encourage you to reconsider and rejoin the European Union.') I was, I realised, now going to be sitting every week in the Cabinet and the National Security Council. I would be summoned to receive my seals of office and be made a privy councillor by the Queen.

I was particularly proud of the thought of becoming Defence Secretary – it was a serious job, dealing with a military which I admired more than almost every other institution in British life, and I was honoured that she took me seriously enough to give me such a role. But none of it was quite how I had imagined my path. This was to be my sixth ministerial role in four years. Five years of punishment for my rebellion, a stumbling progress through reshuffles, was being rewarded with preferment off the back of a colleague who had been sacked. Theresa May's government was on its knees, and I felt I would have very little time to get anything done.

I tried to think what I needed to ask from the prime minister in order to have the best start at the Ministry of Defence, drawing on my conclusions as chair of the Defence Committee: I felt we needed to focus more on the army, and less on the navy, more on Europe, and less on the Pacific. I didn't like the waste of money on aircraft carriers, I wanted us to learn from the US Marine Corps, which had formed a much larger and more effective deployable fighting force on a smaller budget; I favoured more UN deployments, more units with area expertise in the Middle East and Africa, and more focus on the threat from Russia. I planned to use my brief meeting with the prime minister to sketch out my plans, and secure the beginnings of a mandate for reform.

When, half an hour later, a smiling aide led me into the Cabinet Room, I strode in with my chin up, chest out and shoulders back, resisting a strong temptation to salute the prime minister. She sat on the far side of the Cabinet table, exactly where she had sat when she had made me prisons minister. Her eyes flashed, and there was a hint of a smile. She did not rise to greet me. I smiled back and realised how much I liked as well as admired her, not least for what she had tried to do with Brexit. But I had never seen her so tired.

Three years earlier, she had informed me of my appointment as a Minister of State with the repressed excitement of a game-show host. But now she seemed to be simply pushing ahead out of duty.

She had sat in this room at that long table and replaced too many ministers, endured too many betrayals from those that she had once trusted, dealt with too many barbs and pleas from ministers who were seeking to distance themselves from her fading authority. She could not muster any drama now. 'I would like you,' she said simply, once I had sat down, 'to become Secretary of State for International Development.'

'Thank you, Prime Minister,' I said, trying to clear my disappointment at not getting the Ministry of Defence, 'of course I will do it.' Someone else I surmised was being reshuffled to Defence – probably the previous development minister. I was rewarded with a smile, which reminded me of how she looked when I had first saved her from an exhausting evening walking around tables in my constituency: a brief smile of relief. I was almost tempted to leave it at that. But I knew that this was my only chance to secure a mandate for reforming international development. I plunged on. 'I would like to request firstly, Prime Minister, that we use the DfID budget to double the number of staff on the ground, train them in languages and deepen their country expertise.'

'If you put that in writing,' she said, 'I can look at it.'

I felt I needed more than that. 'It will be neutral in terms of budget, Prime Minister – it is all within the 0.7 per cent – and I think it will protect the department from criticism and allow us to do much more. To create the kind of foreign and development policy that we have discussed in the past . . . It's essentially just extending what we did with the Africa strategy to the rest of the world.'

'I am certainly prepared to look at it,' she repeated.

'I would need some support with the Treasury.'

'Why?'

'Well it won't cost anything. But I believe they fear that other departments will be jealous if we increase staffing . . .'

'Okay . . .' she said, sounding a little puzzled.

And, I added, seeing another possibility, 'I think we could transfer money within the department to double our spend on climate and the environment.'

She looked at me but said nothing to that. I sensed I had

outstayed her patience. I thanked her, told her the proposal would be with her by the end of the week, shook her hand, and stood up. She gave that smile again, relieved perhaps this time that I had stopped negotiating, and wished me luck.

The whole conversation had taken less than five minutes. I would be lucky, outside of a brief intervention in a Cabinet meeting, if I got to discuss my portfolio with the prime minister again. It felt not as though I had been recruited to do a job, or joined her team, but instead as though she had, with distant benevolence, awarded me a prize. And not for the first time I wondered whether these ministerial roles were often anything more than symbolic gifts in exchange for loyalty – a chance to receive gold seals of office, attend the acclamation of the new monarch, be called the Right Honourable for the rest of your life and enter the House of Lords, as much as a responsibility for managing a departmental budget. But I had, I felt, got enough in that brief exchange to say to my department that I had shared a plan with the prime minister. At least, she had not objected.

I walked out of the black door of Number 10 and was guided to a new expensive electric Jaguar. A bank of journalists were shouting questions and taking photos. I smiled as politely as I could and got into the car. Instead of turning right out of Downing Street towards the Ministry of Justice, we turned left, up Whitehall. Everything that had been about to happen in my diary – my meetings with a High Court judge and an expert on Islamist radicalisation; my preparation for the Ten Minute Rule Bill on child cruelty, and my explanations of why we would not be supporting Violet-Grace's or Tony's Law – were all dropped in an instant on my successor. I had missed the meeting on Dartmoor prison now and would never be able to be sure I had convinced them not to close it.

We drove under Robert Adam's dolphin-topped screen, through the carriage gates into the courtyard of the Old Admiralty. A small group, led by the permanent secretary, escorted me up the side stairs. In the corridors a couple of people smiled and said, 'Welcome back.' Instead of turning into my old office, we went across the hall, to the grand new office, into which I had persuaded Priti

Patel to move three years earlier. As I sat down, I realised that I was still wearing my electronic tag on my ankle and, being back in the Department for International Development, had no equipment allowing me to take it off.

In my first meeting, in my new role, I was briefed by the permanent secretary, a tall, quiet diplomat whom I had known in the Foreign Office and then at the UN in New York. I told him that I had only two objectives: to double the number of DfID staff, and to double DfID's spend on climate and the environment. He listened to my overly optimistic account of my meeting with the prime minister, and said he would draft a letter to be sent to her for signature that day.

Then I asked the director generals, the next most senior officials, to come to see me. Unlike the permanent secretary, they were DfID veterans, and unlike him they opposed both my ideas. They had spent many months on my last posting in DfID arguing against my push for more staff, more language training and more involvement in monitoring and implementation. One of them had been arguing with me for fifteen years. They still wanted less of it all. And my new push on climate and environment seemed to be particularly unwelcome. I quoted a World Bank report which suggested that, if we did not address climate change, we would face 300 million more people in poverty in a decade.

The senior director general replied testily that 'by moving our immediate poverty work to climate, you are sacrificing the poor of today for the sake of the poor of tomorrow'.

The director generals controlled all the operations of the department. Their power to block any initiative was tremendous. Three years, even eighteen months earlier, I would have continued this discussion, trying to work through the arguments, persuade them of my logic, and manoeuvre them slowly into line. But this was my sixth ministerial appointment. I knew now that change in the British government did not come from winning arguments on merits.

Instead, without clearing it with Number 10, or the Treasury, or the permanent secretary, I went on the leading TV politics show that evening and I told viewers that under my leadership, climate

cataclysm would be our top priority, and the biggest single justifica-
tion for retaining the 0.7 per cent development spend. I made the
same statement to a *Guardian* journalist the following day. No reprimand came from the Treasury or Number 10. So the day after, I
used the opportunity of a response to an international-development
committee report to make a formal written commitment to increase
environmental spend. At the weekend, I tweeted that I would be
doubling DfID spend on climate and the environment. I was no
longer trying to act as a fellow civil servant arguing the case – I was
a politician who had made a promise publicly and repeatedly to
voters. I was claiming a public mandate.

My predecessor had agreed the Single Departmental Plan for the
next three years, just before she left. It rehearsed the DfID nostrums
with which I had struggled for twenty years. But she had not had
time to sign it. It was submitted to me for signature; I said I would
rewrite it.

Here even the permanent secretary balked. 'I'm afraid there is no
time, Secretary of State, it is due this week.'

'I will ask for an extension directly from the prime minister. We
will deliver in five weeks.'

'There is really no need, Secretary of State. It is only a formal
document. No one reads the Single Departmental Plan. It won't
constrain you in any way. I wouldn't waste your time.'

I disagreed. The old plan had been quoted against me repeatedly.
The new one would be too. I asked for climate and the environment
to be inserted. The senior director general tried to suggest that this
was not possible, that the International Development Act limited
the department's activities to poverty alleviation. But I knew that
the department had also signed up to the Sustainable Development
Goals, perhaps thinking that no one would read them either. I used
the goals to insert a new pillar called 'Planet' and put the phrase
'climate cataclysm' into the opening of the report. I followed it with
a commitment on transforming staffing, which came out in the
strangled compression and prolixity of a government report as
'more engagement with projects on the ground, and more local
expertise, and better-informed regional cadres'.

I lost the battle on jargon – the report went out in largely incomprehensible form – but I had, at least, a hook to which to attach new projects.

Now, I was not only a departmental minister: I was a Cabinet minister and privy councillor, with my seals of office given to me by the Queen, in a solemn ceremony in Windsor Castle, responsible for an entire department. Once a week, I entered and left Cabinet, through a bank of cameras and flashbulbs, as though I were on the red carpet at Cannes. Pictures of me and my Cabinet colleagues were printed on the front pages, columns tried to draw significance from whom we were seen leaving with, as though this was the Kremlin in 1979 and all information had to be guessed from positions on the stage at the military review. Inside, things were drabber. We congregated in the hallway near a plaster pillar, which I assumed was a Victorian fake with no structural function, around a coffee urn and a plate of digestive biscuits. Then we went to our prearranged seats at the table.

Cameron had loved the idea of rewarding people who were not Secretaries of State with a seat at the Cabinet table. Theresa May had reined this in a little. But still, in addition to the twenty-one Secretaries of State including me, running full departments, were at least nine others. Thirty was far too many for a sensible meeting. The practice was for us each to speak in turn, only once, rather than debate. There was almost no to and fro to test our ideas, no opportunity to persuade or compromise. It felt as stilted as reading statements at European Council meetings. We might as well have sent recorded statements and stayed away.

A number of my colleagues were already planning to take Theresa May's place, and seemed to want to use their speeches to sound prime ministerial with lengthy *tours d'horizon* which stretched well beyond their departmental boundaries. Michael Gove, the Secretary for Environment, Food and Rural Affairs, was the only candidate who managed to remain almost natural, always leaving his intervention till just before the very end, so he could summarise the other contributions with a neat witticism.

As a Secretary of State, I was entitled to bring in two paid special advisers from outside the Civil Service, to sit in my private office and represent me to Number 10 and the department. For development issues, I brought in Scott Liddle, who was languishing in the lower middle reaches of the Civil Service, where he had taken himself on the romantic assumption that it would allow him to grasp the spirit of the age through technical involvement in the Brexit negotiations. Scott was a six-foot-five redhead, fluent in Arabic and Farsi, who had spent two years with the International Committee of the Red Cross translating for prisoners in Libya, Algeria and Iraq. He had run our Turquoise Mountain operations in Afghanistan, and set up our operations with Syrian refugees in Jordan. I brought him in in part because he symbolised the new kind of field officer I wanted to recruit into DfID. He checked the progress of my reforms when smoking Ghanaian Rothmans on the pavement outside the department building and picking up gossip from other smokers, as though he were confirming rumours in the Aleppo souk.

For my chief of staff, I took Lizzie Loudon. She had been Theresa May's press spokesperson before joining me. Where Scott was large, quoted Virgil, and dressed in Boggi Milano suits, Lizzie was tiny, wore trainers and jeans to most formal meetings, spoke quietly and not in Latin. She had worked in the Downing Street culture formed by the legend of Alastair Campbell, which put an overweening communications director at the heart of every policy meeting, frequently suggesting the policy itself, and then using threats, obscenities and witchcraft to 'win' the narrative. The approach was less Alastair himself, and more a *Thick of It* caricature of how people believed he had once behaved. But it had captivated a generation. With this approach, the language was military. Messages must be 'disciplined'. The truth should be 'rationed'. The story should be 'gripped'. It should be 'pinned to the grid'. Journalists could be 'destroyed'. Articles were to be 'killed'.

But Lizzie didn't follow that model. She listened carefully in policy briefings and asked a few quiet questions. She didn't try to form policy. Instead, she encouraged me to talk in detail about policies to journalists. When I came to her with a minor scandal, she didn't try to destroy the story. Instead she encouraged me to admit what I had done and apologise clearly, rapidly and calmly. She warned me about the pushier or trickier journalists, but she was never tricky or pushy in return. She insisted that I honour the promises that she had made on my behalf, and never let down one journalist for a better offer, still less play them against each other. And as a result, although she never offered to kill a story, she was able to put rumours to bed, set the record straight and get a fair report, simply because journalists knew she never lied to them. She made us all more honest.

The best way of explaining what I was trying to do on the environment, Lizzie suggested, was to take journalists onto the ground. And we might as well start with the *Daily Mail*, as they were the department's leading critics. So I set off round Kenya, where I was photographed tickling the hairy lower lips of the only two remaining Northern White rhino, flopped in a boat through the last sections of coastal mangrove, and strolled through low-density cattle ranches, pondering predators. At the largest wind turbine array on the continent, I announced DfID's 'biggest single direct commitment to tackle climate change'.

The head of our DfID office in Kenya saw the point of this initiative. He used the climate money I had secured for him to make DfID the most influential environment donor in the country, brought President Kenyatta onside and helped to make Kenya central to the global climate conference. All of this was better than anything I had envisaged. And a reminder of how, regardless of the grand strategy, results depended on inspiring individual civil servants.

The National Security Council was a smaller affair than the Cabinet. Only seven of us were members. But it happened around the same Cabinet table, with the prime minister still at the centre, and the chancellor beside her, and the fringes now occupied by generals and intelligence officers, rather than other Cabinet ministers. Used to the US equivalents, I was surprised to discover no screens, no PowerPoint presentations, and few staff. I had known most of the security chiefs for fifteen years or more, because we had all been

closely involved, as younger, more junior, sometimes cheekier, players in Iraq, Afghanistan and the Balkans. I knew many of them
much better than I knew the politicians. And I enjoyed seeing them
now in their grandeur as Chief of the General Staff, or Chief of the
Secret Intelligence Service. But they must, like me, have despaired
about the quality of our discussions. For National Security brought
out some of the pompous sides of my colleagues. I watched one
Cabinet minister deliver an extempore lecture to patient ambassadors on a country he had visited twice, 'Iran you know is a much
more important country than some people realise,' and remind
senior intelligence officers, with thirty years of service in the Middle East, of the difference between Sunni and Shia.

Membership of the National Security Council meant that I had at
last, in theory at least, the power to do the things I had been struggling to do for three years as a minister, and nine as an MP – change
our policy in north-west Syria, and transform our intelligence posture. But, of course, it didn't work like that. Somehow the
intelligence agencies, who had told me they reported to the National
Security Council, now clarified that in fact they reported in one direction to the Foreign Secretary, but in another direction to a
subcommittee, which reported to the National Security adviser,
who in theory reported to the prime minister, who of course did
not have the expertise or time for such details.

This might have meant that the NSC focused only on larger
issues of strategic policy. But in practice, we seemed often to avoid
the larger issues such as the shape of our intelligence footprint or
global requirements and instead discussed particular tactical deployments, which I suspected in the US system would have been decided
by a two-star general. And as always, the lack of knowledge amongst
my political colleagues, the complexity of the subject and the
opaque committee structures, meant that there was little that I
would have recognised as civilian control and accountability over
the defence, intelligence and security services in these underwhelming proceedings.

Nevertheless, the council remained, in the public eye, a thing of
great mystery and prestige, presented as one of the deepest secrets

of our state. And each time I walked out from Downing Street after one of our meetings, apparently deep in thought, the cameras could capture the idea of a minister fresh from the profound mysteries of national security.

Meanwhile, Ebola cases in the eastern Democratic Republic of the Congo (DRC) had doubled in a month. Chris Whitty, the Chief Scientific Adviser to the Department of Health, came to see me. He made medical research sound complex and uncertain.

'What about a vaccine for Ebola?' I asked.

'Well there is a lot of work on vaccines – but vaccines take many years to develop, test and approve, and then it takes a long time to produce significant doses.'

'So there is no vaccine . . .'

'There is – the Canadians developed one five years ago.'

'But it doesn't work?'

'No. It seems to work – it was used in Liberia and Guinea in 2015.'

'Okay but, if there are no serious side effects, and there is only a question as to whether it is 70 per cent or 95 per cent effective, why not just roll it out now?'

'It doesn't work like that. The agencies may be in a position to approve it in another six months.'

'Five years after it was developed?'

'That's about normal for vaccines.'

'Couldn't we start manufacturing and stockpiling just in case it is approved?'

'It doesn't quite work like that, manufacture is complicated. I'm afraid we cannot rely on a vaccine. But there is some experimental vaccination in Congo.'

'So how does this end?'

'The outbreak may burn itself out. That has happened before.'

'But—'

'But this outbreak seems to be spreading quicker and faster than normal. A grandmother and a five-year-old have just died in Uganda – having apparently picked it up in Congo. It is a very open border.'

'How is it spread?'

'Direct contact through broken skin, or the mouth and nose, with the blood, vomit, faeces or bodily fluids of someone with Ebola, or who died of Ebola.'

Here one of the Congo team broke in, 'Traditional funeral practices involve the whole crowd embracing and kissing the dead body.'

'And then what happens?' I asked.

'Well, fever, muscle pain and a sore throat, then vomiting, and internal and external bleeding. The mortality rate can be as high as 90 per cent but with treatment you can bring that down.'

'How much?'

'Basically, if you contract the disease and get to hospital, you only have a 50 per cent chance of dying – usually from multiple organ failure.'

Jeremy Farrar, the director of the Wellcome Trust interjected to explain that, in his view, Ebola was not the main problem. The real problem was that it was distracting attention and resources from malaria, tuberculosis and HIV / AIDS, which would kill far more people.

'A great deal,' Chris Whitty added, 'is still unknown about what is happening, whether contact tracing is possible or even desirable. The WHO has been reluctant to declare a global emergency. There is a chance that the disease has already spread too far to be contained.' He agreed that there was an argument for acting. But there was no certain answer on whether acting would work. And we should not rely too much on the idea of a vaccine.

Everything I had seen with crises in Iraq, or Afghanistan, or in flooding, suggested that the tendency of government was always to be too slow. Acting was costly and uncertain. There would always be requests for more time and more study. People would hope the problem might solve itself, or that Britain didn't need to be in the lead. They would be terrified about the economic and social costs of trying to suppress pandemics. But I didn't believe that it made sense to wait for more evidence, or worry that we might be overreacting or overspending. It seemed to me that a pandemic needed an extreme and urgent response, rapid decisions and a great deal of money.

In Cabinet, I challenged the slower approach being taken by the

Department of Health; doubled the DfID contribution to Ebola; went to Geneva to win over the WHO; made a formal statement to Parliament and, flying to the G7 Development meetings in Paris, went for a long walk with my friend, Mark Green, the USAID administrator, and worked with him to encourage other donors to double their commitment to Ebola too.

Then I travelled to the outbreak: back to DRC which I had last visited for my Brexit conversation with President Kabila. We came by land from Kigali in Rwanda, to a sprawling depopulated series of parking lots and sheds, which marked the border with DRC. At the gate, health workers were checking temperatures and manning hand-washing stations. In Goma I donned a yellow surgical gown and joined health workers, who were working in full surgical kit, with no air conditioning. They needed breaks every hour. I watched them taking off their equipment, revealing drawn faces glistening with sweat. A trained observer stood by me, checking their procedures and talking me through the steps they needed to take to avoid dying of Ebola.

'Look, first he must inspect the equipment for visible contamination or tears, then he disinfects his outer gloves and removes the apron – rolling from inside to outside. Next he must disinfect gloves again, remove his shoe covers, and then, after disinfecting again, take off his outer gloves. Now he removes – and disinfects – the disposable hood; takes off his respirator – disinfects again. Now, he is removing his gown and coverall – see he must touch only the inside of the gown and use a mirror to make sure he is not touching the skin. Now gloves, washable shoes, inner gloves, new gloves. Now I will inspect him and he will go for a shower. You don't have to watch the shower . . .'

We took a small plane over the Virunga volcanoes to Butembo. In Beni, great transparent plastic bubbles had been wrapped around the tents in which the patients lay. We passed two tents in which patients had just died. In a third, we stopped by a woman wrapped in a bright red acrylic blanket from China, printed with a tiger. She was moaning in pain. We had met her two-year-old in the crêche outside the camp. She was far too sick to speak to us.

In the cubicle beyond her was a man sitting up in a chair. He smiled and stood up to speak through the plastic sheet. He had contracted the disease two days earlier.

'So far, so good, boss. A little fever and muscle pain and sore throat.'

'And some vomiting?' interjected the doctor beside me.

'Yes, a little vomiting I am afraid,' he smiled. 'I know what is coming. You see,' he said, turning to me, 'I am a nurse.'

'Here?' I asked.

'No, in a rural clinic – I know these guys,' he raised his eyebrows at the doctor and nurse with me.

'How did you get it?'

'Treating a patient.'

'I am so sorry.' I was only now beginning to realise that he was telling me that he might soon die. 'Do you know how it happened?'

'No, you never really know. I wear the equipment. I follow the twenty-one steps. But sometimes you never know. It's difficult you know to be sure. There can always be a small tear, somewhere you didn't quite disinfect, and you know later you touch your nose?'

As we walked away, I noticed the lines of exhaustion in the doctor's face. In the last major outbreak in West Africa almost 200 doctors and nurses had died trying to treat the disease.

'How do you think he got it?'

'You know the procedures in these rural clinics are not always very strong – there is not much equipment – and they don't like to throw it away.'

'What do you think will happen to him?'

'We don't know. It is early still. But he knows well that the mortality rate is 50 per cent. It is not a good way to die.'

'You must be very brave.'

He shrugged.

In the centre of the facility was an area of sandbags, to which the doctors and nurses could retreat in the event of an armed attack. There had been more than 400 attacks on healthcare facilities in this area of Congo since the Ebola outbreak. It didn't seem that they could move the patients with them to the sandbag area.

I travelled to a village where the latest outbreak had been traced. My driver was an Ebola sceptic.

'Well to be honest, sir, there are some questions, some real questions, which maybe have not been answered about this disease and where it came from. Even I can hear on the radio and see on Twitter people explaining that this is not a real disease – this is a conspiracy from the government about the elections.'

'But people are dying.'

'Maybe – but who is to say whether it is really Ebola?'

At the village I finally saw the experimental vaccine. We stood not far from the house of a woman who had just died of Ebola. Kept at a two-metres distance from me by an anxious WHO employee, were all her relatives and close contacts coming in for their jabs. Beside me stood a WHO doctor from Mali, in gold-rimmed sunglasses and a beautifully pressed embroidered shirt. He spoke fast in colloquial French, making dismissive comments about all that surrounded us. He gestured at the lines: '*L'ignorance est écrasante. C'est l'incompétence omniprésente. Ils manquent complètement de systèmes ou des processus dans ce pays.*' ('The ignorance is overwhelming. Incompetence is everywhere. They completely lack systems and processes in this country.')

But the lines proceeded smoothly and quietly. The vaccine had been partly funded by DfID. It was being kept at minus eighteen degrees in a country with little electricity, and seemed to be proving effective. But everything felt raw and fragile. Just as it was being contained in Butembo there had been another case reported that day in Beni, which had been declared clear a week earlier. And there now seemed to be cases in Goma.

And then there was the politics. Vaccine development and refrigeration were logistics; but vaccinating was trust. If Ebola spread, it would not be because of lack of evidence on vectors and morbidity. It would be because the Congo government had no legitimacy. A fight between the army and a Hutu group, fifteen years earlier, had become a fight with a Tutsi group. Rwanda, Uganda and Angola were involved. So were child soldiers and sex slaves; illegal miners and smugglers of cassiterite, gold, and coltan; the Banyamulenge ethnic group and two Islamic jihadi movements. Analysts talked of the insurgents in an alphabet soup: FARDC, FDLR, CNDP, ADF and M23.

There were 21,000 UN peacekeepers in DRC and a hundred had been killed. Despite repeated ceasefires and peace deals the war continued, and would do so until some settlement could pacify neighbours; address religious and ethnic tensions; tackle the war economy; control conflict minerals; and find some way of restoring the credibility of a corrupt central government, which was 2,000 miles away, and provided almost no services to the people. Persuading people to take protective measures, seek treatment or accept a vaccine in these circumstances was difficult. Lifting people out of poverty in eastern DRC, through conventional development projects, seemed close to impossible.

I flew out to the west via Kinshasa. There I saw Félix Tshisekedi, whom I had last encountered as a marginalised opposition leader, apparently facing a complete refusal of Kabila to hold an election, and who had now been backed by Kabila after the election. We sat in the neat surrounds of the presidential waiting room at the airport. Our meeting was warm. He was thoughtful. But the Congolese Health Ministry was still blocking the deployment of the next vaccine. They claimed they needed more time to recheck the work of the Swiss and American doctors. Outside, I could see a private jet, from which emerged a group of young Turkish men in beautifully cut blue suits, apparently on their way to buy a mine.

22

Leadership

(April–July 2019)

Each of the three parts of my job, considered separately – international development, Cumbria, the chance to shape Brexit – comprised an extraordinary vocation, a privilege. In DfID, as in prisons, I was working with staff whom I admired, and for people in desperate need. My priorities in the Africa strategy, Ebola and climate, would likely survive my departure. But I had now moved through four different departments, and six different ministerial portfolios, in less than four years. I had learned how irrelevant prisons were to the party, to the national debate, to what passed as politics in Britain. Every day made me more and more conscious of how difficult it was to achieve any fundamental change.

I had mastered some parts of the art of politics, and I had developed some administrative cunning and deftness. I knew better how to get my agenda through a department. But as I developed a reputation, I felt that I was being overvalued for things I did not value, such as my ability to remember facts and speak at the despatch box without notes, and undervalued for things I rated, such as my judgements on Afghanistan, my work in Cumbria, or my operational management of the Prison Service. My ambition, my sound bites, my excessive deference to Cabinet ministers and exaggerated courtesy to colleagues made me uneasy with myself.

I spent far too much time in the middle of the night brooding about such things. My visits to my constituency or prison wings or DRC were a relief in reality. But back in London, I felt increasingly exhausted and often ashamed. This may have been why five or six times a month I got migraines that forced me to stagger through meetings, half-spaced out on ineffective painkillers. Yet at the same time I continued to feel awe for the idea of political life. I felt Parliament and country mattered more than almost anything. That, if I were repelled by something so fundamental to our civilisation, then the fault lay largely with me. I remained desperate to vindicate the years I had ploughed into this rebarbative profession.

Two years had now passed since I had seen the edge of the first conspiracies: Andrew Mitchell's speech to the One Nation, and the first advances of Boris's team. Theresa May had survived longer than anyone had predicted. And she had not yet signalled when she would stand down. But the failure of the Brexit votes marked the end. The sharks were circling. Dominic Raab had begun openly recruiting supporters for his leadership bid in November. It was now April and he and Boris Johnson had each declared that they had raised well over £100,000 for their campaigns. And everyone knew that this was only the tip of the millions that donors had been told to hold back for later stages of the race. With money came professional campaign teams. And behind them the parliamentary whipping operations.

Last time the Conservatives had been in government, the MPs alone had chosen the party leader, selecting from among colleagues with whom they had worked for many years, like monks electing one of their members to be the abbot. It was a system that had not favoured original outsiders, and had almost blocked Churchill from becoming prime minister. But it had also excluded some rascals.

The decision, however, was no longer purely in the hands of the MPs. A new system had been established after the John Major government, but never yet used when in government, to elect a prime minister. This system only allowed MPs to select a shortlist of two candidates. The final decision would be made by about 100,000 party members. It was a beauty contest, in which the ultimate judges were not the MPs or the voters of Britain but instead the 0.2 per cent of voters who belonged to the Conservative Party: directly choosing for the first time in history, not simply a party leader but a prime minister. A mirror image existed in the Labour Party where members, far more left-wing than the general population, had in 2015 chosen Jeremy Corbyn.

The first to reach out to me to support his leadership campaign was Jeremy Hunt. He received me in the Foreign Secretary's chambers, one of those high coffered-ceilinged suites, ablaze with red and gold portcullises, in which the great officers of state reside. It would have been difficult to tell I was only one amongst dozens of MPs, scheduled to parade through his room in the designated afternoon left free in his ministerial diary for recruiting supporters. There was no sign of the Shropshire landowner who led Hunt's whipping, or the spreadsheet focused on a hundred names. He seemed to be doing this only for me.

He began on foreign policy and then said he admired my approach to prisons, it reminded him of his approach to the NHS. He knew I was a member of the One Nation group. He too was a believer in 'moderate, modern, compassionate One Nation conservatism'.

And then suddenly his language became stilted, the subject abruptly changed and, with the phrase 'I have highlighted the scandal of illiteracy, which is a blight on opportunity and a cause of lost potential which we should no longer tolerate' – we were into his leadership pitch. 'As an entrepreneur who has been doing deals all my life,' he continued, 'as the Culture Secretary who delivered the Olympics, and as the Foreign Secretary who negotiated the peace talks in Yemen, I can secure a better Brexit deal.'

'I see,' I said.

'From my conversations with European leaders,' he continued confidently, 'it is clear to me that there is a deal to be done. They want us to come up with proposals.'

This I didn't believe. Unless his proposals involved putting a border in the Irish Sea. And he had spent two and a half years in the Cabinet, with his face pressed against the Brexit impasse.

'What about the backstop?' I asked.

'European leaders have told me they recognise that the backstop could not get through Parliament.'

'Do you think we could fall back on a customs union?' I asked.

'No. We can find a solution that delivers the benefits of the customs union without signing up to the current arrangements . . .'

I was troubled, and perhaps he sensed this, for his next comment was about defence. Again, perhaps his briefing had reminded him that I had been chair of the Defence Select Committee.

'I'd like to look at increasing our spending on defence and overseas activities to at least 4 per cent of GDP . . .'

This implied almost doubling our current expenditure. 'To the same level as the US?'

'It's not sustainable that the US spends 4 per cent of its budget on defence and we spend 2 per cent.' He spoke about standing up against China and Russia for the defence of democratic values.

I was unsure whether he fully understood the scale of what he was suggesting. It had been more than forty years since the UK last spent 4 per cent on defence, at a time when the UK armed forces had well over 340,000 people, more than twice their current size. It would be a commitment, on the cusp of Brexit, to spend a fortune extra every year.

I left, wary, wondering if this could really be a future prime minister. And I found myself pondering three questions, which I imagined all the other 316 MPs asked in the same situation: Would he make a good prime minister? Would he give me a serious job? And above all – for nothing mattered if he didn't – would he win?

Michael Gove was next. He invited me to dinner at a hedge fund in Sloane Street. There he announced to the table that he would take land from the dukes, tax the public schools, increase inheritance tax and abolish the Brigade of Guards. And he demanded to know who had a better army and agriculture, Israel or the UK?

'You don't sound like much of a Tory, Michael,' I said.

'I am not a Tory,' he said, to cheers from the table, 'I am a Whig.'

From around the room came an outpouring of bright ideas and radical solutions to every aspect of British life, some of which seemed profoundly silly. As people drank more, someone asked me why I thought I was a Tory.

I said I believed in love of country, respect for tradition, prudence at home, restraint abroad. The table laughed. Was I then a defender of the dukes and the Anglican Church, worse too of the BBC and, though people were too polite to say it, Europe? I went home early.

★

'Boris Johnson,' Andrew Mitchell said, summoning a grand tone as I fell into step with him outside the Commons library, 'is an internationalist and social liberal as well as being liberal on immigration.'

'Surely,' I bridled, 'you can't trust him on international development.'

'He has promised that the 0.7 per cent is safe and DfID is safe,' said the former International Development Secretary.

'Who to?'

'To me personally. And I will be proud, as the secretary of the One Nation, to say that Boris Johnson is a One Nation Conservative. And if Boris wins you may find me,' he said, a little wickedly, 'as your successor in DfID.'

Andrew knew, of course, that Boris Johnson had been fired twice from jobs for lying, that he lied to many of us much of the time, that he had no eye for detail, had achieved close to nothing as Foreign Secretary, was entirely lacking in respect for public office, was not notable for his seriousness, or dignity. But every day, he seemed to be signing up more and more supporters, and the more there were, the more they attracted.

I was puzzled by his emerging coalition. Three or four truly believed that Boris was the only person who really rated or understood them in Parliament – Nadine Dorries, for example, who had found in Boris everything she sought in the Conservative Party, her ally in the fight against 'left-wing snowflakes who were taking Christ out of Christmas', and someone who was prepared to mock the look of women in burqas.

But the workhorses of his campaign were senior figures who felt they had been unjustly fired by Cameron or May, and who trusted Boris to right the wrong. Prominent among these was Gavin Williamson, once their opponent and a Theresa May loyalist. Finally, the ERG gave the ideological heft to a candidate who was not known for the consistency or detail of his opinions. They saw Boris Johnson as someone who could kill Theresa May's Brexit, and get a different Brexit done.

Three groups, then: those who loved him; those who saw him as a vehicle for revenge, and restoration; and those who thought he was a useful idiot. But these groups, perhaps fifty MPs in total, were not enough. To triumph they needed to win over the centre ground of the party. And that was more challenging.

The majority of Conservative MPs were not Brexit ideologues, in fact they had voted Remain. At least half were untouched by scandal, did not nurse deep resentments towards the previous administrations, and liked to see themselves as part of the moderate One Nation tradition. They had never had a conversation of more than a minute with Boris Johnson. What could he offer them? How would he win over the understated, uncontroversial and competent?

Michael Gove and I met again at the Green Chip club – a group initially set up to support more centrist 'Cameroon' conservatism. I began by saying, in great agitation, that the entire survival and reputation of our party depended on beating Boris Johnson. I said that he had made promises to all of us that contradicted the promises he had made to others. He had told one person at the table that he was in favour of the softest of soft Brexits; another that he would never vote for a no-deal Brexit. But I had also heard a third roaring that afternoon: 'This man looked me in the eyes and promised we're going out with no-deal.'

I said that I had sat in meetings in which Boris had told me that DfID was a giant floating cashpoint in the sky, which had to be abolished. And yet he had told Andrew Mitchell he would protect it. I was also sure Johnson had implied that he would give Andrew Mitchell my job. ('I need you on the team – *cent pour cent* – it is a cause of national indignation and scandal that you are not yet in the government . . .').

We had, I said, to beat Boris. If no one else would stand publicly against him, I would. The man who had compared my defence of Theresa May's deal to an Iraqi general defending Saddam raised a laconic eyebrow from the end of the table. I could see that he thought I was hysterical. And was talking too much. I finished with a plea for the customs union.

Michael suddenly said from the other end of the table: 'Just imagine a jihadi broke into your house and the choice was either to let a jihadi kiss Shoshana or something worse, which would you do?'

I could not understand the analogy. But more than that I could not believe the use of my wife's name, or the imagination behind it, and I was very angry. Someone thought for a moment I was going to hit Michael Gove.

It was at about this moment that Nicky Morgan, a former Education Secretary, created a One Nation caucus to challenge 'Brexit ideologues'. I turned up to the meeting, hoping that it might have the potential to stop no-deal, and prevent the ERG and Boris Johnson from capturing the Conservative Party. Looking around the oak-lined room on our first meeting, however, I found the gathering a little troubling. I could see that her 'One Nation' branding had attracted the 'liberal centre right': MPs who were more likely to speak in support of climate and international aid, and less likely to be in debates on immigration.

But many MPs who would be crucial to a real One Nation campaign were missing. Three powerful voices, on the Remain side, including the minister Anna Soubry, had resigned from the party. Nick Boles, one of the brightest and most energetic of our generation and a fierce opponent of Boris, had walked out in disgust over the failure to get his compromise Common Market amendment across the line, and now sat as an Independent. Three more former ministers of talent and power were not there because they were focusing their energies on fighting deselection. As the right of the party was strengthening and coalescing, the centre seemed to be shedding and moulting.

Also, as Richard Benyon who was sitting beside me observed, we looked a 'little nice'. Too many people in the room were known chiefly for their thoughtfulness and courtesy. We were supposed to be taking on Liz Truss, Priti Patel and Nadine Dorries, and challenging the religious certitude of Steve Baker, Jacob Rees-Mogg's Instagram-enhanced languid reassurances, the D-Day invocations of Mark Francois, the Vulcan arguments of Redwood, and the encyclopaedic confidence of Kwasi Kwarteng. We felt like a book club going to a Millwall game. Third, and more worrying, we did not seem to have attracted many of our natural allies. Where were Cameron's trusted aides, his inner circle, who had backed his modernising project against Boris? Or for that matter, where were middle-of-the-road Remain voters, who had not been close to Cameron, like Ben Wallace?

Still, over fifty colleagues were in the room. It was a start. Our chair, Nicky Morgan, began by saying that 'There is no easy way to define One Nation conservatism. It's a bit like defining Britishness.' We chuckled dutifully. She said that she felt it was about healing divisions. She would be asking MPs to sign up to a code of conduct. She got some banging and 'hear hears' when she attacked the *Daily Mail*, the *Daily Express* and the ERG for increasingly portraying moderate voices as traitors and 'enemies of the people'.

When she opened the floor to questions, I said I thought our top priority was to coalesce around our own One Nation leadership candidate to beat Boris. And fast. She, however, said she would be deferring the question of leadership candidates to the next meeting.

We met again in the same room a week later. Our numbers, I saw, had grown by one: Matt Hancock. But the way he worked his way around the room implied that he was more interested in our supporting him than in him supporting us. I began by suggesting that we should at least agree that we were all opposed to a no-deal Brexit. A few people nodded. Then a woman said, 'We can be One Nation Conservatives without taking a position on Brexit. I for one remain agnostic about no-deal.' I tried to argue. Nicky Morgan cut me off. She suggested that I was getting ahead of the agenda, and we should turn to writing our manifesto. No one seemed to disagree with this. The idea, she explained, was that it would list our views on the environment, on international aid and respect for the constitution.

'And on Brexit?' I asked.

She scowled at me and continued. We would publish it and challenge all candidates including Boris to sign up to our One Nation values. Did everyone agree?

I didn't. 'The problem,' I said, 'is they will all sign up to it. Even Boris Johnson will simply endorse this kind of thing, and call himself a One Nation Conservative.'

'He is,' Andrew Mitchell observed.

I glared at him. 'Boris will sign up to whatever you like, in theory, but it won't mean anything . . .'

'We will have to ensure it means something then,' said Nicky briskly.

'How? We have no way of holding them to such agreements. He will feel no shame about making promises to win, and then breaking those promises to stay in power. Look: our best hope is to have our own candidate, whom we know and trust, not to try to kite-mark eleven other candidates. One of us in this room should run.' I looked at Nicky Morgan and Amber Rudd, the two recent One Nation Cabinet ministers in the room. I didn't look at Matt Hancock.

'I think,' a younger member observed, 'that we can be One Nation Conservatives without all backing the same candidate.'

'Then we will lose the party and a moderate Brexit,' I said. Few seemed to want to meet my eye.

It was not that they necessarily disagreed with me, but they were sensing power ebbing away. Somehow, although the core of the ERG barely numbered fifty MPs; although the majority of Conservative MPs had voted for Remain; and 200 had continued to back the prime minister's attempts at more moderate deals, this One Nation group was beginning to doubt that the moderate centre of the party could win. The Tory Party in Parliament and the country was moving away to the right, and I was asking people to risk their chance of a ministerial job under a new prime minister, for an impossible loyalty and a doomed cause.

But I did not think we were doomed. We alone, the MPs, decided who made it onto the final ballot. There were enough of us out there to at least stop Boris and ensure that a One Nation candidate was presented as a choice to the Conservative Party. We could still shape this.

'And no-deal?' I asked.

'One Nation conservatism isn't just about Brexit,' someone repeated. Others nodded.

'Not everyone in the room agrees with you about Brexit, Rory,' Nicky concluded to gentle 'hear hears'. She suggested that, rather than taking a position against no-deal, we might ask all candidates to 'explain their decision to us, and how they've weighed up the risks'.

I said we were like frogs in slowly heating water. No-confidence votes, I reminded the room, had been snapping at the heels of colleagues. The emerging leadership candidates, Boris Johnson, Dominic Raab and Andrea Leadsom, were signalling that, if they took over, everyone would be obliged to accept a hard Brexit position. We would be purged.

'Calm down, Rory,' someone drawled from the back of the room, 'you're getting hysterical. Leadership candidates are not going to deselect One Nation Conservatives and, even if they tried, it wouldn't be supported by local associations. Would your association deselect you?'

'No,' I said, but I was not so certain.

David Gauke was the one MP who I was confident would make a good prime minister. He was tough, skilfully adept at unpopular decisions, practical and moral, modest and natural, a good listener and an astute and elegant observer of politics, generous, provocative and witty. He was young, had been a minister for seven years, served in the Cabinet in three different roles, he loved Parliament and the party, and had every chance of eventually becoming at least Chancellor of the Exchequer. And yet he had recently repeatedly put his principles in front of his career. And done so quietly and with little swank. He was the best boss I had known.

I encouraged him to run. Many MPs, flushed with ambition, might have embraced the idea at once and asked me to help organise their campaign. But David Gauke simply thanked me, said he would take some soundings, came back in a day and said he didn't have the support. I was saddened. I guessed the public and the media would have warmed to him. Colleagues would have sensed his depths, his intelligence, his toughness and his sense of humour. And because he would have backed sensible policies, he would have succeeded. But David was convinced he could not mobilise the MPs. And probably in this, as in many things, his judgement was right.

Instead, he suggested that I should run. But this seemed an even less probable proposition. I was not a long-serving Cabinet minister like David Gauke. I had not been planning and preparing a campaign for the last six months like Dominic Raab or Boris Johnson. He suggested that even if I did not win, I could stand for the principle of what he wanted to call the 'liberal centre right' for younger voters, voters in the south, and Scottish voters. But I was reluctant for anyone to run simply as a symbol. I still felt Boris Johnson must and could be defeated.

I approached Nicky Morgan. Although I had been disappointed by the equivocations in her One Nation caucus, I sensed a strength in her, and the courage to be unpopular. But, as we discussed the party, I became uneasy about the direction in which her mind was moving, the company she was now tempted to keep, and the compromises which she was now proposing in the name of 'unifying divisions'. I worried she was becoming exhausted by the long Brexit fight. So I went to Amber Rudd.

A fellow Cabinet minister, she was the most obvious candidate for the One Nation wing of the party. She had been Home Secretary, which counted in a party where prime ministers were almost always chosen from those holding one of the great offices of state. She was opposed to no-deal, and had fought hard for a moderate Brexit. She knew her own mind; 'a fucking pro' in the eyes of her special advisers. I was not sure how bold she was as a minister, or whether she was as comfortable as David Gauke in detailed and difficult debates with officials. But she had made an honourable decision to resign from the Cabinet, because she had inadvertently misled Parliament. This suggested that, although she could be at times a nimble and even cynical politician, the Ministerial Code mattered to her more than her job.

For all these reasons and more, including her sense of humour, she had a formidable bank of moderate support behind her. She had started discussions around a leadership campaign almost two years earlier. David Cameron backed her. She had funding. She was senior enough for every MP to feel comfortable they would not be diminishing themselves by coming in behind her. The only point made against her was that she held a marginal seat, which she might lose. But the party had a long record of being able to find safe seats for its senior figures. Churchill himself had once lost a seat.

She told me, however, that the Tory Party was unlikely to elect a Remainer before the Brexit deal was done. And she was a Remainer.

'So you are not running,' I said.

'Cheeky of you, Rory, I'm not sure I am saying quite yet.'

I was now prepared to bet she was not running. If she were, she would have tried to recruit me.

'And, if you don't run, can we rely on you to support another One Nation Conservative?'

'I don't think I am going to share all my inner strategies with you, Rory, just now . . .'

It was around this time that I became first aware that the dark eye of the Boris Johnson campaign was sweeping in my direction. A fellow DfID minister from 2016 was now acting as the chair of his campaign. I remained an admirer of his, and was ruefully intrigued by his ability to shift so skilfully from sitting with MPs complaining about civil servants, to sitting with civil servants complaining about a minister. I had been sorry that he had lost his seat in Theresa May's 2017 election. And, if I had had to guess, I would have thought we had a sort of mutual respect.

But someone from Boris's team was briefing a journalist against me. In an article, Andrew Mitchell was quoted generously about my appointment to DfID. But alongside him was an anonymous person, described as a former colleague, 'who observed Stewart when he was Minister of State at DfID from 2016–18', and found that some of the senior officials there 'literally hated him'. He accused me of 'not listening to advice'; 'saying things that weren't realistic'; 'going with ideas he's just made up on the back of a napkin' (I didn't pause to wonder whether a napkin might not have two identical sides) 'and horrifying the civil servants who were sitting beside him as he spoke'. He predicted that my appointment as DfID Secretary would be 'a disaster' and 'could well lead to the death of thousands of the world's poorest people'.

Increasingly anxious about the idea of a Boris-led hard-Brexit party, I gave an interview to *The Times* making the case for a middle ground. I suggested that his willingness to countenance no-deal implied a lack of seriousness and moral principles, adding that I would find it 'deeply worrying' to stay in a Tory Party with him as leader. I said that if Boris were a classical figure at all, he reminded me more of a libidinous pagan poet than a Roman senator.

Boris, who knew his Catullus, called me in to see him. In his office, I was kept waiting in his antechamber by an apologetic secretary. He came out walking toward me, shirt half-untucked, tie askew. It was a different Boris, his eyes looked smaller, his lips narrower, his expression more sour.

'I don't understand,' he mused, a rough edge to his voice, 'why you are saying these things about me . . .'

I explained that I thought he was encouraging the ERG to press for a hard Brexit that would wreck the economy, and shatter the peace in Northern Ireland.

'At the moment, Rory, I have to tell you . . . in all candour,' he said, his voice suddenly changing register to deep and statesman-like, 'none of us wants a no-deal outcome. We don't want a disorderly Brexit.'

'What deal do you want?' I asked.

'We all know the deal. As the man says, "Let's not get stuck in the weeds": Max Fac, Malthouse Compromise, Brady Amendment . . .'

I looked at him. It was difficult to believe, as he spouted this list of alternative Brexit schemes, that he didn't know that these were all different proposals, each of which might destabilise Ireland in a different way, or that the EU would in any case reject them all. He caught my expression and scowled, briefly. I felt I was somehow becoming, in his mind, one of those prim pedantic figures who had disapproved of him in his youth: a housemaster, don, or editor. He shook his head and now tried another smile, 'Come on, we all agree, no? I mean what do you want?'

'The prime minister's deal.'

'Apart from that . . .'

'A customs union.'

'No. You can't mean that. Not a customs union,' he shook his head again.

'How are you going to get round the problem of the borders within the UK and Ireland without either the backstop or a customs union?' I asked.

'Come on – we will get a transition period – a standstill with WTO terms until such time as we have negotiated a free trade agreement.'

'Boris, transition and WTO are completely different,' I said, more aware than ever the way I said 'Boris' seemed patronising. Nevertheless, I explained again that transition was zero tariff; WTO was by definition defaulting to the worst terms available. Our car industry, which exported 90 per cent of its cars, would face 10 per cent tariffs. Agricultural tariffs could reach 40 per cent. 'And in any case,' I continued, 'there can be no transition period without an agreement signed.'

He brushed this aside. 'The fact is anyway we don't want no-deal. I'm not advocating no-deal. So why do you say these things? I'm a One Nation Conservative.'

'If you are prepared to come out and say you are not in favour of no-deal, I will stop saying these things.'

'Well, you heard it here – I'm not in favour of a disorderly Brexit.'

'Say publicly that you have ruled out no-deal, and I will cease criticising and you will find many other people in the One Nation will quieten down too.'

He shook his head. I left.

All the people who were expected to dominate the leadership race – Jeremy Hunt, Michael Gove, Sajid Javid, Dominic Raab and Matt Hancock – understood the arguments I had made against Boris Johnson, because they had sat around Theresa May's Cabinet table, long before I joined. All understood a no-deal Brexit was a sudden, cliff-edge plummet with no transition into the worst trading terms in the world. Terms that would be far more damaging to Britain than to the EU. They, therefore, must have grasped that a no-deal Brexit was not a negotiating position: it was like threatening to cut your own foot off, if you didn't get a deal. Second, they understood that the EU would never allow a customs border between Northern Ireland and the Republic of Ireland, because of its impact on peace in Northern Ireland. Therefore the government faced a choice of either accepting some sort of customs union backstop for the whole of the United Kingdom, or creating a border in the Irish Sea. This had been explained to them literally hundreds of times.

But to my astonishment, as their leadership campaigns took wing, they began in different ways to deny all these things. Michael Gove and Matt Hancock were the most moderate in their language. But ultimately all were prepared to threaten the EU with a no-deal Brexit. All claimed that the UK could leave all customs and regulations alignment with the EU, without having to erect any border in or around Ireland, while preserving the full benefits of access to the European markets. And that they could achieve this by 31 October or, at worst, by the end of the year. Furthermore, none of them was prepared to say that Boris Johnson was manifestly unsuitable to be prime minister.

It was this that shocked me most profoundly. Nine years in politics had been a shocking education in lack of seriousness. I had begun by noticing how grotesquely unqualified so many of us were for the offices we were given. I had found, working for Liz Truss, a culture that prized campaigning over careful governing, opinion polls over detailed policy debates, announcements over implementation. I felt that we had collectively failed to respond adequately to every major challenge of the past fifteen years: the financial crisis, the collapse of the liberal 'global order', public despair, and the polarisation of Brexit.

None of this was helped by the British media – which was either unblinkingly hostile, like the *Guardian* and the *Mirror*, or absurdly credulous and enthusiastic, like almost all the remaining press. The

tone and style of reporting was made worse by the polarising algorithms of Facebook and Twitter. Even in the less partisan papers,
editors wanted page-views, which left little room for journalists to
scrutinise the practical defeats and occasional triumphs of careful
administration, still less events outside the United Kingdom.

Many of the political decisions which I had witnessed were
rushed, flaky and poorly considered, the lack of mature judgement
was palpable, the consequences frequently catastrophic. And yet we
had continued to win elections. 'Politics' dominated the news – but
it was treated as a horse race where all that mattered was position –
and to enquire after the character or beliefs of a politician was
considered as absurd as to ask the same of a horse.

But to put an egotistical chancer like Boris Johnson into the heart
of a system that was already losing its dignity, restraint and seriousness was to invite catastrophe. As the heir to fifteen years of crisis,
he would be able, like Jeremy Corbyn, to appeal to a deep nostalgia
for an imagined lost Britain, reject all traditional consensus as an
establishment conspiracy, deny the complexity of society and economy, and misrepresent what Britain shared, or what it could
realistically be.

He would be able to generate a tissue of evasions, half-truths and
lies, to mobilise a right-wing voter base; and destroy what was left
of the moderate One Nation tradition in the Conservative Party. He
would polarise an already divided country. He would damage our
economy and constitution; create a weeping wound in Ireland and
further alienate Scotland. His government would be ever more
allergic to detail, indifferent to the truth, increasingly shameless in
their support for a shameless leader, and incapable of responding
deftly or thoughtfully to the problems of the modern age.

A hundred or even 200 out of 300 MPs in the party must have felt
this too. But neither David Gauke, nor Amber Rudd, nor Nicky Morgan would run. Nor would half a dozen other senior representatives
of the One Nation wing. Some sensed that they could not win.
Others that by trying to do so they would antagonise colleagues,
polarise MPs, alienate the party members, and destroy their future
careers.

23

Standing Up

Shoshana and I went for a run around Hyde Park. In Cumbria, the brown leaves were still on the beech, the oak and lime were barely buds, and the ash apparently dead. But in London, every leaf was thickening, and the leaves were dulling from the translucent lime of spring to the waxier sage of summer. I complained about my meeting with Boris.

'Does he make you depressed about Britain?' she asked.

'I don't know. Depressed about Boris, but Britain? As I keep saying, we have never been so healthy and educated. We are at peace. Cumbria is one of the most beautiful places in the world. London's the greatest city on earth . . .' I paused. 'Why is it so depressing?'

'I don't know,' she said. 'And we don't know how permanent this is.'

'It feels like we are just walking to a Boris coronation. And we are meant to be a serious country.'

'Does this mean you are thinking of running for the leadership?'

'Yes, of course,' I said. 'Except it would obviously be a disaster. I have no team.'

'We could build the team,' she said.

I had, like many MPs, thought I could be prime minister one day. I had imagined, however, that promotion through the ministerial ranks would come through some sort of competition, defined by ambition, and luck, yes, but also ability. The sort of progress that Boris and the Romans called the *cursus honorum*.

But I was beginning to sense the significance beyond snakes and ladders – how to stand was to make a choice, for a cause. And yet I could still only see any path dimly. It seemed impossible to trace the contours and edges of something as absurdly vast, multiform and inconceivable as a country like Britain. Faced with the problems of the nation, I felt the same sense of shallow half-understanding that I experienced reading a primer on astrophysics.

I accelerated round a middle-aged figure in Lycra, hobbling on her rollerblades. On the grass a group of thick-set middle-aged men in shorts and bibs were running between orange cones. Large Saudi men in ironed jeans were passed by graceful runners with reflective flashes on their shirts and women in saris pushing twin buggies. 'I am tempted,' I said, apropos of not very much, 'to say my vision for Britain is this park.' Horses trotted heavily along the great seventeenth-century avenues towards Kensington Palace, and we now passed a toddler in a bear hat, who was holding on to the leash of a miniature dog, while squatting to pick some daisies.

'Maybe this is Britain? Diversity. Free to everyone. A bit of history and beauty. And,' I offered, 'goose poo.' Shoshana jogged carefully around the Egyptian geese. 'If I just remain where I am, and concentrated on my brief I could stay in the Cabinet.'

'But I don't think you really like being a politician. What would Michael Ignatieff say?'

'I don't know. Last time I talked to him he said that I mustn't be tempted to run a children's crusade.'

'A children's crusade?'

'I know, right?' I shrugged, 'I think he means don't do something naïve, and ultimately catastrophic. Or maybe he means be careful about not becoming a joke.'

'You won't be a joke.'

'Andrew Mitchell said, if I stayed twenty years, I would be Foreign Secretary.'

'And how is that going for him?'

We jogged on past the pleasure boats. I glanced left towards the sprawling mass of the horse chestnuts, their candles still tight and pink.

'And the clearer I am about my beliefs,' I continued, 'the more bridges I am burning.'

★

The next day, on the train to Cumbria, while the children watched *PAW Patrol* on an iPad, Shoshana and I tried to work out what a manifesto, a vision for a 'moderate Conservative Party', might look like. I had often written manifestos for Cumbria and visions for a department. Years of walking, living, listening, reading had shown me borders and government, landscape and Parliament. But a country? I wasn't so sure. Whatever united the kingdom it was no longer the idea of ancient settlements, martial glory, and immemorial institutions on which our myth of national identity had originally been built.

Britain was now, perhaps had always been, a place in hectic motion. A country that we were told had closed its industries and gone big into banking. A place that was now gambling on a new existence outside the European Union, and a closer relationship with China, at a time when the old political orders seemed ever more fragile, and energy security and food security ever less secure. An economy 80 per cent based on elusive intangible services; buoyed by an improbable housing bubble, and entirely dependent for its health and care on immigrants, whom citizens seemed to wish to exclude.

But these were the facts suitable for a column in the *Financial Times*. My most visceral experience of the country came through the doors on which I knocked and canvassed. Behind each I found a proliferation of separateness, of people tending exotic plants, interested in travel, deeply informed about car mechanics, or property management, Himalayan climbing routes, or yoga, but rarely interested in their neighbours, or the deep history and textures of their local soil. Local energy there seemed to be in large measure, local identity less so.

These were the people whom I had spent nine years asking what they wanted from their politicians. How many people? I had averaged perhaps forty meetings a week in London, a dozen a week in the constituency. Twenty weeks canvassing in my seat and other seats. It seemed likely that I had shaken at least 100,000 different-sized hands, of different degrees of moisture and roughness, looked into 200,000 eyes, listened to 100,000 different British voices. Probably many many more.

'What do people want?' Shoshana asked.

At a metaphysical level I could not say. Most voters seemed unsure what was on offer, or what the point of the whole thing was. 'At a practical level,' I suggested, 'probably fixing the things that bug my Cumbrian neighbour in his daily life. Stop hospital car parking charges; stop incentivising traffic wardens to give unnecessary tickets; stop mobile phone companies from ripping people off. Stop nuisance telemarketing. People are fed up with officials tearing up the roads and not fixing them. We have to be much better at governing. And stopping people from being mugged. And we need to fix the horrifying way we deal with the elderly, although that's a £100 billion-a-year project . . . And not give knighthoods to people who don't pay taxes, like Philip Green. Look . . . the point is not talking about these things but doing them.'

Shoshana began to write:

- I'll make sure that people who don't pay British taxes don't receive honours
- I'll abolish hospital car parking charges on day one
- I'll make sure people feel safe in their communities
- And I'll make the unfinished revolution of social care my number one priority

I meant these things. But it hardly felt like what a political vision was supposed to be. Hardly the stuff of black-and-white posters of political leaders in high schools – peering grandly above a political quote. I looked out of the train window at a collection of iron crosses in a field: it appeared to be a Gothic horror park, a Halloween installation, but it might have been a cemetery.

'You have to speak about the environment,' said Shoshana, 'your work at DfID, you are the tree guy, you are the only candidate talking about climate cataclysm.'

So, I took over the laptop and wrote, 'We should be the world leader on the environment. Climate change is the biggest existential threat of our times.' And added:

- Gigafactories and battery development here
- Research and development at British universities

- Climate conference
- I'll plant 100 million new trees

And looked out of the window again.

'Come on what else really matters to you?'

'Is this really the way to write a manifesto?' I asked.

She ignored me. 'What else do you really care about?'

'Bringing the country together again? Stopping the polarisation of Brexit against Remain; Scotland against England; young against old, north against south.'

'And what are you going to do about it?'

'A new Secretary of State for Scotland. Getting infrastructure built in the north, the Leeds–Manchester line, for example.'

'Okay . . .'

'Oh and robotics and AI are going to devastate our workforce, we need to provide the funds for everyone to retrain in midlife.'

I had spent decades criticising politicians for their empty manifestos and platitudinous jargon. And now I had produced a cake mix of random frustrations with daily life, iced with grand intonations about climate change, and decorated with a railway line and a banality on artificial intelligence. I could already imagine, 'Fair, Green, United', picked out in coloured icing sugar.

'This is the problem,' I said. 'Everything pushes politics into visions and abstractions, makes us feel we should be drafting the US Declaration of Independence, when what is going wrong in Britain is much more basic. It's not so much about what we do but how we do it. Getting on with it. Or maybe, in fact, it's about what we don't do? Not making unrealistic promises that can't be kept about tax or Brexit. That's part of why the public is sick of us.'

Shoshana said nothing.

'It's about determination, energy, passion . . . can I . . . can I not just say I want to make Britain a better and happier place?'

She smiled and still said nothing.

All that night, I dreamed about colleagues that I saw little of. I was walking down the oak-lined corridors of the Commons, and had tried to greet them, but they seemed wary of me. Someone from the Whips' Office had asked, 'What is your game?' I wanted this man to approve of me. But his glance suggested that he had somehow found me out. I woke, dry-throated. Getting up for some water I remembered an older member saying to me, 'I can see you in five years' time, you will be Michael Heseltine, elegantly pouring ordure on the party.'

The following day back in London, at the dining table, Shoshana and I tried to work out whether it was actually possible for anyone who was not from the hard-Brexit wing of the party to become prime minister. We mapped out the likely development of the Brexit votes and the party's reaction in boxes and arrows, like a 'design your own adventure game' that eventually spread across six sheets of A4 paper, testing each scenario and assumption along the way. By the end I felt we had a detailed sense of the immediate choices ahead. But the conclusions were not encouraging.

We predicted that, even if Theresa May managed to negotiate a deal with Labour, we would struggle to get more than thirty Tories to vote with her. They would be defined as toxic traitors, the deal would fail, enraged associations would choose a no-deal Brexiteer, and a hard-Brexit candidate would then fight the election on the right. All this I imagined had been Amber Rudd's and Nicky Morgan's conclusions too, even if they hadn't stretched it over ten pages of flow chart.

'It doesn't look very promising.'

'Except you don't like being a politician very much anyway,' said Shoshana. 'And you often say that the only person who can sometimes get things done is the prime minister . . .'

'The press will go after us,' I observed.

'Of course they will. But you're going to be running on what you believe in. And you're only going to get in minor trouble for that. You're not going to get in major trouble for that.'

'. . . just getting any of this together – even beginning to build a team.'

'I'll take six weeks off work. We'll do it together.'

★

Two *Times* journalists asked me in an interview whether I would consider standing to be prime minister after Theresa May. The normal advice was to avoid the question. Answering 'yes' is perceived as disloyal to the prime minister. And declaring too early gives time for other campaigns to sabotage you. But I felt my loyalty to the prime minister was clear and there was merit in answering questions. I said I thought I would be standing. I said the same in a *Spectator* interview, which I did in Hyde Park, hoping to point again to the park as a symbol of modern Britain. *The Times* tried to take my ideas seriously. The *Spectator* reported it as a faux pas, ignored my policies, stuck in a couple of my observations on British life, which seemed to them fey and eccentric, and padded the article with a summary of my CV before Parliament, lifted from Wikipedia.

Meanwhile, Shoshana was under way. She had been a middle-school maths and science teacher; she had studied astrophysics; she was an all-American rower; had taken over Turquoise Mountain and grown it into a $10 million-a-year operation, with 400 employees; completed the restoration of 160 buildings in Kabul, and then restored buildings in Myanmar; and was training and supporting Syrian refugees in Jordan. She even spoke decent Farsi. But she had never been a member of a political party and had never worked on a political campaign.

Starting now, six or even nine months behind the other campaigns, if we were to stand a chance to win, we needed to move very fast. On the first day we opened a campaign bank account, and asked the farmer's daughter from Cumbria, who ran my constituency office, to create a spreadsheet of all Conservative MPs, and to start filling it in with their likely voting intentions. Shoshana put Tommy, who had worked closely with us in the charity, in charge of setting up all our financial procedures and mastering our reporting requirements, and then, in charge of media and social media as well (he and I had made BBC documentaries together in Afghanistan). By day three, we had recruited a neighbour, a playwright, a former literary agent, three journalists, and almost everyone who worked, or indeed had ever worked, with us in Afghanistan or in my parliamentary or constituency offices.

I began my canvassing of colleagues by approaching my parliamentary private secretary, a young recently elected MP who acted as my parliamentary assistant. He was supposed to be the main interface between the ministry and Parliament – detecting any sign of disquiet with an aid programme, organising meetings with colleagues, and looking after the political side of my life. He was engaging, teasing, arch and intelligent. I felt lucky to have him. But curiously he had stopped attending departmental meetings and stopped replying to my WhatsApps. When I reached out to him, expecting an apology, he simply said that he had been busy.

Two days later, however, he suggested that we have dinner. We met in a dark basement room in the Athenaeum Club. He told me that I was the Pete Buttigieg of British politics, investing it seemed a lot of glamour in this US political candidate, and that he was very excited to hear about opportunities in my campaign. Flattered, after a long day, I was very frank with him about how early we were in the process, but I said I was very keen for him to join and could offer him a very senior role. The next morning, when I phoned to follow up, he told me he was backing Matt Hancock. I guessed he had already passed on to Hancock what I had told him about our leadership campaign.

At home, the team doubled in size every three days. A classicist, who had been captaining a boat to rescue migrants in the Mediterranean, came back to lead on social policy. My best friend, Felix, who had written a book on the theory of money, worked on our economic policy with one of the smartest people I knew from banking. Joel, from my parliamentary office, clipped my radio and TV interviews and posted them. Tommy, our friend from Afghanistan, along with running finance, operations and media, now took on building a website.

The first political professional to join us was a young, tall, good-looking Scot to whom my mother had introduced me ten years earlier, when he was a parliamentary candidate. He had put his drive, charm and knowledge of US electoral techniques into setting up a political consultancy. He asked us whether we had a 'path to victory', whether we had focused on 'the mid-air stall' and wondered if we were thinking 'triangulation'. We had not. Did not. Probably would not.

Then my Scottish strategist was joined by a friend, who had been for some time the only Conservative columnist on the *Guardian*. And subsequently, to my delight, two members of Theresa May's Number 10 team, one of whom was a polling specialist. I gathered all these people in our living room, some on the floor, some on the sofa arms, and began to draw different policy ideas on a flip chart in multicoloured pens. The Scottish strategist interrupted and said I needed to sort my position on Brexit.

I looked around the room surprised. 'There shouldn't be any ambiguity or problem about my position. I support Theresa May's Withdrawal Agreement.'

'What happens when that fails?' asked the former *Guardian* journalist.

'Well I would settle for a customs union: an arrangement like Turkey.' Turkey was not in the European Union, but it was in the customs union.

There was a silence. People glanced at each other. The journalist had voted Remain and supported a second referendum. The Scottish strategist had voted for Brexit. Neither seemed very excited by my position. The Scot coughed, 'I wouldn't advise saying that, Rory.'

'What would you say?'

'I don't think it's necessary to mention Theresa May and the Withdrawal Agreement. And I wouldn't use the phrase "customs union". You need,' he pointed out, 'to win over the Conservative Party members, your only focus ultimately should be on those roughly 100,000 people. Look,' he continued, 'I know you didn't vote Brexit, but you have to make it clear you are in favour of Brexit . . .'

'Yes, I accept the result of the referendum, I just think—'

'So just say you're a Brexiteer now. We all are,' said the Scot. I glanced at the journalist who was poker-faced. 'As for your pitch: Turkey is not too bad. No one thinks Turkey is in the European Union. But some may also think of it as not the kind of country we want to be. Could you maybe say you are in favour of a free trade deal? How about "Turkey for now . . ."' He repeated the phrase 'Turrrkey for now.'

It sounded like a Christmas offer.

None of these people were paid. But some would need to be soon. So I asked my best friend, Felix, the economist, to be the chair of the campaign, and he ran a fundraiser on the third day. We had no idea how much money we needed. He thought £70,000. I guessed double. Some campaigns were apparently happy to take £100,000 from a single donor. We decided, however, to limit any single donation to £10,000.

Charlie, who was a comedy producer, contributed, so did Robert, who was a farmer and an 'assistant village postmaster'. My cousin Charlie contributed, partly from the proceeds of his new patent milking machine, and friends whom I had known for thirty years, Khaled and Edward. These were people I knew and trusted.

I also received a cheque for £10,000, with an offer to send more, from a Kenyan businessman whom I had met a few months earlier at a Conservative fundraiser, at which he had delivered a moving, eloquent speech on Conservative values. He phoned me the day after the money arrived. He told me why he thought my campaign was not being properly run and would not succeed. He advised me to come in behind Dominic Raab to whom he had also sent money. He then suggested he could be useful to the Foreign Office, and outlined his plans for Middle East peace. I thanked him and emailed him to say that I was returning the money.

On day four, I took a break and travelled 350 miles back up to the constituency, to lay stone paths above Ullswater with the 'Fix the Fell Volunteers'; discuss climate change with Penruddock primary school; do a Penrith surgery; and then race back down again to London. And then, at almost midnight, I joined the twelve people who were still scattered around our house, peering at laptops, phones, spreadsheets, website designs, policy documents and income projections, among the cold congealing remains of a Lebanese takeaway.

'The only thing, Rory that really matters,' the Scot said, looking up, 'is winning the support of MPs – it is they who choose the candidates presented to the associations. Get calling.'

My canvassing of MPs began in the Pugin Room, with twelve separate half-hour meetings and twelve half-drunk cups of tea, followed by another twelve the following day, prioritised by our new spreadsheet. I hoped that I might recruit the co-chair of the One Nation dining club, who asked some thoughtful questions. He didn't tell me that he had already agreed to chair Matt Hancock's campaign. Then I saw Luke, a neighbour from Scotland, one of my closest friends in Parliament, smart, honest, capable. But he too didn't join us. I feared that he too was committed elsewhere, but he wouldn't say where. I pitched to the Attorney General in his wooden labyrinth by Central Lobby. He discussed Hobbes, shooed his assistant out of the room, produced a good bottle of wine and told me he was not intending to back anyone.

On my way up again to Cumbria, this time to judge tray-bakes, and attend a Penrith Climate Jury, I diverted to Edinburgh and saw Ruth Davidson, the Scottish Conservative leader. We agreed, it seemed, on almost everything. I told her that, if she came in behind me, I could see her being in the Cabinet in a foreign policy position, in Defence or DfID. She seemed particularly excited by the idea of DfID.

'How did it go?' asked the Scot.

'Well, I think.'

'Did she sign up?'

'No. Not exactly.'

'Get back up there again.'

Meanwhile, Shoshana had rented some office space. Tommy and his crew had built a campaign website and hired a director, cameraman and editor to follow me around. We had a 'grid' laying out the timetable for our policy announcements. We guessed the final leadership vote would now be held, as it had been when David Cameron ran, at the party conference in October, which gave us five months. Which was just as well, since I was still working full-time as a new Secretary of State, attending Cabinet and the National Security Council, chairing African investment conferences, pushing on Ebola, and making the 350-mile trip up and down to the constituency.

In mid-May two rural MPs, both children of MPs, shrewd and funny, agreed to join our campaign. One was Nicholas Soames. His support, announced in a long article in the *Daily Mail*, made a real difference, not simply because he was Winston Churchill's grandson, but because he had a considerable network, and real reserves of experience and political cunning, which he could put behind the campaign. I was very grateful that someone with a reputation for picking winners should have taken the risk of endorsing someone who was such an outsider. It suggested how angry he was beginning to feel about the party's lurch to the right.

I asked the second why she was backing me, and Victoria Prentis simply said, 'Don't be silly, Rory. You stand for everything I believe in: the Union, the countryside. And hopefully you don't support HS2?' she added as an after-thought.

'Well . . .' I said evasively, for the high-speed rail line was the greatest boast of the *Guardian* journalist and ex-special adviser who was helping to run my campaign. It would ruin part of the landscape of her constituency but would make journey times shorter to mine.

'That's right,' she said firmly, 'I will just tell everyone you don't support HS2.' And left.

Meanwhile, others continued to try to shape my campaign. The Scot tried to convince me to say I was taking Remain off the table, but not 'no-deal'. I resisted because I wanted to take both off the table. Rob Rinder, a lawyer and television personality, took half an hour out of his diary to tell me my cuffs were too long, as was my jacket. I should have had two buttons instead of three. My shirts were too baggy. My shoes were from another generation. He was too appalled by my green tie to be able to comment on it. I changed the tie but resisted the rest. He endorsed Matt Hancock.

A few days into our campaign, the Conservatives were wiped out, first in the local elections and then in the European elections. Most

MPs told me that they were still undecided, but that they were looking for someone who could mollify, ease and unify the party. Perhaps because of this tone, all the potential candidates were still being polite to each other. Dominic Raab claimed to have discovered an Eleventh Commandment of Ronald Reagan: 'never speak ill of a fellow conservative'. Even I had ceased my attacks on Boris Johnson on the understanding that he would announce his opposition to no-deal. Eight colleagues were clearly intending to run for the leadership, but because Theresa May had not yet announced her resignation, our leadership war remained a phony one.

I met Dominic Cummings, the central architect of the Brexit campaign, and the inventor of the slogan 'take back control', on Pall Mall. I had never met him before. I found a slight man with a permanent frown. In his T-shirt, jeans and sneakers he looked more like an advocate for Occupy Wall Street than a former aide to Conservative ministers.

The Athenaeum Club, where I had proposed meeting, wouldn't let him in in his jeans and sneakers, so we walked up Haymarket together in bright sun, passed the red and yellow bubbles of the M&M shop on Leicester Square and someone dressed as the Tin Man. The charcoal artist on the pavement seemed to be drawing caricatures that looked a lot like Dominic Cummings. I took him to Joy King Lau, on Leicester Street. He had been gruff and opinionated on the walk, but to my surprise, he seemed happy for me to order in the restaurant.

As he worked his way through prawn dumplings, he asked smart focused questions on the ten-prison project, and our use of checklists. By the time the pork buns had arrived, we were agreeing about what needed to be fixed in the Civil Service. I was surprised that this man, who was apparently fixated on A/B testing and public opinion, didn't seem to mind that voters cared little for Civil Service reform.

I was beginning to see why he had been so appealing to some Conservative ministers and leaders. In a culture defined by consensus, timidity and process, he was entirely confident and unabashed about everything. He could listen, but when he spoke, his certainty was astonishing. No question, however complicated, ever evinced a pause. He did not seem to be someone likely to change his mind. When I mentioned that I was thinking about going on holiday, he told me exactly where I should go and for how long.

'The answer to your campaign,' he said, 'is "don't get stuck in the weeds".' I remembered Boris Johnson using the same phrase two weeks earlier, but since I couldn't imagine him having any time for Johnson, I wrote if off as a coincidence. 'Present yourself as the outsider. Get your teeth into something like procurement for three months, demand proper systematic follow-up from the permanent secretaries. The media will start paying attention. Do a Facebook live. Take questions on your prison reforms for two hours. If the media don't cover it, post saying "This is something that the media won't cover – but I'm sharing it with you."'

I was struggling to work out how to reconcile 'don't get stuck in the weeds' with his advice to spend three months focused on government procurement regulations. Although I didn't doubt his passion for the issue. 'Is that really,' I asked, 'your advice for the leadership campaign?'

'No, your campaign,' he said, picking up a napkin and writing on it, 'should have only this slogan: *get Brexit done, beat Jeremy Corbyn, unify the country.*'

After lunch we walked back along Piccadilly talking about the other candidates. He said that he would not be endorsing anyone but I was relieved that someone so associated with the Brexit right still seemed willing to engage, and I was more relieved that he seemed to share my total contempt for Boris Johnson. I was impressed by the bracing tricolon, which he had handed me. The next time I did an interview I said that I wanted to *get Brexit done, beat Jeremy Corbyn, unify the country.*

Two days later, Sajid Javid announced his bid and said that he would 'get Brexit done, beat Jeremy Corbyn, unify the country'. The day after, Dominic Raab said the same thing. Then it was Boris Johnson's turn. Every candidate, it was now clear, had met Dominic Cummings, and seemed unconsciously to be folding their pitch into his three ideas. While he, at least in public, remained above the fray. I dropped the slogan but remained impressed.

The following morning, Friday 24 May 2019, Theresa May announced she was resigning, and that the new PM would be in place by 24 July – not, as we expected, in October. Instead of almost five months to build and run a leadership campaign, I now had two. The same afternoon, Boris ,who had told me he was opposed to leaving with no-deal, promised that he would leave on 31 October 'with or without a deal'.

I spent the night wondering how Boris thought he could leave by 31 October when Parliament would obviously block him, or could prevent no-deal crashing our economy, or could extract a new deal which did not involve a border in the Irish Sea. And in the early hours of the morning I concluded that he was not a man of Odyssean cunning: he could do none of these things. My anger and contempt, however, was increasingly blended with fascination. I remembered his charm and his proclivity, his eye for the main chance; his beefy shoulders; and the irrepressible chaotic energy that lifted his unruly hair. But I clung to two truths. First, he had lied directly to me about his attitude to no-deal. Second, if his lies took him to victory, his mendacity and misdemeanours would rip the Conservative Party to pieces, unleash the most sinister instincts of the Tory right, and pitch Britain into a virtual civil war. All with a shake of his moppy head, and a grin of small uneven teeth.

24

Pinocchio

I arrived at Broadcasting House for the *Today* programme at six in the morning to find Lizzie quietly waiting for me in reception: her white trainers, neatly crossed beneath her skinny black jeans, a Pret cappuccino for me in one hand, and in the other her phone, apparently alive with WhatsApps and texts and emails with different bids from different media, all to be balanced through the day. As we went up together, she gave me the headlines. The other candidates were worrying about when and how to announce their candidacy. I didn't need to worry. I had already done so a month earlier. She agreed with my friend, the former *Guardian* journalist, that this was the moment to be clear about my principles.

The interviewer asked me whether I would refuse to serve under any of the others. Most candidates would, I thought, have avoided this kind of question so as not to shut down future options or deals. But this seemed a moment to answer.

'I could not,' I said, 'serve in a government whose policy was to push this country into a no-deal Brexit. I could not serve with Boris Johnson.' I explained that he had reassured me that he would not support a no-deal Brexit; and had broken that promise. I said I thought his politics 'would be a huge mistake. Damaging, unnecessary, and I think also dishonest.'

Amber Rudd followed me onto the show. She was asked three times whether she thought Boris was an honest politician, and three times, she refused to answer. She said: 'I'm not going to start maligning any of my colleagues.'

I doubled down. I insisted on *BBC Breakfast* and Sky that I could not serve in a Boris Johnson government. My comments began to lead the news. Iain Duncan Smith, the former party leader, gave an interview to LBC saying I was 'stupid' for refusing to serve under Boris Johnson. I tweeted back 'Why exactly?' and got a million views on Twitter. I followed up with a tweet which ran, 'The star name will not always be the best choice. There may be times when Jiminy Cricket would be a better leader than Pinocchio.'

My stance was now the first item on the *Six O'Clock News* as well. 'The fight has begun with one of the candidates accusing Boris Johnson of offering a damaging and dishonest Brexit plan. Rory Stewart said he wouldn't serve.' Dominic Raab and Matt Hancock had chosen the same day to announce their leadership bids. But their announcements were buried. Lizzie began to hear from colleagues that they blamed me for breaking their momentum.

The next morning, the *Daily Mail* ran the headline: 'Rory Stewart brands Boris Johnson a LIAR in thinly veiled Pinocchio tweet.' The *Sun* said that the leadership race had exploded into life. Matt Hancock's attempts to introduce his policies on the morning round were derailed by questions as to whether he would serve under Boris. Since his run depended on being on the left of the party, and bringing in the One Nation vote, he found it difficult to say he would. But, because he was anxious about his future, he found it difficult to say he wouldn't.

Meanwhile, *GQ* ran a large piece arguing that only I could save the Tories. 'Rory Stewart has an aptitude for dealing with complex problems and yet managing to appeal to both sides in a deeply divided country.' It listed everything I had done on broadband, the environment, flooding and prisons, and called me 'an enlightened choice for a country desperate for stability and in need of self-respect'. How much of this extreme flattery was the independent conclusion of the writer and how much some piece of wizardry by Lizzie Loudon I could not tell, and she was too modest to say. A morning shaped by my anger at Boris Johnson, and an irritable exchange on Twitter, had somehow become a strong leadership launch. Except nominations were to close in ten days' time and I still had only two MPs endorsing me.

On the Monday, I wrote a letter to all Conservative MPs, touching on everything from my father's wartime service to my time in

Afghanistan, making the case for building 2 million affordable homes, and 'making our hospitals our schools our communities our people and our environment the envy of the world'. But the letter had no discernible impact, apart perhaps from reassuring them that I had enough of an operation to draft a pitch, the budget to print some letters, and a team to deliver some envelopes. Next, I sent out WhatsApp messages to 150 colleagues who had not yet declared. A quiet intelligent MP, who had been one of David Cameron's advisers, didn't even bother to reply. This seemed a bad sign.

So I decided to get out of Westminster and sent a tweet saying that anyone who wanted to, could find me in Costa Coffee in Barking in East London. I was gambling that, if I could prove the public would get behind me, MPs might follow. I started with Barking because it had the strongest Leave vote in the country, and I was considered a Remainer. People were already outside the coffee shop when I arrived. The first looked like a postcard in Trafalgar Square: broad-shouldered, shaven-headed in a sleeveless T-shirt and shorts, with a British bulldog at his heels. He wanted to talk about the drugs being sold opposite the Tube station. A second person came up to talk about disabled access, and another about medieval archaeology, a fourth discussed the import of cobalt from Europe, and a fifth mental health. A formally dressed man said he had been mugged of his watch, just outside his house, fifty yards away. A woman wanted to talk about what might be done to 'bring back the things she loved'.

Perhaps, if I had been their constituency MP, I would have felt powerless and depressed. But now I felt a shape and power in these encounters. For years, my ministerial and parliamentary life had been structured in half-hour slots, in which I met people at their most prepared, and most confrontational. My interlocutors often had local requests which I could not grant, or twenty years of fury embedded in fifty typed pages on the iniquities of American foreign policy. But now I was simply standing in the sun, far from the tea-stained cups in the Pugin Room, learning about cobalt or local violence. I was able to think about what a new prime minister might or might not do about these things. I remembered that I had not said enough in my manifesto about community policing .

The contrast between the grand pretensions of a leadership campaign and the reality of a candidate for prime minister chatting in the Costa in Barking seemed to amuse Twitter. Ever more people began retweeting and turning up. Some for a laugh. Some with an earnest commitment. One man travelled forty-five minutes from Shoreditch to ask me to sign my book. Tommy's film crew arrived. A young Afghan came over and we spoke a little in Dari. This was posted on Twitter and watched about 300,000 times. People seemed to like watching a Conservative speaking Dari.

The next day, I moved on to Lewisham, a Labour stronghold in South London. I chatted at a fruit stall to an older cockney, whose family had run his stall for over a hundred years. Behind him was a group of Afghan men from Kunar, a dry province of a land-locked country, who were running a lobster and whelk business. An elderly man told me he was one of a family of seven crammed in a council flat built for two. No one raised Brexit. But Jon Snow of Channel 4 arrived and filmed me in the market and interviewed me in a taxi. People watched these films and criticised me for not wearing a seat belt in the taxi, and for not having a good answer to Snow's suggestion that I sounded like a figure from the imperial past. But, strangely, rather than harming me, these blunders seemed simply to raise my public profile.

The next day, I went to Kew Botanical Gardens. It was pelting with rain and I stood in a creased blue mackintosh. Tommy's cameraman suggested that I do a more polished piece to camera asking people to come and see me there, but that I should hold up my hand, while he filmed, as though I were recording a selfie. This was a poor idea. The first reply when we posted it – 'Are you pretending to hold the camera?' – got about 23,000 likes. I replied 'yes', which got another 2,000. The clunkiness of this Tory politician standing in a mac in the rain, inviting people to come and see him, while faking a selfie, went viral and got almost 2 million views. *BBC Breakfast* played the clip and interviewed me about it.

Rather than wrecking my campaign, selfie-gate now accelerated

it. Viewers seemed to find my admission of faking, or even my faking itself, authentic. I was benefitting, I sensed, from the same forces
that rewarded Boris for his incompetent and transparent dishonesty.
The same people watching me for a laugh were picking up glimpses
of my approach and policies along the way. I had fallen down a
Twitter hole into a political wonderland. My Twitter followers
increased by 50 per cent in a week. At Euston station I was stopped
by a man who wanted to video me on a station bench. He posted
my lengthy, and slightly complicated, answer on the customs union
on YouTube and it got 2 million views; my rivals' polished and carefully produced statements on their EU position didn't top 50,000.

Three days of excitement on Twitter seemed to force the *Telegraph*, Boris Johnson's paper, which had until now ignored me, to
move into the attack. They now said that my ideas on Brexit were
'truly ludicrous – like Conan's Doyle's touching belief in the Cot-
tingley Fairies'. But an article in the *Spectator*, by someone who had
worked with me in the Prison Service, praised me for 'a rare and
attractive seriousness of purpose which has not elided into crippling
self-regard and is built on authentic foundations. He is a good man
in a tight spot.' And the political editor of the *Sun* said, 'Today's political gold is authenticity. @rorystewartuk's anarchic street
romps . . . captures that best . . . Keep this up, and Rory could define
this whole contest.'

I kept walking. A *Telegraph* journalist came with me on the train
to Wigan and Warrington. Boarding the train, I sent out a tweet
asking if people would contribute to the campaign and received
hundreds of donations within minutes – many for £5 or £10, with
larger donations of over £1,000 from the owner of a shoe shop; a
glass manufacturer; an art dealer; the British–French founder of a
company working on the Internet of Things; and a Cumbrian
farmer. A man who looked about twenty approached me and said
he wanted to give me five pounds in cash, for which I was very
grateful, but which later sparked a long chain of WhatsApp messages with the team about how to declare this gift. To my relief, we
were now fully funded and I was able to stop taking money. At a
red-branded Virgin Trains table, over a red-branded Virgin Trains

coffee, and a red-branded Virgin Trains raspberry-filled macaroon, I tried to interest the *Telegraph* journalist in my social care policy. She took notes, but with little enthusiasm.

She glanced down at the notes she had prepared. 'Have you ever taken drugs Rory?'

'No,' I said, 'unless you count smoking an opium pipe at a wedding in Iran.' She thanked me politely for the interview and got off at the next stop.

In a Warrington shopping centre, a woman tried to convince me that no-deal would have Europe 'snapping at our heels'.

'You,' said the man beside her, 'are nostalgic for warm beer and rickets and wanting to remember the war again.' I managed to get them, I thought, to part in good humour.

These meetings, on foot in different parts of the country, were exposing me to random individuals, from every political persuasion, unscripted. But they were also increasingly part of an unreal world, because my rising profile meant that I was followed everywhere by journalists, and camera crews. Gary Lineker, a Remain voter with 7 million followers, was commenting on my tweets, and so was Arron Banks, one of the major Brexit funders. The office sent me a note saying that in the last few days I had received 26,700,000 impressions; my profile had been visited 1,780,000 times and I had been mentioned 110,000 times. For years my reputation had been as a rather over-earnest, details-focused minister. Suddenly I was becoming a minor celebrity. Each of my walks and street encounters reappeared in newspapers or was posted raw to Twitter, where 100,000 people eavesdropped on a personal encounter. And, while MPs had happily consigned my earnest letters to the wastepaper basket, they seemed to notice me on Twitter.

On 29 May the *Telegraph* led its front page with 'Rory Stewart admits smoking opium in Iran'. Then, having extracted all it could about my iniquity and hypocrisy, it led the next day with the 'exclusive story' – that I would be unable to be prime minister because my drug use would ban me from entering the United States on diplomatic business. Cartoonists began to enjoy themselves. One showed a citizen staring in disbelief at the leadership list and wondering 'if

Rory Stewart has any opium he could spare me'. *The Times* portrayed me shouting 'What are they smoking?' and the *Guardian* was developing a vision of me riding a camel in robes, away from a lounging Boris Johnson, portrayed as a Turkish pasha with a hookah.

The following day, Michael Gove, who had made stern moralistic judgements about drug-users and threatened them with ferocious jail time, was revealed as having snorted cocaine. Boris was quoted in his own alchemic blend of omission, denial, self-exoneration and fabrication, saying, 'I think I was once given cocaine, but I sneezed, so it did not go up my nose. In fact, I may have been doing icing sugar.'

None of this was helping me to communicate my policies. In Edinburgh I took one of Dominic Cummings' pieces of advice and recorded a tweet saying that, since the media would not report my social care policy, I would bypass them. Shoshana filmed me explaining it, walking down the street. The tweet on my vision for social care immediately generated 600,000 views, three times the readership of the *Daily Telegraph*, and thousands of replies developing it, challenging it and fleshing it out. Again, I tried to brief *The Times* with an 'exclusive' interview on my proposals for the National Citizen Service. They instead ran on a colleague comparing me to a suicide bomber. So I talked in a rain-drenched doorway in Derby, explaining the policy, posted it, and immediately had 1.2 million views, five times the readership of *The Times*. Twitter could find audiences that the editors thought didn't exist. And as my amateur video on a moderate Brexit reached 3 million views, I began to sense that social media could be a weapon not only for the populists, but also for what I was starting to perceive as a more radical centre.

Meanwhile, in the single week since Theresa May had announced she was stepping down, and while I was continuing to do my street walks, no fewer than thirteen colleagues had announced that they were running for the leadership. We now included a backbencher, two junior ministers, and a cluster of present and former Cabinet ministers, including four who had run against Theresa May in 2016, each with our own financial backers; branding; social media strategy; political consultants; manifestos and dreams, each fishing for what now seemed to be less than a hundred undeclared MPs' votes. It was a less predictable field than the Grand National and almost as large. The newspapers and TV covered little else.

Boris Johnson remained the overwhelming favourite. His silhouette shimmered like a mirage in front of us all, and his campaigning style beckoned us into a children's movie, a land of fairy tales, and buildings with plywood fronts, where cartoon figures appeared beside human actors. His vision was increasingly echoed by the other candidates. Jeremy Hunt and Sajid Javid, who had voted multiple times for Theresa May's deal, now opposed it entirely, and presented the moderate Brexit they had voted for four weeks earlier as a conspiracy to Remain. Almost every candidate, echoing Boris, promised to magic a radically different deal from Brussels, which would avoid all problems around the Irish border, and all refused to rule out the threat of no-deal.

Almost all the candidates cloaked this pessimistic negation of possibility with fantasies of unbounded affluence. They promised a Britain which flickered like an unreliable screen between Jacob Rees-Mogg's vision of a Victorian past, and the alternative hedge-fund vision of a Singaporean future. All the candidates were promising extravagant tax cuts and vast additional spending at a time when the government was still borrowing. Such promises, in a party that prided itself on balancing the budget, would have been almost unthinkable in previous leadership contests. But Boris Johnson was proving that saying and doing things which previous leaders had been ashamed to do, would be rewarded. The Conservative Party in the country, instead of being shocked by the complete abandonment of fiscal prudence in the midst of Brexit, seemed to be delighted.

Returning to London, I tweeted that I was on my way to Speakers' Corner, the lecture ground for cranks for 200 years. Perhaps 300 were waiting for me when I arrived: teenage political enthusiasts in waistcoats; mothers out for a stroll; commuters who had stopped on their race down Park Lane, and were leaning back on sleek racing bikes. As the crowd grew, I could not be seen so I hoisted myself up and sat on a spiked railing and shouted as loudly as I could – my rhetoric of moderation and understatement sitting oddly with my roaring voice and exaggerated hand gestures, as I tried to hold a crowd thirty yards deep.

I said again that I was seeing the same themes in the rhetoric of both the hard Brexit and the second-referendum campaigners. Both were only interested in votes, Parliament and the constitution when it helped them, and when it didn't they seemed happy to bypass such things. And almost everyone was making reckless disastrous economic promises. I refused to promise tax cuts or unfunded spending increases. I shouted, 'You only vote for me if you want moderation and compromise.'

Yet, while championing restraint and moderation, I was showing neither in my attitude to Boris Johnson. The centre of my campaign was against him. He seemed the only truly dangerous one of the candidates. He alone could cloak a darker narrative in clowning. He alone allowed the public to indulge ever more offensive opinions under the excuse that some of it might be a joke. I could not contemplate Boris engaging with the future of their health system. Or writing the instructions to the nuclear submarines. But his omissions and equivocations still seemed to be convincing people that he was lying to everyone else, while being truthful with them.

Boris Johnson referred to foreigners as people who cooked 'goat curry on campfires' and wore veils that made them look 'like letter boxes'. He said, 'Islam will only be truly acculturated to our way of life when you can expect a Bradford audience to roll in the aisles at *Monty Python's Life of Muhammad*.' But he said it in a way that let racists believe he agreed with them, and others to convince themselves he was only joking. So too when he sneered at 'bum-boys in tight pants'. The same approach allowed him to call himself a One Nation Tory, while launching a culture war for a right-wing political base; and to say that 'over my dead body will there be a border in the Irish Sea' while offering an 'oven-ready Brexit deal' that contained exactly that. His supporters watched him as though they were delighting in the genial accidents in a 1950s cartoon, where

Boris could sprint, in every episode, like the roadrunner off a cliff –
and experience some surprise but little consequence. And yet I still
believed that the Conservative Party in the country had not completely changed. And that in the end no one would accept such
nonsense.

David Gauke's and Ken Clarke's agreement to endorse me gave my
campaign a solidity to offset the effervescent shimmers of Twitter.
I knew that other campaigns were having to make extravagant
promises of cabinet positions in future governments to gain support. When I texted my former boss, however, he had made no
demands: Gauke's endorsement came in a simple WhatsApp, 'Okay
I'm in.' Ken Clarke didn't have a mobile phone. I reached him on his
landline in Nottingham, and he said simply, 'Of course, old boy. I
think we ah-agree on everything, or if we don't, I don't know about
it, and you would be the best prime minister of this lot.'
    Ken Clarke was the longest-serving MP in the House, had held
two of the four great offices of state and had himself run three
times to be leader, narrowly missing out on each occasion. I was
proud to have the pair as economic advisers, and they immediately
wrote a lengthy article in the *Financial Times* endorsing my economic policies, and attacking the fiscal recklessness of the other
candidates. But this was not a race that was going to be won in the
op-ed sections of the *FT*. What surprised me and mattered most to
me was that the people whom I admired more than any other MPs
were prepared to put their reputations behind me.
    In Northern Ireland, continuing with my walks, I found Brexit
dominated every conversation. At a kitchen table in a border farm,
a few miles outside Enniskillen, I ate jam scones and looked up a
steep slope, crowned by a giant sycamore, and heard that 80 per
cent of the lambs in Northern Ireland relied on being exported to
the European Union. In Belfast, I walked with shop owners and
heard how a border in Ireland would disrupt supply chains, raise
prices and drive small suppliers to the wall. In Fermanagh a doctor
explained how Ireland had developed a single health economy
around the open borders. Thus it seemed a hard Brexit threatened,

sometimes subtly and sometimes brutally, to undermine structures long taken for granted.

In Derry/Londonderry, my guide was blunter: 'Peace is not a state, it's a process. A journalist was shot in this town a month ago. Earlier this year there was a car bomb here,' he pointed, 'where you are standing now. Yesterday, a bomb was found under a policeman's car in Belfast. The Troubles were ultimately about the border. The Good Friday Agreement removed that border. A hard Brexit risks reinstating it.' But I returned to Westminster, still unsure how to explain these points to a British population that often seemed to know little, and care less, about Northern Ireland.

The day I returned, on 4 June, the 1922 Committee announced a new electoral system. To be nominated, we would each require the support of not two but eight MPs. We would need the support of seventeen MPs three days later, then thirty-three MPs five days after that, and then the last-placed candidate in each round would be eliminated. Despite the grandeur of their names, I had so far signed up only four MPs. I would need to double that for the nomination, then double it again by 13 June, and double it again by 18 June. They also clarified that only two candidates would be presented to the party in the country. Which meant in practice there would be only one slot free against Boris Johnson.

One of the junior ministers in the leadership race immediately announced his withdrawal. I saw him outside Portcullis House, and I had never seen him so angry. He had raised a great deal of money for his campaign, before discovering that he lacked the MP support to continue. He felt the rules had been deliberately skewed to make it impossible for smaller candidates to establish themselves, and win over the party in the country, as David Cameron, a new MP, had done in 2005.

'The entire rules, Rory, are stacked against insurgent candidates like you and me – it is an establishment stitch-up.'

I said I hoped he would continue to support other insurgent candidates. He chose to endorse Boris.

Another new MP, James Cleverly, was also struggling to stay in the race. He was worldly, at ease with social media, and a Brexiteer.

We didn't agree, of course, on many policies but I needed someone like him to show I was serious about reuniting the party. I told him that, as a double act, one Remainer, one prominent Brexiteer, we had a decent chance. But he kept on saying that he had significant financial backers; that they wanted him and only him as the candidate, and would not consider a partnership. The new rules broke his campaign as well. He announced that he would be dropping out. I called him again but he said, flatly, that he had chosen to endorse Boris. We were down to eleven.

The day that our first polling came out, JJ, my friend the pollster, solemnly informed me, in the convoluted language of opinion measurement, that 'Rory Stewart was the most unifying candidate and the top choice of PM for eighteen-to-forty-five-year-olds, and the only candidate in the top two with all key voter groups that the Conservatives had to win back from Labour.' I was perceived by the public as a whole (including Remain voters) as 'the best candidate to handle Brexit', as well as 'the best candidate to get onto the issues that people really care about here at home'. I also led the pack in twenty of twenty-four attributes the public were looking for in a PM. I never quite worked out what four attributes I was missing, and wasn't sure I wanted to know.

Our key volunteer in Parliament was now running endless iterations of a spreadsheet in which each of the 317 MPs was now marked with their Brexit votes, their meetings with any of our team, and their affiliations. He sent me to the nine MPs who had endorsed James Cleverly and the other junior minister that had dropped out. Both candidates had promised their supporters to Boris, when they endorsed him. But to my delight half their supporters agreed to nominate me instead.

Our next move was to create a form on our website to get constituents to write to their MPs, urging them to back me in the leadership race. Thousands of emails and letters were sent. MPs were cross but impressed. One of Boris's supporters started writing back to every letter saying that no one should support me because I neglected my constituency. This broke a lot of unwritten rules. I confronted him, showed him in my diary how much time I spent in the constituency. He said he was in his constituency much more than I was. I said I was the International Development Secretary, that my constituency was 350 miles away, and his was an hour from Westminster. And I asked how much time precisely Boris Johnson spent in his constituency. He kept on writing, and backing Boris.

The hustings held by the One Nation group of centrist MPs was probably my most important event. At least eighty of my potential voters were seated in that room, and I needed to win almost all of them to make the final round against Boris. I began by saying that I was the only candidate prepared to rule out a no-deal Brexit; the only candidate rejecting the fantasy of a 'better deal' from Brussels; and the only candidate prepared to sign up to fiscal rules, to refuse to promise tax cuts or make vast unfunded spending pledges, which would destroy confidence in our economy. I said that the Brexit policy being pursued by Boris Johnson and Dominic Raab, and increasingly echoed by almost every other candidate, would tear the Conservative Party apart. If they wanted the party in the country to be presented with a One Nation candidate, they needed to support me. A few people cheered loudly. But not enough.

After my speech, Nicky Morgan asked me if I would sign a piece of paper committing to the manifesto on One Nation values.

'I was the only leadership candidate who was in the meetings that drafted these values,' I said, signing them. 'But, the problem is even Boris Johnson would be quite happy to sign this.' I read excerpts out loud. 'He will even claim he believes "in a civilised, open respectful political debate and strengthening the health of our society and democracy". That is why we need a One Nation candidate.'

The One Nation had insisted that the proceedings should be kept private and that no one should brief the press, so I had kept the doors closed, and told my supporters not to stand with the journalists in the corridors. When the BBC asked what I had said as I walked out, I excused myself. They reported this sourly, 'No member of Stewart's team was there to talk to us, and he didn't want to talk to us afterwards either.'

Boris Johnson gave the speech after me. His team wedged the door open so that the journalists could hear what he was saying, and Gavin Williamson gleefully briefed them before and after his remarks, while another member of his team handed his full written speech to the *Guardian*. To the sound of loud approval from his supporters by the doors, he told the One Nation that the party needed to 'stop banging on about Brexit and put that bawling baby to bed; pacify it and recapture the political agenda with One Nation conservatism'. He said he would rule out both an early general election, and proroguing Parliament to push Brexit through. He pulled out a pen and signed with a flourish to all the One Nation values, ticking off that he would 'reject narrow nationalism', 'be a leader in international development' and 'believed in universal human rights and the rule of law, an independent judiciary, and Parliament'.

In individual meetings with another nineteen uncommitted MPs, I secured four more. And – hoping to win over the bloc of thirteen Scottish MPs – I kept pressing the Scottish Conservative leader for her support. She wrote an article for the *Mail on Sunday*. It started promisingly: 'Rory's the sort of man whom you believe could not only explain the finer points of Plato's *Republic* . . . but he could do so while repairing a car engine with little more than a wrench, a pair of tights and some baling twine.' But she concluded 'Stewart-mania' was 'like Nick Clegg-mania' – nothing more than a temporary media sensation. And she endorsed Sajid Javid. Out of the other leading One Nation voices left in the party, Amber Rudd now endorsed Jeremy Hunt, Damian Green endorsed Matt Hancock, Nicky Morgan endorsed Michael Gove, while Ken Clarke and Nicholas Soames had endorsed me. The One Nation had allowed itself to be irredeemably split.

An MP who had been the strongest in encouraging me to run six weeks earlier continued to sit in on our internal discussion, but held back from publicly endorsing me. 'My final request,' he said, 'is for you to ensure that there would be no costs to EU nationals establishing residency in Britain.' I didn't like this pork-barrel politics but I did not dislike the policy. I costed it, found it would cost a few hundred million, consulted with the team and called him back an hour later to say, yes. 'But,' I added, 'I now need you to endorse me. This has been going on too long. I need you across the line.'

'Oh, I'm sorry Rory,' he said, 'I have already decided to endorse Michael Gove.'

But the encounters that troubled me most were with those who were gravitating towards Boris. His supporters never attempted to defend Boris's character or his ability to govern, only his ability to win. It was as though they were selecting not a Head of Government but a campaign mascot. 'How can you possibly support him?' I asked an apparently sensible Yorkshire MP, whom I would have trusted with almost anything.

'Because he is a winner.'

'But he will make a terrible prime minister.'

'No one will be prime minister, if we don't win the next election.'

All of us were distributing opinion polls to potential supporters. The latest opinion poll from the *Observer* showed me as the most popular candidate with the general population. I used this to argue that I was now the candidate most likely to win a general election. But Sajid's own polls emphasised his lead among younger people and minorities, Michael's focus groups his credibility as a proponent of Brexit. Jeremy could demonstrate that he had the most endorsements from MPs.

But the ultimate choice would be made not by the public as a whole, but by the more than 100,000 members of the Conservative Party, and they did not love us. They loved Boris. He had been the favourite from the very beginning. I might now be second to him in the betting odds, but he was a favourite by an astonishing margin. If you had bet a pound on me, and won, you would make six. If you had bet a pound on Sajid and won, you would make twenty. If you had bet five pounds on Johnson, you would make two. In the cartoons, he was consistently portrayed as four times the size of the rest of us – we were on a desert island, for example, in the *Times* cartoon, and the four of us were scrawny figures at the water's edge, while he was a giant balloon of tight inflated pink flesh, filling the centre, and pushing us into the sea.

25

Pro-rogue

Continuing my journeys, which were now branded on Twitter as #RoryWalks, I walked to Poplar, one of the poorest parts of London. I came down a side street on to a housing estate and saw in the rough grass a white tent pitched over the body of a dead man, and an air ambulance, rotor blades spinning, waiting to take him away. I listened to an older man describe how he had walked out of his mosque and seen this man lying on the ground, bleeding to death from a knife wound. This image sat with the line of broken windows in cell after cell in Liverpool prison, and the blood on the floor in Birmingham in my mind: a reminder of how unforgiveable and shameful so many things remained in modern Britain. And how little was being done to fix them. I felt all of our politics should begin with a sense of shame – an explicit account of the horrors we faced.

The next day I answered DfID questions in the House. Quentin Letts from *The Times* watched me and wrote:

Mr Stewart . . . appears to be doing everything he can *not* to be elected leader of his Party. Sir David Amess (C, Southend West) wondered what further opportunities Mr Stewart saw for Southend businesses in the developing world once we have managed to leave the EU. Sir David, a Leaver, is one of life's remorseless optimists. He always wants ministers to be upbeat. Mr Stewart replied mirthlessly that while there might be some trade potential around the world, 'I would just warn, when people start talking about a no-deal Brexit, that we need to be very careful in specifying what kind of tariff levels people are talking about and with whom they are negotiating, because certainly farmers in my constituency, the automotive sector and the aviation sector will suffer terribly if we end up with the wrong arrangements.' Sir David gave the frown of a boy who has offered his friend a pineapple chunk only to have it coldly refused.

Oh well, what about Mr Stewart's vision for his departmental spending? Surely this would give him a chance to mention the sort of aid projects that Conservatives hold dear, such as airports, schools, medical supplies and distributing copies of *The Laws of Cricket* to inquisitive pygmies? Er, no. Answering questions from the Lib Dems' Jo Swinson (East Dunbartonshire) and Labour's Emma Dent-Coad (Kensington), Mr Stewart said that he wanted to double spending on climate change prevention because the world faced a 'climate cataclysm'. He also wanted to double 'the effort that the department puts into that issue'.

A *Telegraph* journalist, watching the same event, seemed more interested in my looks. He offered 'eyes: alert, beady, constantly darting. And that face: gaunt, hard, bony. Like a Gurkha's.'

On 9 June, a YouGov poll showed me ahead of Boris Johnson and all the other candidates 'on which of the candidates would make a good prime minister'. Meanwhile, Boris kept doubling down on his promise to take Britain out of Europe by 31 October. Since there was no majority in Parliament for it, he could not. Unless, that was, he broke his latest promise to the One Nation, forcing the Queen to prorogue Parliament.

I sent out a tweet asking, 'Can every candidate – starting with Boris Johnson – please now personally clarify that they completely rule out proroguing Parliament? Locking the door on Parliament would be offensive, undemocratic and ultimately futile. Please confirm you would not do it. Clearly and precisely.'

The response from the Boris team was to send four separate people to see me telling me that I was being 'a populist'; that Boris would never even consider proroguing Parliament; that he had said as much to the One Nation hustings; that it was grotesque of me to suggest he would even contemplate it. I said that, if he were prepared to confirm that publicly, I would stop attacking him.

He didn't. So I said that, if he tried to lock Parliament, I would walk the MPs across Parliament Square and convene a second Parliament. Parliament was not a building, it was people.

Adam Boulton on *Sky News* said, 'What is it about Stewarts? They're always trying to set up alternative parliaments.'

One of Boris Johnson's campaign managers wrote to me saying, 'I hope you won't mind me adding that I would serve with any Conservative leader. But I do think we need to be very careful to use language during a potentially divisive leadership contest that doesn't trash our brand. Can I be completely upfront, I've been a little taken aback by some of yours on TV. We must not trash our party in the process of exchanging ideas.'

When I was invited to address a Eurosceptic group of MPs, the antipathy towards me in the room was uniform. Only half a dozen people seemed to meet my eye. Iain Duncan Smith, who had called me 'stupid' in one interview and 'a narcissist' in another, invited me to a second hustings. I did my best to find common cause with him on his attempts to sort out the bewildering complexity of the benefits system. I answered questions on faith and on defence reasonably well. But only a dozen of what were supposed to be eighty members bothered to turn up to hear me. And I was beginning to sense that they perceived me as part of the elite that had sneered at them (just as Cameron had described the Brexiteers in UKIP as 'loonies, fruitcakes and closet racists'). That they would never reconcile with someone like me, or trust me.

'I wonder,' emailed Michael Ignatieff when I described the scene, 'whether you have ever taken on the criticism that is levelled at you and will be levelled again, viz. that you are a self-publicizing adventurer who can't be trusted: too vain and too naïve to understand that politics is (a) a team sport that rewards loyalty and punishes cleverness, and failing to grasp (b) that the prize in politics goes not to those who are "serious" but those who are good at exuding confidence and reassurance, conveying the illusion of control and mastery, even when they are pedalling furiously to keep afloat. You don't want people to come away thinking that you believe you are too clever for this sordid game.'

Returning to canvassing, I hoped to add Robert Buckland, a Welsh MP who represented an English seat, to their numbers. He was a romantic Tory of the left. In the era when the leadership seemed fixed on open-necked shirts and Davos, he wore heavy and old-fashioned suits that seemed to demand a waistcoat. When he talked about the Union between England, Scotland, Wales and Northern Ireland, it was half-mystically, like a donnish Jesuit reflecting on the holy mystery of the Trinity. He liked to sing music-hall ballads to colleagues. In his endearing fogeyishness, and theatrical irony, he would have made an affectionate school history master, carefully attentive to the progress of his boys.

'Don't call me a Brexiteer,' he boomed at me down the table. 'I am a Remainer till I die.' His view of Boris Johnson and the Brexiteers seemed to be a combination of astonished disdain, and moral outrage. He made no secret of the fact that his greatest ambition, as a lawyer, was to become Lord Chancellor, but a Lord Chancellor, it seemed, in the mould of Thomas More from his favourite movie *A Man for All Seasons*, an unbending guard of rectitude.

Characteristically, he was also intrigued by the fact that my distant ancestor was an MP called Richard Rich, the villain of *A Man for All Seasons*, who had betrayed Thomas More in exchange for promotion to become Attorney General for Wales and ultimately Lord Chancellor. Robert liked to quote More's comment: 'Why Richard,' he took to saying to me, 'it profit a man nothing to give his soul for the whole world . . . but for Wales???'

But on 11 June, two days before the first ballot, he co-wrote a piece in *Conservative Home*, 'We are looking for a prime minister . . . who will be realistic and honest . . . and who will be able to unite the nation behind any deal that is done. We believe that person is Boris Johnson.' Boris Johnson had it seemed promised him the post of Lord Chancellor.

The other campaigns had done their launch events in the meeting rooms of hotels and conference centres, with podiums, a few political journalists, some select MPs in the front row, and excessive numbers of coloured leaflets piled on folding tables. We chose a circus tent on the South Bank. It was my friend Charlie's tent, and the only large venue we could secure and afford. As I walked across Westminster Bridge and along the South Bank, JJ handed me a draft of a speech, focused on fiscal rules; ideas on social care, and policy towards Scotland, but I put it aside. I hadn't seen the tent before. A screen had been set up outside for the overspill; 20,000 people were apparently already watching the live-stream.

I had overpacked the days with walks and interviews and canvassing colleagues, and I had not had time to think through the speech. Pacing among the Portaloos and lighting equipment and stepping back and forth over the guy ropes, by the temporary fencing, I tried to get my thoughts in order. This was where actors paced before they walked onto that stage, and perhaps an actor was what I and all the other candidates were becoming. What mattered was not the reality of our characters or the real impact of our policies, but how people perceived us. We were each swimming; through a million immiscible layers of prejudice and illusion; through a polluted ocean of public opinion, storm-whipped by social media.

If public opinion was simply random eruptions of sentiment, then the temptation was to address it through a game of whack-a-mole. This was why Boris was making promises to Northern Irish Unionists to break Theresa May's Brexit deal; and would break those same promises to secure a new deal with the EU, and break his promises to the EU when it suited him too. That's why he was promising the One Nation he would not prorogue Parliament, while also promising the Brexiteers to leave on 31 October, which required proroguing Parliament. That was why the other candidates were implying that you could retain totally free access to the European markets, and have total freedom to make your own trade deals; or were proposing independent trade deals with Australia, while also insisting on no-border on the island of Ireland, and no border in the Irish Sea. And promising more spending and lower taxes and unprecedented growth, regardless of our borrowing. And suggesting that all such paradoxes and contradictions could be mystically and miraculously ('homoousian-istically', Boris might be tempted to say) resolved. And it was working for them. Perhaps this was nothing new: 'A prince,' Machiavelli insisted, 'could not keep his word, nor should he.'

Perhaps my idea of a different politics based on slightly more truthful conversations was too rooted in face-to-face encounters in Derby and Warrington and in speeches to halls. Perhaps I had not fully grasped the difference between an approach that might work for a mayor, possibly even among the 40,000 citizens in a city state, as opposed to the strategy for a mass democracy. I was trying to be the prime minister in an age of populism and social media, appealing to the 65 million highly individual minds of this mysterious, recalcitrant, elusive online nation – a country in motion – always inverting its history, and discarding its heroes. But I was behaving as though the task was to persuade in a public argument. Perhaps we were called on only to be circus beasts trudging through an alien planet, with quite different rules of gravity.

An aide came out to tell me that the event was starting. Gillian Keegan – calm, engaging, direct and one of the MPs from the new intake whose support I was most proud to have – walked onto the stage to introduce me. Peeking through the red curtains, I could just make out through the glare of the spotlights a cavernous space. Beside the stage on folding chairs were Ken Clarke and Nicholas Soames, and some of the Remain campaigners who haunted College Green. Further back, I thought I could see my son Sasha, aged four, already with his hand up to ask a question. Behind him on the rows, that reached backwards into darkness, were some surprisingly elderly women in rainbow-coloured ponchos; a scattering of hipsters, and a man in a massive EU-branded top hat.

Gillian on stage was talking about listening and truth. She made a joke about a 'big tent' of supporters, and moved aside. I stepped out. I was, I saw, in a circular space with the audience surrounding me. Above my head a vast red velvet canopy reached high enough to accommodate a tightrope walker. The whole audience seemed to be smiling. I glanced at the mirrored walls and the polished teak floor and I imagined Boris on this stage: politically incorrect, unstable, with a hint of weight, slapstick and danger in those tree-trunk legs.

'For weeks now,' I began, 'I've been travelling around this extraordinary country. Derry to Derby, from Edinburgh to Peterborough, Woking, Wigan, Warrington. And everywhere I've been, I've been listening to you. People have asked why I wanted to be prime minister, to take up a poisoned chalice, particularly now. But this is exactly when I feel I need to be prime minister. We have to make a choice between two different paths for our country. A choice between fairy stories and the politics of reality.'

I said, 'I'm going to start with that great prancing elephant in this circus tent . . . I'm not thinking about the leading leadership contender . . . I'm thinking . . .' By now the audience were applauding line after line as though this were a stand-up routine. I paused, repeated myself over the catcalls and continued, 'I'm thinking about the phrase "no-deal". It's not just no to a deal. It's no to trade. It's no to Europe. It's no to reality . . . This prophet is not a real prophet. He is a prophet of negativity. He is a prophet of no. It is the great word of all false prophets through the ages.'

I talked about love, and loving the reality of a place. I rejected tax cuts or pretending that we were going to get some better deal out of Europe. I talked about filth and poverty; our Union with Scotland; our National Security Council, and our Parliament. I said it was not good enough to debate prison as though it were an abstract question, we needed to recover a sense of anger and shame. I spoke about what it meant to meet an eighty-eight-year-old woman who was looking after a ninety-three-year-old, doubly incontinent, husband.

Finally, I talked about my father. I explained he had been a battle-school instructor, who had spent two years in the Second World War training soldiers to crawl, run in small groups, and provide covering fire. But when he arrived in Normandy his commanding officer had ordered them to march slowly line abreast across the field, into the German machine guns. It was, my father said, as though nothing had changed since the advance of the Old Guard at Waterloo. An entire company of the Black Watch was killed or wounded before they were a quarter of the way across that field.

My father didn't see this as courage. True courage was not the opposite of cowardice, but the golden mean, between cowardice and foolhardiness. To promise vast spending when the country's finances were wrecked was not the virtue of generosity, it was the vice of profligacy. To claim to be able to miraculously cut the knot of the Brexit negotiations was not the virtue of the great-souled man, it was hubris. Courage in government was not about marching, line abreast, into the guns. And nor was it about sitting still. It was about moving thoughtfully and skilfully, employing hedgerows and covering fire, and reaching the objective intact.

I tried to talk about rediscovering a different British tradition – what I called an energy that came from prudence; shame; seriousness; action, and the wisdom of practical judgement.

It wasn't a perfect piece of oratory. Speaking without notes, I had headed off down curious rabbit holes, pacing back and forth for a long twenty minutes, with repetition and phrases which out of context had a stagey grandiloquence. I hadn't needed to talk about how I had 'planted 5,000 trees, stuck my hand in the earth, teased out the roots, squeezed each tree into the soil, staked it; tubed it; watered it', nor to weave in King Canute and King John. But I didn't really regret a word. After nine years of feeling suffocated and silenced in politics, I had finally, with all the showmanship and embarrassment, found a political voice.

My team brought in the press clippings the next morning. To my surprise the *Telegraph*, which had attacked me for nine years, had written, 'Rory Stewart gave a speech that blew his Tory leadership rivals out of the water.' Robert Peston, the ITV presenter, had tweeted 'Rory Stewart electrified this tent. He delivered the most coherent and lyrical launch speech of any candidate. On this showing the Tories have found a proper star.' James O'Brien, the radio presenter and journalist, had written, 'For good or ill, Rory Stewart would absolutely annihilate Jeremy Corbyn in a general election.' Generally, faced with this type of praise I felt queasy, both overvalued and misunderstood, guilty at having got away with something. But on this occasion, I felt I had come into my own.

*

Meanwhile, Britain remained a mess. There was a housing crisis; incomes were stagnating; adult social care was hardly functioning, and the Union itself was under strain. We hadn't invested sufficiently in research or education or infrastructure, or how to respond to a world in which AI and robots would replace millions of existing jobs. Our economy was weak, and we were borrowing tens of billions of pounds more every year. And we had built our economy on financial markets that left us almost no room to borrow more. Abroad, the whole international system was creaking under new forces of populism and increasingly aggressive authoritarianism. And that was before we began to consider what the long-term impacts of Brexit might be, or what might happen if China invaded Taiwan.

The other candidates continued to press for more tax cuts, regardless, it seemed, of the impact on borrowing, or public services. Gove wanted to reduce VAT. Johnson promised a tax cut for English higher-earners (somehow neglecting to notice that this would not apply to Scotland, and would in effect be subsidised by Scottish taxes). Hunt was going to slash corporation tax, while doubling defence spending. Raab was for cutting the basic rate of income tax.

I wrote an op-ed for the *FT* in which I said that I would not be making unfunded spending commitments, and proposed that as Conservatives we should commit to a new fiscal rule: 'that public-sector net debt as a percentage of GDP will decline each year over the three years of the next spending review'. Theresa May's chancellor, Philip Hammond, who was increasingly contemptuous of Boris Johnson, the hard Brexit fantasies and the reckless spending promises, followed up by asking the other candidates to sign this fiscal pledge. None did. But the support of the chancellor behind veteran Treasury figures such as Ken Clarke and David Gauke carried less weight than I hoped with colleagues.

In the vote held two days after my launch speech, three more candidates were eliminated for failing to obtain the requisite first-round votes; my support more than doubled, and the latest *Conservative Home* poll finally showed me now in second place to Boris Johnson with the party membership. (Previous polls had just shown me leading with the general population.) The *Spectator* reported, 'Rory has now messed up everyone else's campaign – Took the supporters from Hancock – Made Jeremy Hunt and Sajid Javid' s media output seem lame – Took out Michael Gove's reputation as the one person who could take the fight to Boris.' But I still needed to sign up far more MPs.

Two days later, Matt Hancock also announced he would be dropping out of the race. We had started with thirteen candidates, we were now six. Four days of the race remained. Sunday would see the first television debate, Tuesday the next round of voting and the second TV debate, and the final ballots would be held on the Wednesday and Thursday. By Thursday afternoon one of us would be in the final two against Boris Johnson.

I had planned to spend the Sunday, the day of the first debate, entirely in preparation. But Matt Hancock asked me to come and see him at his home near Kilburn in North London, so I cancelled all the morning preparations. We walked together around a nearby park. The weather was beautiful. Some passers-by glanced at us with apparent interest.

If I could secure his endorsement, I had a chance of unifying much of the liberal centre of the party and entering the first debate with real momentum. So, I did my best to recruit him. I talked about how I had admired his energy in government. He seemed, I said, to be one of the only truly active Secretaries of State in the Cabinet. I spoke about how close our campaigns had been in tone and ideas, how our supporters came from the same side of the party. How much difference his endorsement could make.

And we talked about Boris. He had committed publicly and repeatedly to rejecting Johnson's policies. He had implied he would find it difficult to serve in his Cabinet. When Boris had said, 'Fuck business,' he had replied, 'Fuck fuck business.' He had said Johnson's flirtation with proroguing Parliament went 'against everything those men who fought their way up those beaches on D-Day died for'.

Returning to the team who were waiting to brief me for the leadership debate, I told them that I was pretty sure Hancock would at least prefer me to Michael Gove. They winced and said it was more likely that he had been deliberately trying to waste the time I had set aside for debate prep.

Matt announced his decision in *The Times*. He said: 'I have reflected on what is needed in the national interest, and how the approaches of the candidates fit with my values. Having considered all the options, I'm backing Boris Johnson as the best candidate to unite the Conservative Party, so we can deliver Brexit and then unite the country.'

Still, I felt in good match condition, as I practised questions with David Gauke and the campaign team. We arrived early at a studio built between the old wharfs of the London docks. It was perfect, a bright June evening, the sun still high in a pale blue sky, so I went for a walk with Shoshana along the canals, and together we rehearsed some of the arguments again.

Entering the studio, I found the candidates' podiums arranged in a semicircle, and the audience on chairs, in a circle right around us. With its soaring roof, and audience in the round, it felt a little like the circus tent in which I had launched the campaign. Each of us took our position at our assigned podium, fiddled a little with the water glass, and laid down our phone. I was at the far left, with Michael Gove, Jeremy Hunt, Sajid Javid, and Dominic Raab on my right. Each of us, I noticed, was a man in his late forties or early fifties in a blue suit and white shirt. But there was no Boris Johnson. He had decided to skip the debate – presumably because he was in the lead and didn't want to take any risks. Channel 4 had left his empty podium in position as a reminder of his absence. We all looked nervous. Sajid, in particular, seemed to be swallowing hard.

The show began with the presenter trying to list our places of birth to show where we were 'from': Aberdeen, Rochdale . . . They skipped me, presumably because they didn't know how to say I was 'from Hong Kong'. The format was questions from the audience.

The first question was, 'How could we defeat Jeremy Corbyn?'

Here Michael Gove began. He sounded stiff, and a little nervous, like a schoolboy at a debating championship, who was experimenting with a fighting talk, slightly at odds with a geekier manner. 'I,' he said, 'was able to take Jeremy Corbyn comprehensively to pieces. That's what we need in a leader . . .'

'How would you get Brexit done, Michael Gove?'

'I have delivered, in the three jobs that I have done, I have shown I can do the impossible . . . who's the person Corbyn's most terrified of facing? That's me.'

Perhaps in a conventional TV interview, seated, looking into the camera, without a live audience, these lines might have worked. But he delivered them with an expectant pause, as though anticipating applause, which the audience declined to deliver.

When Dominic Raab spoke, he said that in order to get Brexit done by 31 October it might be necessary to prorogue, or shut the doors of Parliament. I interrupted. I said prorogation was deeply undemocratic, disturbing, and futile. When Tony Blair had tried to do it during the Iraq War, Parliament had simply assembled across the Square. The audience applauded for the first time.

Dominic Raab shot back that my idea of a citizens' assembly was Venezuelan. This comparison had perhaps performed well in an expensive focus group, because he repeated it twice and called me Maduro. I ignored him. The audience did too. Instead, I squared up to him and began asking him questions myself. The contrast between Dominic Raab, three inches taller than me, ripped and ready from weights and boxing gym, standing toe to toe with my scrawny figure, must have been arresting. Increasingly almost every challenge I made to him was applauded.

The other candidates, perhaps drawn by the applause, began increasingly to align themselves with me against Dominic Raab. 'You don't deliver on democracy, Dom, by trashing democracy,' said Sajid Javid.

'I will always stand up for our democracy,' said Michael Gove.

Dominic Raab turned to point out that, if the other candidates would not prorogue Parliament, they were giving up on a new Brexit deal by 31 October. But they brushed this aside. Each of them would get a fresh deal from Brussels. Michael because, as he kept reminding us, he 'could do the impossible'; Jeremy because he was 'an entrepreneur'; Sajid because he had 'led large negotiations'. And above all, they insisted, because they would keep no-deal on the table. Their repeated insistence on the impossible began to sound increasingly surreal. Encouraged by the applause in the room, I pointed out that we were witnessing a competition of machismo – 'Everyone is saying, "I'm tougher." It reminds me of when I'm trying to stuff three bags into a rubbish bin, and my wife says, "It's never going to fit," and I say to her, "Believe in Britain, believe in the bin!"' #Believeinthebin began trending.

Finally, we were asked what our weaknesses were. Dom said his weakness was his determination to get things done. I said I hardly knew where to start and listed many.

In the polls after the debate 33 per cent of viewers concluded that I had done best; with Jeremy Hunt at 18 per cent; Dominic Raab at 10 per cent; Sajid Javid at 9 per cent, and Michael Gove at 6 per cent. The *Telegraph* concluded, 'Rory Stewart is the only serious threat to Boris Johnson and the TV debate proved it.'

Matt Hancock, in endorsing Boris, had hoped to deliver his supporters to Boris. But the majority of his supporters now came over to me. I was also benefitting from the other candidates experiencing what my Scottish strategist described as their 'mid-air stall' – while my vote was doubling, theirs were hardly moving. The votes of four or five MPs on Tuesday evening, however, could still have a disproportionate impact. If one more MP voted for Dominic Raab rather than Sajid, Sajid would be eliminated, and this would help me immensely, for I was confident that I would pick up many of Sajid's supporters and move comfortably ahead of Michael Gove. And, if Michael Gove then dropped out, many of his One Nation team supporters would I thought come back to me and I could move ahead of Jeremy Hunt into the final run-off against Boris Johnson. But if Dominic Raab was eliminated first, and Sajid remained in, Raab's Brexit voter would go directly to Boris Johnson, and the One Nation vote would remain split four ways.

The following morning, Michael Gove's team reached out, perhaps having seen the poll that put their candidate at 6 per cent, saying that Michael was now open to merging his campaign into mine. He requested a 'very private' meeting at his chief of staff's

Chelsea house. I turned up for an early breakfast in a town house with dark grey carpets and sparse furniture, coffee, pastries, and Michael at his most excessively polite. He produced five reasons why we would be the perfect couple, and paid tribute to my momentum. He said that he was not averse in theory – 'in theory', he emphasised – to the idea of coming in behind me. But he thought there 'might also' be an argument for me to come in behind him. We agreed to come to a decision after the next round of voting. 'But we must,' he said, 'keep the meeting secret.'

Two hours later, I was called by journalists saying that they had been briefed that I had gone to see Michael Gove, had thrown in the towel, and would now be endorsing him. This appeared on the news. My phone filled with panicked and furious messages from my supporters, who said I had killed my campaign. I raced to Millbank studios to explain to a dozen radio and television stations that this was untrue and that I was still in the running. Walking out onto the street, I faced the largest assembly of press I had ever encountered: journalists national and international, six rows deep. I stood there for half an hour answering question after question, emphasising that I was still in the race. This seemed to kill the story. Until another MP apparently insisted, on the basis of 'an off-the-record briefing', that I was indeed backing Michael Gove. More messages flooded in from my more recent supporters, saying this story alone – regardless of its truth – had cost me their vote: 'Way to go, Rory, way to wreck a campaign . . .'

All of this could only have come from Michael's team – and I guessed that this had been the plan from the start. I suggested to Michael that we speak. We agreed to meet just outside Speaker's House in Parliament. He shook hands and apologised and said that there had been a misunderstanding. He hoped our agreement to work together could stand. Oddly, however, a cameraman had been tipped off. A photograph of us meeting again, in the curious pose of two minor Mafia bosses, Michael bowing slightly to me, appeared in *The Times*.

That afternoon, I went to our next rally, on a stage at the South Bank. It was a blazing June afternoon, and the largest gathering of my supporters to date, spilling out from the arena onto the embankment – the crowd younger and more diverse. People shouted that they had travelled from Derby and Scotland to be there. Richard Benyon, who stood beside me, said it was the first time he had seen so many young people re-engaging with the party. And then slightly undercut the compliment by saying it reminded him of the early days of David Cameron. Theresa May's deputy prime minister, David Lidington, introduced me on the stage. Endorsing me and looking at the crowd, he said, 'Rory alone is the true One Nation and Unionist candidate – he has demonstrated that there are no "no go" areas in the country which we aspire to lead. That we are the National Party or we are nothing.'

When I was interrupted by a heckler, I jumped down from the stage and moved into the crowd to join him, with the now ubiquitous television cameras capturing the whole interaction from the angry challenge to a final embrace. Then I wove my way apologetically through a line of people queuing for selfies, back to the House of Commons to continue canvassing MPs.

Michael Gove found me outside the cafeteria as I was rushing to another meeting, and detained me to say he needed to apologise again. 'I am afraid Rory I have written an article for *The Times* which might be misconstrued. I very much hope when you read it that you will not be offended. I very much want to keep the option open of working very closely with you.' Then I received a call to say that my mother had been taken suddenly ill. I called the hospital but she was still in intensive care and the doctor said she could not speak. I headed up to my office for another round of meetings with colleagues.

I began with three of Matt Hancock's supporters who still seemed undecided. First to see me was the chair of the One Nation, a passionate Remainer who was opposed, I believed, in every fibre of his body, to the culture wars already signalled by the Boris campaign. This was the second time he had agreed to meet with me. I appealed as strongly as I could to everything that he had said in thirty One Nation dinners about Boris, the centre left of the party, and about the European Union. But I could hardly recognise the figure in front of me – he sat hunched in the miniature arm-chair, refusing to meet my eye, and repeating 'I'm afraid I am not ready to commit.'

'Well, at least, you wouldn't declare for Boris,' I insisted.

There was a silence. And then he muttered that Boris had looked him in the eye and promised that he would never include the threat of a no-deal Brexit in the manifesto.

Next, there was a younger MP who had worked with me – clever, charming, ambitious, and an early supporter of Matt Hancock – who had voted Remain, and long emphasised his absolute opposition to a no-deal Brexit. In my office, I explained that I was in danger now of losing the race by one vote. I needed him. He equivocated. I said very forcefully that this was the moment to show his character. 'You need to stand up and be counted.' I immediately saw the humiliation and anger in his eyes at being addressed like this. I apologised quickly, blaming exhaustion and stress and the final push. But it was too late. He stood and repeated stiffly that he would think again. Later he released a video endorsing Boris Johnson with the desperate sincerity of a hostage.

Finally, I saw a woman who was one of the few MPs who had moved from being a colleague to a friend – who had come to my house, teased me with references to Persian poetry, and who had shared some of the strains of her personal life, and a long and difficult French book on the Taoist concept of *wu wei*. I felt kinship with her and trust. But when we spoke, she seemed close to tears. She said that she didn't quite believe she was doing it, but she could not support me, even in a secret ballot. That I had to understand that she had a family, that her whole career was now at stake. That her heart said yes but . . .

The next morning, I switched on my phone to find each campaign running a different attack on me in a different paper. An MP in Jeremy Hunt's campaign wrote 'Rory's the man of the moment for the chattering classes and arch Remainers . . . Stewart, who went on a gap year to Afghanistan, is making the party a laughing stock outside the Westminster bubble.' A long article from an MP in Johnson's team accumulated references and names and atmosphere in a swirling *J'acccuse*: 'Stewart might have been a spook but he is more Austin

Powers than 007. Short, white, male, upper-middle-class and entitled, Stewart is so postmodern, so cutting edge . . . he's almost deified by his eclectic cross-section of followers, drawn from the establishment, encompassing superior, ex-Treasury mandarins, like Nicholas Macpherson, ITV's breathless Robert Peston, who does little to disguise his embarrassing man-crush, to more aggressive Tory haters like Gary Lineker and Professor Brian Cox and their hordes of snarky followers on social media.' I was, he concluded, 'a charming huckster with a mysterious past who captivates the town with his easy manner and silver tongue – a heady mix of showmanship, hypocrisy and artifice'.

The *Spectator* insisted that it was me, not Boris Johnson, who was the archetypal politician, 'all presentation and little substance'. Another journalist insisted in a blog that I was a liar who had entirely invented my walk across Afghanistan. A *Telegraph* article entitled 'Rory Stewart the Florence of Belgravia years', was topped with a picture of me aged eighteen wearing a silk Chinese jacket. It made insinuations about my relationship with Shoshana; reminded readers that I had called my constituents 'primitives'; and concluded that 'the army boys nicknamed him Florence of Belgravia because of [Rory's] propensity to want to compromise with the very terrorists who were killing British troops'. Michael Gove, not to be outdone, had taken the front page of *The Times* to argue that it would be a profound mistake to vote for me – and had persuaded two of my One Nation colleagues to go on the record attacking me.

The final debate was now a few hours away, and I was not able – as I had been with the previous debate – to spend four hours around a table practising questions. Instead, I had to focus on turning out the vote – insisting to every MP that I was now the only person with a hope of beating Boris Johnson. Ken Clarke went missing and only appeared, walking painfully slowly down the upper corridor, minutes before the voting doors were closed. Despite all that had happened in the last twenty-four hours, I doubled my vote again. Sajid Javid and Dominic Raab came behind me, but Sajid was ahead of Dominic. If Sajid had come behind Dominic or received one less vote, he would have been eliminated, and then our spreadsheets suggested I would have picked up fourteen of his voters, moving ahead of Michael Gove. But Sajid got just thirty-three votes – the minimum threshold for the next round – and although Michael Gove's and Jeremy Hunt's votes had stalled and frozen, both still remained ahead of me.

Everything now depended on delivering a second TV debate as good as the first. It still seemed possible that Sajid, whom I had beaten in the most recent voting round, would be the next to be eliminated, and that enough of his votes would then go to me to take me in front of Michael, and that I would gain enough of Michael's votes to move in front of Jeremy, through to the final against Boris. At least the betting odds seemed to accept this logic, for they now put me in second place to Boris at 6/1, with Jeremy third at 18/1, then Michael, and then Saj. I would then have six weeks to tour the country, to meet the associations. Six weeks to convince the party that Boris Johnson could not be the answer, and become the prime minister.

There was barely an hour between the end of the voting and the second debate. In a rational world, I would have prepared for the debate with someone who understood Boris Johnson's mannerisms and techniques, to practise when and how to interrupt him. And above all to be prepared for how that sleepy form could deploy, with precise comic timing, arcane knowledge, abstruse vocabulary, and a staggering willingness to insist on the untrue. But I had used up all my potential preparation time trying to rally those last few MPs' votes.

I already sensed that this debate would be very different to its predecessor. The *Spectator* claimed to have discovered that given a choice between focusing on 'stopping Boris or stopping Rory', the other campaigns had decided they needed to use this debate to 'stop Rory'. I needed to focus on the seating arrangements, consider what would happen if the questions did not focus on Brexit, practise moving from addressing a TV audience to addressing my fellow panellists, and concentrate on what I had said in the last month, which might be quoted against me. I would have liked an opportunity to practise against people who were playing the other characters, to capture the grandeur of Jeremy Hunt, the affability of Sajid Javid, the barbs of Michael Gove. And try them in every combination against me.

But we did not have the time for any of this. Instead, I had pushed on with my pavement campaigns, mass rallies and press interviews, leaving only small gaps to have thirty individual canvassing conversations with colleagues, call intensive care to check on my mother, and take my third triptan of the day which was having no impact on the migraine drilling remorselessly into my left temple.

A colleague telephoned to say that I must use the debate to demonstrate that I was the only person able to take the fight to Boris Johnson. 'You alone can rile him,' he said. 'If you get him on the defensive, you will see a different, meaner character emerge. And so will the public. He is not used to being challenged. Destroy him in the debate and you will be unstoppable.' But two of my closest supporters were pleading with me to be more statesmanlike. 'Don't interrupt or be aggressive. The momentum is with you, don't blow it. Use the debate to reassure MPs that you are a unifying figure.' They showed me an article by Adam Boulton of Sky, who had written, 'all to play for now for Rory Stewart who needs to convince in debate that he's a constructive disrupter not a splitter'.

Shoshana had a Turquoise Mountain engagement and could not be with me for the final half-hour of prep. David Gauke advised that I should just keep doing what I had been doing. I should let the audience see that there was nothing Conservative about all the unfunded tax cuts and spending pledges from the other candidates. I should demonstrate that Boris's policies were peculiarly senseless; that it was impossible to secure a better deal from Brussels, and 'leave on 31 October'. In other words, I should avoid prepared lines, and talk simply about things I believed in. The emperor had no clothes, and I could pin Boris relentlessly to reality. 'How will you leave on 31 October against the consent of Parliament? How will you deal with the Irish border? How, Boris? How?' It seemed encouraging that Boris had skipped the last debate and tried to avoid this one.

26.

Quaestor

We marched, five candidates together, into the studio and looked around. Technicians pinned us with microphone wires to five widely spaced, low-backed bar stools. The stools curved from the presenter's podium round to the side of the stage: Boris Johnson at the near end, me at the far. From their positions, Boris Johnson and Michael Gove would be able to address both the screen and our colleagues at the same time. But if I chose to face the screen, I would be turning my back on my colleagues. There was no live audience.

The presenter, Emily Maitlis, swivelled between cameras, responding to commands in her earpiece. Images of clocktowers and doors flashed across the giant TV screen – the 'Our Next Prime Minister' logo glowed on the floor in front of us. Lee from Norwich loomed into focus. Boris Johnson was given the first question.

'Could you guarantee to get Brexit through by 31 October?' This was what Boris had promised to do, although he knew that it was impossible, because Parliament would prevent it. I would have preferred Lee to have asked, '*How* can you get Brexit done by 31 October?' But 'how' was not really, it seemed, a question in this political moment.

As Boris began to answer, it seemed as though someone had smeared ponderous reasonableness over the less reliable aspects of his personality. His hair was cut, he was in a smart dark suit and there were no jokes. 'You are absolutely right, Lee, to ask that question because we must come out on 31 October . . . I think the British people are getting pretty fed up . . .' I scribbled on the paper beside me, 'How, Boris? How are you going to leave by 31 October?'

'Politicians need to take their responsibilities and act maturely and soberly,' he continued, wandering around the question with the solemnity of a politician at a war memorial.

I waited for Emily Maitlis to interrupt and point out that Boris could not leave by 31 October, unless he locked the doors on Parliament. But she didn't. Instead, she called on Jeremy Hunt, who reassured Lee that he had asked 'a very important question'. If Hunt didn't secure a better deal, he *would* accept a no-deal Brexit before 31 October. But, if he had a deal, which was about to be completed, he might take *a little* longer. Maitlis let this pass too and turned to Michael Gove.

'Look, Lee, I share your frustration. But if we're *almost there* on 30 October,' purred Gove, 'and we just need an extra couple of days to do it, who could object?' Gove peered through his spectacles. He sounded far more confident than he had been two nights earlier. Perhaps he had been practising, or perhaps he flourished on the absence of the live audience with all its empathies, antagonisms and enthusiasms. At any rate, he was in his benign-headmaster mode. 'You occasionally have,' he twinkled, 'extra time in football matches to slot home the winner . . .' I waited for Emily to say that 2 November was no more realistic than 31 October. Instead she turned to Sajid Javid, who agreed with Boris that it was fundamental that we left by 31 October. Finally she came to me.

I turned awkwardly round to Lee, and away from my colleagues.

'Lee, we need to leave the European Union as quickly, efficiently and legally as possible. But we also need to be honest with you.' They were all, I said, wrong. It would not be possible to negotiate a new and better deal with the European Union by 31 October. Nor would it be possible to leave with no-deal on that date. Our best hope was still to convince a majority in Parliament to pass a version of the existing compromise deal, which had been negotiated with the EU. That is what I wanted to do. Lee, who had been nodding at all the other replies, stopped nodding.

Emily Maitlis decided this was her chance to challenge: 'I put it to you, Rory Stewart, that you are pushing the same deal, which failed not once but three times.'

I answered that there was no alternative to getting an agreement through Parliament. That was the fact of our constitution. 'In the end we are in a room,' I said, 'with one door and the door is called

Parliament and I am the only person here trying to find the key to that door, the others are staring at the walls shouting "Believe in Britain".'

Emily Maitlis looked bemused. Michael Gove jumped in.

'But we have run into that door already three times. We've got to have a different route out.'

I began to reply that there was no other route out – Parliament was the only legal route in our democracy. Emily Maitlis cut me off. Michael Gove filled the gap, burbling again about how, if his deal was not quite ready on 31 October, 'it might be worth spending a few more days getting it through'.

'Can you just raise your hands if you guarantee to leave on 31 October?' asked Emily.

Sajid half-raised his hand. The others ignored her. But they didn't stop talking about the issue. This conversation suited them. The longer we spent talking about imaginary dates, the less time they would have to spend analysing the desperate problems in their fantasy alternative Brexit deals. Boris continued smoothly and sympathetically 'I think there is a wide measure of consensus . . .'

I felt like I had lost possession of the ball and was watching the opposing players passing it back and forth, while they ran the clock down. I had to interrupt. I asked Boris, 'How?' But it seemed that my microphone was partially muted and the cameraman, unsure perhaps who had spoken, closed in again on Boris, who kept ploughing on.

I leant right forward and tried a second time, 'How?' Again I was barely audible. Marooned on the edge of the stage, I felt a light year away. I longed to be able to go toe to toe with Boris, as I had with Dominic Raab two nights earlier. Instead all the viewer could see was a close-up of Boris speaking on in a congenial drawl, about how he was 'taking the solution to the Irish border issues, putting that into the implementation period'. Perhaps there was a hint of my half-muted heckling in the background.

'Boris,' I said more loudly, 'there is no implementation period without an Irish backstop.' Here at last the camera turned to me. I had possession of the ball again and an open goal. Just one more question, I felt, would collapse Boris's credibility on Brexit. But before I could shoot, Emily stopped the exchange, and ruled that it was now Sajid Javid's turn to speak. He repeated that we needed to leave by 31 October. Emily brought the first Brexit answers to a close.

Eleven of the sixty minutes had gone. The next question came from Carmella from Bristol. She asked, 'Why are you even contemplating a no-deal Brexit?'

Emily turned first to Michael Gove, who began, 'Now, I do agree that a no-deal Brexit would create some economic turbulence . . . but we are a great country and we can get through it . . .'.

I wanted to shout that a no-deal Brexit was not only catastrophic: it was also now impossible, Parliament would not accept it, any more than they would accept a different Brexit deal, or leaving on 31 October. I interrupted again, 'How, given that Parliament does not consent to no-deal, how are you going to deliver no-deal against the consent of Parliament?'

Michael ignored me. Sajid said, 'You prepare for no-deal precisely because you want a deal.' Jeremy turned to Carmella, who had told us her husband was in the property business, and said, 'Your husband will know that the only way you can get a deal is to be prepared to walk away.'

All the candidates knew that this 'debate' bore no relationship to anything Parliament had been doing or discussing for months. And yet they continued to insist they could magically do the impossible. Four Cabinet ministers, however, were insisting on this alternative reality, the presenter was accepting their assumptions, and it was beginning to seem as though it was I, not they, who was desperate and deluded. I felt outmanouevred, migrained, exhausted and hot. I took off my tie – a gesture which, I sensed, made me look not so much casual as slightly unhinged.

Carmella came back in, 'No one can give an answer . . .'

'My answer is—' I began, but Boris brushed me aside with the ease of a pub bore, 'No one wants a disorderly no-deal Brexit . . .' he said.

Finally, after the other candidates had spoken for six whole minutes, Emily turned to me. But we had now run out of time. 'Very briefly, Rory Stewart, very briefly . . .' she said.

'If I were prime minister,' I replied, 'there would never be a no-deal. It is so unnecessary and damaging. It is not even a credible threat . . .' I had managed fifteen seconds. Emily raised her hand to stop me. Michael Gove was interrupting that my proposal on Brexit was 'serving up the same bowl of cold porridge'. Sajid too was challenging me but I could not hear what he was saying. Jeremy Hunt called me 'the no-Brexit candidate'. As I tried to answer Jeremy, Sajid interrupted me again, and the camera cut me off and closed in on Emily so the viewers could only hear my voice, faint in the distance, with the others shouting over the top of me. 'Rory Stewart,' said Emily loudly, 'we cannot hear anything – can you please hold back.'

And with that we arrived at the final question on Brexit. 'Can the candidates please explain how you will solve the issue of the Irish border?' Boris agreed strongly with Michael, Sajid and Jeremy. He said, 'You can solve the question as the UK comes out of the EU during the implementation period, whilst we negotiate the free-trade deal.'

This was jargon cloaking impossibility. The EU had insisted on the backstop as a condition for granting an implementation period. I shouted out, 'Boris there is no implementation without a backstop.' And Emily finally echoed my challenge, 'You're not going to get an implementation period if you won't sign up to a backstop,' she said, but Boris just kept speaking. Emily asked, 'Can you hear me?'

'I can tell you why they will give us an implementation period,' Boris said, and burbled about how the EU would be all too happy to make concessions to get us out.

At last, she turned to me, and I had my final chance to turn the debate on Brexit. I had two choices. I could simply turn to the camera and say clearly, 'All these people are lying to you, Emily, I need two minutes to explain the Irish border since the future of our country is at stake. And you are going to have to give me two minutes to do it.' But I thought instead that my priority was to expose

Boris Johnson as a charlatan who did not understand the details of Brexit. So I decided to use my minute to cross-question him. 'Boris,' I began, 'a farmer in Enniskillen is sending 80 per cent of his sheep across the border to the Republic. What are your tariff levels going to be on that border?'

'Rory, if I may say with the greatest respect . . . there will be no tariffs, there will be no quotas. What we want under GATT 24, is in the context of that trade . . .'

I leant in for what I thought was the kill. GATT 24 was a complete fantasy, irrelevant to the case. 'Boris . . .' I began. But then, apparently deciding that my ten-second question was my full minute intervention, Emily cut me off and handed the stage back to Michael Gove. As I closed my eyes, trying to recover some equilibrium, Michael took over the show in the slow voice of a family doctor. 'I've worked in Northern Ireland,' he said, 'and I know there are several things we need to do. We need to get the institutions back and running . . .' Sajid was nodding with polite interest but I found myself looking straight at the ceiling, my face drained of colour, stretching as though to rid myself of a demon. In the alien vacuum of the studio, marooned at the very edge of the stage, with no live audience to persuade, I felt like a satellite falling out of orbit.

Was this actually, I wondered, how it was going to end? With Michael running down the clock with anecdotes about County Down and Donegal? He spoke for a minute. Then, given another chance by another question, added another thirty seconds on his affection for the Irish agricultural minister, Simon Coveney.

I interrupted, 'There is no reality to this. No reality.' But my mike had been muted and Michael continued on about his Irish friends. 'There is literally no reality here,' I said, feeling that I was almost shouting, 'Europe has made it clear that the extension that Boris is talking about is conditional on the Withdrawal Agreement. None of these people are explaining *how* they are going to do it—'

Emily cut me off again: 'We have heard from each of you. We have heard your view on *how*.' And with that she brought the Brexit debate to an end. I had lost.

My posture and comments now simply amplified my despair. Everyone else was leaning in, nodding genially and collegiately at each other's remarks, while I had ripped off my tie, was arching my back and was alternately staring up at the ceiling or grimacing at the floor. For almost thirty years the British state had absorbed all my most romantic illusions about public service. But now at the culmination of my career, I felt trapped in the clichéd predicament of a poorly cast contestant in a low-budget reality TV show. My speeches, instead of adapting to the mood of the studio, were becoming stiff and pedantic: I was going from misreading the space, to insulting it.

When an ex-Conservative, and now Brexit Party voter, asked what tax cuts we would offer, the other candidates enthusiastically promised many. Jeremy Hunt said that 'all we needed to do' was double our growth rate to the US growth rate and 'we would have an extra £20 billion'. I told Emily that I would not be cutting any taxes. 'I believe the way that we get everybody back and reunify the country is by being honest and realistic.' By turning to address the presenter, I was turning away from the man who had asked the question, my colleagues, and the camera.

'And,' I continued, 'the thing that slightly depresses me in this debate is everybody, I feel, is *promising* things. They're promising they're going to get a new deal out of Brussels, which they're not going to get. They're promising to get a new deal through Parliament, which they cannot deliver. And now all four together have promised nearly £84 billion worth of tax cuts.' I persisted, 'I'm going to be very straight with people. I don't think this is the time to be cutting taxes because I'm not thinking about promises for the next fifteen days. I'm thinking about the next fifteen years.' Perhaps, if I had been in front of a live audience, even this might have generated applause.

But there was no audience, only our isolated figures projected onto 3 million television screens. My voice became flatter, my message bleaker, 'Our country is suffering huge pressures on public services. *If* I can deliver a good safe, moderate Brexit – and that's a big *if* – I would be spending the money not on tax cuts, but on investing in our public services. And I would not be committing to tax cuts or spending when we don't have—'

The questioner now snapped back that Jeremy Hunt 'got it' and that I was 'completely out of touch'.

Bizarrely both the *Times* and YouGov polls after the debate recorded me as the winner by a large margin. Twitter seemed to enjoy the question of whether I had removed my tie to sing, or in preparation for a fist fight. But the MPs and lobby journalists had witnessed my turn against too many of the instincts of the Conservative Party and knew that I had just performed a suicide routine. In just one hour I had destroyed my hope of beating Boris and with it my hope of getting a sensible Brexit deal done, or of creating the politics I had imagined. I sat in the green room still not quite able to understand what had occurred.

When exactly had I lost the debate? When I had failed to speak clearly about Ireland? When I chose to focus on the depressing reality of Parliament, rather than emphasising the opportunities which could come with passing a more moderate Brexit deal? Or much earlier when the format had been agreed? Had I simply been too tired to control my temper? Or had my bleak, rebarbative tone somehow revealed I was already losing faith in the Conservative Party, and my belief in the entire system that had propped us on these unstable bar stools?

In the lobby of Broadcasting House, a friend from *Newsnight* stuck a microphone in my face demanding an explanation for my 'lacklustre' performance. A *Times* photographer asked me to stay still while he stood, a foot from my face, shooting frame after frame, each loud click exploding another flashlight. I stared into this clattering strobe for four minutes until I asked him if he could stop. One MP rang to say, 'I'm sorry but I won't be voting for you again. The sparkle has come off.' Another MP preferred to give an interview saying 'Rory completely bombed. He was absolutely awful. What we were left with after that debate was a bit of roadkill that was still twitching but in need of being put out of its misery.'

I was eliminated in the votes the next day, followed by Sajid Javid and Michael Gove. Jeremy Hunt went through alone to the final contest. Every poll now showed that Boris Johnson had three times the Conservative Party votes of Jeremy Hunt. And Boris Johnson had inherited my lead in the broader country too. I, and what remained of the One Nation tradition, declared for Jeremy Hunt. But it was no longer up to us, the vote now rested with the Conservative Party members. And they would vote for Boris Johnson.

Five months later, I travel up to Penrith to march alongside Sasha in the Remembrance Day parade, with my one medal on, behind veterans who are wearing many. Shoshana and Ivo are already in the church. Boris Johnson, having failed to prorogue Parliament, or deliver Brexit by 31 October, has called an election for December. I am no longer a Cabinet minister, having resigned as soon as Boris Johnson became prime minister on 24 July. I am no longer a Conservative, since Boris Johnson has thrown twenty-one of us out of the party for continuing to vote against a no-deal Brexit. But I would not be prepared, in any case, to campaign for him or his manifesto. Since I am unwilling to run as an independent in Penrith against people I have worked with for a decade, I will soon no longer be a Member of Parliament. I read the lesson in St Andrew's Church. I am sitting in a pew next to the councillor who purged me from the association, and, on Boris Johnson's orders, banned me from local events.

My house in Cumbria is rented as a constituency home, with financial support from Parliament, so it can no longer be our home. After the service, I remove the toy tractor from the floor, and the red helium balloons from the rough kitchen rafters. The yellow and blue wellington boots go into a box.

Returning to London, I run to be mayor, as an independent. It is hard to run alone: short of money, humiliated by contemptuous donors, struggling to find a slogan which is both true and effective, asking so much from the volunteers, and battling for the smallest gains in the polls, against the machines of the established political parties. That campaign ends when Boris Johnson cancels the mayoral elections, for Covid reasons.

★

In Penrith high street, five older Conservative Party members, in their thick scarves and boots, gather for the sake of civic duty and party power. In a nearby field, sheep scatter over the ground where they buried Flavius Martius, the representative for Penrith and the Border, 1,770 years ago. He too, one of the *honestiores*, 'an honourable member', canvassed electors, heard complaints about roads and taxes, and justified the laws sent from a distant capital. The inscription on his tomb – 'local senator and quaestor, of quaestorian rank' – proclaims his power, not his power failures.

The agent pulls the canvassing sheets and the rosettes out of the supermarket bag which protects them from the rain. The leaflets, optimistically thick as a pulpit bible, strain against their rubber bands. They have been designed by experts in Westminster, who claim to have worked with someone who worked for Obama's campaign. Beneath the three-word slogan are boxes, into which the new parliamentary candidate has inserted photographs of himself visiting a primary school and shaking the prime minister's hand. As in my old leaflets, broadband, parking and a better infirmary are presented with the colourful bubble ticks usually reserved for *National Geographic* children's magazines, or special offers at the supermarket.

A pair of canvassers continue down a side street. One knocks and pushes a leaflet through a door, the other waits to discuss residents' parking, or a foreign war. On a loud television a politician is being interviewed. A curtain closes. An unseen terrier rages beneath the letter box. The doorbell plays the chimes of Big Ben.

I am living now in my home in Scotland. Every morning, for five months, I wake at six and take a Thermos of tea out on a long walk. A sudden cold spell has killed the leaves on the chestnut-leaved oaks, crinkling them to brown dust. In April, the wild cherry blossom runs along the branches of a hundred trees. The rain, which could clear the flowers in a single storm, has held off, so that the branches blaze for weeks. I stroke the lime-green brush of the spruce, and the soft tangerine-smelling leaves of a grand fir. I sit under a hawthorn watching pigeons swaying in birch trees. One morning, a roe deer, leaping from the lower field, lands next to me.

Startled eyes meet startled eyes and then he is away, hurdling my outstretched leg, the veins straining against the tight surface of his frightened body.

Sasha, now five, and Ivo, two, spend a lot of time on the trampoline. I injure my ankle trying to avoid the strokes of a plastic sword. I persuade the boys to plant some oaks, and they watch me ramming fence posts into the ground and stringing them with barbed wire. Sasha writes a long story about a red car. I plant an irregular sequence of yews, which the deer eat. I read about the Japanese concept of *wabi-sabi*, and *The Tale of Genji*, which makes me think about those Japanese councillors who retire from the court, to make gardens and prepare tea.

Dramatis Personae

First elected 1970
Ken Clarke (born 1940), MP for Rushcliffe. Son of a watchmaker and jeweller. Minister under four Conservative prime ministers, and continuously in office from 1979 to 1997. Variously Secretary of State for Health, Home Secretary, Chancellor of the Exchequer, Lord Chancellor and finally 'Father of the House'. Remainer.

First elected 1983
Nicholas Soames (born 1948), MP for Crawley from 1983 and for Mid Sussex from 1997. Son of an MP, grandson of Winston Churchill. Minister of State for the Armed Forces under John Major. Remainer.

First elected 1987
Andrew Mitchell (born 1956), MP for Gedling from 1987 and for Sutton Coldfield from 2001. Son of an MP. Chief whip, and enthusiastic Secretary of State for International Development. Remainer with Eurosceptic tendencies.

First elected 1997
Philip Hammond (born 1955), MP for Runnymede and Weybridge. Son of a civil engineer. Worked in housebuilding, manufacturing, healthcare and oil and gas before entering Parliament at the relatively late age of forty-one. Secretary of State for Transport, and for Defence, Foreign Secretary, Chancellor of the Exchequer. Remainer.

First elected 2001
Boris Johnson (born 1964), MP for Henley from 2001 to 2008 and for Uxbridge and South Ruislip from 2015. Son of a Member of the European Parliament, and an artist. Journalist, editor of the *Spectator*, TV

celebrity, mayor of London, and Foreign Secretary. Brexiteer. Leadership candidate in 2019.

David Cameron (born 1966), MP for Witney. Son of a stockbroker, and a magistrate. Straight from Oxford into the Conservative Party, party leader within five years of his election, prime minister within ten. The youngest prime minister for 200 years. Remainer.

George Osborne (born 1971), MP for Tatton. Son of a baronet who manufactured and sold wallpaper and fabrics. Straight from Oxford into the Conservative Party as researcher, aide and then MP. Chancellor of the Exchequer from 2010 to 2016. David Cameron's closest ally and co-ruler of the Conservative Party. Remainer.

First elected 2005

Richard Benyon (born 1960), MP for Newbury. Son of an MP. Environment minister under David Cameron. Remainer.

Jeremy Hunt (born 1966), MP for South West Surrey. Son of an admiral. Management consultant, entrepreneur, publisher, Japanese-speaker. Secretary of State for Culture, Media and Sport, for Health and Social Care, and Foreign Secretary. Remainer. Leadership candidate in 2019.

Michael Gove (born 1967), MP for Surrey Heath. Adopted at four months old. Oxford contemporary of Cameron and Johnson, journalist and writer, Education Secretary, chief whip and Environment Secretary. Brexiteer. Leadership candidate in 2019.

David Gauke (born 1971), MP for South West Hertfordshire. Son of a policeman. Lawyer, Chief Secretary to the Treasury, Secretary of State for Social Security, and then Lord Chancellor. Remainer.

First elected 2010 – joined with me

Sarah Wollaston (born 1962), MP for Totnes. Daughter of a sailor and aircraftman. GP and medical academic. Chair of Health Select Committee. Not promoted under Cameron or May. Remainer.

Amber Rudd (born 1963), MP for Hastings and Rye. Daughter of a stockbroker. Banker, businesswoman, Secretary of State for Energy and Climate Change, Home Secretary, Social Security Secretary. Remainer.

Nadhim Zahawi (born 1967), MP for Stratford-on-Avon. Son of a Kurdish businessman. Born in Baghdad, established and sold polling company, consultant on Iraqi oil, not promoted under Cameron, junior education minister under May. Brexiteer.

Jacob Rees-Mogg (born 1969), MP for North East Somerset. Son of a journalist. Founder of a hedge fund, worked in Singapore, long-time Conservative candidate. Catholic, Edwardian voice and clothes. Not promoted under Cameron or May. Brexiteer.

Sajid Javid (born 1969), MP for Bromsgrove. Son of a bus driver and small-businessman. Banker, trader and then head of operations for Deutsche Bank Singapore. Secretary of State for Culture, Media and Sport, for Business, Innovation and Skills, for Housing, Communities and Local Government, and Home Secretary. Remainer, with Brexit leanings. Leadership candidate in 2019.

Steve Baker (born 1971), MP for High Wycombe. Son of a carpenter, and an accounting clerk. Engineer in the Royal Air Force, then software engineer, not promoted under Cameron, junior minister for Brexit under May. Brexiteer.

Priti Patel (born 1972), MP for Witham. Daughter of owners of a chain of newsagents. A background in PR and communications. Secretary of State for International Development. Brexiteer.

Dominic Raab (born 1974), MP for Esher and Walton. Son of a food manager, and clothes buyer. Oxford boxing blue, lawyer, latterly in the Foreign Office, then chief of staff to a Conservative shadow minister. Secretary of State for Exiting the European Union. Brexiteer. Leadership candidate in 2019.

Kwasi Kwarteng (born 1975), MP for Spelthorne. Son of an economist, and a barrister. Historian, prolific author, banker, not promoted under Cameron, junior minister for Brexit under May. Brexiteer.

Liz Truss (born 1975), MP for South West Norfolk. Daughter of a maths professor, and a teacher. Economist at Shell and Cable & Wireless, believer in libertarian economics. Environment Secretary, Chief Secretary to the Treasury. Remainer turned Brexiteer.

Matt Hancock (born 1978), MP for West Suffolk. Son of the owners of a computer software company. Briefly an economist at the Bank of England, then George Osborne's chief of staff and favourite, minister in the Cabinet Office and then Secretary of State for Culture, Media and Sport. Remainer. Leadership candidate in 2019.

First elected 2015
Rishi Sunak (born 1980), MP for Richmond (Yorks). Son of a doctor. Worked for Goldman Sachs, and then a hedge fund, married to the daughter of the founder of Infosys. Not promoted under Cameron. Junior minister in Local Government under May. Brexiteer.

First elected 2017
Gillian Keegan (born 1968), MP for Chichester. Daughter of an office manager. Not made a minister under May.

Glossary

The House of Commons
The elected chamber of Parliament, and the chief legislative body in the United Kingdom, which emerged through the thirteenth and fourteenth centuries to represent the shires of England to the monarch. It passed laws and voted on taxes – particularly relevant when the king or queen required money for foreign wars. Its power was transformed when, in 1649, members of the House of Commons convicted and executed the king. The monarchy was restored in a weakened state, and from the late seventeenth century onwards, the House of Commons was the most powerful body in the kingdom. From 1535, also the Parliament of Wales, from 1707 the Parliament of Great Britain, including Scotland, from 1800 the Parliament of the United Kingdom including Ireland, and from 1927 the Parliament of England, Scotland, Wales and Northern Ireland. In the eighteenth and nineteenth centuries it was a debating club for the wealthiest men in the country – many of them related to each other.

Member of Parliament (MP)
One of the 650 elected members of the House of Commons. Unpaid in the eighteenth and nineteenth centuries. When I became an MP we were paid £65,738 a year (or £56,363 with a pension contribution). This was then slightly less than a senior head teacher, less than a general practice doctor, and much less than the most senior civil servants. But about three times the minimum wage. This is, and always has been, a very large legislative assembly. The US Senate, for example, has only a hundred members.

General election
An election for the House of Commons. These are triggered by a prime minister dissolving Parliament. David Cameron introduced

fixed-term parliaments of five years but in practice prime ministers continued to be able to dissolve parliaments at will – as Theresa May did in 2017 and Boris Johnson did in 2019. In the eighteenth and early nineteenth centuries only about one in seven adult males were eligible to vote. Successive reforms to the suffrage gave votes to 60 per cent of men in 1884, all men over twenty-one and all women over thirty in 1919, and equal voting rights to women in 1928. Members are elected through a first-past-the-post system, in which whoever receives the most votes in a *constituency* is elected – even if they receive far less than the majority of the votes. I stood for election in 2010, 2015 and 2017. Parties with widespread national support but no concentrated support within a constituency can end up with little representation in Parliament. Thus in 2015, the Scottish National Party won 4.7 per cent of the vote and fifty-six seats, the Lib Dems won 8 per cent of the national vote but only eight seats, UKIP won 12.6 per cent of the national vote but only one of the 650 seats.

Prorogation
The ending of a parliamentary session. Parliament cannot meet and vote until a new session begins. Boris Johnson used the Queen to prorogue Parliament in 2019 to prevent Parliament voting on Brexit. This was ruled to be illegal by the Supreme Court.

Constituency
The geographic area which selects its single representative for Parliament. The number of voters in an average constituency is about 70,000 people. The constituencies range from city constituencies of about a mile square to vast remote rural constituencies. Their boundaries are decided by the Boundary Commission to balance population size and historical identities. My constituency was Penrith and the Border.

Penrith and the Border
The largest and most sparsely populated constituency in England, and the heart of the vanished kingdom of Cumbria. Its centre is the Eden Valley, a sandstone rift valley. It is surrounded on three sides

by mountain ridges: the Howgill range to the south, the peaks of Helvellyn and Blencathra to the west, the Pennine ridge to the east. Its northern border is formed by half the English–Scottish border. It took me about six weeks to cover most of the villages in the constituency on foot. A tenth-century tomb reputed to contain the last king of Cumbria lies in Penrith churchyard. His father's treasure is supposed to be buried on its western border and its eastern border is marked by the place where Eric Bloodaxe, the last Viking king of York, was killed in 942.

House of Lords

The second chamber of Parliament, originally containing the princes, hereditary aristocrats and great churchmen of the kingdom. Once relatively small it is now one of the largest parliamentary bodies in the world because of the tendency of recent PMs to create more and more life peers – retired generals and ambassadors; business people; detective novelists; scientists; sports stars; judges; and many, far too many, retired politicians. Queen Elizabeth I created eighteen lords in her forty-four-year reign. Tony Blair created 400 in a decade. And David Cameron the same. It has over 1,000 members who continue to wear ermine-edged scarlet robes. But it has lost much of its historic authority and now retains only limited powers of scrutiny and delay. During the late 1990s devolved assemblies were created in Scotland, Wales and Northern Ireland with devolved powers over health and education but only limited powers over law and taxation. There is no such assembly in England, which is instead ruled directly by the House of Commons.

Safe seat

A constituency traditionally dominated by a single political party, which it would be very unusual for someone from that party to lose.

Backbencher

An MP who is not a minister (part of the governing party but not of the government). They sit on the benches in Parliament behind the ministerial front bench.

Select committee

A group of about a dozen backbench MPs who are elected by other MPs to shadow the work of particular government departments. They hold televised 'evidence sessions' with expert witnesses on thematic areas, cross-question ministers and senior civil servants, and publish reports. To join a select committee you have to be elected by the MPs from your own party. To become a committee chair you have to gain the most votes from all MPs, regardless of party. Chairs were in my time paid about £10,000 a year extra on top of their parliamentary salary. I was elected to the Foreign Affairs Committee in 2010. I was elected as chair of the Defence Committee in 2014.

Whip

A dozen MPs selected to control the party parliamentary business on behalf of their party leader. The government whips get government legislation passed by cajoling MPs to vote for their party. They can have influence over promotion. They liaise with the opposition on legislation. They do not speak in Parliament or in the media. The plumbing or sewage system of the House of Commons. I was never a whip.

Pairing whip

The whip charged with deciding which MPs can be excused from particular votes. (With a significant majority it is not necessary for every MP to be present for every vote – instead the whips allow certain MPs permission to miss votes to go back to their constituency or attend key events. They also often make an agreement with the opposition whips so that each party agrees to absent a voting member at the same time.)

Three-line whip

A vote which is considered of vital importance to the government, and where all MPs are expected to vote in line with the government. Most votes in my time were three-line whips.

Free vote
A rare occasion where MPs are allowed to vote in accordance with their conscience.

Confidence vote
A vote which if lost would mean the resignation of the prime minister and the dissolution of Parliament.

Withdrawal of the whip
A punishment in which an MP is suspended from their political party. This can be because they are suspected of committing a crime or simply because they have rebelled against a three-line whip. Generally the whip is restored before an election so that the MP can run on behalf of the party (as happened with the 'Maastricht rebels' – Eurosceptics who defied John Major's government). Boris Johnson, however, used this power in 2019 to strip the whip off his major internal opponents, and then held an election, in which they were prevented from running as party candidates. By doing so, he effectively expelled them from Parliament. This is what happened to me and to twenty other Conservative MPs who voted to block a no-deal Brexit.

Parliamentary private secretary (PPS)
An unpaid part-time position for MPs, serving as a liaison between ministers and other MPs. Generally appointed by the whips, and seen as the first rung for promotion. They must always vote with the government. If they rebel, they lose these positions. So they are a good way for the government to shore up its vote. They do not have ministerial powers. I was never a PPS.

Ministers
All ministers are Members of Parliament. This is unlike the US system, where there is a separation of powers between executive and legislature, and the equivalents of ministers may come from anywhere. In my time one junior minister in each department was

usually drawn from the House of Lords, but all other ministers, and all Secretaries of State, were members of the House of Commons.

Parliamentary Undersecretary of State (PUS)

The most junior minister in a department. A paid position with formal powers, a Civil Service staff, a government office, and responsibility for one part of the ministry's business – reporting to a Secretary of State. Often simply called a minister. A PUS – like a committee chair – then earned about £10,000 a year on top of their MP's salary. In 2015, I became parliamentary undersecretary in DEFRA. I was referred to as the environment minister – or flooding minister.

Minister of State

The middle of the three ranks of ministers. Not very different in practice to a PUS, but paid more, and often with a slightly more senior civil service staff. In DfID in my time, for example, there was one Secretary of State, one Minister of State (me) and one parliamentary undersecretary. In Justice, there was one Secretary of State, one Minister of State (me) and two parliamentary undersecretaries. But my portfolios were generally about the same size and importance of those of the other junior ministers. We received £30,000 on top of our ministerial salaries. I was Minister of State in DfID, the Foreign Office and the Ministry of Justice.

Secretary of State

The top of the ministerial tree. In charge of their own department. Appointed by the prime minister. Attends Cabinet, and in certain roles the National Security Council. They, not the junior ministers, make the ultimate decisions in the department: signing off the departmental plan, and setting the budget. But they don't usually get to select their junior ministers. I was in the Cabinet and on the National Security Council as Secretary of State for International Development.

Cabinet

The group containing the Secretaries of State, and a few additional senior ministers, chaired by the prime minister. Cabinets were traditionally teams of rivals, containing most of the senior figures from all spectrums of the party, who were closely consulted on policy. Since Tony Blair the role of the Cabinet has weakened. I was in the Cabinet.

Prime minister

Head of government but not head of state. A member of the House of Commons. Like all other ministers, the PM has to combine governing the country with the duties of an MP in their own constituency. Traditionally a 'first among equals'. Since Tony Blair, the PM has begun to behave more presidentially – often ruling less through 'Cabinet government' and more through their own office in 10 Downing Street. In my time David Cameron, Theresa May and Boris Johnson were prime ministers.

Leadership candidate

An MP who runs to be leader of their party. In 2016 and 2019, the winner automatically became prime minister. The rules for the election of a Tory leader are set by the 1922 Committee of backbenchers. In 2019, the rules were that you required the support of eight MPs to be nominated. Then you entered a series of rounds, in which the last-placed candidate and anyone failing to meet a minimum threshold was eliminated, before voting was held again. To avoid elimination you would need the support of seventeen MPs by 13 June 2019, then thirty-three MPs by 18 June. The two winners would be presented to the Conservative Party members in the country for a final vote.

Conservative Party

The 'oldest and most successful' political party in the world. Emerged from the eighteenth-century 'Tory' Party. The Conservative Party has been in power either alone, or in coalition, for over seventy of the last hundred years. Traditionally on the side of the establishment, defence and property. The party of Winston Churchill. But capable of reinventing itself – whether pushing for the expansion of suffrage under its nineteenth-century leader, Benjamin Disraeli; or for radical privatisation and deregulation under Margaret Thatcher. The parliamentary party consists of the Members of Parliament who 'take' the Conservative whip. The party as a whole is composed of any citizen who is willing to pay the membership fee, which in my era was £50 a year. But few wish to. The party which numbered about 2 million in the early 1950s numbered just over 100,000 in my period, and was considerably older, whiter and more pro-Brexit than the general population.

Head of state
The monarch (queen or king), who rules by hereditary right, in direct descent from monarchs of England and Scotland, who in turn were descended from rulers who assumed power not long after the Roman withdrawal from Britain in the fifth century AD. During my time, Queen Elizabeth II. Now her son, Charles III.

Special adviser (SPAD)
Secretaries of State are able to bring in a couple of special advisers from outside the Civil Service. The media SPADs are often former journalists or PR and comms staff from think tanks. Other SPADs are often young, and fiercely ambitious, seeking to become MPs. David Cameron and George Osborne were SPADs, as were their opposite numbers on the Labour benches, Ed Miliband and Ed Balls.

Civil servants
In the UK civil servants, right up to the most senior level, immediately below the ministers, are professional, impartial, and are not political appointees. This is also true for almost all ambassadors. They remain while politicians come and go, serving all parties. They are politically neutral. The mantra in my time was 'civil servants advise, ministers decide'. But civil servants have been in the departments much longer, there are many more of them, and they generally know much more than ministers about their portfolio. And since many of the departments I served in had only three or four ministers, and thousands of civil servants, their power is considerable. I started my

career as a civil servant. The senior-management stream of the Civil Service is usually organised from the most junior up into deputy directors, directors, director generals and permanent secretaries. In the odd cases where they have to be ranked against the military for protocol or seats on planes, they are the equivalents of colonels up to generals. The permanent secretary is the most senior civil servant in a department. They are often a knight or a dame, at the very peak of their career, traditionally in their fifties, with thirty years of Civil Service experience behind them. The head of the permanent Civil Service then earned about £200,000 a year – more than the prime minister.

The British constitution

An uncodified series of laws and conventions, developed over many centuries, and with only limited 'separation of powers'. Some of the conventions – such as the principle that a minister who lies to Parliament must resign – are difficult to enforce. Parliament is sovereign (traditionally said to be able to 'do everything except make a woman a man, or a man, a woman' – although it has become increasingly interested in that issue as well). There is no equivalent of the US written constitution standing above Parliament. The prime minister and all ministers are Members of Parliament. The PM controls Parliament through the party whips. The House of Commons is sufficient to do anything – including, as David Cameron attempted to do, to abolish the second chamber of Parliament – *provided* the PM can secure a simple majority of votes.

Acknowledgements

The writing of this book was made possible by the Jackson Institute (later School) of Yale University. I owe a particular gratitude to its director, Jim Levinsohn, who invited me to teach politics and international development after my departure from politics. The bulk of the book was completed at Yale, and is shaped by conversations with colleagues there: Emma Sky – particularly – who inspired so many ideas, not least on our walks together through tidal marshes, but also Bryan Garsten, David Engerman, Beverley Gage, Sunil Amrith, James C. Scott, Iain Shapiro and (at Chicago) Jonathan Lear. I would like to thank Reid Hoffman for his long support and friendship. And Roger Pauli for his patient generosity and insights.

John Hatt has been with me through every stage of my political career and the writing of the book – giving many hundreds of hours of his time, on everything from the title to the cover, the commas and the ending – and despite, as he insists, disagreeing with me about almost everything. Stephen Brown went carefully through every draft, transforming and clarifying the structure and narrative, spending hours on the phone with me as I tried to debate every point, and shepherding it into a better place. Patrick Mackie read multiple drafts and his suggestions for improvements were brilliant and expressed with great wit, tact and delicacy. I felt very lucky to benefit from the intelligence, trust and creativity of Bea Hemming, my editor at Penguin Random House. I was also very fortunate in the patience and understanding of Scott Moyers at Penguin Press as he came to terms with the manuscript for a very different American audience.

All these people identified very fundamental problems with the book, many of which I did not fully understand, even late in the process and which I have failed to address adequately. Stephen's book, for example, would have given a much clearer, more open account of my emotional journey and discoveries. Patrick's would have been much more condensed, aphoristic and original. John Hatt's book would have been called *Power Failures*. All would – given more time – have led me to create something much better, and shorter.

Michael Ignatieff shared profound and raw reflections on how he and I were each struggling in different ways to reconcile to the pain of politics, and tried to get me to clarify my journey from naivety to experience. Johnny Tusa brought the eye of a historian, the nous of an effective administrator, and much heart and care to his criticisms – and saved the reader from a very slow beginning. Julian Glover was rapidly insightful, and drew to my attention a dozen dimensions of political background that I had missed. Larissa MacFarquhar with tact and grace pointed out the examples of self-obsession, complacency and lack of sympathy in my accounts of others. Alastair Campbell encouraged more generosity towards my adversaries. David Gauke brought context, and pushed for more empathy, and humour, and more analysis of the reasons for decline. Again in almost every case I struggled to respond adequately to their insights.

Clare Alexander has been my agent and friend for twenty-three years and is the perfect combination of frankness, patience, loyalty and energy. Jenny Dean brought real focus and improvement to the final stages of the book and its production. Peter Martin mused on how Tacitus would have written it differently. Ben Crewe and Kevin Beaton kindly read carefully the sections on prisons and offered corrections of fact and interpretation. Harriet Hall spent hours entering my handwritten corrections on two drafts of the manuscript. My mother engaged thoughtfully with almost every aspect of the book and the career that preceded it, and encouraged both with love and generosity. She and Dolly Yang did a magnificent job of proofreading the 1,000 pages of the first draft, identifying errors on every page, and would greatly have improved the final version too, if they had been allowed to do so. Sasha and Ivo were kind about the weeks I spent apart from them struggling with the book, and Sasha saved me from an underwhelming title.

Finally, Shoshana lived alongside this from the first stumbling passages composed at a cold table in a Scottish garden, through the index cards laid flamboyantly out on the dining room in Yale, to the days closeted in front of a giant monitor in Amman. She heard half the passages read aloud at lunch or dinner. She was alert to the storyline, tone, and my descriptions, and consistently wise in her suggestions. She did not lose faith and patience as every deadline was missed and it dragged into its third year. But most importantly she lived through the nine years described in the book and I would not have begun to have survived them in the way I did, without her.

Index